Feydeau, First to Last

GEORGES FEYDEAU, by Leonetto Cappiello

Feydeau,

FIRST TO LAST

EIGHT ONE-ACT COMEDIES

Translated and
with an Introduction by
Norman R. Shapiro

Cornell University Press

ITHACA AND LONDON

First published 1982 by Cornell University Press.
Published in the United Kingdom by Cornell University Press Ltd.,
Ely House, 37 Dover Street, London W1X 4HQ.

International Standard Book Number 0-8014-1295-1
Library of Congress Catalog Card Number 81-15182
Printed in the United States of America
*Librarians: Library of Congress cataloging information
appears on the last page of the book.*

*The paper in this book is acid-free, and meets the
guidelines for permanence and durability of the Committee
on Production Guidelines for Book Longevity of
the Council on Library Resources.*

TO THE MEMORY OF DAN SELTZER—

actor, teacher, friend—who
got it all started.

Contents

Introduction

Feydeau, First to Last: An appropriate title when one considers that Georges Feydeau is the first of the French *farceurs* of his generation to last successfully in the modern repertory. The first of the many *fin-de-siècle* purveyors of light Boulevard comedy—Gandillot, Gondinet, Valabrègue, Capus, Grenet-Dancourt, and many more, today all but forgotten—to become a theatrical "classic" in his own right. And not only in France. Immensely popular during his lifetime (1862–1921), Feydeau has steadily grown in admiration, abroad as well as at home, since his "rediscovery" in the early forties, after a relatively brief period of that posthumous semi-obscurity to which so many popular artists fall victim.[1] Virtually unknown outside his native land three decades ago, except to specialists, he is admired today by theatergoers of the Western world, connoisseurs and laymen alike, as the very master of his genre, and, according to many, as the foremost French comic playwright since Molière.[2] Today Feydeau enjoys a celebrity bordering on adulation. And a well-deserved celebrity—his craftsmanship, wit, and intuitive flair for the comic are, indeed, without peer—although he himself would probably find it hard to fathom, considering himself an entertainer, as he no doubt did, without high-flown pretensions to artistic eminence. But

1. Although *La Dame de chez Maxim* was revived at the Odéon as early as 1938, it is the revival of *Feu la mère de Madame* at the Théâtre-Français, in 1941, that is credited with having marked Feydeau's rebirth of popularity. (See Jean Bergeaud, *Je choisis...mon théâtre* [Paris: Editions Odilis, 1956], pp. 248–249.) In 1947, *Occupe-toi d'Amélie* was successfully recreated at the Marigny by Jean-Louis Barrault and Madeleine Renaud. Three years later the same artists added *On purge Bébé* to their company's repertoire. The revival of *Le Dindon* at the Salle Luxembourg, in 1951, occasioned considerable controversy among hidebound traditionalists, but not enough to blunt Feydeau's renewed vogue.

2. See, for example, Jean-Louis Barrault, *Une Troupe et ses auteurs* (Paris: Vautrain, 1950), p. 51; and Marcel Achard's introduction to Feydeau's nine-volume *Théâtre complet* (Paris: Le Bélier, 1948–56), vol. 1, p. 7. Critic Georges Pillement's early praise is typical: "Feydeau was considered a wit, his *bons mots* were the delight of the gossip columnists, he was one of the best-known figures of the Boulevard. It is only today, however, that we realize he was a veritable dramatic genius, one of the great comic authors of all time" (*Anthologie du théâtre français contemporain*, vol. 2 [Paris: Le Bélier, 1946], pp. 51–52). (This, and subsequent translations, are my own.)

9

the fact remains. Today his plays (comedies, vaudevilles, farces—call them what you will)[3] are always being performed somewhere.

Feydeau, First to Last: An appropriately punnish title when one is dealing with a playwright for whom typically Gallic wordplay, unabashed and unblushing, was such a favorite preoccupation throughout his career. And, all the more obviously appropriate too, since this volume contains Feydeau's first and last extant plays—one-acts, like the six others here included.[4] Typical examples of an all-too-often-neglected staple of his dramatic production. For, if Feydeau's name is synonymous today with farce elevated to artistic respectability, it is primarily so—especially for English-speaking audiences —thanks to a rather small handful of frequently performed works that have entered the repertory. Big plays, for the most part. Veritable extravaganzas. Tours de force (or de farce) for actors, directors, designers alike. Anticipations, in their own way, of that "unbridled farce" that director Charles Dullin, a generation or so later, would see as the potential salvation of a moribund, overly sophisticated French theater.[5] Constructions typical of the minutely ordered build-up of insignificant cause into gigantic, often nightmarish effect, spread over three (and sometimes more) acts of mounting frenzy before the inevitable happy, if gratuitous, ending. In the face of such masterful "machines," it is easy to overlook the fact that one-acts account for over a third of Feydeau's theater, that he opened and closed his career with them, and that they continued to provide grist for his comic mill throughout.

No other reasons, it seems to me, should be needed to collect a number of these more modest Feydeau endeavors in English versions. They represent a substantial but little-known aspect of his work, showing both its termini, *a quo* and *ad quem*, and thereby deserve to live their own transplanted lives outside the French text of his *Théâtre complet*. But there is another, more practical reason as well: to provide a bridge from page to stage. For the numerous English-speaking actors and directors eager to try their hand at the difficult art of farce—far more difficult than it appears—they offer scripts of the "master" much more accessible and much less demanding (of time and expense, though certainly not of talent) than his bigger and better

3. Feydeau, recognized today as the master of "farce," never used that term himself to designate his plays, first preferring, among others, the term "vaudeville"—with its French, not Anglo-American implications—and, later, the simple terms "comedy" and "play."

4. Two plays were left unfinished at his death: *Cent millions qui tombent* and *On va faire la cocotte*. The manuscript of a one-act drama, *L'Amour doit se taire*, apparently a first juvenile effort, is in the possession of his grandson, actor Alain Feydeau. (See Jacques Lorcey, *Georges Feydeau* [Paris: La Table Ronde, 1972], p. 64.) Regarding other works not usually included in the Feydeau corpus, see my article "Georges Feydeau: Note sur deux énigmes résolues," *Revue d'histoire littéraire de la France*, 1980, no. 1, p. 90, note 3.

5. Dullin is quoted in Frederick Brown, *Theatre and Revolution: The Culture of the French Stage* (New York: Viking, 1980), p. 327. On the other hand, Feydeau's comedies, demanding clockwork timing and technique, are the antithesis of the improvisations that Dullin was also to espouse.

known. Not every school theater or community playhouse wants, or is able, to tackle the intricacies of, say, *La Puce à l'oreille* ("A Flea in Her Ear"),[6] with its huge cast of virtuoso performers, its costumes, and its scenic bag of tricks. (And, sad but true, many of those who do want to, shouldn't: Feydeau's glitter has more than once been tarnished by well-meaning overreachers, amateur and professional as well.) The present plays offer such groups a happy alternative to avoiding Feydeau altogether, or to biting off more than they can artistically and technically chew. For those English-speaking readers and audiences to whom Feydeau's name is synonymous only with slamming doors and madcap romps from bed to bed, through seamy hotels, I hope these little comedies—*multum in parvo*, as Dupont might say, in *Gibier de potence*—help round out the picture. And for those, ever diminishing in number, to whom his name still means nothing at all, I hope they succeed in whetting the appetite. Just one caution: for those who appreciate farce, the taste can become an addiction.

If Feydeau was obviously devoted to the one-act from first to last, it is not always the product of the same aesthetic or personal demands throughout the whole of his professional life. Rather, it seems to have answered different needs at different stages of his career. Nor are all his one-acts cast in the same mold. Despite all the detectable and delectable similarities of Feydeau wit and style, there is a world of difference—or a lifetime of difference— between the sentimentality of a *Notre futur* (1882?) and the frivolity of a *Par la fenêtre* (1882?), on the one hand, and the bitter humor of a *Hortense a dit: "Je m'en fous!"* (1916), on the other. As we shall see, his early one-acts grew out of the salon entertainments of his day, when dramatic monologue and intimate *saynète* were the social genres *à la mode*. In sharp contrast, the one-acts produced at the end of his career, studies in marital frustration pushed to the extreme, reflect his very personal, though stylized, skirmishes in the age-old battle of the sexes. Strindberg, of sorts, in a comic key, but resounding with dissonant, less-than-humorous overtones. Between the two extremes, Feydeau would exploit the one-act at odd moments, turning to it, it would seem, when he felt the need to retrench from an overextended technique, or whenever he had to fill a gap in his creativity and keep his name before the public with a minimum of effort. For that reason it is not always possible to be sure if his mid-career one-acts really date from the times when they were first performed. Some may, in fact, have been earlier efforts, dusted off and polished up for an ever-growing, ever-admiring audience. An exact chronology, therefore, is difficult to establish, despite valuable biographical studies that now exist to guide the Feydeauphile, who, until fairly recently, had to unearth the facts for himself from a variety of disparate

6. I cite the title of John Mortimer's frequently performed adaptation, although the French original, with its distinctly physical connotations, might better be rendered as "Ants in Her Pants."

sources.[7] Still, certain broad lines can be drawn, and it will be useful to follow them in a brief examination of the plays in this volume.

It is customary to divide Feydeau's career into four periods. His earliest plays, as I have said, were a natural outgrowth of the Parisian society that lionized him in his youth. Son of the socially prominent intellectual Ernest Feydeau, handsome, himself a talented actor,[8] he quickly became known for his witty dramatic monologues, in prose and verse, examples of a genre that seems dated to us, but one that was to spread like a virtual epidemic during the last two decades of the century.[9] And along with monologues, a host of duologues and other unassuming *saynètes*, slender dramatic playlets by the known and the less known, tailored to the dimensions of the fashionable drawing-room.

Our first three plays—*Notre futur*, *Par la fenêtre*, and *Amour et piano* (here respectively, if not overly respectfully, rendered as *Ladies' Man, Wooed and Viewed*, and *Romance in A Flat*)—fit squarely into this tradition. For the sake of scholarly accuracy, a digression is in order concerning their chronology. Aside from the usual uncertainty about any play's date of composition—production or publication dates providing only a *terminus post quem non*—there are a few other specific problems concerning these three early works. *Par la fenêtre* is usually considered Feydeau's first extant playlet, his first excursion into a genre a little more ambitious than the monologue. The date given by most sources for its initial performance is the fall of 1881, and the place, the northern resort town of Rosendaël. Jacques Lorcey, however, much of whose biographical research is based on docu-

---

7. In addition to the detailed Lorcey biography already referred to, Leonard Pronko's study *Georges Feydeau* (New York: Frederick Ungar, 1975) gives an overview of the playwright's career. Two other recent works—Arlette Shenkan's *Georges Feydeau* (Paris: Seghers, 1972) and Henry Gidel's *Le Théâtre de Feydeau* (Paris: Klincksieck, 1979)—are more specialized and less strictly biographical.

8. Lorcey (chapter 3) recounts in some detail the playwright's youthful successes as an amateur actor. A decade later, riding the crest of the theatrical wave, even after he had given up the idea of becoming a professional actor, Feydeau continued to indulge his talents: "The most novel amusement in the salon was provided by a group of habitués, young men and women warmly received by Madame Arman de Caillavet since the marriage of her son. They were all mad about the theater and loved to stage little plays. Their charming troupe was led by Georges Feydeau, the young playwright at the very height of his success, and by Robert de Flers. . ." (Jeanne Pouquet, *Le Salon de Madame Arman de Caillavet* [Paris: Hachette, 1926], pp. 174–75).

9. Abetted by the talents of such popular artists as the Coquelin brothers and Félix Galipaux, the monologue was all the rage. One dramatist of the time complained that the monologue "reigns endemically in Paris. Nobody escapes it. . ." (Abraham Dreyfus, *Jouons la comédie* [Paris: Calmann-Lévy, 1887], pp. iii–iv). One of Feydeau's own early monologues, *Un Monsieur qui n'aime pas les monologues* (published in 1882), with typical Feydeau whimsy, jokingly condemns the genre: "Monologues! Who ever heard of such a thing! If I were the police department I'd make them illegal. They're phony! Super-phony! A man in his right mind doesn't talk to himself. . . ."

ments previously unavailable, places its composition and production a full year later.[10] Since *Amour et piano*, usually considered Feydeau's second *saynète*, dates unquestionably from January 1883, according to all sources, it has always been taken for granted—and Lorcey continues to make the assumption—that *Par la fenêtre* (whether presented in 1881 or 1882) and *Amour et piano* (1883) are numbers one and two. A difficulty, however, arises, and one that has apparently escaped notice: namely, the fact that the modest *Notre futur*, seldom accorded any importance at all by Feydeau critics, must also date from this very early period. Although not mentioned by any sources as being performed until 1894, on an intimate little Parisian stage, and supposedly left unpublished until its appearance many decades later in volume 6 of the *Théâtre complet* (1952), the playlet did, in fact, originally appear in print in 1882 (in the company of works by many better-known contemporaries), in a popular *saynète* collection of the period.[11] If, therefore, both *Par la fenêtre* and *Notre futur* date from 1882 at the latest, there is no compelling chronological reason as yet brought to light to assume that the latter was not actually Feydeau's first, as I choose to believe, though certainly not by much. The playlet's very nature would seem to support my hypothesis. Looked at with hindsight, it is clearly not "typical Feydeau." For all its charm, and even with its "surprise" denouement, it is written in a much more sentimental vein than was to become his wont. Few, if any, of Feydeau's later heroines will give way to outbursts of authentic tears, as poor Valentine does in her first disillusioning foray into romance. Crocodile tears, yes. Or tears of spite, of anger, even of rage. But seldom, if ever, the real thing. His typical females will quickly become a more cynical lot, much more like Valentine's social-butterfly cousin, the wordly-wise Angélique.[12] It is as if, after a first tentative venture into sentimental comedy, Feydeau quickly realized, even if only intuitively, that delicate emotion was not to be his cup of tea, and that the robust humor of imbroglio, albeit tempered with not a little wit and frequent social wisdom, was where his talents lay. *Par la fenêtre*, also a duologue, would put him right on track. And *Amour et piano* would follow, essentially a delicate little *pas de deux* as well, though with the further development of an added minor character.

Questions of precise chronology aside, it is clear that this trio of early endeavors was conceived of salon inspiration and with salon audiences in mind. (Even the piano in *Amour et piano*—a rather cumbersome prop for a

10. Lorcey, pp. 75–76.

11. *Théâtre de campagne*, vol. 8 (Paris: Ollendorff, 1882). There is even evidence that it was also performed, at least informally, some time prior to 1885. An edition of a Feydeau monologue, *Le Colis*, appearing that year, included a publisher's advertisement for "*Notre futur*, one-act *saynète*, as performed by Mlles Reichemberg and Bartet of the Comédie Française."

12. Angélique is named Henriette in the original. The purist should be warned that I have found it expedient for a variety of reasons to change some of the characters' names, and that I refer to them throughout as they appear in my versions.

twenty-minute trifle—suggests a ready-made drawing-room decor.) In content each is essentially one-situational: variations on the theme of mistaken
motive or mistaken identity. And in technique each unhesitatingly exploits
the unrealistic conventions of monologue and aside; dramatic devices common to their period in general, and to the salon comedy in particular, in
which the inherent intimacy of the situation—the proximity of an audience
sympathetically predisposed, almost by definition—makes it all the more
tempting to ignore the "fourth wall."[13]

Still, limited and unambitious as these early playlets are, we should not be
surprised to see in them, here and there, the seeds of things to come. *Par la
fenêtre* does, in fact, introduce us to a number of Feydeau themes and
characters in germ. The women stand out especially, as they will all through
his theater. Hector's jealous wife, though never seen, prefigures the many
willful heroines of Feydeau's later plays, especially those at the end of his
career. We meet her in this collection again, closing the circle, as the
fully-developed, flesh-and-blood Marcelle, in *Hortense a dit: "Je m'en fous!"*,
product of Feydeau's baleful middle-aged experience rather than of his more
benign youthful imagination. There, like Hector's wife, she will fire her
maid too, but for reasons far more basic to her shrewish personality than this
early example of newlywed pique, and with far more disastrous results to the
marriage. As for Emma, Hector's tempestuous next-door neighbor, she will
prove no less typical. She is only the first of the many emancipated Feydeau
females bent on avenging their husbands' peccadillos.

The men in the playlet—both the seen and the unseen—are equally pro-
totypic of many future Feydeau characters. Hector, the butt of his wife's
groundless suspicions as well as of Emma's unorthodox demand, passive up
to a point, will mature into the several harried husbands of the late plays, of
whom Follbraguet in *Hortense*, the last, is the *ne plus ultra*, literally as well
as figuratively. And Emma's Brazilian spouse, the fiery Alcibiades, whose
jealousy sets the comedy in motion, though only a bodiless allusion in *Par la
fenêtre*, will take concrete form in such extravaganzas as *Un Fil à la patte*[14]
and *La Puce à l'oreille*. There he will bluster across the stage, incarnation of
the swaggering Latin *rastaquouère*, soldier of fortune (and of lady's boudoir),
a common figure in French society and literature since the Second Empire.[15]
Here he, in the wings, and Emma, on stage, are only the first of the legion
of foreigners to parade through Feydeau's theater. Eccentric caricatures, for
the most part. Reflections of the real-life cosmopolitan fauna of a Paris

13. For a detailed study of Feydeau's use of these dramatic devices, see Gidel, pp. 319–27.
14. My version, entitled *Not by Bed Alone*, appears in *Four Farces by George Feydeau*
(Chicago: University of Chicago Press, 1970).
15. In the theater, one thinks, for example, of *Le Brésilien*, the one-act comedy by Henri
Meilhac and Ludovic Halévy (1863). It is probable that Feydeau, who knew Meilhac and
admired his plays, was familiar with that one. At any rate, he was obviously familiar with the
phenomenon.

quickly becoming the magnet of Europe. Examples of what one journalist, not without a little hyperbole, has recently called Feydeau's "systematic xenophobia," apparent in "all those ridiculous Russians, Belgians, and South Americans" that people his comedies.[16]

The unseen Alcibiades also serves the purpose of allowing Feydeau to poke fun at one of the social foibles of the age, and one that he was apparently to take great pleasure in deriding—to wit, the duel. It would be difficult to exaggerate the vogue of this anachronistic relic of chivalric ages long since dead; one of the available means, in the nominally egalitarian, bourgeois-dominated republic, for some—those aspiring to social distinction—to be "more equal than others." Indeed, duels were the order of the day, and the art of fencing flourished. Even otherwise level-headed individuals were willing and often eager to cross sabres at the drop of a glove. As one observer of the period notes, "Between 1895 and 1905, hardly a day went by without a duel hitting the headlines of the Boulevard."[17] Such an institution, rife with the potential for a personal aggrandizement begging to be deflated, was a favorite target of the humorists of the *Belle Epoque*. It is no surprise that Feydeau was to join their number.[18] Unlike some later comedies, however, in which the duel plays an important part in the imbroglio, the threatened combat in *Par la fenêtre* is referred to only briefly. But it is so delightfully bizarre in Alcibiades' supposed choice of weapons— hand drills, no less, *à la brésilienne*—that Feydeau's attitude, even in this early work, is clear. It will be so again, a decade later, in *La Dame de chez Maxim*, when the harassed Doctor Petypon, menaced with an absurd duel against his will and better judgment, proposes the weapon he knows best: the scalpel.[19] Feydeau will, in fact, go on to use the duel for comic effect in

16. Pierre Enckell, "Un Tandem inusable," *Les Nouvelles littéraires*, 21–27 February 1980, p. 28. Xenophobe or not, Feydeau was clearly aware of the influx at its height, as an often-quoted letter to journalist Jules Huret, written in August 1897, humorously shows: "Where am I?—For the last week, abroad, in Paris! But not for long; I'm afraid I might forget my French" (Jules Huret, *Loges et coulisses* [Paris: Editions de la Revue Blanche, 1901], pp. 289–90).

17. André Billy, *L'Epoque 1900* (Paris: Tallandier, 1951), p. 384.

18. One thinks especially of *raconteurs* such as Aurélien Scholl, and of popular *chansonniers* like Léon Xanrof, whose songs filled the repertoire of the famous Yvette Guilbert. As for Feydeau, the fact that his stepfather, critic Henry Fouquier, and his father-in-law, fashionable portraitist Carolus-Duran, were themselves well-known swordsmen, does not seem to have prevented him from making his own little thrusts at the institution.

19. The choice of bizarre and absurd weapons, replacing the heroic sabre or pistol, had been a common device among duel parodists for decades. It is more than likely that Feydeau knew the one-act comedy by Labiche and Martin, *La Main leste* (1867), in which, for example, the weapons are cups of milk:

LEGRAINARD. . . . as the offended party I have the right to choose the weapons, and I've chosen a duel with cups of milk.
REGALAS *bewildered*. What ... We're going to drink milk?
LEGRAINARD. Don't joke, monsieur! This is very serious. I've scratched the sulphur off of seventy-two matches into one of these cups. . . . The one who drinks it will have long,

about half of his plays, making fun of its principles (as well as its principals) in varying degrees—from passing pleasantry to integral element of plot—and for a variety of reasons: the usual triviality of its motives, the pseudoheroic affectation of its adepts, their thirst for publicity and recognition. He will even make sport of the overly enthusiastic second, like Marollier in *La Dame*, a Bergsonian puppet-type more concerned with rigid formalism and ceremonial protocol than with a supposedly bruised *point d'honneur*.[20] But if the heroic combat in *Par la fenêtre* is only a *duel pour rire*, in *Hortense*, a far cry from Feydeau's early frivolity, we shall see the duel (or at least the threat of one) as a culmination of Follbraguet's mounting misfortunes, and one with potentially serious consequences. It is Feydeau's final humorous indictment of the institution. Not of poor Follbraguet, certainly. (After all, like Hector, he doesn't seek the duel, the duel comes seeking him.) But of the society that had made of the *affaire d'honneur* an often laughable product of the overblown ego.

But if *Par la fenêtre* prefigures many of Feydeau's later comedies, it is not only for its foreshadowing of certain characters and its modest attempts at passing social commentary, but also, and more basically, for the absurdity of its premise. (Where but in the universe of a Feydeau-type farce, with its special rules of logic and its own brand of cause and effect, will strange ladies appear and ask their neighbors to make love to them?) The same may be said of *Amour et piano*. To be sure, we shall see all its characters again, in different guise and in different circumstances. Lucile, the well-bred *ingénue* in her first brush with romance, but—like Valentine, in *Notre futur*—not quite ready to blossom into womanhood, will appear frequently in Feydeau's repertory. Her inept domestic, Baptiste, fresh from the country, agog at Parisian ways and properly malapropistic, will develop into the boor of *Les Pavés de l'ours* (as we shall see in this collection), well-meaning bull in his

---

horrible convulsions, until he drops dead. . . . I'm the offended party, so... I have my choice. I take the white cup. Here, you swallow the blue one.... [Scene xiv]

The folly of the duel would never be parodied in a more outrageous choice of weapons than in a one-act vaudeville by Feydeau's little-known but prolific contemporaries Lebreton and Saint-Paul, *Mademoiselle le docteur* (1900), pitting two hypochondriacs against each other:

MOUFLARD. I have the choice of weapons! '. . . I choose Doctor Kockey's laxative pills! . . . Here!
TRIBOLIN. Laxative pills?
MOUFLARD. Yes. You only need three to have instant results. We'll take thirteen each. . . . [Scene xi]

20. Marollier and his like are not constructions of Feydeau's imagination. A contemporary authority on the duel warned of the danger posed by such "professional seconds": "We see, all too often, the swashbuckling second, who thrusts himself upon us, come hell or high water. . . . It's his job to take the minor row, hawk it about, exaggerate it, and turn it into a major incident. Then he appears and offers his services as absolutely the only one who can set matters straight. . . . God save us forever from this duel-procurer, this panderer who lives off the duels of others" (Gabriel Letainturier-Fradin, *L'Honneur et le duel* [Paris: Flammarion, 1897], p. 72.).

master's amorous china-shop, as well as into less destructive domestics, both male and female. As for the would-be *roué*, Edouard, the fatuous provincial dandy seeking to add his ripple to the social whirl of Paris, no less agog but more adept, he too will have a number of future Feydeau incarnations. We meet him soon again as the philandering professor in *Gibier de potence*, less of a dandy but no less of a provincial, and, like Edouard, in quest of that surefire badge of wordly success, a Parisian actress-mistress. And we shall continue to see his ilk—developed, expanded, and nuanced—scattered through Feydeau's theater: the provincial, of both sexes, dazzled by the social and intellectual prestige of Paris.[21] We shall also see Feydeau, throughout his career, aim his barbs, in passing, at many other social and intellectual phenomena that could easily degenerate into modish faddism. (Like the duel in *Par la fenêtre*, for example.) He does so too in *Amour et piano*, with a deflating little pin-prick at the host of Parisian aesthetes (and pseudo-aesthetes) who had recently discovered the music of Wagner, and who were already beginning to worship *en masse* at his altar.[22] Not that Feydeau was a philistine. Far from it. Only that, as a humorist, he could never resist cutting affectation of all kinds down to realistic size.

But contemporary allusion and stock characters aside, as with *Par la fenêtre*, what strikes us most in *Amour et piano* as "typical Feydeau" in germ is the folly of the imbroglio. Mistaken identity compounded, and giving rise, before the inevitable disentangling, to a series of comically suggestive double entendres, tame by any standards—his day's as well as ours—but titillating in their implied naughtiness, especially given the virginal innocence of the sweet young thing entangled. Tame, especially, for a Feydeau who will not shrink, later, from placing his boudoir adventurers and adventuresses into bed together, long before Hollywood would sanction such proximity. Clearly Feydeau will be no prude. What has come to be known as "bedroom farce" was no genre for the bluenose. But neither will he be a pornographer.

21. Nowhere in Feydeau's plays is the snobbish imitation of Parisian manners ridiculed more deliciously than in *La Dame de chez Maxim*. Throughout the entire second act, in which she is mistaken for Madame Petypon, "Môme Crevette" succeeds in imposing her colorful cabaret argot and actions on a group of staid provincial ladies eager to accept her vulgarisms as authentic Parisian *bon ton*. So much so that they vie with one another in the elegance with which, like her, they kick a leg over a chair and exclaim "Eh! allez donc, c'est pas mon père!" (untranslatable, but roughly the equivalent of "Your father's mustache!"). Doctor Petypon, constantly on guard lest "La Môme" reveal her true identity, parries her faux pas by assuring the good ladies that "it's all the rage in Paris! ..." (Act II, scene iv).

22. While Wagner, as arch-idealist and mystic, did not become the demigod of the budding Symbolist movement until a few years later, with the founding of the *Revue Wagnérienne* in 1885, and although the great Wagnerian battle, marked by polemics and parodies, was not to begin until the famous Paris performance of *Lohengrin* in 1887, the controversial composer had become a topic of heated dispute as early as 1879, when Pasdeloup presented the first act of that opera at one of his concerts. The modest allusion to Wagner in *Amour et piano* is not Feydeau's last. Two years later, in the monologue *Le Colis*, the narrator recounts how his mother-in-law was "Wagnerized" at a concert—put to sleep by his music.

Indeed, at times he will stretch "good taste" to the limit, but never beyond.[23] It may even be argued that much of his broadest, most explicit "bedroom farce" is essentially moralistic. After all, those who lust illicitly, in the mind or in the flesh, are usually plunged into a variety of infernal mortifications, physical and mental, to reap the wages of their sins, at least temporarily. (Though I realize that this defense, used at least since the Middle Ages with works of dubious "morality," generally fails to convince.) Understandably still rather timid in an early trifle like *Amour et piano*, Feydeau is content to imply and let his spectators infer. "Honni soit qui mal y pense," as one journalist quipped at the performance.[24] And certainly in the context of this doubly youthful opus—both by and about the young—an ounce of inference is worth a pound of explicitness.

The last play of the early grouping, *Gibier de potence* (here adapted as *Fit to Be Tried, or, Stepbrothers in Crime*), represents something of a transition. Feydeau's first ambitious three-act comedy, *Tailleur pour dames*, will not be performed until 1886.[25] An immediate success, it will mark the beginning of what may be labeled his "second period," that of his emergence as a budding comic dramatist. *Gibier de potence* clearly points the way. Feydeau's first multicharacter comedy, it is longer and already far more complex in plot and structure than its slender one-act predecessors, and far richer in what will be his typical comedic devices. It is not clear, however, by how much it actually preceded the composition of *Tailleur*. Lorcey, in his generally authoritative biography, indicates that *Gibier* was completed early in 1883 and first performed on a small Parisian stage on June 1 of that year.[26] The script of *Tailleur*, he tells us, was finished a full two years later, after a year of army service, and was shown, during the first weeks of 1885, to Feydeau's director-friend Samuel, who enthusiastically snapped it up on the spot.[27] Another version, however—from a contemporary source—suggests something more of a struggle for the young playwright in getting his work accepted,

23. Possible exception might be made for the late three-act play, *Le Circuit* (1909), a collaboration with the young Francis de Croisset, parts of which are in very dubious taste. But Feydeau's contribution was probably minimal. Henry Gidel even refuses to recognize it as belonging to the Feydeau corpus (Gidel, p. 11).

24. Quoted in Lorcey, p. 77.

25. Many sources—the catalogue of the Bibliothèque Nationale and the Le Bélier edition among them—unwittingly give a false impression of Feydeau's early career by giving this date as 1887. (See my article "Georges Feydeau: Une date essentielle corrigée," *Revue d'histoire de théâtre,* 14 [October–December 1962], 362–64.)

26. Lorcey, p. 78. The date cited in volume 6 of the *Théâtre complet* and elsewhere, 23 December 1884, is actually that of a second performance. (See Lorcey, p. 83.) I suspect that the play was probably written, or at least begun, in the first half of 1882. A lengthy reference to *Othello* was most likely suggested by a production of Louis de Gramont's translation at the Odéon during April and May of that year.

27. Lorcey, pp. 82–83.

and seems to place *Tailleur*'s composition rather closer to *Gibier*'s, namely some three years before its triumphal premiere in 1886.[28]

Whomever we choose to believe, *Gibier de potence*—unlike its immediate or not-quite-immediate successor, *Tailleur pour dames*—shows a fledgling Feydeau still clinging to the security of the one-act nest. But clearly he is maturing for more ambitious flight. To be sure, conventional monologues, asides, and sly confidences to the audience have not vanished from his technique. Nor will they do so all at once (though they will become less and less evident as he gradually develops a more realistic stagecraft, perhaps influenced in the 1890s by the dramatic *vérisme* espoused by Antoine of the Théâtre Libre, vigorously though Feydeau might deny it).[29] The opening scene of the hapless Dupont is a long monologue that still smacks unmistakably of the salon, much as did Angélique's in *Notre futur*, Hector's in *Par la fenêtre*, and Edouard's in *Amour et piano*. As for the customary asides and the remarks to the complicitous audience, the action would be virtually impossible without them.

In other respects, however, *Gibier de potence* marks a definite advance. Its expanded cast of characters develops some types only lightly sketched in the preceding playlets, or left altogether invisible in the wings—Dupont and Pépita—and introduces others as yet unmet—Camembert, La Mole, and Bloarde. We meet them all again in future incarnations. And not unexpectedly. Like some artists—his contemporary Toulouse-Lautrec comes to mind—Feydeau the social observer will not be one to paint a single portrait and send his model packing. Dupont is a fleshed-out and middle-aging Edouard, though no less fatuous a provincial (for all his Latin), and no less intent on paying court to a Parisian actress. As ingenuous bungler and innocent butt,

---

28. "It took M. Georges Feydeau three years to have *Tailleur pour dames* performed. . . . Feydeau needed no less than the friendship of Fernand Samuel, daring director of the Renaissance, to enable him to unpigeon-hole the three acts that had been drowsing untouched for some time" (Guy de Saint-Môr, *Paris sur scène, 1886–1887* [Paris: Piaget, 1888], pp. 227–28.).

29. Feydeau's younger contemporary and protégé, dramatist René Peter, assures us that Feydeau had no use for the naturalistic technique of Antoine. For him, *vérisme* eventually led away from veracity rather than toward it. "In the theater," Peter quotes Feydeau as saying, "even the most accurately observed, the most *real*, . . . everything is, and can only be, *convention!*" (Peter, *Le Théâtre et la vie sous la Troisième République, première époque* [Paris: Editions Littéraires de France, 1945], pp. 251–52). We have to wonder, however, if his disaffection was not more with the avant-garde faddism of many of Antoine's enthusiastic and idealistic followers—a natural butt of Feydeau's aversion—than with his stagecraft. While Feydeau's early comedies abound, as we have seen, in those unrealistic conventions that were anathema to Antoine, he will, as I say, gradually abandon them in favor of a greater realism. (A notable exception will be Hubertin's two-page drunk scene in *La Main passe*, a monologue if ever there was one, but unlike the typical earlier monologues in that his drunken soliloquy, almost by definition, is not intended to take the audience into his confidence.) In addition, the precision and elaborate detail of the mature Feydeau's stage directions seem to be a page from Antoine's book; and the late one-act conjugal comedies are not, technically speaking, unlike the Théâtre Libre "slices of life," albeit with a difference.

he points the way to the luckless Bouzin, suffering antihero of *Un Fil à la patte*, whose only crime will be his pretentious advances to actress Lucette Gautier, by her own admission toast of the Paris stage, flesh-and-blood sister to Edouard's unseen actress. Pépita is something of a Lucette-in-the-making. Perhaps she is not yet quite as cynical or wordly-wise—though, as we shall see, she has no trouble wrapping her husband around her little finger, either before or after marriage—but she is well on the way. Feydeau will develop the character years later in the notorious "Môme Crevette" of *La Dame de chez Maxim*, whose brash, flamboyant, but lovable vulgarity will make her name a Parisian household word for over a decade. Pépita, more reserved than "La Môme," and certainly more domesticated—even if not by her own choosing—needs no excuse like Emma's vengeance to indulge her extramarital fancy. She too will have many descendants: liberated Feydeau ladies for whom marriage will be no guarantor of morals. (Though it should be said, in passing, that her escapade, under Camembert's very nose, is only implied, unlike the more blatantly outrageous affairs of many a later heroine.)

The other major characters in *Gibier de potence* are all making their first bow, but certainly not their last. Camembert, the cuckold, will spawn a hearty lineage, the veritable backbone of Feydeau's future theater. Given the preponderance of the *cocu* in French farce, from the Middle Ages on—for whatever deep-seated psychological reasons—it was inevitable that Feydeau should eventually portray him. And frequently. And not without considerable nuance. For, if Camembert suspects Pépita's probable involvement, other horned husbands will be less aware: Chouilloux, for example, in *On purge Bébé*, who learns of his wife's infidelity only in time for the traumatic revelation to rebound, as expected, on the innocent Follavoine.[30] Nor will they all react in one and the same way. Some, like Chouilloux, will give vent to their rage, demanding the redemption of their honor at swords' points; while others, like Savinet, the wine-merchant in *Le Système Ribadier*, will accept their horns docilely, less concerned for their blemished manhood than for their professional prestige. Still another, Chanal, the congenial bourgeois of *La Main passe*, will, after the first shock, react with a rare good sense and good humor, evoking our sympathy rather than our derision. Camembert, the first, is a curious case. Astute enough to have his eyes opened to Pépita's liaison (by Othello, no less!), he is still too blind to see how she had hoodwinked him into a marriage of convenience—her own, of course. The reason is clear. Without his awareness there would be no plot: intent upon revenge, he sets in motion a plan that will have unforeseen results. (Unforeseen and unimaginable in the ordinary scheme of things, but perfectly logical in Feydeau's emerging universe.) The rather bland La Mole, Pépita's lap-dog lover, is Feydeau's first "other man." But, given the

---

30. My version of *On purge Bébé* appears in *Four Farces*, under the title *Going to Pot*.

number of cuckolds to come, he will, *ipso facto*, not be the last. All will display much the same variety as the husbands they so blithely wrong. As for Bloarde, the grocer-cum-cop, he too is a Feydeau first. Caricature of the ex-military man imperfectly turned civilian, he is probably a projection of the young author's anticipation of his upcoming army service. According to Lorcey, Feydeau had finished *Gibier de potence* while waiting to join the ranks for his twelve-month stay.[31] Be that as it may, the character would develop, full-blown, almost a decade later, into the assorted army types of *Champignol malgré lui*, the immensely successful Feydeauesque nightmare that portrays the tribulations, corporeal and spiritual, of a would-be philanderer and his almost-cuckold victim, enmeshed in the mindlessness of military authoritarianism. In *Gibier*, Bloarde, for the few moments he bellows about as a surrogate police chief, relives the glories of his military past with a dogmatic, monolithic devotion to duty. At the same time he cannot forget that he is a grocer. On the contrary, he plies his civilian trade at the most inappropriate moments, in the midst of chaos, embodying that kind of professional rigidity, single-minded and mechanical, that will characterize a variety of Feydeau obsessives cut from the same cloth: a Marollier, the "professional second" in *La Dame de chez Maxim*, a Planteloup, the insistent police chief in *La Main passe*, determined to solve a nonexistent crime, and many others of their stripe. Like Dupont, the professor, inopportunely spouting his Latin as if by reflex. And, to a lesser extent, like poor Camembert as well.

For Camembert, the herb doctor with a puffed-up opinion of the value of his calling, prefigures many other professionals rather similarly inclined—such as the antimicrobian Doctor Paginet, hero of *Le Ruban*, who covets a decoration for his misguided efforts, and, in a less scientific (or pseudoscientific) realm, Follavoine, manufacturer of chamberpots in *On purge Bébé*, imbued with an idealized conception of the product of his labors. As one would expect, Feydeau has Camembert's self-important notions properly deflated, not only by Pépita's sarcastic teasing, but by our own recognition of his obvious simplicity. The good "doctor," after all, is scientifically naïve, to say the very least, ready to see a medical miracle in his premature paternity. Priding himself on being a man of science, he has far less excuse for his blindness than will others; for example, the simple domestic Etienne in *La Main passe*, victim of a similar misconception (so to speak).

Camembert also provides Feydeau with an opportunity for another jab at contemporary pretension: in this case, the mania for unmerited decoration. Just as Emma's reference to the duel in *Par la fenêtre* is only the first of many, so too the allusions here to the decoration craze. Indeed, in *fin-de-siècle* France, many a self-respecting bourgeois yearned to sport an imposing

31. Lorcey, p. 78.

ribbon in his buttonhole. If the prestigious *Légion d'honneur* or *Palmes académiques* were beyond reasonable expectation, he could at least aspire to one of the host of newer high-sounding honors created to satisfy egalitarian elitists.[32] "Aux grands hommes la patrie reconnaissante," as the Panthéon loftily proclaims. Even if the *grandeur* was often debatable. And if no home-grown honor was within reach, there was always recourse to a seemingly endless array beyond the borders. Like the impressive titles of a pseudono-bility conferred, for a price, by hard-pressed foreign governments, the exotic decoration was quite an acceptable substitute, rather easily acquired. Poor Camembert, ashamed of his naked lapel, mumbles sheepishly that his wife, after all, does know a Rumanian prince, and . . . The implication, to Fey-deau's audience, would be clear. And all the more ironic since Camem-bert doesn't seem to realize what services she will probably have to perform to get him his medal. (Like the heroine of the late farce *Occupe-toi d'Amélie*, whose father is promised an impressive decoration in return for her *services exceptionnels* to the lecherous Slavic prince.)[33] A few scenes earlier, Pépita turns Camembert's expectations to advantage. She pretends—improvising with a brio that Feydeau's characters will develop into an art—that her diamond brooch, gift from a passionate admirer, had really belonged to her father, who used to pass if off as a foreign decoration, having none of his own. She knows the stratagem will strike a responsive chord, and that Camembert, similarly unberibboned and unbemedaled, will easily accept it. The decora-tion mania, though lightly touched on in this early play, will reappear, like the duel, in a variety of situations. And those affected by it will feel varying degrees of Feydeau's good-natured ridicule. Doctor Paginet, in *Le Ruban*, will embody it to the fullest, reminiscent of Molière's miser Harpagon in his willingness to sacrifice even his family to his obsession; by a delightfully ironic twist, he will finally see himself decorated, but only by mistake.[34]

32. Between 1870 and 1900 over thirty new decorations were created by the French govern-ment, among them such intriguing examples as medals of Acts of Courage, Forest Service, Penitentiary Administration, Indochina Customs and Excise, National Highway Sanitation, and Epidemic Control, to name but a few. "Ribbons there will be aplenty, ribbons for everyone, and of every color," comments one observer of the phenomenon. "It seems, judging by the Frenchmen's thirst for decorations, that the day will come when every little baby born in France . . . will have, amid its dimples, a spot above its left nipple, reserved for future medals and rosettes" (Robert Burnand, *La Vie quotidienne en France de 1870 à 1900* [Paris: Hachette, 1947], pp. 163–64.).

33. Although the situation was already something of a cliché, it is not improbable that Feydeau had in mind another Slavic nobleman equally lavish with his country's decorations, a character in the popular three-act vaudeville *Niniche* (1878), by Alfred Hennequin, whose work he knew well and would subsequently study.

34. Other comic contemporaries exploited the theme as well, especially in the wake of the *Affaire Wilson* of 1887, a scandal involving the son-in-law of President Jules Grevy, convicted of trafficking in *Légion d'honneur* medals. It may seem hypocritical that Feydeau himself actively sought the rosette of the *Légion d'honneur*, finally receiving it in 1894, the same year as the

In brief, then, although *Gibier de potence* is slighted (if not ignored altogether) by most Feydeau critics, I see it as a significant link in his development. It is hard to imagine the leap from an *Amour et piano* to a *Tailleur pour dames* without a *Gibier de potence* or its like in between. Not primarily for the characters it develops or introduces, or for the modest social allusions, all common to many a humorist of the period. Nor for the expanded punning and wordplay, promise of things to come. It is, rather, for the burgeoning complexity of its structure. Pépita's affair, Camembert's revenge, and Dupont's ambition all become entwined—thanks to an unseen malefactor and his unfortunate victim—in a case of multiple mistaken identities, an imbroglio that will be typical of the mature Feydeau. (Though, as one might expect from such an early effort, not wholly unflawed.) The complexity of plot results in other complexities as well. We witness, for instance, the earliest examples in Feydeau's theater of what I might call the "impromptu explanation," euphemism for the tall tale invented on the spot. Pépita's explanation of her diamond brooch, for example. Dupont's and La Mole's extravagant mutual fabrication, a few scenes later, is already a masterpiece, appropriately absurd, of contrived deceit growing more and more involved and entangling its inventors. Feydeau's theater will be rich in such protracted prevarications, as characters caught in a web of circumstance struggle for their freedom. Doctor Petypon, for example, in *La Dame de chez Maxim*, will be obliged throughout the play to pile lie upon lie—or "explanation upon explanation"—in his frantic attempts to hide "Môme Crevette's" identity; the embodiment, like so many a Feydeau hero, of the truth of Scott's well-known couplet, "Oh, what a tangled web we weave/When first we practice to deceive!" In *Gibier de potence* the web is still made of gossamer. In later plays Feydeau will be weaving it of cable.

As a result, we are not surprised to find in his later, "well-made" Scribean constructions—*Champignol malgré lui*, *La Dame de chez Maxim*, *La Puce à l'oreille*, and others—an abundance of unabashed physical action. In post-classical theater it is difficult to ensnare and enmesh a helpless character in nothing more than words and ideas, however powerful. (At least, it was so before, say, the theater of a Beckett.) As the ultimate examples of such mechanistic farce, Feydeau's extravaganzas will be visual in the extreme, prototypes of what one unsympathetic critic—Feydeau's own stepfather,

---

premiere of *Le Ruban*, ironically enough. (Though who ever said that a comic author must never ridicule follies he sees in himself? If that were the case, Molière might never have written *L'Ecole des femmes*, with its aging Arnolphe, victim, like Molière himself, of an amorous generation-gap.) At any rate, years later—older and perhaps wiser—Feydeau was to revert to character by refusing the promotion from *chevalier* to *officier* because it entailed a modest fee. "Either they give me the rosette because I deserve it," he is said to have remarked, "or they sell it to me, in which case I don't want it. Not even for fourteen francs" (Achard, p. 11).

Henry Fouquier—would disparagingly term "Hennequin's theater of a hundred doors."[35] We are not dealing with the wordy, socio-cerebral comedy of a
Shaw or the equally wordy, poetico-philosophical comedy of a Giraudoux.
Despite the frequent, irrepressible glints of wit, the *mots*, the unforgettable
characters, the barbs of social commentary that will distinguish Feydeau's
farces from the *strictly* mechanistic, action is still paramount. Comedy for
the eye as much as, or more than, for the ear. A complex collaboration of
meaning and motion. And with action, "business." And with "business,"
props. And with props, more action, as his precise, often intricate stage
directions attest; directions that become an integral part of the mechanism.
Which is why the director of a typical Feydeau farce has to be as much a
choreographer as an interpreter of lines, and oftentimes more. True, *Gibier
de potence* is rather modest in this respect. It is certainly no "machine,"
no extravaganza. But it points the way. With its physical confrontations, its
sight gags, its props—Dupont's puppy, his coat, his recalcitrant umbrella
(foreshadowing the luckless Bouzin's in *Un Fil à la patte*)—Feydeau takes
a giant step toward that visual comedy that will be his hallmark for the
next quarter-century, through the height of his career.

    The period inaugurated by the success of *Tailleur pour dames* had its ups
and downs for the young Feydeau. Enough downs, it seems, to justify the
cynical prophecy of one of his contemporaries, Jules Prével, who wryly
observed as he left the premiere: "Tonight they've let you have your success,
but they'll make you pay for it."[36] Enough downs also to lead him, some four
years later, to a brief hiatus, a two-year "exile" from the public for artistic
introspection. It would be during this period, if we can believe dramatist
René Peter, that Feydeau devoted himself to studying three comic masters:
Hennequin *père*, Labiche, and Meilhac.[37] In the meantime, following *Tailleur*'s warm reception by both public and critics, he would try his hand at
several more three-acts and even a pair of operetta libretti.[38] He would also
continue to produce his witty monologues—old habits die hard, especially
successful ones—as well as two one-acts, a genre to which he had clearly
become attached.

    35. "Le Krach du théâtre," *Figaro*, 18 November 1891. The reference is to the intricate
vaudevilles of Alfred Hennequin (1842–1887), considered by contemporaries as the prototype of
the genre.
    36. See Achard, p. 9.
    37. Peter, p. 48.
    38. One of the three-acts, *A qui ma femme?*, has never been published or produced. The
manuscript is in the possession of Feydeau's grandson. (See Lorcey, p. 95.) As for the operettas,
the three-act *La Lycéenne* (1887), with music by Gaston Serpette, would seem to have been an
attempt to consolidate the success of *Tailleur* with a popular genre, the collaboration of a
popular composer, and a popular theme: the humorous incursions of the spreading feminism.
The other operetta, *Mademoiselle Nounou*, apparently produced in 1890, remains rather shroud-
ed in uncertainty. (See my article "Georges Feydeau: Note sur deux énigmes résolues," p. 90,
note 3.)

The fifth play in this collection, *C'est une femme du monde* (here adapted as *Mixed Doubles*, for reasons that will be all too apparent) is one of the latter. Produced on March 10, 1890, it is one of Feydeau's last two "pre-exile" comedies, and one of his early collaborations with Maurice Desvallières.[39] It is one of those one-acts that appear to have been dictated by practical career considerations. Later, as I have suggested, he would turn to the one-act to fill a gap in his creativity and keep his name before the public. With this play he seems, rather, to be retreating to security, as if he felt the need to retrench from an overextended technique. The comedies that had followed *Tailleur pour dames*—among them the first two collaborations with Desvallières: *Les Fiancés de Loches* (1888) and *L'Affaire Edouard* (1889)—had, bearing out Prével's prophecy, been rather disappointing. Even if René Peter exaggerates in calling them *fours*[40]—flops—and even if they have been largely vindicated since in modern revivals, there is no denying that for Feydeau they were a disappointment, especially after the promise of *Tailleur*. Perhaps an occasional less ambitious work was in order, more modest in scope and less boisterous in technique. Which is not to suggest that Feydeau was about to abandon the comedy of imbroglio, already his trademark in *Tailleur* and its less-than-successful successors, or that he was to return to the intimate sentimental genre abortively attempted in *Notre futur*. On the contrary, *Le Mariage de Barillon*, the three-act comedy that joined *C'est une femme du monde* in a double bill, is a veritable romp.[41] But a romp more tightly constructed, more rigorously logical in its mechanistic development than the several preceding *fours*. Perhaps it was intended to satisfy the demands of those critics, like straightlaced Auguste Vitu of the *Figaro*, who had called for more "logic" from the youthful playwright. "I think that he would work to better advantage," Vitu had written, "if he took the trouble to develop his ludicrous entanglements and link them together by some kind of logic."[42] As a pair, then, these two plays, each in its own way, seem to signal Feydeau's efforts to court the critics and convince them that *Tailleur* had been no flash in the pan: the one, by polishing and tightening

---

39. Feydeau had met his future principal collaborator in 1887, the same year in which he had met his future wife, the beautiful Marianne Carolus-Duran. Both relationships were marked for eventual rupture. A half-dozen years and some eight productions later, Feydeau and Desvallières reached a parting of the ways, and the artistic collaboration came to an end, to be revived only briefly in 1905. (Less easily ended, the marital collaboration was to wait until 1916.) Desvallières (1857–1920), author in his own right of many comedies, monologues, and operettas, is credited by many with helping channel and discipline Feydeau's youthful, unbridled inventiveness. While it is impossible to evaluate his contribution—in this comedy or others—it is unfortunate that most Feydeau enthusiasts tend to ignore it altogether. Desvallières himself, we are told, keenly resented his lack of recognition. (See René Peter, *Théâtre et la vie sous la Troisième République, deuxième époque* [Paris: Marchot, 1947], pp. 42–43.)

40. Peter, *première époque*, pp. 250–51.

41. My version, entitled *On the Marry-Go-Wrong*, appears in *Four Farces*.

42. From a review of *La Lycéenne*, in *Figaro*, 24 December 1887.

his flamboyant technique; the other, by discreetly retreating from it, to the comfort of a more conservative one-act.

I am not implying that *C'est une femme du monde* lacks the expected Feydeau complexity. Only that it is a complexity on a smaller scale, situational, not slapstick. No sight gags, no essential visual "business," no slamming doors pounding out a counterpoint to the confusion. (Unlike its partner, *Le Mariage de Barillon*, to which it provided an appropriate counterpoise.) It is one of those rare Feydeau comedies that can be enjoyed almost as much in the reading as in the seeing.[43] Its structure, easily appreciated on the page, is like a kind of simple musical composition, the basic ternary A B A, opening and closing with the maître d'hôtel's "theme." In the middle, a B section, extensively developed, admittedly rather contrived and predictable. Not the traditional lovers' triangle, to be sure, but a properly improper "lovers' square." A naughty chiasmus. What the French would call a *chassé-croisé*, made all the more compact by the neat relationship between "themes" A and B.[44]

Like most other light comedies of the period, Feydeau's own included, *C'est une femme du monde* offers a number of social insights. Obviously its *raison d'être* is not as a social document. Still, it seems to me that the element of contemporary social sport—"satire" would be too ambitious a term—is more important in this play than in its predecessors. The reason, I think, is in the very predictability of the plot. For all their passing social allusions and social caricature, such playlets as *Par la fenêtre* and *Gibier de potence* are, as I have observed, more notable for the absurdity of their plots and their resolutions. We are never quite certain just how they will turn out. (Even *Amour et piano*, simple as it is, is not wholly predictable.) By contrast, in *C'est une femme du monde* Feydeau seems hardly to be trying at all to conceal the denouement, even from the beginning. We suspect the relationships among all the characters, and feel little surprise when, at the end, our suspicions are confirmed.

The interest—and the humor—lies rather in the sketches of certain social fauna and their interactions, and, by implication, of the milieu that produces

43. This is not to imply that all of his plays might not be read with pleasure. It is only a question of degree. One recalls the prophecy of dramatist-critic Catulle Mendès, who, admitting Feydeau's talent, took him to task for wasting it on "plays that will be performed four or five hundred times running, and revived four or five times as well, but that will never be *read*" (*Le Journal*, 18 January 1899; quoted by Gaston Sorbets in the first edition of *La Dame de chez Maxim*, in *La Petite Illustration*, 1 August 1914–17 May 1919). Today Mendès is a curio. His works are neither read nor performed, while Feydeau's are both, and their attraction shows no signs of waning.

44. The musical analogy has been offered before, though for Feydeau's more complex, geometric plays. "There are moments when—all things, let me say, being unequal—the progression of an act of Feydeau offers the same secure feeling of satisfaction in surprise as the workings of a Bach fugue" (Béatrix Dussane, *Notes de théâtre 1940–1950* [Lyons: Lardanchet, 1951], p. 221.).

them. This comedy offers Feydeau's most explicit tableau, to date, of the contemporary world of Parisian easy virtue. True, his earlier efforts had (implicitly, at least) already portrayed individuals of dubious conventional morality. Emma's request of Hector is for no innocent amusement; Edouard has not come seeking his actress for a game of checkers; clearly Pépita and La Mole are no saints. And mistresses, lovers, wronging husbands and wronged wives—assorted inamoratos and inamoratas—weave through the fabric of the comedies that followed, as early as *Tailleur*. But nowhere in such a concentrated dose. A society in microcosm, *C'est une femme du monde* presents a tableau of infidelity rampant: two braces of heroes and heroines, mistresses blithely cuckolding their no-less-blithely two-timing lovers. Cads and cadesses all, albeit unbound by the bonds of matrimony— which, in any event, would certainly not have stopped them. (Their humorous antics will sound a more serious echo in the elaborate mate-swapping of *La Main passe*, a dozen or so years later.) In this comedy Feydeau plays no favorites. He delights in spoofing both the *demi-monde* would-be society ladies as well as their respectable bourgeois lotharios. The former, *cocottes* turned *coquettes*, awkwardly struggling through a maze of verbose affectation to keep their masks from slipping, are clearly the principal butts of his humor. But the latter obviously amuse him too: self-important, convinced of their irresistible charms, sure that in their private dining-room love nest (backdrop for many a later Feydeau adventure) they will easily wear down their "society ladies'" resistance. Pompe-Nicole is even more the *roué* than Bordeleau, yearning for the spice of danger and challenge to excite his jaded romantic palate and feed his self-image. But both lovers deserve the mortification of their egos. And, to their credit, both accept it gracefully in the end, convinced that a good meal—literal, not figurative—is worth even more than a good affair. At least, until the next time.

C'est une femme du monde is also the first of several Feydeau comedies to reflect another social phenomenon: divorce. After many years of agitation and argument pro and con, the *Loi Naquet* was finally enacted in 1884, reestablishing civil divorce in France. Society quickly felt the results. As one observer put it, writing in the same year: "Thanks to Monsieur Naquet, the consoler of those who were not born with the knack for lasting marriage, the courts are about to have their work cut out for them."[45] And the prophecy came true. As for the theater of the period, serious and comic, both before and long after, it is filled with theses on the one hand, imbroglios on the other, and a host of passing allusions, light and heavy.[46] Playwrights were

45. L. Sevin-Desplaces, in Charles Simond, ed., *Paris de 1800 à 1900*, vol. 3 (*1870–1900*) (Paris: Plon, 1901), pp. 280–81.
46. Typical are the following popular plays of the period: Augier, *Madame Caverlet* (1876); Sardou and Najac, *Divorçons* (1880); Bisson, *Les Surprises du divorce* (1888); Brieux, *Le Berceau* (1898); Bourget, *Un Divorce* (1908). The list could be expanded to comprise several

adding a new string to their bows. Their characters need no longer suffer infidelity in silence, or resort to adultery, comic or dramatic. In this play, true to the spirit of the Boulevard humorists, Feydeau's allusion to divorce is properly lighthearted, providing a topical twist to the denouement. It will be so, too, in others of his plays. Only with *La Main passe*, in 1904—a more serious comedy of marital disillusion (and, indeed, dissolution)—will it take on a much less frivolous dimension, as if Feydeau's own domestic difficulties gradually begin to project themselves onto his creations. Eventually the specter of divorce will hover over the five late plays of conjugal discord. In this volume we shall see the ultimate results in *Hortense a dit: "Je m'en fous!"* Not in the play itself, but in its predictable post-curtain climax: Foll-braguet-Feydeau's own real-life divorce. With that hindsight provided, we can see an almost prophetic irony, as Lorcey suggests, in the fact that his first two plays produced after marriage, *Le Mariage de Barillon* and *C'est une femme du monde*, "dwell rather heavily on the benefits of divorce and on marital misfortune."[47]

Feydeau's subsequent two-year absence from the boards—his voluntary "exile"—came to an end with a bang in 1892, with the production of no less than three successful comedies. From that point on, success followed success, virtually unabated. To list all the plays produced during this period is, with few exceptions, to name all the best-known "machines" that were building his reputation then, and on which it primarily rests today. By the end of the century his most ambitious play was to be the celebrated masterpiece *La Dame de chez Maxim*. And also his most unqualified triumph. The critics were to vie with one another for superlatives, as *La Dame* would quickly become the classic of its genre, spreading Feydeau's name far and wide.[48] But Feydeau, by his own admission, did not always give birth to his progeny without a painful labor. *La Dame* did not see the light of day—or of the footlights—until January 1899, though conceived and, most likely, largely completed two years before.[49] His most recent creation had been *Le Dindon*, produced in February 1896. Already addicted to the sweet smell of success (and the sweeter smell of cash, for his growing financial needs and specula-

---

dozen—many more if one were to include the scores of works by utter unknowns, and the transient offerings of humorists and cabaret *chansonniers*.

47. Lorcey, p. 106.

48. "Is there any town today," asks Gaston Sorbets, in the play's first edition, "even tucked away in the most far-flung province, where that phrase ["La Dame de chez Maxim"] fails to bring back the happiest memories?"

49. Feydeau's laziness had become legendary. In a frequently-quoted passage he admits: "I may as well confess it: I hate work. . . . The theater has become the rule, my duty. It is my trade. . . . No, I am not one of those who enjoy giving birth! . . . When the work is done, what a relief! I regain my freedom" (Adolphe Brisson, *Portraits intimes*, vol. 5 [Paris: Armand Colin, 1901], pp. 15–16). *La Dame* was a case in point, taking two years to polish, although it had already been accepted by the management of the Théâtre des Nouveautés as early as 1897. (See Jules Martin, *Nos auteurs et compositeurs dramatiques* [Paris: Flammarion, 1897], pp. 214–15.)

tions), Feydeau was not about to let the public forget him for three whole years while finishing, reworking, and polishing his *magnum opus*. A trio of one-acts would be called to fill the breach. Two of them—*Les Pavés de l'ours* and *Dormez, je le veux!* (rebaptized *The Boor Hug* and *Caught with His Trance Down*)—are the next comedies in this collection.

As with Feydeau's earliest one-acts, chronology poses a problem with these. While the former was produced in 1896 and the latter in 1897, I suspect that they were, in fact, written in reverse order. Flugel, in the first, seems clearly to be a fleshed-out development of the lightly sketched Max, in the second.[50] I suspect, too, that at least one of the plays, if not both, was written several years earlier and dusted off for Feydeau's purpose. The unscrupulous hypnotist-servant Justin, the villain of the piece in *Dormez, je le veux!*, is a virtual double of a similar scoundrel in a one-act playlet, *Le Fluide de Jean*, published in 1891 by Maurice Hennequin, son of one of Feydeau's comic idols. Feydeau, who had met the younger Hennequin early in the same year, was subsequently to collaborate with him on *Le Système Ribadier*—also a spoof of the current rage of hypnotism and its potential for skullduggery—one of the three successful comedies that marked his reemergence in 1892. Whether Feydeau got the idea of Justin's hypnotic dodge from Hennequin or vice versa, it seems reasonable to assume that these several hypnotism comedies date from roughly the same time.[51] *Le Système Ribadier* being the most complex, and its stratagem being the most elaborately developed, it would seem that *Dormez, je le veux!* most likely preceded it. All of which would tend to place that play around 1891 and, in any event, prior to *Les Pavés de l'ours*, though by how much we can only conjecture.[52]

The two plays, whatever their chronology and whatever Feydeau's reasons for producing them when he did, are a coherent and contrasting pair. Both are rich in Feydeau's verbal humor and his typical situational inventiveness. But while both are variations on the age-old master-servant theme, *Dormez, je le veux!* is basically a visual comedy. Justin's character and stratagem are essential, of course. But they really exist only to provide an excuse for

---

50. In the originals, both domestics are examples of "those ridiculous Belgians" referred to by Pierre Enckell, Germanicized in my version for obvious reasons: anti-Belgian humor would be lost on Americans.

51. Given Hennequin's playlet and his collaboration on *Le Système Ribadier*, I lean toward the supposition that the hypnotism idea was his. In any event, he and Feydeau were not alone in exploiting it. From the late 1860s on, as the work of Charcot and others began to rescue hypnotism from its mystical associations with Mesmer, its literary vogue became immense. By the mid-1880s it was not only inspiring serious works like Maupassant's *Magnétisme* and *Le Horla*, and Claretie's *Jean Mornas*, but had been seized on by Boulevard humorists like Grenet-Dancourt, Galipaux, Najac, Allais, and scores of others, who worked the mine for its comic potential, treating hypnotism as semi-science, semi-spirit, and—like Feydeau and Hennequin in their comedies—often confusing fact with fancy.

52. The over-zealous scholar should not see in the reference to Freud an aid in dating. It is my own slightly anachronistic liberty, replacing the name of the less well-known Charcot.

the physical action: the zany antics of his unsuspecting victims, and his eventual "duel" with his outraged antagonist.[53] On the other hand, *Les Pavés de l'ours*, though not without its visual moments and its less-than-subtle touches—Madame Prévallon's provocative stammer, for example, typical of many a Feydeauesque physical imperfection—is more of a character study, if I may use such a high-sounding term in the context. The results of Flugel's boorish good intentions are themselves less important, I think, than the foibles that precipitate them. Whereas Justin is the product of a transient fad, Flugel is an unforgettable type. The one gives us belly-laughs; the other, a more reflective chuckle.

The two contrast also in their embodiment of the theme. The master-servant comedy is as old as the Greek and Roman theater. In France it is as venerable as the first extant farce, the thirteenth-century *Le Garçon et l'aveugle*. Whether in his eventual *commedia dell'arte* incarnations, in Molière. Beaumarchais, Goldoni, or beyond, the servant, by whatever stock name he is called—Scapin, Arlecchino, or many others—is a social inferior; a kind of archetypal *puer* vis-à-vis the symbolic (if not always senescent) *senex*. He compensates for his social status by his presence of mind and his intellectual resourcefulness. By traditionally abetting his master's amours, he proves at least to his own satisfaction that social position is no measure of his worth. If Justin is a distant descendant of Molière's Scapin, it is only because of his inferior station, his superior wit, and his efforts at compensatory self-aggrandizement. Certainly not for any desire to serve his master's needs. In this he is spiritually closer to the scurrilous likes of Lesage's Crispin and Frontin, reflections of early-eighteenth-century rumblings of upward social mobility. Flugel is his opposite in practically every respect. Justin is the clever, cynical Parisian; Flugel, the dim-witted, ingenuous provincial. No scheming Arlecchino he! If Flugel is a naïve "diamond in the rough," as Casimir keeps insisting, then Justin, to extend the metaphor, is a worthless stone, but polished to perfection. And if Justin thinks only of manipulating Boriquet to serve his own ends, well-meaning Flugel is selfless to a fault. His sole concern is to serve his new master. The results of their adventures are likewise symmetrically opposite. Boriquet is trying to marry his fiancée, and despite Justin's efforts to scuttle his love life, he wins out in the end (though through no fault of his own). Casimir, on the other hand, is trying to shed his mistress,[54] but through Flugel's misguided altruism his best-laid plans go

---

53. It was certainly such unsubtle, external humor that provoked the usually conservative Catulle Mendès (though probably against his better artistic judgment) to admire the play as "one long guffaw from beginning to end," and to see in Feydeau a playwright "wonderfully endowed with joy and burlesque inventiveness" (*L'Art au théâtre*, vol. 1 [Paris: Charpentier, 1897], p. 180).

54. In this he is reminiscent of other fickle Feydeau lovers—foremost among them, Bois-d'Enghien in *Un Fil à la patte*, produced in 1894. The date leads us to wonder if *Les Pavés de l'ours* may not have been a "spin-off".

awry. Justin's failure is Boriquet's success, while Flugel's apparent success—ironically, he thinks he has put everything to rights—is Casimir's debacle. Flugel succeeds only in wreaking havoc. The nasty Justin may be mildly satanic, but his damage is undone before the curtain falls. Poor lovable Flugel, on the other hand, paves his road with good intentions. The damage, we may assume, will eventually be righted, but not before much tearing of hair and much gnashing of teeth.

Casimir's mini-hell is nothing compared to the torments suffered by the heroes of the typical Feydeau extravaganzas—the Champignols, the Bouzins, the Petypons. As more than one critic has pointed out, Feydeau's theater is cruel when stripped of its humor.[55] As creator of a self-contained little universe, he seems to delight, almost sadistically—aware of his godlike prerogative to dispense, capriciously, comic damnation or salvation—in playing a kind of cosmic cat-and-mouse with his creations. This is certainly what Pierre Enckell must mean when he accuses Feydeau of having a "basic scorn for his characters," a *mépris général* that produces more hysteria than gaiety, and that comes closer to derision than to good-natured ridicule.[56] Feydeau's suffering characters, like those of virtually every farce since the Middle Ages, are unfortunate victims. As I have observed elsewhere, "To some extent all farce portrays its characters as victims, from *Pathelin* to Ionesco and beyond, with Chaplin and the Keystone Kops thrown in—victims of something or someone, whether brickbats or bullies, one's adversaries or oneself, comic quid pro quos or cosmic misadventures. Feydeau's theatre, from beginning to end, is no exception. From his earliest farces . . . it presents an array of hapless victims whose suffering—sometimes deserved, more often gratuitous—runs the gamut from mere embarrassing misunderstanding to physical discomfort, panic, and unbridled, unspeakable frustration."[57]

Nowhere in Feydeau's theater is this victimization more concentrated, more intense, than in the late one-acts that mark his "final period," that of the "untamed shrews," to quote Marcel Achard,[58] of which *Hortense a dit: "Je m'en fous!"* is—regrettably—the last. There is a kind of curious irony here. For, if the characters trapped in Feydeau's imbroglios are victims of his whimsy, if he plunges them into grotesque situations and lets them thrash about in a crescendo of desperation until he charitably plucks them free, in

55. See, for example, Paul Morand, "Champignol parle au nom des dieux," *La Parisienne*, no. 10, October 1953, pp. 1424–25; and Jean Cassou, "Le Génie systématique de Feydeau," *Cahiers de la Compagnie Madeleine Renaud–Jean-Louis Barrault*, January 1956, pp. 55–61.
56. Enckell, p. 28.
57. Introduction to my version of *Hortense a dit: "Je m'en fous!"*, in *Comedy: New Perspectives*, vol. I of *New York Literary Forum* (Spring 1978), pp. 275–76. I have discussed the same question in detail in "Suffering and Punishment in the Theatre of Georges Feydeau," *Tulane Drama Review*, Autumn 1960, pp. 117–26.
58. Achard, p. 17.

these final plays he is obviously himself the victim. The parallel between these tableaux of marital misadventure and his own domestic life, even unto certain specific details, is too well documented to remain hypothetical or to need restating.[59] Feydeau's own divorce and subsequent mental breakdown are clearly no coincidence. Perhaps this is why, of all his plays, these are the only ones in which the victimization remains not only unresolved, but with little, if any, hope of ultimate resolution. The curtain that falls on Follbraguet and his brothers-under-the-skin has not solved their problem. Perhaps, too, this personal dimension helps explain why, after such resounding triumphs as *La Dame de chez Maxim*, Feydeau chose to turn once again to the modest one-act, though this time with less farcical, even serious overtones.

Elsewhere I have suggested several plausible reasons: Feydeau's legendary laziness (hard though that may be to reconcile with his meticulous craftsmanship), his awareness that "Hennequin's theater of a hundred doors" was falling into disrepute,[60] his midlife need for artistic renewal—a kind of artistic menopause—or, indeed, his need for something of a sublimation, a therapeutic working-out of his own domestic problems.[61] While all these reasons, and probably others, may have played their part, I should think, given the circumstances of his personal life, that the last was the most compelling. Be that as it may, Feydeau's change to a more serious form of comedy was not wholly unprepared. We have seen that even before *La Dame de chez Maxim*, as early as 1894, with *Le Ruban*, he (and Desvallières) had attempted to portray characters more at home in so-called "higher" comedy, even considered worthy—though not without many a raised eyebrow—of the conservative Odéon, one of the national Parisian theaters. After *La Dame*, two other plays pointed in the same direction: *La Main passe* (1904), with its semiserious treatment of divorce, and *Le Bourgeon* (1906), a curious mixture of farce and drama, delicately handling the difficult theme of a young seminarian's struggle with his devil in the flesh. Nor was the change an abrupt one. Two other farces, among them Feydeau's broadest and most successful—*La Puce à l'oreille* (1907) and *Occupe-toi d'Amélie* (1908)—showed that he was still fully in command of his intricate Chinese-puzzle technique when and if he chose to use it.

Of the five conjugal comedies, *Feu la mère de Madame* (1908) was the first. Whatever the reasons for the change in style had been, its warm reception by audiences, and especially by prestigious critics, determined

---

59. Feydeau's son Jacques, for example, was undoubtedly—and admittedly—the "villain" of *On purge Bébé*. (See Lorcey, pp. 202–3.)

60. It seems more than coincidental that, after the appearance of the pessimistic article on the condition of the "vaudeville" by his stepfather, critic Henry Fouquier, Feydeau was never again to use that term in designating his works.

61. *Comedy: New Perspectives*, p. 278.

what was left of Feydeau's career.[62] Aside from two generous collaborations with youthful protégés and the two farces left unfinished, his last productive years were devoted to these painful reflections of his own disintegrating marriage. *Hortense*, to my mind, is by far the most painful. I find it hard to understand the curious opinion of Jacques Lorcey, who, failing somehow to see it as the marital tableau that it is, considers it rather as a simple return to Feydeau's earlier blatant farce: "The author wanted to hark back to his first loves, and peppered his little comedy with vaudevillesque scenes, madcap but very superficial, that make us yearn for the vein of 'conjugal comedies.'"[63] *Hortense* is, on the contrary, the natural and inevitable culmination of its four predecessors. It shares with them a few innocent off-color moments —typical by now—and a few passing topical allusions common to all of Feydeau's comedies to some extent. More important, like them, it is a play of imbroglio, albeit a restrained, psychological imbroglio, with small cause mounting to huge, frustrating effect, but with none of the vaudevillesque jack-in-the-box devices that Lorcey suggests. Especially like them, too, it leaves its victim still enmeshed and struggling; a victim not only of his wife's harassment, but, from a more cynical viewpoint, of his own—and his creator's—misguided belief in the possibility of successful marriage. We know where his struggles, onstage and off, are destined to lead.

Marital love is hardly an issue in most of Feydeau's theater, except as a prelude to the inevitable infidelities and attendant escapades. It plays no active role. But in the late conjugal comedies it plays an important role indeed, at least negatively, by its very deterioration. *Hortense* closes the door on it altogether, with Follbraguet's final slam. In the earliest playlets of this collection, young love is felt as a positive presence, despite the none-too-serious obstacles that stand in its way. In *Notre futur* we can assume that, after her initial adolescent disillusionment, Valentine will meet a nice young gentleman—perhaps one of the guests at Angélique's posh soirée. In *Par la fenêtre*, if Hector's jealous spouse prefigures the shrewish Marcelle, it is only a dim foreshadowing. At this point in Feydeau's career theirs is only a minor spat; they will certainly kiss and make up after the curtain. We can even imagine that Edouard and Lucile, the young couple of *Amour et piano*, will meet again under less accidental circumstances, and that their budding romance—in "A Flat" or elsewhere—will take its course. In *Hortense*, however, there is no room for such optimism. It is Feydeau's parting shot, his final cynical statement about the potential for marital bliss. Perhaps he had not meant it to be quite the last word. We know that he had planned, at least vaguely, to incorporate the late plays in a series to be entitled *Du*

---

62. Besides *On purge Bébé* (1910) and *Hortense a dit: "Je m'en fous!"* (1916), the other plays of the group are *Mais n'te promène donc pas toute nue!* (1911) and *Léonie est en avance (ou Le Mal joli)* (1911).

63. Lorcey, p. 243.

Mariage au divorce ("From Marriage to Divorce").[64] Perhaps one more was intended to complete the cycle and portray the couple's actual break-up, yet further literary revenge against the insufferable spouse. If so, it was not to be. But Feydeau, in his theater as well as in his life, had already amply illustrated colleague Alfred Capus' dictum that "there's nothing like marriage to separate so many husbands and wives."[65]

He was not the first. And he would not be the last.

Like most translations, the ones in this volume can do with a few words of explanation. Translation being, by definition, an act of artistic choice, translators are prone to a kind of paranoia, often feeling the need to defend that choice against potential criticism. This is especially true when the theater is involved. More than with other genres, the translator of plays is faced with the obligation not only to be "faithful" to his original, but also to bring it to life on stage. And for audiences sometimes far removed in time or place, or both. Most especially in comedy, where cultural and temporal barriers frequently make topical allusions, wordplay, and the like, virtually inaccessible. There are two extreme solutions: the translator can hew to the original with a rigorous, scholarly fidelity that will, from the theatrical point of view, result in rigor mortis. Or he can "adapt" the original to death, wrenching it out of its milieu to varying degrees—updating it, tinkering here and there with the plot, Americanizing the idiom with an assortment of "wows," "cools," "gee whizzes," and such. (I exaggerate to make my point, but not by much.) The first solution may produce a faithful document, accurate and useful to historians of literature, but moribund as theater. The second may result in witty and lively dramatic works, but ones in which the hand of the playwright is hardly visible, and his voice only dimly heard.

I try to walk the tightrope. Convinced that to be slavishly faithful to the likes of Feydeau is to be unfaithful to his spirit, I take my full share of liberties. But if I often call my versions "adaptations," it is only my translator's paranoia showing. It is not because I really stray very far from his originals. Belgians will become vaguely nondescript Germanics. Names will occasionally change to fit American actors' mouths (while retaining their Gallic flavor), or to adapt themselves to Feydeauesque wordplay. Contemporary allusions may be appropriately altered. Puns will be recast—a necessity that should need no defense—or find themselves displaced, or become expanded to compensate for others best left unattempted. I even plead guilty, on occasion, to adding a gag or amplifying a situation. But only in what I have come to know as the "Feydeau spirit," and never, I hope, enough to falsify his intent.

64. Achard, p. 17.
65. Quoted in Francis de Croisset, *La Vie parisienne au théâtre* (Paris: Grasset, 1929), p. 140.

In this collection the most extensive examples of liberties taken occur in my version of *Gibier de potence*. Extensive because, in addition to the usual names, puns, allusions, and the like, a few small changes have had to be made for the sake of dramatic consistency and accuracy. I have already suggested that the play is not without flaws. Although Feydeau was quickly to gain fame as the master of tightly knit, geometric farces—precision-built constructions that might be seen, metaphorically, as anticipations of the machine-age Futurism of Léger and company—he was not above an occasional lapse in the earliest days of his career. *Gibier* contains several that he surely would not have allowed himself once he had hit his stride. Some are obvious oversights: a few inaccurate stage directions, props picked up that were never set down, imprecisions of the type that the more mature Feydeau—who was to "orchestrate" his plays in the greatest detail—would simply never commit. Some, however, are more basic. For example, in the original, we see Camembert writing his denunciatory note to the police at four in the afternoon. But in fact he never sends it. At five, Bloarde arrives supposedly in response, letter somehow in hand, and says that the police chief had received it at lunch that day. Inexplicable inconsistencies. Or again, when La Mole brings Pépita the evening paper, she reads that the infamous murderer is still at large. Yet Bloarde informs her later that he had been caught that very morning. Such lapses and a handful of others could, I suppose, be considered intentional. Conscious little tidbits of delightful absurdity. But nothing in the comedy reinforces that possibility, and certainly Feydeau's later meticulous stagecraft would seem squarely to contradict it. Hence my liberties, somewhat greater in *Gibier* than elsewhere, but I think no less defensible. I hope that purists will not take them for license. I am sure that actors and directors will not do so. And, for that matter, I doubt that Feydeau would do so either.

Likewise I think he would not object to the obvious liberties I have taken with his titles. A cursory glance will show that they are less than literal. The plays they introduce in this volume are appearing for the first time in my (or, to the best of my knowledge, any) English-language versions, except for *Par la fenêtre* and *Hortense a dit: "Je m'en fous!"* The former was originally translated in my collection *Four Farces by Georges Feydeau* and is reprinted by permission of the University of Chicago Press; the latter appeared in the first number of the *New York Literary Forum* (Spring 1978). I thank the publishers for permission to reprint them.

My thanks also to Wesleyan University for its support in this and other projects; to Robert Kiely, Master of Adams House, Harvard University, for his cordial hospitality; and to the many friends and colleagues always generous with their suggestions and their good judgment: Evelyn Simha, Caldwell Titcomb, Herbert Myron, Estelle Stinespring, Seymour O. Simches, Sheila Hart, Lillian Bulwa, Maurice Charney, Jeanine Plottel, Dudley Knight, Joan

Dayan, Laurence Senelick, and a host of others. Above all, to my father, for his unflagging encouragement, and to the memory of my mother, for inspiration lasting long beyond her passing.

My special thanks to director H. Stuart Shifman for his splendid premiere of *The Boor Hug*, at the Wesleyan Center for the Arts, in October 1980. His superb student cast—Paul Caruso, Andrea Corney, Cheri Litton, Jon Sperry—proved by their talent, enthusiasm, and especially their uncompromising hard work, that an Equity card is no prerequisite to virtuosity. To all associated with that production—foremost among them, Sharon Jones, Chris Lanier, Sylvie Stewart, Pamela Tatge, Frank Wood, Grete Fries, Michael Haney, Tracy-Jake Solomon, Fritz deBoer, Michael Schler, Bill Ward, and Jerry Zinser—my hearty appreciation. Michael Haney's delightful premiere of *Ladies' Man*, six months later, with Sharon Jones and Pamela Tatge, confirmed my admiration for the theatrical achievements of Wesleyan undergraduates.

My acknowledgments would be incomplete without mention of the late Daniel Seltzer, good friend and multitalented man of the theater, who, years ago, while I was still a student, first suggested that I try my hand at translating Feydeau, and to whose memory this collection is affectionately dedicated.

NORMAN R. SHAPIRO

Cambridge, Massachusetts

LADIES' MAN

·

Notre futur

CHARACTERS

Angélique

Valentine

A richly furnished drawing room. Upstage center, a double door. On the rear wall, left, a clock. In the right wall, downstage, a fireplace. Above it, a mirror, flanked by two lighted candelabra. Down right, parallel to the footlights, a divan. In one corner of it, a wicker sewing basket. Down left, a small table. On either side of it, facing the audience at appropriate angles, an armchair. On the table, an unfinished embroidery and a newspaper. Other lavish furnishings—carpets, chairs, pictures, etc.—ad lib.

At rise, the stage is empty. After a brief moment, the double door opens and ANGÉLIQUE *appears, wearing an ornate gown and covered with diamonds.*

ANGÉLIQUE, *standing in the doorway, back to audience, talking to someone offstage.* Yes, yes, Toinette... Candles... Everywhere, understand? Lots and lots of candles... And this time please don't forget to light them! (*She turns and enters the room, sighing.*) Ah! Candlelight... I simply adore it! It absolutely brings out the best in my complexion! (*She goes over to the mirror, admiring herself.*) You ravishing creature, you!... And that exquisite gown!... Stunning!... Utterly stunning!... (*Primping.*) Oh! It's going to be a triumph! I can feel it in my bones... (*Coyly.*) "Why, Monsieur de Neyriss... You naughty boy! I didn't know you cared ..." (*Reveling in her expected conquest.*) They'll all be simply green with envy!... Women can be so insufferably jealous!... (*Changing her tone, suggestively.*) And men can be so... (*Coquettishly, as she continues to admire her reflection.*) Well, who can blame them?... Oh! I can hardly wait!... (*Looking at the clock.*) Eight fifteen... Another whole hour! (*She sits down in one of the armchairs, down left.*) Sixty whole minutes with nothing to do! (*She gets up and paces back and forth for a moment, then sits down in the other chair.*) Really... Time just stands still when you wish it would fly!... Absolutely still! (*She gets up, goes over to the*

39

clock to check the hour more closely, and shakes her head.) And when you wish it wouldn't... (*She crosses down right and sits on the divan.*) It's not that I'm nervous... I mean, I certainly have no reason to be nervous... It's just that... Well, after all, marriage is a serious proposition! I think I have every right to feel a little... a little... (*She gets up and goes over to the mirror, primping.*) Especially when the man is a handsome young devil, and... and the woman is the widow of a tired old general with one foot in the grave... (*Realizing the absurdity of her last remark.*) That is, both feet now... But even when poor Antoine was alive, there wasn't much life in him! (*Going back to the divan.*) It's not that I'm blaming him... It's just that, when it came to... (*Pointedly.*) affection... Well, he wasn't exactly... how shall I put it?... the soul of generosity!... (*She begins pacing again.*) Heaven knows, it wasn't his fault, poor dear! But still... A young woman can't live on I.O.U.'s for long! There comes a time... Whereas, with Monsieur de Neyriss... (*She sits down in one of the armchairs, sighing.*) Ah! Gaston... I'm sure that's no problem! I'm sure he must be... (*Emphasizing.*) generous beyond belief! So young, so handsome... After all, he's from Marseille... No ice-water in those veins! Not from Marseille!... (*Getting up.*) The only question now is, will he come?... I wish I could be sure... (*Pacing again, reflecting.*) Actually, I haven't seen hide nor hair of him for days... (*Reassuring herself.*) Still, that's no reason... (*Stopping in front of the other armchair, categorically.*) I invited him and he's coming! He wouldn't dream of missing an opportunity like this! Not when he loves me the way he does... Not when he's planning to ask me to marry him!... (*She sits down.*) What better time than tonight, I mean?... The music, the champagne... (*Getting up, going over to the mirror, admiringly.*) The candlelight... Of course! Tonight... It's perfectly obvious... Why, just the other day... last week... in the sitting room... (*She sits down on the divan.*) I was sitting... (*As an afterthought.*) Naturally... And he practically asked me then and there!... He really did!... I was on the Morocco love seat... the brown one... And the dear boy absolutely threw himself at my feet!... Why, if Toinette hadn't come bursting in just at the wrong moment, I'm sure he... (*The doorbell rings.*) Oh my! Who can that be? (*Looking at the clock.*) It can't be a guest already!

Voices are heard offstage.

MISS SMITH'S VOICE, *with a pronounced English accent.* If you're sure you don't want me to stay...

VALENTINE'S VOICE. No, no... Sank you, Mith Thmiss... (*Correcting herself, enunciating.*) Thank you, Miss Smith... You're a dear... Bye-bye...

ANGÉLIQUE *gets up as the double door opens and* VALENTINE *appears. She is simply though tastefully dressed.*

VALENTINE, *at the threshold.* Oh, these English names! I'll never—

ANGÉLIQUE, *surprised, going to greet her.* Valentine!

VALENTINE, *entering.* Angélique!

ANGÉLIQUE, *kissing her.* Precious!... You're early!

VALENTINE, *teasing, with a little laugh.* You sound disappointed!

ANGÉLIQUE. Hardly, love... Just a little surprised... The guests aren't arriving for almost an hour, and—

VALENTINE, *interrupting.* I know... That's why... I wanted to talk to you before they all got here.

ANGÉLIQUE. Oh?

VALENTINE, *moving down right.* Just the two of us... in private...

ANGÉLIQUE, *following her.* Good heavens! That sounds serious!

VALENTINE. Serious? That's hardly the word, I'm afraid! (*She sits down on the divan, sighing.*) I need your advice...

ANGÉLIQUE, *sitting down beside her.* Well, for goodness' sake... Tell me...

VALENTINE. I mean... there are some things I just can't discuss with Mamma...

ANGÉLIQUE. No... I'm sure...

VALENTINE. And certainly not with... (*Nodding toward the door, articulating.*) Miss Smith...

ANGÉLIQUE. No...

VALENTINE. But with you... After all...

ANGÉLIQUE. Of course, love... Please... That's what cousins are for!

VALENTINE. Exactly!... (*Innocently.*) Especially older ones... (*Realizing her faux pas, as* ANGÉLIQUE *stiffens slightly.*) That is, even if they don't look it...

ANGÉLIQUE, *with mixed emotion.* Thank you...

VALENTINE. Like tonight... You do look lovely tonight, I must say!

ANGÉLIQUE, *with a note of pique.* Much obliged! At least for tonight...

VALENTINE. Now, now... Don't tease! You know what I mean!... (*Rephrasing.*) "You look even lovelier than usual..." There!

ANGÉLIQUE. I do?

VALENTINE. And that gown is an absolute masterpiece! Really!... You're going to put everyone else to shame!

ANGÉLIQUE, *standing up, pirouetting.* Do you think so?

VALENTINE. Oh, I'm sure of it!... Why, I'm going to feel like a poor little Cinderella! Just look at me...

ANGÉLIQUE, *sitting down beside her*. Nonsense, precious! You look utterly charming! Simplicity becomes you...

VALENTINE. And those diamonds! Angélique... I've never seen so many in one place before!... I'd give anything to be able to wear diamonds like that!

ANGÉLIQUE. On a sweet young thing like you?

VALENTINE. No, I suppose you're right... It's different when you're a widow ... (*Innocently*.) And so much more mature...

ANGÉLIQUE, *aside*. Again?

VALENTINE, *sighing*. It must be wonderful... Being a widow, I mean...

ANGÉLIQUE, *with a wry laugh*. Yes... Only don't let the young man you marry hear you say that!

VALENTINE, *reproaching herself*. Oh my! That was a terrible thing to say, wasn't it!... Me and my foolish talk!... Every time I open my mouth ... Really!... Or else I'm so afraid I'm going to say something awful that I just don't say anything! And that's just as bad!

ANGÉLIQUE, *with a gesture*. Silly!

She gets up, goes to the table, down left, and picks up her embroidery.

VALENTINE. But no one ever taught me all the right things to say... (*Admiringly*.) The way you do, for instance...

ANGÉLIQUE, *sitting down in one of the armchairs*. Well...

VALENTINE. Or how to talk to young men...

ANGÉLIQUE, *embroidering*. It's really not so difficult... (*Aside*.) When you're so much more mature!

VALENTINE. It just never comes out the way it should, somehow... Why, take Monsieur de Mercourt, for example... Right here, last week...

ANGÉLIQUE. Philippe?

VALENTINE. Yes... You know what happened?... He came up to me, out of a clear, blue sky, and said: "Ah, mademoiselle! You're a vision of loveliness!"

ANGÉLIQUE. Dear boy!

VALENTINE. And can you guess what I answered?

ANGÉLIQUE. "Thank you," I imagine...

VALENTINE. Oh yes... I said "Thank you!"... But that's not all...

ANGÉLIQUE. Oh?

VALENTINE. I said: "Thank you, monsieur! So are you, I'm sure!"

ANGÉLIQUE, *with a little laugh.* You didn't...

VALENTINE. You can just imagine how it sounded! (*With a shudder.*) He thought I was making fun of him! He turned on his heel and left!

ANGÉLIQUE. No!

VALENTINE. Yes!

ANGÉLIQUE, *sympathetically.* Tsk tsk tsk... Poor Valentine... That's innocence, precious! It's a virtue, you know!

VALENTINE. Yes, well... That's all well and good... for somebody else! But I'm tired of being virtuous! I... (*Unthinking.*) I want to be like you!

ANGÉLIQUE, *somewhat taken aback.* Valentine! Really...

VALENTINE, *angry with herself.* See? That's just what I mean! I can't seem to help it... No matter what I say... Please! You've simply got to teach me...

ANGÉLIQUE. Of course, love... I'll try... (*Holding her embroidery on her lap, after a brief pause.*) But certainly that's not what you came to ask me...

VALENTINE, *embarrassed.* No... It's not...

She pauses.

ANGÉLIQUE. Well?

VALENTINE. It's... It's not easy to explain... It's about a... a...

ANGÉLIQUE, *laying the embroidery down on the table, beside her.* A man!

VALENTINE, *with a start.* What?... How on earth did you know?

ANGÉLIQUE, *laughing.* How indeed!

VALENTINE, *naïvely.* That's amazing!

ANGÉLIQUE. Call it woman's intuition!... Besides, only a man could make you blush that flattering shade of red!

VALENTINE, *putting her hands to her face.* Oh...

ANGÉLIQUE. Now then, what's the name of this lucky young gentleman?

VALENTINE. His name?... Oh no... (*Mysteriously.*) I couldn't... Not just like that...

ANGÉLIQUE. Good! I love a mystery!... Well then, what is he like?

VALENTINE. What is he... (*Rapturously.*) Oh, Angélique!... He's... He's simply the most handsome, the most perfect...

ANGÉLIQUE, *aside.* Ah yes! Aren't they all!

VALENTINE. Besides... You'll meet him and you'll see for yourself!

ANGÉLIQUE. I will?

VALENTINE. Yes... Tonight...

ANGÉLIQUE. Here?

VALENTINE, *putting her hand to her mouth*. Oh my... I hope you don't mind... I invited him... I thought...

ANGÉLIQUE. Good heavens! I must say, that really does sound serious!

VALENTINE. Oh, it is! It really is!

ANGÉLIQUE, *not without a touch of irony*. True love!

VALENTINE, *missing the intent*. Oh yes! I'm sure! It just couldn't be anything else...

ANGÉLIQUE. And he feels the same way, this young man of yours?

VALENTINE, *as if it were obvious*. Of course!... Why else would he ask me to marry him?

ANGÉLIQUE, *a little surprised*. Marry him?

VALENTINE. Yes... Just the other day...

ANGÉLIQUE, *trying not to be too disillusioning*. But they all do, precious! That doesn't prove a thing! It doesn't mean they love you!

VALENTINE. Oh, but he meant it... I could tell... The way he asked me ... The look in his eyes, his voice...

ANGÉLIQUE. Valentine...

VALENTINE. Why, it was right here... Last week... Just after Monsieur de Mercourt...

ANGÉLIQUE. The party for the countess?

VALENTINE. Well, whoever she was... Anyway, the two of us were dancing ... (*Dreamily.*) I'll never forget! It was a waltz... My favorite... At least, it is now!... And before I knew what was happening, he was waltzing me off into the little room... (*Pointing offstage.*) You know...

ANGÉLIQUE. The sitting room?

VALENTINE. I guess...

ANGÉLIQUE, *aside*. That must be their favorite spot for such things!

VALENTINE, *with a little shiver of emotion*. All alone... Just the two of us... And he sat me down on your Morocco love seat...

ANGÉLIQUE, *with a slight start*. My what?

VALENTINE. Your love seat... The brown one... You know the one I mean...

ANGÉLIQUE. Oh yes... Yes... (*Aside.*) I swear! These men are all alike! (*To* VALENTINE.) Be a dear... (*Pointing toward the divan.*) Get me my sewing basket, won't you?

VALENTINE, *going over and bringing her the basket*. And then, as soon as I was sitting down, Monsieur de...

　　She catches herself.

ANGÉLIQUE, *quickly*. Monsieur de...?

VALENTINE, *smiling, coyly*. The gentleman took my hands in his and... and...

She pauses, embarrassed.

ANGÉLIQUE, *rummaging in the basket*. And?

VALENTINE. And he absolutely threw himself at my feet! (*She kneels down in front of* ANGÉLIQUE.) Like this!

ANGÉLIQUE. No!

VALENTINE, *sighing, romantically*. Oh, Angélique... There's nothing in the world like seeing a man at your feet! Really... If you don't know what it's like, I couldn't possibly explain it!

ANGÉLIQUE, *wryly*. I think I do, thank you!

VALENTINE, *embarrassed*. Of course you do! What am I saying?... You see?

ANGÉLIQUE. Quite all right, love... No offense...

VALENTINE. There's simply nothing like it! A handsome young man... in front of you... on his knees...

ANGÉLIQUE. Strange how our husbands don't share your enthusiasm! (VALENTINE *sighs, oblivious to her remark*.) Well now, you were saying...

VALENTINE. Yes... There I was, on the love seat...

ANGÉLIQUE, *aside*. Appropriately named!

VALENTINE. And there he was...

ANGÉLIQUE. Kneeling at your feet...

VALENTINE. Exactly!... And telling me things, as sweetly as could be...

ANGÉLIQUE. Things?

VALENTINE. All kinds of things... Some that I didn't even understand... But I knew if I did understand them I would like them!

ANGÉLIQUE. Dear child...

VALENTINE. And I didn't dare say a word! Really... I was simply so... Oh! I just knew that the minute I opened my mouth I was sure to say something stupid! So, whatever he said, I just smiled and said "Yes..."

ANGÉLIQUE, *putting down the basket*. You just... (*Concerned*.) Valentine! You didn't...

VALENTINE, *getting up, innocently*. Did I do something wrong?

ANGÉLIQUE. Well I'm sure I don't know! "Yes" is a dangerous word with some men!

VALENTINE. But what else could I do? I told you... I didn't dare... You should have heard him... (*Imitating his voice*.) "Ah! Mademoiselle...

From the production of *Ladies' Man* at Wesleyan University, May 1981, directed by Michael Haney (photograph by the director).

You're beautiful, and I love you..." (*In her own voice.*) "Yes..." (*Imitating.*) "Ah! Valentine... Valentine..." He called me "Valentine"...

ANGÉLIQUE. So I see...

VALENTINE, *imitating.* "Valentine, you're superb... You're magnificent... (*In her own voice.*) "Yes..." (*Imitating.*) "You can make me the happiest man in the world... You can make all my fondest, most cherished dreams come true..." (*In her own voice.*) "Yes..." (*Imitating.*) "My heart is ablaze... consumed with the flames of wild, passionate desire..." Or something like that...

ANGÉLIQUE. No doubt!

VALENTINE, *imitating.* "And no one... No one... Only you can quench the raging inferno that your eyes have set afire in the depths of my soul..." (*Naïvely.*) That part I really didn't understand at all! But then he said... (*Imitating.*) "Ah! Valentine... Valentine..."

ANGÉLIQUE, *with another touch of sarcasm.* He called you "Valentine"...

VALENTINE, *continuing.* "Joy of my heart... Light of my life..." (*Stopping, correcting herself.*) No... I think "light of my life" came first... Then... (*Imitating.*) "Mistress..." (*Trying to remember exactly.*) "Mistress..."

ANGÉLIQUE, *with a start.* What?

VALENTINE, *continuing.* "Mistress of my fate..."

ANGÉLIQUE. Oh...

VALENTINE. "Marry me, Valentine! Say you'll be my wife!"

She pauses.

ANGÉLIQUE. And?

VALENTINE. And I said "Yes..." What else could I do?

ANGÉLIQUE. Oh! Men!... They can be such unprincipled cads!... They'll promise you anything to get what they want!

VALENTINE, *with conviction.* Oh, I know! Believe me...

ANGÉLIQUE, *jumping to her feet.* You do?

VALENTINE, *embarrassed.* Well... Yes...

ANGÉLIQUE, *suspecting the worst.* How?... How do you know?

VALENTINE. Please... Angélique...

ANGÉLIQUE. Don't "please Angélique" me!... You're hiding something, aren't you? Something absolutely frightful... You and that... that young satyr of yours!

VALENTINE, *misunderstanding.* "That young..." Oh no! Really... He's as French as you or I!

ANGÉLIQUE, *ignoring her remark.* And don't think you're getting away without telling me!

VALENTINE. But...

ANGÉLIQUE. Out with it, Valentine! What are you hiding?

VALENTINE. I... Oh dear... I... (*Pathetically.*) Do I have to?... Just like that?... (ANGÉLIQUE *nods.*) But... (*Resigned, sighing.*) Oh... (*Leaning her head on* ANGÉLIQUE's *shoulder.*) Better you than Mamma, I suppose!... I think I'd absolutely die if I had to tell her!

She pauses.

ANGÉLIQUE. Well?

VALENTINE, *bowing her head.* Angélique... (*Hesitating.*) I... He... We...

She pauses again, obviously distressed.

ANGÉLIQUE. Yes?

VALENTINE. We... We...

ANGÉLIQUE, *sharply.* Valentine! You didn't!

VALENTINE, *head still bowed, softly.* I... I'm afraid we did...

ANGÉLIQUE. No!

VALENTINE. And now I'm going to have to marry him, whether I want to or not!

ANGÉLIQUE, *embracing her, tenderly.* Oh! Precious... You poor, dear, innocent child!... You mean you actually...

VALENTINE. Yes... We... (*Abashed.*) We kissed!

ANGÉLIQUE. You what?

VALENTINE. We kissed!

ANGÉLIQUE, *heaving a sigh of relief.* Oh! Thank heavens! (*She sits down in one of the armchairs, picks up the newspaper from the table, and begins fanning herself.*) I thought... I... Well, never mind what I thought... It's not important...

VALENTINE. But...

ANGÉLIQUE, *replacing the newspaper on the table.* So, love... your young man gave you a kiss!... My my my!

VALENTINE, *sitting down in the other chair.* Yes... Isn't that awful?

ANGÉLIQUE, *exaggerating.* Oh my! I should say!... Why, if I were your confessor, I would tell you it's a sin!...

VALENTINE. Oh!

ANGÉLIQUE. But just between you and me, love, I wouldn't worry!... Men will do that sort of thing! (*Sighing.*) I know!... It's really not your fault...

VALENTINE. It's not? Are you sure?

ANGÉLIQUE. Positive! (*Picking up her embroidery.*) There's a lot more to marriage than kissing!

VALENTINE, *aside.* There is?

ANGÉLIQUE, *laughing.* If we had to get married each time one of them kissed us... Well...

VALENTINE, *aside.* What else, I wonder...

ANGÉLIQUE. So I really don't think you have to be too concerned...

VALENTINE. And... and you really don't think I'm just the most frightful...

ANGÉLIQUE, *shaking her head.* Tsk tsk tsk... Not at all!... Why, the general, rest his soul... the general always used to say: "Love is the best excuse!"

VALENTINE. He did?

ANGÉLIQUE, *aside.* Not that he had much to excuse himself for! (*To* VALENTINE.) And I certainly agree!

VALENTINE. But... What should I do when I see him tonight? What should I say?

ANGÉLIQUE. Well, first try not to say "Yes"...

VALENTINE. I mean, what if he wants me to elope with him, or something?

ANGÉLIQUE. It's the "or something" I'd really be worried about, precious!

VALENTINE. The what?

ANGÉLIQUE. The first time they're only unprincipled cads, but the second time they can be out-and-out scoundrels!

VALENTINE. But what do I do when he asks me to dance? I can't very well say "No!"

ANGÉLIQUE. Well, you could...

VALENTINE, *growing more and more emotional.* It's not as though we're strangers! The man did ask me to marry him, after all! (*Almost about to whimper.*) And even an unprincipled cad and... and an out-and-out scoundrel wouldn't do that unless he meant it... Would he?

ANGÉLIQUE, *gently.* I do believe you're serious, Valentine! I think you really love him! (*There is a pause as she waits for an answer.*) Do you?

VALENTINE, *meekly, turning aside.* I don't know... I'm not sure... (*Looking at her.*) But I do know I'd like to!

ANGÉLIQUE, *with a knowing smile.* I think that's all the answer I need!... And does he love you?

VALENTINE, *enthusiastically.* Oh yes! He adores me!... I can tell... I just know...

ANGÉLIQUE. Then there's really no problem! I'll speak to your mother...

VALENTINE, *clapping her hands in anticipated joy.* Would you?... Will you?...

ANGÉLIQUE. Of course!... And if she gives her blessing, I can't see any reason why you shouldn't get married!

VALENTINE, *delighted.* Married? Me?... (*She jumps up and throws her arms around* ANGÉLIQUE's *neck.*) Oh! Angélique, darling! You're just the most wonderful cousin in the world!

ANGÉLIQUE, *trying to protect her toilette from the affectionate assault, with a touch of irony.* Anything to oblige!

VALENTINE, *still trying to hug her.* And I'll never forget it!

ANGÉLIQUE. I'm sure...

VALENTINE. Never, never, never!

　　She gives her a kiss.

ANGÉLIQUE, *finally disengaging herself, adjusting her coiffure.* I take it you rather like the idea of being married!

VALENTINE, *ecstatic.* Like it? I... Oh! I can't wait! Just the thought of it... Hearing everyone call me "Madame"... and wearing diamonds... and... and going to the Opera... Oh!

ANGÉLIQUE. I must say, your notion of wifely duties is a trifle... (*She pauses.*) Well... you love each other, and that's all that matters.

VALENTINE. Oh yes! Yes, we do!...

ANGÉLIQUE. And that's why I'll speak to your mother, first thing... (*Reflecting, good-naturedly.*) Of course, it might help if I knew the young man's name!

VALENTINE. His... (*Putting her hand to her mouth, hesitating.*) Do you think it's all right?

ANGÉLIQUE. Do I think... (*Smiling.*) Well really, love... I can't just go up to her and say: "Oh, by the way, Jacqueline... your daughter asked me to tell you that she wants to get married to some man or other..."

VALENTINE. No... That would never do... But... (*Deciding.*) Well, I suppose... I mean, now that you've promised to help... There's really no reason to hide it, is there?... It's... it's Gaston de Neyriss...

ANGÉLIQUE, *thunderstruck.* Who?

　　She throws her embroidery down on the table.

VALENTINE. Monsieur de—

ANGÉLIQUE, *jumping to her feet, interrupting.* It can't be! That's impossible!

VALENTINE, *puzzled.* What?

ANGÉLIQUE. It must be someone else!

VALENTINE. Someone... (*Innocently.*) No, no... I'm sure... It's Gaston... Gaston de—

ANGÉLIQUE. Don't be absurd! It can't be!

VALENTINE. What do you mean, "It can't..."? It is, I tell you!

ANGÉLIQUE, *categorically.* And I tell you it isn't!

VALENTINE. But...

ANGÉLIQUE. He doesn't love you!

VALENTINE. He... Of course he does! He said so!

ANGÉLIQUE. He never said anything of the kind! He couldn't...

VALENTINE. But Angélique... Really...

ANGÉLIQUE. He couldn't...

VALENTINE. He—

ANGÉLIQUE. He simply couldn't!

VALENTINE. But he did!... I'm sure!... And... and I'm going to be his wife!

ANGÉLIQUE. Well, so am I! So there!... Now what do you say to that?

VALENTINE, *nonplussed, sitting down.* You... He... You're going to... You are?

ANGÉLIQUE. I am!

VALENTINE. You and... and my Gaston?

ANGÉLIQUE. Quite!

VALENTINE. He... he asked you to marry him?

ANGÉLIQUE. He... Well, practically... He's as good as asked me... He's asking me tonight!

VALENTINE. Tonight?... But... he's already asked me... Last week! I told you...

During the succeeding exchange, ANGÉLIQUE *paces between the divan and the fireplace, stopping every now and again to primp nervously in front of the mirror.*

ANGÉLIQUE. Besides, what's the difference? With men like that marriage is a mere formality!

VALENTINE, *dejected.* It is?

ANGÉLIQUE. It's love that counts! And he loves me... madly...

VALENTINE, *almost pathetically.* But he asked me...

ANGÉLIQUE. And anyway, it's perfectly obvious... He's not the man for you! You're much too young!

VALENTINE. But Gaston is young too!

ANGÉLIQUE. Him? Young?... Really, Valentine! You must be joking! He's thirty if he's a day!

VALENTINE. Well...

ANGÉLIQUE. Youngish, perhaps... But not young enough for you! (*Looking at herself in the mirror.*) Whereas...

VALENTINE, *beginning to resist.* And besides, I don't see why that's any concern of yours!

ANGÉLIQUE. Valentine!

VALENTINE. You promised to speak to Mamma...

ANGÉLIQUE, *adjusting her coiffure.* Me? Speak to your mother?... I wouldn't dream of it!

VALENTINE, *getting up.* But you promised!

ANGÉLIQUE. And have you hate me?... Have you utterly loathe me for ruining your future?

VALENTINE. For ruining my—

ANGÉLIQUE. For letting you marry a man who doesn't love you!

VALENTINE. But he does, I tell you!

ANGÉLIQUE. Valentine! Be sensible!... Do you think you're the only woman in his life? Look at me...

VALENTINE. I know... (*Simply.*) But he loves me... That's the difference...

ANGÉLIQUE, *growing impatient, aside.* Impossible child!... (*To* VALENTINE.) Don't you know how many women he's probably running after?

VALENTINE, *annoyed.* Oh!

ANGÉLIQUE. Dozens, believe me!... I know his type! He doesn't have a faithful bone in his body!... Is that the kind of man you want for your husband?

VALENTINE, *giving her tit for tat.* Is that the kind of man you want for yours?

ANGÉLIQUE, *caught short.* I... That's right! Change the subject!

VALENTINE. But that *is* the subject!... What's good for the goose is good for the... (*Adapting the proverb in mid-sentence.*) for the other goose! I really don't see the difference!

ANGÉLIQUE, *rather curtly.* The difference is... In the first place, Valentine, we're not talking about me! And even if we were... There are simply certain things... A widow knows more than a callow young child!

VALENTINE. I'm sure...

ANGÉLIQUE. And besides, you don't love him!... You can't! You hardly know him!

VALENTINE, *petulantly.* Don't say that!... I do!

She crosses over to the divan, turning her back to ANGÉLIQUE.

ANGÉLIQUE. You only think you do!... And you certainly don't want to marry him!... Not really!... All you want is... (*With a shrug.*) to wear diamonds, and... and go to the Opera!

VALENTINE, *turning to her.* That's not true! I do love him!... (*Almost whimpering.*) I... I do! I do!

ANGÉLIQUE, *sitting down in one of the armchairs.* Love?... At your age you don't even know what that means!... Puppy love, perhaps!... But it's all bark, no bite!... (*Trying to pacify her.*) Believe me, precious! I know... I've been through it!... You see a handsome young man... (*Aside.*) Well, youngish... (*To* VALENTINE.) And before you know it, he's all you can think about... Nothing else, day and night... And then, heaven help us, if he happens to flatter us... to say something nice... an innocent little compliment... Why, all of a sudden we're sure he wants to marry us! And we keep expecting him to ride up on his white horse, and climb up to our balcony, and... and carry us off! Like in all the stories!... But life doesn't happen that way, Valentine! Real love is very different!... Believe me!... Very, very different!

VALENTINE, *softly, but a little bitterly.* That's not the way you were talking before! (*Imitating.*) "I'll speak to your mother... I can't see any reason why you shouldn't get married!"

ANGÉLIQUE. I... I've had time to think...

VALENTINE. Rather quickly, I'd say!... In fact, only since I mentioned Monsieur de Neyriss!

ANGÉLIQUE. And what is that supposed to mean?

VALENTINE, *obviously repeating an overheard cliché.* Only that a lawyer pleads best for himself!

ANGÉLIQUE, *playing the part of injured innocence.* That's right! Blame me for trying to open your eyes!... For telling you the truth, and trying to protect you!... Instead of thanking me... instead of... (*In a huff.*) Oh!... Well, go ahead! Marry him!... You'll have a very loving husband!... Loving every other woman he can get his hands on!

VALENTINE, *still at the divan.* Angélique! That's... that's hateful!

ANGÉLIQUE, *reaching out to her, attempting to be conciliatory.* Really, Valentine...

VALENTINE, *turning aside, curtly.* Oh... leave me alone!

She sits down on the divan, back to ANGÉLIQUE.

ANGÉLIQUE, *losing patience.* Fine! Go ahead... Sulk to your heart's content!... Only please be good enough to let me know when you've finished!

She sits down in her chair. There is a long, heavy pause, during which both women pointedly ignore each other. After a few moments, ANGÉLIQUE *casually picks up the newspaper from the table, fans herself, then begins to read with pretended interest. Suddenly something in the paper catches her eye.*

ANGÉLIQUE, *jumping to her feet, with a start.* Oh! Good God!... I... It can't be!... I don't believe it!

VALENTINE, *turning to her.* What on earth...

ANGÉLIQUE. Monsieur de Neyriss... He's...

VALENTINE, *anxiously.* He's what?

ANGÉLIQUE. He's getting married!

VALENTINE, *jumping up in shocked disbelief.* Married?

ANGÉLIQUE, *holding out the paper.* Look! See for yourself! (*Reading.*) "Impending nuptials..."

VALENTINE, *falling back onto the divan.* Oh!

ANGÉLIQUE, *reading.* "We are happy to announce the forthcoming marriage of Monsieur Gaston de Neyriss and Mademoiselle Brigitte de Grossegeld, beautiful heiress to the Grossegeld gypsum fortune..." (*Appalled.*) Beautiful?... She's crosseyed!... (*Reading.*) "When asked if there was any truth to the report that the bride-to-be's father, eminent industrialist Baron Maximilien de Grossegeld, was providing a dowry in the millions of francs, the gallant Monsieur de Neyriss, always the perfect gentleman..." (*Incensed.*) Oh yes! Perfect!... Simply perfect!... (*Finding her place, reading.*) "...the gallant Monsieur de Neyriss..." (*Skipping over the offending phrase.*) Blah blah blah... (*Reading.*) "...smiled and replied: 'I really wouldn't know. We never discuss money. I only know that I'm in love with his daughter...'" (*Flinging down the paper.*) Oh! That... that swine!... That utter swine!

VALENTINE, *who has been listening, benumbed, on the verge of tears.* It... it's just not possible... Not my Gaston...

ANGÉLIQUE. *Your* Gaston... Ha!... (*Snidely.*) Yours, mine, hers... whoever's!... (*Angrily.*) Oh! Men... They're all alike! Every last one of them!

VALENTINE, *weakly.* He told me he loved me...

ANGÉLIQUE. Not worth the powder to blow them to kingdom come!

VALENTINE. And he wanted to marry me...

ANGÉLIQUE. Maybe now you'll believe me! A man like that... (*Pacing angrily back and forth.*) And you wanted me to help you... to talk to your mother... to let me ruin your life...

VALENTINE, *sighing.* Angélique... Darling...

ANGÉLIQUE. Oh yes! Now it's "Angélique darling!" But before, when I tried to tell you... when I tried to warn you that the man was a... a... (*Fighting back her own emotions.*) Oh!... No! You wouldn't listen! You thought I was being selfish... only thinking of myself... (*With a tear in her voice.*) As if... as if I would ever marry a man like that!

She pats her eyes with a handkerchief.

VALENTINE. Angélique...

ANGÉLIQUE. I don't know why I don't just say: "I told you so!"

VALENTINE, *sadly.* Please...

ANGÉLIQUE. Because I did, you know... I did...

VALENTINE. I know, but...

ANGÉLIQUE. Well, maybe next time you'll pay more attention...

VALENTINE, *pathetically.* Please, Angélique... Don't scold... I had no idea... He seemed so... I mean, I thought he... I thought...

She pauses, shaking her head.

ANGÉLIQUE, *going over to her, taking her hand, gently.* Yes, I know... I know... (*Patting her hands, affectionately.*) After all, I thought so too, precious...

VALENTINE, *sighing.* Oh...

ANGÉLIQUE *stands comforting her for a moment. Then, after a final sigh, she affects a resolute, business-as-usual manner.*

ANGÉLIQUE, *striding up to the mirror.* Well now... that's that!... It's over and done with!... (*Primping.*) He's not the last young man in Paris, now is he?

VALENTINE, *getting up, trying to emulate her, as defiantly as possible.* I should say he's not!... And he's not so young, either! Why, he's practically thirty!

ANGÉLIQUE, *with a nostalgic, almost imperceptible sigh.* Yes...

VALENTINE, *hands on hips.* And I'm not going to miss him! Not even a little!

ANGÉLIQUE. I certainly hope not...

VALENTINE. You'll see!... I won't... (*Fighting back the tears.*) I won't... I really won't...

She begins to sob quietly.

ANGÉLIQUE, *turning to her.* Why... Valentine, love... you're crying...

VALENTINE, *turning aside, with a whimper.* No I'm not!... I'm not doing anything of the kind!

ANGÉLIQUE, *joining her, tenderly.* There, there... I know... It's no shame to shed tears... The shame belongs to the one who makes us shed them!

She embraces her and gives her a kiss.

VALENTINE, *drying her eyes.* That's right! And... and he doesn't deserve them!... (*Composing herself, mustering a forced little smile.*) See?

ANGÉLIQUE, *sympathetically.* Tsk tsk tsk... I'm afraid your first love hasn't
been a huge success!... (*Trying to console her.*) But look at it this way... If
things had turned out better, think how much worse they'd be!

VALENTINE, *quizzically.* Please?

ANGÉLIQUE. Why, you might have become Madame de Neyriss... (VALEN-
TINE *heaves a melancholy little sigh.*) And that's a fate we wouldn't wish
on anyone!

VALENTINE, *weakly.* No...

ANGÉLIQUE, *sarcastically.* That is, except the beautiful Mademoiselle Brigitte de Grossegeld!

VALENTINE. You're right! (*As if reciting a lesson.*) And now I only want to
forget him!

ANGÉLIQUE. Completely!

VALENTINE. Every day I'll try to forget him more and more! And... (*Naïvely.*)
And finally I'll forget him so much that I'll... I'll hate him!

ANGÉLIQUE. Hate him?... Oh no, love! No, no! Don't you dare!... That's
the worst thing you can do! You'll just love him all the more!

VALENTINE. Oh no... I wouldn't...

ANGÉLIQUE. Just like the rest of us... We women are all alike!... No, no...
Don't hate him, don't blame him...

VALENTINE. But...

ANGÉLIQUE. None of that!... Because the more you condemn him for what
he's done, the more you'll love him for... (*With a little shrug.*) for just
being himself. Our love finds a reason to forgive them... It always does...

VALENTINE, *with a sigh.* Oh...

ANGÉLIQUE. No, no... Just forget him! It's really the only way!

VALENTINE, *determined, but still drying her eyes.* I will!... I will!... (*She
pauses for a long moment, closing her eyes tightly, as if making a supreme
effort, then opens them, smiling.*) There!... (*With a determined nod.*)
I have!

ANGÉLIQUE, *smiling.* And after a little while, when there's no more love
left... nothing to make you forgive him... You'll see... you won't even
give him a second thought! Believe me!... And you'll thank your lucky
stars that you shed your tears in time!

She gently pats VALENTINE's *eyes with her handkerchief.*

VALENTINE, *tenderly.* Thank you, Angélique... I... I won't cry... I promise...

ANGÉLIQUE, *with forced joviality.* Well, I certainly hope not!... I mean,
think of our guests!... Tears? On that pretty face?... What on earth would

they say?... All those handsome young men... (VALENTINE *smiles*.) Fine!...
Now give me a kiss! (*They embrace*.) There!... (*She looks over at the clock*.)
It's time we were dancing! (*Taking* VALENTINE's *hand, apostrophizing*.)
Well, Mademoiselle Brigitte de Grossegeld... You can have him! With
our compliments!

VALENTINE, *smiling, pretending not to understand*. Whoever do you mean?

ANGÉLIQUE, *playing along, pretending to forget*. Why, Monsieur... Monsieur... (*Laughing*.) Monsieur de What's-his-name!

VALENTINE. Oh, him...

They go to the door, hand in hand. VALENTINE *exits*. ANGÉLIQUE
stands in the doorway for a moment, back to the audience.

ANGÉLIQUE, *calling offstage*. Candles, Toinette... I thought I told you...
Lots and lots of candles...

CURTAIN

WOOED AND VIEWED

•

Par la fenêtre

CHARACTERS

HECTOR

EMMA

A well-furnished drawing room. Upstage, a door leading to the hall. Down right, a window. Close to it, a chair. Up left, a fireplace and mantelpiece appropriately decorated. Up right, a door leading to HECTOR's study. Center stage, a table set for lunch. Chairs and occasional furniture ad lib.

At rise, HECTOR, in shirtsleeves and apron, has just finished setting the table. walks in from kitchen, with Glass of water and silverware. Food on table.

HECTOR, *alone.* There! Not bad for a beginner, if I do say so myself! (*He looks down at his apron.*) Lucky I'm alone... If anyone saw me like this, who knows what they'd take me for? (*He flares out his apron and makes a mock curtsy.*) Well, they'd be wrong! Believe it or not, I'm a lawyer... Really! Not that I ever had much to say about it, heaven only knows... My mother's the one who decided it all. One day, there I was with my governess... I'll never forget, I was just eight months old... Anyway, there we were. Mother took one look at me, up and down, and all of a sudden it came to her: "He's going to be a lawyer!"... So now I'm a lawyer. It was as easy as that... It was the same thing when I got married. You think I had anything to say about it? Not a bit. It was Mother again... She's the one who decided it all. "Hector, I have just the girl for you! Just the girl!" And that's how it was... Now, don't misunderstand. I'm not complaining, mind you. My wife couldn't be prettier... Really... (*Reflecting.*) Of course, she's not exactly perfect. Once in a while she... (*Becoming more confidential with the unseen audience.*) Well, frankly, she's jealous. But when I say "jealous"... Take yesterday, for example. I was talking to Rose... She's our maid... I mean, she was our maid... But I'll come to that... Anyway, I was telling Rose to go do something or other, and all of a sudden my wife gets all red and begins to make a scene. Why? Because I was looking at Rose while I was telling her what to do... Just looking at her, understand?... Talk

61

about being jealous!... Well, a little later on, when I wanted my slippers, I looked straight at my wife... straight at her... and I said to Rose... she was standing behind me... I said: "Go get my slippers!" I figured that way my wife wouldn't say I was looking at Rose again. Well, she was fit to be tied... My wife, that is. What a scene! She said I was ordering her around in front of the help. So she fired Rose on the spot and went running back to her mother's. And that's how I happen to be home all by myself... Well, not exactly by myself. Our downstairs neighbor, Madame Scandale, probably hasn't closed her eyes for a minute, just so she can tell my wife every move I make. (*He looks down toward the floor and addresses the unseen neighbor.*) Sorry to disappoint you, you old windbag! Wish you had something to tell, don't you! (*To the audience.*) There hasn't been a soul in here but me, and I haven't stepped outside since she left. (*Thumbing his nose at the floor.*) So there!... And now I'm going to have my lunch... without my wife. (*Defensively.*) Well, so what? I love her... Of course I do... I'd do anything for her... I'd lay down my life. Still, I don't want to starve to death waiting for her to come back. At least, not on an empty stomach. (*The doorbell rings.*) Ah! Speak of the devil... (*Another ring.*) I'd know her ring anywhere. (*Several more rings.*) All right, Antoinette! I'm coming!

He leaves, upstage. A moment later EMMA *enters through the same door, in great excitement.*

EMMA, *with a Latin accent.* Well, it's about time! Didn't you hear the bell? (*standing at door*) (*ringing bell over and over*)

HECTOR, *following her, replying as graciously as possible.* Why yes, madame, but—

EMMA, *mocking.* "Why yes, madame, but..." But what, imbecile? (*Grab Him*) (*Let go Enter*)
She strides down right and peers out the closed window.

HECTOR, *taken aback.* I beg your pardon, but— (*stand still*)

EMMA, *without turning to look at him.* Come, come! Announce me! (*Standing at edge of platform*)

HECTOR. Announce you? (*stands at door*)

EMMA. To your employer, of course!

HECTOR. My employer?... But I am my employer... I mean—

EMMA, *still looking out the window.* What are you talking about? Stop mumbling! Are you an idiot?

HECTOR, *removing the apron and putting on his coat.* No, my good woman, I'm a lawyer! (*Insistent + perturbed*)

EMMA, *finally turning around.* A lawyer? (*mockingly*)

HECTOR. Exactly!

EMMA. You... you mean... *(turning around)*

HECTOR. Precisely!

EMMA. Oh, monsieur! What can I say?... And here I was, calling you an idiot, and thinking you were the... Oh! *(Acting as if she gave a shit)*

HECTOR, *courteously.* Please, think nothing of it. After all, it's hard to tell when you don't know someone.

EMMA. But you will accept my apologies... *(Non chalantly) Not looking*

HECTOR, *bowing.* Really, you needn't give it another thought, I assure you... (EMMA *regains her composure.*) Now then, madame, is there something I can do for you?

EMMA. Yes, monsieur, there is. In fact...

    She removes her hat and coat, and places them on a chair.

HECTOR, *aside.* Good God! She's planning to stay! And there's my lunch getting cold!

EMMA, *nervously.* Monsieur...

HECTOR. Madame?

EMMA. Are you... Monsieur, are you... how shall I say?... (*Emphasizing.*) noble? *(Turning to him)*

HECTOR. Am I...

EMMA. Noble. *(Turn to him)*

HECTOR. Well really, madame, with a name like "Hector Bouchard" I'm hardly what you would call... Of course, I do have an aunt who once married a duke, but she—

EMMA. No, no, no! You don't understand. When I say "noble" I mean... I mean spiritually. *(walking towards him)*

HECTOR. Oh? Well, spiritually... I suppose I'm as noble as anyone else. (*Aside.*) Now what on earth is she getting at?

EMMA. Fine! Then I'm going to ask a favor of you. *(borrowing a law book)*

HECTOR. A favor?

EMMA. A big favor... (*She moves very close to him.*) A very big favor...
    She moves still closer. (close book move to him)

HECTOR, *withdrawing before her advances, aside.* If Antoinette could see me now! *(Dodges her advance, by going to glass of water)*

EMMA. You see, monsieur, I'm a married woman... *(chasing)*

HECTOR. Yes, I see... I see. (*He offers her a chair.*) Won't you have a seat? *slipping nervously*

    EMMA *sits down by the table.* HECTOR, *heaving a sigh of relief, sits across from her.* *Emma sits, Hector relieved, wipes his head w/ handkerchief behind her, she looks at him on husband.*

EMMA. Yes, monsieur, I have a husband... *(Hiding Hanky look at him)*

HECTOR. Naturally.

EMMA. What do you mean, "naturally"? *(running from her)*

HECTOR. Well, I mean... naturally. You said you were married, so I assumed... (*Aside.*) She has to spoil my lunch to tell me that?

EMMA, *continuing*. Yes, monsieur, I have a husband... a jealous, jealous, husband! A husband who never gives me a minute's peace. A husband who suspects every move I make... Every move—

HECTOR, *a look of comprehension suddenly lighting his face*. Ah, now I understand! *(Goes to Book Case)*

EMMA. You do?

HECTOR. Of course. Why didn't you say so in the first place? (*Assuming a professional tone.*) You've come to seek my assistance. *(Browsing thru Books)*

EMMA. Exactly!

HECTOR. Ah, well... Wait here, I'll just be a moment. *(goes thru door, returns w/ legal pad...)*

   He leaves, up right, and returns immediately carrying a large, legal-looking volume.

EMMA. Monsieur?

HECTOR, *blowing the dust off the book*. I'll be only too happy to represent you. (*He begins leafing through the volume.*) Now then, madame, have you any reason to suspect your husband's fidelity? Perhaps you have some letters? Anything we might use in our case against him... Any evidence?

EMMA. Evidence? Against him? What on earth for?

HECTOR, *still in a very official tone*. Well, madame, I... I assume you wish to seek a separation. And, as your lawyer, I— *(leaning to her.)*

EMMA. *(Standing)* My lawyer? A separation? Me?... Why, I never said anything of the kind! (*Becoming aggressive.*) I'll have you know I love my husband! I adore him! *(Approaching him in chair, grabbing him)*

HECTOR. Oh? That's very nice... I... But... Precisely what was it you had in mind? Just what is the nature of your grievance against the gentleman? *(straightening collar)*

EMMA. My "grievance"? Why, I just told you. He is a jealous, jealous man. He makes my life miserable! *(Looking out the window)*

HECTOR. I understand, but... There's not very much I can do about that!

   He looks at the audience and shrugs his shoulders.

EMMA, *getting up and addressing him indignantly*. But he has no right to be, I tell you!... No right at all! (*She begins backing him into the*

From the production of *Wooed and Viewed* at Los Angeles City College, February 1978, directed by Dudley Knight (photographs by James Mathews).

corner, up right.) You can say what you want about me, monsieur! You can say anything you like. But as far as *that* goes, my conscience is clear!

HECTOR, *recoiling, losing his aplomb.* But my dear woman, I haven't said a word about you... or your husband!

He mops his brow.

EMMA, *walking over to the window, dramatically.* Me... unfaithful! Me! How could he even bring himself to think such a thing? Me? The very idea... saying I don't love him! And the scenes he makes! Oh!

HECTOR, *aside, going over to the table.* How do I get rid of her? I'm starving!

EMMA, *moving over to him resolutely, as if to announce an important decision.* Monsieur, I have come to you because you are my neighbor. I live just across the way.

HECTOR. Delighted, I'm sure. (*Aside.*) Is she making the rounds of the neighborhood?

EMMA, *sitting down near the window.* And now, monsieur, you will please make love to me!

HECTOR. What? (*He looks at the audience, dumbfounded.*) I beg your pardon... Did I hear you say... you want me to...

EMMA, *getting up and moving toward him, very matter-of-fact.* Yes, if you don't mind... Of course, first I should tell you exactly how I feel about you.

HECTOR, *bowing fatuously.* Oh, madame! Really... (*Aside.*) What a romantic young thing! A Juliet looking for her Romeo!

EMMA, *graciously, but somewhat embarrassed.* Monsieur, I think you are ugly... (Attacking him controlled)

HECTOR, *taken aback.* What? (shocked)

EMMA, *even more graciously.* No, don't interrupt! You're ugly, you don!t seem very bright, you are... well... a little on the chubby side. In fact, you're perfectly ordinary in every way. There's not a thing about you that appeals to me... Not a thing. Absolutely nothing!

HECTOR, *aghast.* But... but... (*He stands agape for a moment, finally regaining his composure.*) You're really much too kind! (*Aside.*) Her compliments do have a style all their own, I must say!

EMMA, *still as gracious as can be.* In a word, monsieur, that is how I see you.

HECTOR, *sarcastically.* Thank you for the portrait. You don't believe in unnecessary flattery, do you!

EMMA. Oh well, I just paint what I see... I'm an impressionist, you might say. Besides, I'm sure you understand... I'm telling you all this so you won't get the idea that I'm interested in you.

HECTOR. Why, the thought never entered my mind!

EMMA, *looking toward the window*. After all, you men do get such foolish ideas... (*With a sigh of determination*.) Well, now that all that is taken care of... Now that you know just where I stand... Let's begin! Come, make love to me!

She sits down again.

HECTOR. Look, if this is your idea of a joke...

EMMA. A joke? I beg your pardon!

HECTOR. You mean to sit there and try to make me believe that... that... No! What do you take me for? (*Impatiently*.) Come now, tell me what you want!

EMMA. What I want? But I told you. I want you to make love to me... Right here!

She points to her chair.

HECTOR. But... but... My good woman, I'm not the slightest bit interested in you!

EMMA, *getting up and moving toward him, sharply*. And I couldn't care less about you! I thought I explained all that!

HECTOR. I don't even know you. I—

EMMA. I don't know you either.

HECTOR. Besides, I'm married.

EMMA. Well? So am I.

HECTOR, *losing his patience*. Now look! Really, this has gone far enough!

He moves behind the table.

EMMA, *crossing down left*. But monsieur... I'm not asking you the impossible. Don't you see? I want to teach my husband a lesson. I want to punish him for all the terrible things he suspects me of... for all those horrible scenes he makes. You can help me, monsieur. Now do you understand?

HECTOR. I can... You want... No, not a word!

He snatches a slice of bread and devours it on the sly.

EMMA, *aside*. Oh, these men! If they're not jealous, they're stupid! (*Aloud*.) Well, never mind. Let's begin anyway. Here, come over by the window.

She opens the window wide.

HECTOR, *moving briskly stage left.* Wait a minute! What are you doing?

EMMA. What does it look like I'm doing? I'm opening the window.

HECTOR. But it's freezing outside!

EMMA. Then go fix the fire. (*Pointing to the fireplace.*) Can't you see it's out?

HECTOR. The fire? The fire's been out since yesterday... And besides, what's the good of lighting it if you've got the window wide open? It's like the North Pole in here! For heaven's sake, close it! (*Aside.*) She's out of her mind... absolutely out of her mind!

EMMA, *pointing to the apartment across the way.* What do you mean, "close it"? How can I close it? If I close it, how will Alcibiades see us?

HECTOR. Alcibi... Who?

EMMA. Alcibiades.

HECTOR. Alcibiades the Greek?

EMMA. What Greek? My husband isn't Greek!

HECTOR. I don't give a damn about your husband!

EMMA, *scandalized, moving toward him with fire in her eyes.* Oh! You forget, monsieur, that you are speaking to his wife!

HECTOR, *thoroughly confused.* What? Who? Whose wife?... Oh, you mean Alcibiades' wife... I see!... Fine! Now close the window!

EMMA, *aside.* He's out of his mind!

She goes back to the window.

HECTOR, *aside.* She's crazy... There's no other explanation. (*In a commanding voice.*) Now look here! Either you close that window or, I'm warning you, I'll... I'll... (*Sheepishly, withering before* EMMA's *menacing gaze.*) I'll catch cold.

EMMA. That's all right... I'll give you a handkerchief. Now then, let's begin.

She pulls HECTOR *by the sleeve over to the window, despite his muttered imprecations.*

HECTOR, *breaking loose.* What a minute! It's freezing over here!

EMMA. Here, take my coat. (*She envelops him in her fur.*) There! Now please, it's getting late. We must begin. (*She sits down.*) Make love to me.

HECTOR, *falling onto a chair by the table.* "Make love to me... Make love..." On an empty stomach?

He snatches another piece of bread.

EMMA, *getting up*. What? You mean you haven't eaten yet? Oh, Monsieur, why didn't you say so? (*Passing in front of the table.*) Of course, I should have realized! The table is set, and... Oh my, how could I be so stupid? What can I say?... (*Suddenly.*) All right then, let's eat!

She sits down at the table.

HECTOR, *incredulous, mechanically repeating her invitation*. "Let's eat!"... (*Getting up.*) I beg your pardon, madame, but—

EMMA. What?

HECTOR. I said... I beg your pardon, but... I don't recall inviting you...

EMMA, *graciously*. Bah, don't let that bother you. I'm not offended... Now then, you sit over here, on my right... like the guest of honor.

HECTOR, *sitting down, with a shrug*. "Guest of honor!" (*Aside.*) In my own house!

EMMA, *pointing to the table*. Oh look, there's only one setting. Call your servant, will you?

HECTOR. My servant?... But I am my servant...

EMMA. What? I thought you said you were a lawyer.

HECTOR. Of course I'm a lawyer. I'm a lawyer by profession... and a house-keeper by necessity. My wife fired the maid yesterday.

EMMA. You don't say! Why, what a coincidence. I just fired my maid too. Isn't it a small world!

HECTOR, *aside*. Not small enough!

EMMA. Well, since you're keeping house yourself... Go set the table for one more.

HECTOR. What? Since when—

EMMA. Go on, go on! You don't expect me to do it, I'm sure! I haven't the vaguest idea where anything is kept... Well, what are you waiting for? Go on!

She stamps the floor with her foot, in a gesture of impatience.

HECTOR, *aside*. Now she's gone too far! (*Aloud.*) Not in a million years!
EMMA. What did you say?

She stamps again, harder.

HECTOR, *aside*. Good God! Madame Scandale! (*Aloud.*) All right, all right! I'm going!

He leaves through the door, up right, casting angry glances in EMMA's direction and muttering under his breath.

EMMA, *getting up and walking over to the window*. And as for you, Alcibiades... Oh! I'll teach you to be jealous! I'll teach you to suspect a wife who has always been a model of virtue!... So, you think I'm cheating on you?... Well, I'll show you! Before I get through, you'll see plenty to be jealous about... and it will serve you right! Yes, it will serve you right! It will! It will!

She stamps again and again, even harder.

HECTOR, *entering and setting another place at the table*. There! (*Shivering*.) This place is like an ice box!

EMMA. Come here, will you? I need your help.

She takes one end of the table.

HECTOR. With what?

EMMA. With this table. We're going to move it over by the window.

HECTOR. Oh no we're not, damn it! That's the last straw! There's no rhyme or reason... Whoever heard of anyone eating next to an open window in the middle of February? It's insane! You're insane! This whole damn thing is abso... abso... (*He tries to repress a sneeze*.) absolutely insane! (*He sneezes*.) There! I hope you're happy. Now I've got a cold.

EMMA. God bless you!

HECTOR, *aside*. God damn you!

EMMA. Monsieur Bouchard, I would like to point out to you that if you hadn't put up such a silly fuss, we would have been finished long ago.

HECTOR, *speaking through his nose*. Madame Whoever-you-are, I'd like to point out to you that... (*He sneezes*.) that... (*Sneeze*.) that... (*Sneeze*.) Fine! Now I've really got it!

He places his napkin around his head and knots it under his chin like a kerchief.

EMMA. Well, you can do what you like. But let me warn you... Unless you cooperate and do what I ask, I'll tell your wife that you've been making love to me. So there!

HECTOR. What? You'll tell my wife... Oh no, you couldn't... You wouldn't do such a thing! You... you...

He sneezes again.

EMMA, *coaxingly*. I won't if you say you'll help me.

HECTOR. But really, my good woman... You're asking me... Just think—

EMMA. I have thought, monsieur! My husband has the audacity to think that I'm unfaithful, and now he's going to pay for it. That's all. He must be punished... and by his own jealousy, too! That will be my revenge!

HECTOR. Yes, but have you thought what might happen?

EMMA, *very matter-of-fact.* Oh, I know what will happen. He'll kill you.

HECTOR, *recoiling.* What? He'll... Just like that?... And what am I supposed to be doing in the meantime?

EMMA. Oh, he'll kill you all right... Unless, of course, you... Oh no! I hope you wouldn't have the nerve to kill my Alcibiades!

HECTOR. But...

EMMA. It's bound to be a duel to the death. It always is. And of course, it will be the kind of duel that we have in our country... With hand drills.

She makes the gesture of turning a hand drill.

HECTOR, *appalled.* Hand drills?

EMMA. Yes, monsieur, hand drills. That's how we fight duels in Brazil.

HECTOR. But... that's disgusting!

EMMA. Disgusting?

HECTOR. It's... it's revolting!

EMMA. You mean, you disapprove?

HECTOR. Of course I disapprove!... Hand drills! Ugh!

EMMA, *with disdain.* I see. In other words, monsieur, you are afraid!

HECTOR. No... But for heaven's sake, I don't know the first thing about carpentry! I can't even hammer a nail!

He paces up and down.

EMMA, *still disdainfully, moving stage left.* Oh, these Frenchmen are all alike!

HECTOR. Now look... Let me suggest something else. Take my advice and file suit for a separation. It's much easier and... much less dangerous for everybody!

EMMA, *with fire in her eyes.* Separation? (HECTOR *draws back as she advances, menacingly.*) What kind of revenge is that? I told you, I love my husband! I adore him! I want revenge, not a separation!

HECTOR, *near the window.* But my dear woman—

EMMA, *following him.* No, that's not what I want at all! (*Forcing him onto the chair by the window.*) Come now, sit down and make love to me.

HECTOR. No! No! No!

EMMA. Look, I'm warning you...

HECTOR. For goodness' sake, be reasonable. You don't just walk into somebody's house and...

While he continues mumbling his objections, EMMA *looks out the window toward her own apartment.*

EMMA, *suddenly aghast.* Oh, my God! My God in heaven! Is it possible?... Alcibiades... with a woman! Oh, that beast! That good-for-nothing! That monster! Oh, that... (*To* HECTOR.) Quick, my coat! My coat! Where's my coat?

She runs round the table looking for her coat.

HECTOR, *following her and joining in the search.* Her coat! Where's her coat?

EMMA, *noticing it on* HECTOR's *shoulders.* You have it on, you idiot! Give it to me!

HECTOR. Oh, so I do!

He gives her the coat, which she puts on in a flurry of excitement, along with her hat.

EMMA. I'll... I'll scratch her eyes out, that's what I'll do! I'll tear her to pieces... I'll...

She leaves through the hall door. A moment later the outer door is heard to slam behind her.

HECTOR, *falling into an armchair, heaving a sigh of relief.* Gone at last! What a woman! My God, what a woman! I'm worn out!... Believe me, if she comes back, she can knock, and kick, and ring the bell to her heart's content... She won't get me to open that door. I've had enough. I've had it up to... to... to... (*Just as he fits the gesture to the word, raising his hand to eye level, he has a sneezing fit.*) to here! (*Sneeze.*) And I had to catch a cold in the bargain! (*Sneeze.*) Damn! (*Sneeze.*) Well, she won't mind if I close the window now! (*He gets up and walks over to the window. Suddenly his eye is caught by something across the way.*) What?... Oh no!... I don't believe it!... It can't be!... But that dress... It's Antoinette's. It's her orchid dress... her famous orchid dress. I'd know it anywhere... Good God! My wife... with that Brazilian! Oh, the snake-in-the-grass! The... the... (*Sneeze.*) And all the time I thought she was at her mother's! Just what does she take me for? Well, she won't get away with this! I'll show her! I'll... I'll... (*Sneeze.*) I'll fight if I have to... Even with hand drills! I don't care... I'll take lessons... I'll practice, I'll train... In two weeks I'll be able to... (*Suddenly struck by an idea.*) No, wait... I have a better idea. I'll get even with her... Oh, yes... but not that way! No... (*He begins pacing back and forth.*) Oh, if only that mad woman would come back now! If only she'd come back!... Oh, how I wish she'd come back!... (*The doorbell rings.*) Aha! Maybe... maybe...

(*He runs out through the hall door. Offstage he is heard greeting* EMMA.)
Come in!... Yes, please... Come right in!

EMMA *enters*.

EMMA, *laughing*. Ah, Monsieur Bouchard... You'll never guess...

HECTOR, *following closely on her heels*. Please, madame, this is no time to
be laughing. We have serious business, you and I.

EMMA. We do?

HECTOR. We certainly do!

EMMA. Why, what on earth is the matter?

HECTOR. The matter, my dear woman... The matter is that... You remember what you wanted me to do a little while ago? Well, now I accept...
and with pleasure! Come over here, by the window.

EMMA. Oh, that! But I don't want to any more.

HECTOR. What? You don't want to... But I do! I want to! I insist! Don't
you understand? Now I'm the one who's looking for revenge. An eye for
an eye! A tooth for a tooth! A wife for a wife!... A hand drill for a hand
drill!

EMMA. But, monsieur...

HECTOR, *moving toward her with determination*. Come to the window.
Come, let me crush you in my arms. Let me smother you with kisses.
Let me... let me make love to you!

EMMA, *drawing back*. Whatever has come over you? Are you out of your
mind?

HECTOR, *at the window*. Out of my mind? Ha ha ha! You mean to stand
there and tell me you don't know about my wife? You don't know she's
two-timing me?... At this very moment!... And with your husband, no
less! Your Alcibiades!

EMMA. Your wife and my... Why, that's absurd!

HECTOR, *growing more and more excited*. Oh, it's absurd, is it? Then tell
me I didn't see her over there! Tell me I don't recognize her orchid
dress when I see it! Tell me—

EMMA. Her orchid dress?... Her... Oh, but you can't be serious! (*Laughing*.)
You must have seen our new maid!

HECTOR. Come now, you can think up a better one than that!

EMMA. But I assure you... In fact, you must know her. Her name is Rose,
and she used to work for you.

HECTOR. Rose? She... You mean, our Rose? The same Rose my wife fired
yesterday?

EMMA. Exactly.

HECTOR. But... That's impossible... She... Is it really?

EMMA. None other. And since I was out, my husband let her in, and he was talking to her. That's all. Now do you believe me?

HECTOR, *sitting down by the table, with a sigh*. Oh, thank heaven! You don't know how relieved I am! Here I was, all ready to think that my dear, sweet Antoinette...

EMMA. Yes, I know. You men are all alike, always getting jealous for no reason at all.

HECTOR, *suddenly jumping up*. Wait a minute! What about that dress? If that was Rose, why was she wearing my wife's... (*He stops short, mouth open, struck by a thought.*) Of course! (*Falling onto the chair.*) Now that's a good one for you! How did I ever forget?... Antoinette gave her that dress a couple of days ago. Of course!

EMMA. You see?

HECTOR. What a relief!... Oh, what a relief!... And to think I could suspect her of... Oh, my! How can I ever make it up to her?... I'll beg her to forgive me, that's what I'll do. I'll throw myself at her feet...

EMMA. That's precisely what you should do, monsieur. In fact, that's what my Alcibiades did just a few moments ago. And I forgave him!

HECTOR. You mean you're not out for revenge any more?

EMMA. Absolutely not! Although, now that you mention it, he did see us over here, you know.

HECTOR, *suddenly terrified*. He did?

EMMA. Oh yes! He even asked me who was that funny-looking little old lady I was talking to!

HECTOR. Little old... You mean, he thought...

EMMA. And so I told him you were the mother-in-law of an old schoolfriend of mine. How do you like that!

HECTOR. Mother-in-law? Me? A mother-in-law! (*Laughing.*) That's a little hard to take! But I suppose it's better than hand drills at twenty paces!

EMMA. And now, monsieur, if you don't mind, I'll be on my way. I only came back to thank you for being so uncooperative.

HECTOR. For being so...?

EMMA. Uncooperative.

HECTOR. How's that?

EMMA. Why yes. After all, if you hadn't been so very... how shall I say?... ungentlemanly, I would have had my revenge on Alcibiades, and the poor dear would never have begged me to forgive him.

HECTOR, *laughing*. I guess you're right.

EMMA. Well, monsieur... Maybe some other time...

HECTOR. Any time at all. Always happy to be of service! (*Bowing.*) Madame!

EMMA, *nodding, about to leave.* Monsieur! (*Several loud knocks are heard on the ceiling.*) My goodness, what on earth...

HECTOR. Oh, don't mind that. It's just the upstairs neighbor. She's cracking walnuts. (*Aside.*) That does it! First thing tomorrow, I look for another place! (*Aloud.*) Madame!

EMMA. Monsieur!

CURTAIN

ROMANCE IN A FLAT

·

Amour et piano

CHARACTERS

EDOUARD

BAPTISTE

LUCILE

A well-furnished drawing room in a middle-class flat. Upstage center, a double door leading to a vestibule. On each side of the door, an upholstered wooden chair. Midstage right, a fireplace. Downstage left, the door to LUCILE's *bedroom. Upstage left, a curtained doorway to her mother's room. Close to it, a coatrack. Midstage left, against the wall, a writing table and chair. Downstage left, a canape and an end table. Upstage right, a piano, facing the fireplace at an angle. Downstage right, an armchair. Other furniture ad lib.*

At rise, BAPTISTE *is standing by the canape, arranging bric-a-brac on the end table.* LUCILE *is seated at the piano, playing her scales with impressive speed.*

BAPTISTE, *after listening for a few moments in rapt admiration.* Bravo! Bravo! (LUCILE *stops, looks up.*) Oh, please, mademoiselle... I didn't mean to interrupt... Mademoiselle can really make her fingers fly... Like the wind, I mean... All that "whoosh whoosh whoosh..."

LUCILE. Thank you, Baptiste. But these are only my scales...

BAPTISTE, *quizzically.* Scales, mademoiselle?

LUCILE. That's right. See?

She illustrates.

BAPTISTE. Oh no, mademoiselle. That's nothing like scales. Scales are for weighing, not for playing... And they don't go "whoosh whoosh whoosh..."

LUCILE. No, Baptiste...

BAPTISTE. Like the wind, on the farm, when it comes through the doors... (*He imitates the whistling of the wind.*) No, that's nothing like scales.

LUCILE. Maybe not... (*Resigned.*) But still, that's what we call them here in Paris... "Scales!"

81

BAPTISTE, *shrugging*. Hmm! I'm not surprised, mademoiselle. No one talks plain and simple anymore. Not like back home...

LUCILE, *putting an end to the discussion*. Very good, Baptiste... (*Standing up, changing the subject*.) Tell me, has Mamma left yet?

BAPTISTE. Yes, mademoiselle. About fifteen minutes ago.

LUCILE. Oh my! What a nuisance!... I bet you can't guess where she went, Baptiste, can you?

BAPTISTE. No, mademoiselle. I can't—

LUCILE, *as if pleased to reveal the news*. To police court, that's where! She got a... (*Emphasizing*.) a subpoena!

BAPTISTE. A "supreme" what, mademoiselle?

LUCILE. No, no... A subpoena... a summons...

BAPTISTE. A summons?... Madame?... The police?...

LUCILE. Oh, don't worry, Baptiste. It's only to be a witness.

BAPTISTE, *relieved*. Aha!

LUCILE. Something about a cab she was riding in the other day... And the driver got fresh and insulted a policeman. And it can't be postponed. So they came and gave her a subpoena. For today...

BAPTISTE. Oh, if that's all... Insulting a policeman... I wouldn't mind getting a "supreme" like that, believe me.

LUCILE, *a little impatient*. All right now, Baptiste... I've got to practice. So please... I can't sit here listening to you all day long...

BAPTISTE, *almost about to object*. Mademoiselle...

LUCILE. You do like the piano, don't you?

BAPTISTE. Oh yes! When it's mademoiselle who's playing! (*Grimacing*.) When I try to myself...

LUCILE, *surprised*. You mean, you play too?

BAPTISTE. Oh no, mademoiselle... But we used to have an old piano on the farm, and—

LUCILE. And you used it?

BAPTISTE. Yes, mademoiselle. All the time. To keep bread in...

LUCILE. To keep... A piano?

BAPTISTE. Back home we can't waste furniture like that just to play tunes on...

LUCILE, *smiling rather condescendingly*. Really, "just to play..." (*Suddenly remembering*.) Oh, that reminds me, Baptiste... I'm expecting a gentleman.

BAPTISTE. A gentleman, mademoiselle?

LUCILE. Yes, a new piano teacher. He should be here any minute.

BAPTISTE. Very good, mademoiselle.

LUCILE. They say he's a little... well, odd, if you know what I mean... But that really doesn't matter. He's terribly famous. Probably the best in all of Paris... Maestro... (*Trying to remember his name.*) Maestro...

BAPTISTE. Mademoiselle's what?

LUCILE. What?

BAPTISTE. What's mademoiselle's "estro"?

LUCILE. I beg your pardon?

BAPTISTE. Mademoiselle said "my estro," and I asked her—

LUCILE. No, no, Baptiste... (*Emphasizing.*) Maestro... That means a great musician... a teacher... You know...

BAPTISTE. Oh... (*Aside.*) More fancy talk!

LUCILE, *still trying to think of the name.* Maestro... Maestro... As a matter of fact... Come to think of it, no one ever told me his name. But I'm sure it's very famous.

BAPTISTE, *trying to be helpful.* Molière, mademoiselle?

LUCILE. Hardly, Baptiste!... (*She gives a shrug.*) Well, anyway... when he comes, he's going to ask if Mamma is here...

BAPTISTE. And I'll tell him madame is out.

LUCILE. No, no... You'll show him in. I'll talk to him myself.

BAPTISTE, *rather shocked.* What, mademoiselle? Without madame...

LUCILE. Don't worry, Baptiste. It's perfectly all right. Mamma said I should.

BAPTISTE. Aha!

LUCILE. After all, a famous maestro... We can't very well keep him running back and forth. He's not just some everyday teacher, you know. (BAPTISTE *shakes his head.*) When you have an appointment with a maestro, Baptiste, it's got to be on time... Unless you're the maestro yourself, that is... Then you can be as late as you please...

BAPTISTE, *aside.* Hmm! That's the job for me! An "estro!"

LUCILE. So... you're sure you understand? When he comes, just show him in. (BAPTISTE *nods.*) All right, Baptiste. That's all. You can go now. I've got to do my scales.

BAPTISTE. Yes, mademoiselle. (*Aside.*) Her and her scales!

He exits, up center. LUCILE *sits down at the piano and returns to her practicing for a few moments.*

LUCILE, *stopping abruptly, sighing.* Oh! I swear... Of all things to have to learn... Do re mi fa sol la si do... Do si la sol fa mi re do... Do re mi... What on earth could be duller? Scales, scales, scales!... (*Resigned.*) Well, if I have to... Nowadays no man will marry you unless you play the piano. Though I can't for the life of me understand why! (*She plays a few more scales, then stops.*) I mean, that can't be why people get married, after all... Certainly not to play scales, heaven knows! (*She begins again, then stops.*) Oh, what a bore!... "Play your scales every day, and you'll have nice limber fingers!..." That's what they say. As if a young lady needs nice limber fingers to make a good wife. Really, I mean... If only we could speak our minds and say what we think! I'd tell any man that wanted to marry me: "Look here, monsieur... I'm going to be twenty, and I don't play the piano... I'm terribly sorry, but I don't expect you to be able to play the flute! No one says marriage is supposed to be a concert. It's supposed to be... to be... well, I'm not really sure... But I know people don't get married to make music!... So, if you want me, just the way I am... no piano, I mean... well, take me, I'm yours! If not, monsieur, there's nothing more to say!..." There! That's what I'd tell him. If I could, that is... But young ladies like me have to suffer in silence...

She heaves a long sigh, as BAPTISTE *enters, up center.*

BAPTISTE. Mademoiselle... There's a gentleman... It's the "estro," I think.

He hands her a calling card.

LUCILE. Ah! My teacher... (*Standing up, reading the card.*) "Edouard Paraquitte"... Paraquitte?... My goodness, what a name! (*To* BAPTISTE.) Show him in, Baptiste... And tell him I'll just be a minute.

She exits, down left. BAPTISTE *exits, up center.*

BAPTISTE'S VOICE. This way, monsieur...

EDOUARD *enters, followed by* BAPTISTE.

EDOUARD, *obviously uneasy.* Thank you, my good man...

He hands BAPTISTE *his hat.*

BAPTISTE, *placing the hat on the coatrack, up left.* Mademoiselle said to tell monsieur she'll just be a minute.

EDOUARD. Ah! "Mademoiselle said to tell monsieur..." She said to tell me... Then you gave her my card?

BAPTISTE. Yes, monsieur.

EDOUARD. And... and what did she say?

BAPTISTE. She said: "My goodness, what a name," monsieur.

EDOUARD. That's all?

BAPTISTE. That's all I heard.

EDOUARD, *nodding*. Aha! I see... Well, thank you... Thank you...

BAPTISTE. Not at all, monsieur.

EDOUARD *takes a coin and presses it into* BAPTISTE's *palm*. BAPTISTE *looks at it in surprise, shrugs, and exits, up center*.

EDOUARD. There! I've done it!... The first step is always the hardest, but... I've done it!... It's not easy to break into Paris society... Especially when you're from Marseille, like me... But here I am, and it's only two weeks. And already I'm on my way... Of course, no one would ever guess that I'm from Marseille. Certainly not by the way I talk. Maybe because I grew up in Dunkerque... Anyway, I'm young, I'm handsome... I'm a millionaire... Well, fifteen thousand francs a year... But back home that's enough to make you a millionaire... Besides, it's enough to make friends with all the right people... And they tell me I'm even more Parisian than the Parisians! I'm sure they're right, too. After all, they should know!... The best tailor, the best barber... Why, I already have princes I can call by name, and a duke I give rides to... Everything!... Well, almost! There's just one thing... the most important... An affair!... That's right... and with somebody special. A celebrity, a name... So I said to myself: "Look, why not La Dubarroy?" No harm in trying. I don't know her, but the way people talk... A good affair with an actress like her... Well, that's all I need. Nothing like an actress for a man's reputation!... So I look up her address, and here I am! As simple as that!... (*Walking around, inspecting*.) Lovely place she's got here!... Chic! That's the word... chic, chic, chic! (*He stops at the curtained doorway, up left*.) Ah! The boudoir, no doubt!... Well... (*Emotionally*.) Later, later...

LUCILE *enters, down left, carrying her music*.

LUCILE. I'm dreadfully sorry to keep you waiting, monsieur. I couldn't find my music.

EDOUARD, *visibly moved, and not a little confused*. Ah!... You couldn't find your... Please, mademoiselle... Not at all... That's really quite all right.

LUCILE. I simply can't do anything unless I have my music. (*Sitting in the chair, down right, and pointing to the canape, down left*.) Please, monsieur. Won't you sit down...

EDOUARD, *complying*. Thank you... (LUCILE *nods politely*.) Yes, there's something about music, mademoiselle. It's so... How shall I put it?

LUCILE. So beautiful!

EDOUARD, *fatuously*. Exactly!... Beautiful!... That says it so well!

LUCILE. As I always say, it's the noblest of the arts! (*Aside*.) That should impress him!

EDOUARD. I couldn't agree more! (*Aside.*) If it makes her happy!

LUCILE. Of course, it's not easy when you're still a beginner.

EDOUARD. I suppose so, mademoiselle... Then again, I wouldn't know.

LUCILE. You mean, you don't remember, monsieur?

EDOUARD. Remember?... Remember what?

LUCILE. Why, when you were a beginner.

EDOUARD. Oh? I really never was...

LUCILE. You never... (*Aside.*) I must say, he's not modest! (*To* EDOUARD.) Tell me, monsieur. What do you think of Wagner?

EDOUARD. Who?

LUCILE. Wagner... I hear he's all the rage.

EDOUARD. You mean Wagner the druggist?

LUCILE, *with a puzzled look.* The what?

EDOUARD. The druggist... From Marseille...

LUCILE. Heavens, no! The composer!

EDOUARD. The composer?... Oh, that Wagner!... (*He faces the audience and shrugs.*) They say he writes music...

LUCILE, *aside.* They say...

EDOUARD, *nodding.* Yes, that Wagner... Of course... (*Aside.*) Time to get down to business... (*To* LUCILE.) Excuse me, mademoiselle—

LUCILE. And Mozart, monsieur?

EDOUARD. I beg your pardon?

LUCILE. Mozart... What do you think of Mozart?

EDOUARD. Well, actually... I don't very often... Now, if you don't mind—

LUCILE. But you must have a favorite composer.

EDOUARD, *aside.* I must?

LUCILE. Mine is Bach. I simply adore him.

EDOUARD. Back? Back from where?

LUCILE. No, no... Bach... Johann Sebastian... Who's yours?

EDOUARD, *hemming and hawing.* My favorite composer?... Hmmm... Ah... Cordillard!... Yes... Cordillard!

LUCILE. Who?

EDOUARD. Cordillard... Jean-Jacques... A friend of mine from home... He writes absolutely sensational songs.

LUCILE. He does?

EDOUARD. Yes... He's the one who wrote "The Sheik from Chicago."

LUCILE. I... I don't think I know it.

EDOUARD. You don't?... It goes like this... (*Singing.*)

"The sheik from Chicago
Is chic as can be,
As chic as the sleek sheiks
Of old Araby..."

(*Speaking.*) That's one of his best.

LUCILE, *nodding.* Aha...

EDOUARD, *eager to change the subject.* But here I am, mademoiselle, talking, talking, talking. And I haven't even told you...

LUCILE. Told me what, monsieur?

EDOUARD. Well... Why I'm here. I mean...

LUCILE, *with a little laugh.* Oh! You don't have to tell me! I'm sure I know!

EDOUARD, *surprised.* You do?

LUCILE. Of course, monsieur... of course I do!

EDOUARD, *aside.* These Parisian women... I must say...

LUCILE. I've been expecting you.

EDOUARD, *astonished.* You've been expecting... You mean, you know me?

LUCILE, *coyly.* Really, Monsieur... (*Sneaking a look at his card.*) Monsieur Paraquitte!... (*As if to say: "Who doesn't know the great maestro!"*) After all...

EDOUARD, *confused, but happy to agree.* After all... (*Aside.*) It's going to be even easier than I thought!

LUCILE, *a little naïvely.* They tell me you're terribly fashionable, monsieur.

EDOUARD, *aside.* They do? (*To* LUCILE, *fatuously.*) Well, mademoiselle... I suppose... My tailor, my barber—

LUCILE. No, no... I mean... prominent... You know, monsieur... socially...

EDOUARD. Oh, I suppose...

He looks at the audience and gives another confused shrug.

LUCILE. No doubt you've been through the Conservatory too?

EDOUARD. The Conservatory?... (*Nodding.*) Aha... (*Aside.*) I've passed by it, I think, but I've never gone in...

LUCILE. And didn't I hear that you won a first prize?

EDOUARD. I what?... (*Reflecting.*) Well, now that you mention it, mademoiselle... But I was only nine. And the prize was in spelling. I really don't see... (*Aside.*) Curious conversation!

LUCILE, *aside.* A little odd, indeed!

EDOUARD, *brusquely.* Mademoiselle... My name is Edouard Paraquitte, and I'm twenty-four years old.

LUCILE, *rather taken aback*. You're... (*Smiling*.) That's... that's a nice age, monsieur.

EDOUARD. Very nice, mademoiselle!

LUCILE. Though, considering what you're here for... I mean, age doesn't really matter, now does it?

EDOUARD. It doesn't?

LUCILE. Of course not!

EDOUARD. But... you have to admit, mademoiselle, the younger the better.

LUCILE. Oh? I don't know... The older you are, the more experience you have.

EDOUARD. Well... Experience... Yes, perhaps, but... Certainly there's more to it than that, after all.

LUCILE. I know what the proverb says, monsieur.

EDOUARD. The proverb?

LUCILE. "If only the old were able!" Right?... But don't forget the rest: "If only the young knew how!"

EDOUARD. Oh, I know how, mademoiselle! I... Really, I know how!

LUCILE, *with a nervous little laugh*. Not you, monsieur! I didn't mean you. I'm sure you know all there is to know!

EDOUARD. You are? (*Aside*.) My goodness! I wonder who told her!

LUCILE. That's why I simply can't wait for you to teach me!

EDOUARD, *startled*. Teach you? I beg your... You mean, you... you want me to—

LUCILE. Of course I do, monsieur! Why else would you be here?

EDOUARD. But... (*Trying to control his obvious enthusiasm*.) Why mademoiselle, I... I'd be delighted! The sooner the better! You're absolutely right. Why else would I be here?... Yes, any time you like... (*Growing more and more excited*.) Yes, I... I... yes...

LUCILE, *noticing his emotion*. What is it, monsieur?

EDOUARD. It's... it's... (*Controlling himself*.) It's just that... (*Abruptly*.) Mademoiselle, I'm a very wealthy man...

LUCILE. Oh?

EDOUARD. And money is no object.

LUCILE. You mean, you only do it for the love of the art?

EDOUARD. For the love... Yes, you might say... (*Gallantly*.) And the love of the artist!

LUCILE, *nodding graciously*. Monsieur! (*Aside*.) Odd, but sweet!

EDOUARD. What I mean to say, mademoiselle, is that I... I won't... That is, you'll find me perfectly agreeable, I assure you.

LUCILE, *puzzled.* Agreeable, monsieur?

EDOUARD. To any... how shall I put it?... to any financial conditions you decide on.

LUCILE. Oh, that!... But... I thought the arrangements were quite clear, monsieur. I thought you understood...

EDOUARD. Arrangements?... No, no... Not at all... That is, I really have no idea... (*Aside.*) She'll probably rob me blind!

LUCILE. Why yes... Four hundred francs a month, four times a week, one hour each time.

EDOUARD, *with a start.* What?... You mean, it's by the hour?

LUCILE. Well, I assumed... Isn't it always, monsieur?

EDOUARD, *with a noncommittal gesture.* Oh... I... (*Aside.*) Who knows, with these Parisians? (*Regaining his composure, to* LUCILE.) Four hundred francs a month, you say? You're sure that's quite enough?

LUCILE, *surprised.* I beg your pardon?

EDOUARD, *aside.* It's a bargain at twice the price!

LUCILE. Isn't that satisfactory?

EDOUARD. Oh yes! Yes, indeed! Perfectly satisfactory! Perfectly, mademoiselle...

LUCILE. Oh, I misunderstood. I thought you said—

EDOUARD. No, no! That's just fine!

LUCILE. Besides, monsieur, if things work out... Well, I'm sure at the end of the month a little bonus wouldn't be out of order.

EDOUARD. A little... Aha! Of course!... (*Aside.*) Now it comes out! (*To* LUCILE.) Of course! A bonus...

LUCILE. And anyway, monsieur, I shouldn't be discussing such matters myself. Really, if you have any questions, you should talk to my mother.

EDOUARD. To your... (*With a broad, knowing wink.*) mother?

LUCILE, *on whom the irony is lost.* Monsieur?

EDOUARD. I should talk to your... (*Emphasizing, with another wink.*) mother?

LUCILE. Yes, monsieur. (*With her little laugh.*) I do have one, you know.

EDOUARD. Aha!... You mean, a real one...

LUCILE. A what? (*Aside.*) What kind of a question... (*To* EDOUARD.) Besides, you must have talked to her already, or you wouldn't even be here.

EDOUARD. Yes, I must have... (*Aside.*) I'm not going to argue at a time like this!

LUCILE. Well, monsieur, you can work things out with her. But I'm sure she won't want to make any changes.

EDOUARD. You're sure she won't want to—

LUCILE. I'm almost positive...

EDOUARD. Well, then... that's that! Let's say four hundred francs a month.

LUCILE. Four times a week.

EDOUARD. Four times a week.

LUCILE. One hour each time.

EDOUARD. One hour each time.

LUCILE. Good!... (*She stands up.*) And now, monsieur, if you don't mind, let's begin.

EDOUARD, *jumping to his feet.* Let's... You mean, today? Right now? Just like that?

LUCILE, *looking around the room for something.* Why yes, I thought... If you're ready, that is... (*Aside.*) Where on earth did I put it?

EDOUARD, *watching her, nodding, aside.* If I'm ready...

LUCILE, *aside.* Ah! It must be in my bedroom... (*Moving down left, stopping, still aside.*) No, no... in Mamma's... (*Turning and moving up left, to* EDOUARD.) Excuse me, monsieur. I'll just be a moment.

She exits, up left.

EDOUARD, *bowing from the waist as she leaves.* Mademoiselle! (*He sighs and shakes his head.*) My, my! I must say, that didn't take long! They certainly don't mince words in Paris! Talk about efficiency... Damn! Just like the army... One, two! Forward, march!... That's progress for you! Nothing like back home... (*Rubbing his hands together, moving around the room.*) Well, so far so good! A nice little affair to get me started, and I'm on my way!

He stops at the curtained doorway, up left, just as BAPTISTE *enters, up center.*

BAPTISTE. Monsieur?

EDOUARD. Ah?... Yes, my good man?

He goes over to join him.

BAPTISTE, *handing him a musical score.* Mademoiselle asked me to give monsieur this book.

EDOUARD. Oh?

BAPTISTE. She calls it "Baking Venison," or something like that.

EDOUARD. She calls it what?

BAPTISTE. "Baking Venison," monsieur. It must be a cookbook.

EDOUARD, *examining the score.* Ah! "Bach Inventions..."

BAPTISTE. Monsieur?

EDOUARD. "Bach Inventions." That's what it says...

BAPTISTE. Does monsieur really think so?

EDOUARD. Of course! Look here!

He points to the title.

BAPTISTE. Oh?... But then it wouldn't mean anything at all, monsieur.

EDOUARD. What the devil does she want me to do with this?

BAPTISTE. Read it, I suppose.

EDOUARD, *flipping through the music.* Read it? How can I read it?

BAPTISTE. Well, mademoiselle didn't say, monsieur. But that's all I can think of.

EDOUARD, *a little sarcastically.* Thank you! Much obliged!

He puts down the music and moves back toward the doorway, up left, as if to exit.

BAPTISTE, *stopping him.* Pardon me, but... Does monsieur know where he's going?

EDOUARD. Well, I thought... No, not exactly... But perhaps you'd like to tell me...

BAPTISTE. That room, monsieur... (*Hesitating.*) That room...

EDOUARD. Yes, my good man... (*He takes a coin from his pocket and holds it up.*) Go on, go on...

BAPTISTE, *aside.* Twenty francs! (*To* EDOUARD.) That's the bedroom, monsieur...

EDOUARD, *nodding.* Quite! The bedroom... The love nest... (*Waxing poetic.*) The temple of Venus...

BAPTISTE. The bedroom where mademoiselle's mother sleeps, monsieur.

He reaches for the coin.

EDOUARD, *pulling the coin out of* BAPTISTE's *grasp, and putting it back in his pocket.* What?... Her mother?...

BAPTISTE, *aside.* Damn!

EDOUARD. You mean... her... her mother...?

BAPTISTE. Excuse me, monsieur?

He holds out his hand.

EDOUARD, *taking another coin from his pocket.* Yes, yes... Here you are!

BAPTISTE, *looking at the coin.* But monsieur, that's one franc!

EDOUARD. Quite all right. (*With a wave of the hand.*) Keep the change.

BAPTISTE, *sarcastically.* Thank you, monsieur!

He exits, up center, grumbling.

EDOUARD. If he thinks I'm going to pay an arm and a leg for that!

LUCILE enters, up left, brandishing a long conductor's baton.

LUCILE. All right, monsieur, I found it.

EDOUARD. Found what, mademoiselle?

LUCILE. Here...

EDOUARD. What is it?

LUCILE, *incredulously.* I beg your pardon?

EDOUARD. I said: "What is it?"

LUCILE. What does it look like, monsieur?

EDOUARD. Why, a stick of some sort.

LUCILE. A stick? (*Aside.*) You'd think he never saw a baton before! (*To EDOUARD.*) Here... Take it...

EDOUARD, *complying.* But... What for?

LUCILE. Really, monsieur. I never do well without one.

EDOUARD. Oh?

LUCILE. Now please... (*Pointing to the chairs on either side of the double door, up center.*) Take one of the chairs, and start beating.

EDOUARD, *going over to one of the chairs, confused.* "Take one of the..." (*Aside.*) She wants me to dust the furniture first?

LUCILE. That's fine! Now we're ready! (*She goes to the piano and sits down.*) I should warn you, monsieur. I'm not very good.

EDOUARD, *aside.* It must be some weird kind of test. Like in the Masons...

LUCILE. Go ahead... You can start beating now.

EDOUARD. But... but mademoiselle... Won't that make a lot of dust?

LUCILE. Dust, monsieur? I can't imagine why.

EDOUARD. Well, I assumed...

LUCILE. All right now, let's begin.

She starts playing her piece. EDOUARD, upstage behind her, begins vigorously beating the seat of one of the chairs by the door, raising great clouds of dust.

EDOUARD, *aside.* A grown man... Of all things...

LUCILE, *without looking up.* Please, monsieur. You're not beating in rhythm.

EDOUARD. I'm sorry. I'm doing the best I can.

He continues beating. After a few moments, LUCILE *stops playing.*

LUCILE, *finally turning around.* Monsieur!... Monsieur! Please!... What on earth are you doing?

EDOUARD. What does it look like? I'm beating the chair.

LUCILE *sneezes.*

LUCILE. But... but...

EDOUARD. Isn't that what you said...

LUCILE. Me, monsieur? When?

She sneezes again.

EDOUARD. When? Just now! You told me to take a chair and start beating...

LUCILE. Time, monsieur... I meant you should beat time...

EDOUARD. Ah!... Beat time... You want me to beat time...

LUCILE. Of course! (*Aside.*) My heavens, what a teacher!

EDOUARD, *wiping his forehead.* Aha! (*Aside, sighing.*) Ay ay ay!

LUCILE. Now we're going to have to start all over again.

She turns her back and begins her piece again, as EDOUARD, *upstage, awkwardly beats time. Little by little, he moves downstage, dragging the chair and beating, until he arrives center stage.*

EDOUARD, *aside.* Good God, is this what they mean by an affair?... And with these actresses! The things they make you do... Stand here beating time, when I don't know the first thing about music... Thank heaven my friends can't see me, that's all... (LUCILE *stops playing, turns around, and watches as* EDOUARD *continues beating time, still talking to himself, aside.*) Who asked her to play? That's not what I came for. She's not even very good... Well, what can I do? I've got to be polite... Anything to break into Paris society!

LUCILE, *standing up.* Monsieur! What are you doing?

EDOUARD. What am I... I'm beating time. You said—

LUCILE. But I'm not even playing... See? I've stopped.

EDOUARD. You're not... (*Sheepishly.*) Aha!... You're right...

He stops beating, embarrassed.

LUCILE, *aside.* I've heard about absentminded professors, but...

EDOUARD. You must be getting tired.

LUCILE. Tired, monsieur?

EDOUARD. I mean, music is very nice, and all that. Still, we shouldn't overdo it.

LUCILE. But I... I've hardly begun...

EDOUARD, *aside*. Hardly begun... (*To* LUCILE.) No, no... Really, that's quite enough for now. You don't have to—

LUCILE. But monsieur... We only have four times a week. And only an hour each time, after all...

EDOUARD. Exactly, mademoiselle! That's just what I was thinking. If you're going to spend the whole hour playing the piano... Well...

LUCILE. Monsieur?

EDOUARD. I mean... how much time will that leave us for... for...

LUCILE. For what, monsieur?

EDOUARD, *beginning to babble*. For... well, for... other things. You know... (LUCILE *looks at the audience as if to say: "He's raving!"*) No, really... That's enough... Believe me, you'll have plenty of time to play when I leave. (*Going to the piano, summoning up his courage.*) Here... Let's just close this up... (*He closes the piano.*) Like that...

LUCILE, *sitting down, aside*. What a curious lesson!

EDOUARD, *putting his chair next to her, and sitting down*. And now, let's have a chat.

LUCILE. Monsieur?

EDOUARD. My dear... if I may... do you like oysters?

LUCILE, *dumbfounded*. Do I what?

EDOUARD. Do you like oysters?

LUCILE, *edging her stool away, uneasily*. Why yes, monsieur. I do... But—

EDOUARD, *taking out a small notepad and writing*. Fine! Then oysters it is... And how about a bisque? A nice oyster bisque?

LUCILE, *obviously growing uneasier by the minute*. I... I don't know. I've never tried it...

EDOUARD. Ah! You'll love it, take my word! (*Writing.*) Oysters, and a bisque... (*To* LUCILE.) There! Now what else would you like?

LUCILE. Really, monsieur... I... I'm sure I don't know...

EDOUARD. Never mind. Just leave everything to me. You won't be sorry...

He scribbles a few more notes, rips out the leaf, and folds it.

LUCILE, *aside*. At least he seems harmless.

EDOUARD. May I ask you for an envelope, mademoiselle?

LUCILE, *pointing to the writing-table, stage left*. Over there... On the table...

EDOUARD *goes over to the table.*

EDOUARD, *sitting down.* You're not doing anything at midnight, I trust?

LUCILE. Monsieur?

EDOUARD. Tonight... After the theater, I mean.

LUCILE. But... I'm not going to the theater tonight...

EDOUARD. Aha! Your night off... That's even better.

LUCILE, *aside.* And they let him out on the streets? All alone?

EDOUARD, *putting the paper in an envelope and writing an address, aside.* "Maxim's, Rue Royale..." There! A private room for midnight! (*To Lu-CILE.*) Could I trouble you again, mademoiselle, to ring for your servant?

He stands up.

LUCILE. No trouble, monsieur...

She gets up, rings, and moves over behind the canape, down left.

EDOUARD. Thank you, my dear.

LUCILE. Not at all...

After a few moments of embarrassed silence, BAPTISTE *enters, up center.*

BAPTISTE. Mademoiselle rang?

EDOUARD. Here, my good man... (*Giving him the letter and a coin.*) Go find a messenger, would you, and have him deliver this...

BAPTISTE. Very good, monsieur.

LUCILE, *aside to* BAPTISTE, *with a note of urgency in her voice.* Please, Baptiste, don't go too far!

BAPTISTE *exits, up center.*

EDOUARD. Now then, my dear. Let's have our little chat... (*He motions to her to sit down on the canape.*) What shall we talk about? (LUCILE *sits down, rather reluctantly.*) I know! Let's talk about you, and... and your success. (*He sits down beside her.*) I hate to admit it, but I still haven't seen it.

LUCILE. Seen what, monsieur?

EDOUARD. Why, *Mademoiselle Froufrou!*

LUCILE, *shocked. Mademoiselle...* I should hope not! That dreadful play!

EDOUARD. I beg your pardon?

LUCILE. That's not for nice young ladies, monsieur!

EDOUARD. Well, I'm hardly a nice young lady, my dear...

LUCILE. No... That's not what I meant...

EDOUARD. And anyway, I'll certainly go see it as soon as I can.

LUCILE. Yes... Do, by all means.

She turns toward the audience with an appropriate shrug.

EDOUARD. But only because of you, you understand.

LUCILE, *quizzically*. Because of me, monsieur?

EDOUARD. Of course! Otherwise, why bother?

LUCILE. You're much too kind... (*Aside.*) Tsk tsk tsk! Poor thing! And he's so young, too.

EDOUARD. After all, your name is on everybody's lips.

LUCILE, *with a start*. It is?

EDOUARD. All the critics adore you! All of Paris is at your feet! (*She looks at him in a combination of pity and amazement.*) Men worship the ground you walk on!

LUCILE. But...

EDOUARD. Yet here you are... in all your glory... And still, so... so simple, so unassuming... Unspoiled by all the praise, all the tribute, the adulation...

LUCILE. But...

EDOUARD. No, you haven't let fame and fortune turn your pretty head. You're so warm, so charming, so generous... Not cold or aloof, like so many celebrities... Why, you made me feel at home the minute I saw you. I came in... I didn't know you... I was timid and self-conscious, and... yes, even a little frightened. But you welcomed me, mademoiselle... Welcomed me with open arms... With music, no less... (*With a faint hint of sarcasm.*) Lots of music... And instead of the dismal failure I expected, here I am on the threshold of a... a glorious triumph!

LUCILE. But... but...

EDOUARD. And as if it weren't enough just being here... just sitting here beside you, instead of being thrown out head first, as I imagined... As if that weren't enough, you're going to do me the honor of your company tonight... Tonight, you and me... And a cozy little dinner, just for two, at Maxim's...

LUCILE. Monsieur...

EDOUARD. Ah, mademoiselle! What more can I say? You're... you're an angel! There's no other word... You're an angel!

LUCILE. But... Monsieur! Please! (*Jumping to her feet.*) Really, that's enough!

EDOUARD, *standing up*. Enough? Enough?... It can never be enough! I'm rich, mademoiselle... Money is no object! You'll have everything you want! Your slightest wish will be my command!... Four hundred francs?

You say four hundred francs a month? Nonsense! Twice as much! Three times... You can name your own figure... You'll have oysters, mademoiselle... Oysters at every meal... Three times a day... If only you'll love me...

He takes her hand in his.

LUCILE, *terrified.* Monsieur... Don't...

EDOUARD. Tell me you'll try to love me! Please... Even just a little...

LUCILE, *trying unsuccessfully to break free.* Monsieur... Monsieur...

EDOUARD. Please... Try to understand... I... I'm... It's... Haven't you ever read *Romeo and Juliet*...

LUCILE. Monsieur...

EDOUARD. *Pyramus and Thisbe, Daphnis and Chloe, Abelard and Heloise*...

LUCILE. Please, monsieur... let me go!

EDOUARD. Yes, that's what I am... (*Dramatically.*) A Romeo wrenched from his Juliet. A Pyramus torn from his Thisbe. A Daphnis ripped from his Chloe. An Abelard severed from his... No, what I mean is... All that matters is that I love you! I'm mad about you, you understand? Mad with love... Mad with passion... Mad, you hear me? Mad! Mad! Mad!

LUCILE. Yes, yes... I believe you! I'm sure... Oh! My heavens...

She tries desperately to pull away.

EDOUARD, *pressing on.* Come, you divine creature! Let me take you in my arms...

LUCILE, *struggling.* Let me go! Let me go!

EDOUARD. Please... Don't be afraid...

LUCILE. Monsieur... Let me go!

EDOUARD. But I'm not going to hurt you. I only want to... Why on earth are you trembling? Is it something I said?... Something I... What did I say? I thought everything I said made such... such perfectly good sense...

LUCILE. Oh yes... Perfectly, monsieur... (*Aside.*) You mustn't contradict them!

EDOUARD, *releasing his hold, sitting on the canape.* Look... I'm sitting down... (*Taking a deep breath.*) See? Everything is all right... We're calm as can be... Nothing to be afraid of... There! We're fine now, aren't we? And we were silly to go and get frightened, now weren't we?

LUCILE, *growing calmer.* But monsieur, it's just that... The things you said... And to me... I mean, really...

EDOUARD, *with a little laugh.* You'd think no one ever told you such things before, my dear...

LUCILE. Certainly not, monsieur!

EDOUARD, *taken aback*. But I thought... I assumed... In the theater, after all...

LUCILE. The theater? What theater?

EDOUARD. What theater?... *The* theater! Your theater! The stage!

LUCILE. Monsieur?

EDOUARD. I mean, I thought... Since you're an actress, and all that...

LUCILE, *startled*. Since what?

EDOUARD. I said: "I thought, since you're an actress, and—"

LUCILE. An actress? Me?

EDOUARD. Of course! Who else...

LUCILE. But monsieur... I'm not! I'm not!

EDOUARD, *jumping to his feet*. You're not?

LUCILE. Me? An actress?... Whatever made you think—

EDOUARD, *beginning to suspect the truth*. You... you mean, you're not La Dubarroy?

LUCILE. La Dubarroy?... Good heavens! No!

EDOUARD. But... You've got to be joking... Tell me you're joking...

LUCILE. I'm sorry, monsieur. I couldn't be more serious.

EDOUARD. But... but... I don't... That is... You mean... Then what am I doing here?

LUCILE. I really couldn't say. I was wondering myself.

EDOUARD, *babbling*. Aha! You were wondering. And... and I was wondering. And... and that means both of us were wondering, now weren't we?... (*Aside*.) I must look like a fool!

LUCILE, *suddenly*. Oh... Wait, monsieur... I think... Yes, I know what happened...

EDOUARD. You do?

LUCILE. Of course... I just remembered... We do have a neighbor who's an actress... Next door... I don't know her name, but I'm sure she's very famous... It must be your Mademoiselle Dubarroy.

EDOUARD. Oh?

LUCILE. You picked the wrong house, that's all. This is number two.

EDOUARD, *agape*. Number...

LUCILE. That's right. Number two.

EDOUARD. And I... Oh my! Next door?... And all the time I thought... I mean... Oh my! Where's my hat?

LUCILE, *getting his hat from the coatrack*. Here you are, monsieur.

EDOUARD. Really, mademoiselle... I don't know what to say...

LUCILE, *very much in control.* Please... Don't give it a second thought, monsieur. We all make mistakes... (*With a smile.*) Why, I even thought you were my new piano teacher!

EDOUARD. A piano teacher? Me?... (*Laughing.*) I can't play a note!

LUCILE. That's why I kept making you listen to me play. And why I kept asking you to beat time, monsieur... (*Coyly.*) Which you did rather badly, if you don't mind my saying...

EDOUARD. Well, what do you expect? It's the first time I conducted...

LUCILE. At any rate, all's well that ends well, as they say.

EDOUARD. And you will accept my apologies, mademoiselle?

LUCILE, *nodding.* Monsieur... And now, you mustn't let me keep you.

EDOUARD, *reluctantly.* Of course... Of course...

LUCILE. You'll find Mademoiselle Dubarroy next door.

EDOUARD, *shrugging.* Oh, Mademoiselle Dubarroy... I... Really, I don't think I'll bother... Not now... But... (*Emotionally.*) I do hope, mademoiselle, that... some day, somewhere... I hope I have the honor of making your acquaintance.

LUCILE, *with a coy little laugh.* Well, people do meet, monsieur. Socially, that is...

EDOUARD. And that... and that I can have the pleasure of continuing... properly, I mean... this... this rather unusual...

LUCILE, *seeing him at a loss for words.* I hope so, monsieur. Perhaps fate will see to it.

EDOUARD. Oh, believe me, mademoiselle. I'll see to it that it does. (*He backs toward the door, up center, bowing from the waist.*) Au revoir, mademoiselle...

LUCILE, *nodding.* Au revoir, monsieur...

EDOUARD, *aside.* Talk about breaking into Paris society! (*Nodding, to* LUCILE.) Mademoiselle...

LUCILE. Monsieur...

EDOUARD, *at the door.* Mademoiselle...

CURTAIN

FIT TO BE TRIED

OR

STEPBROTHERS
IN CRIME

•

Gibier de potence

CHARACTERS

CAMEMBERT

LA MOLE

DUPONT

BLOARDE

FIRST POLICEMAN

SECOND POLICEMAN

PÉPITA

SUZETTE

CAMEMBERT's *elegant drawing room. Upstage center, the door to the hall, flanked by two chairs. Up right, a diagonal wall, with the door to a closet. Up left, in a corresponding diagonal wall, another closet. Against the rear wall, between the hall door and the diagonal wall left, a small console table. Midstage right, a fireplace. Above it, a mirror. On the mantelpiece, a wooden yardstick. In front of the fireplace, a chair, facing the footlights. Next to it, a small end table. Down left, the door to the rest of the apartment. Midstage left, parallel to the wall, a table and two chairs, one on each side, facing each other. On the table, a pen and inkstand, stationery, envelopes, etc. Downstage, far right and far left, an armchair. Other appropriate furnishings* ad lib.

At rise, CAMEMBERT *is seated at the table, midstage left, facing the wall, writing.* PÉPITA *is seated in the chair by the end table, in front of the fireplace, reading a newspaper.*

CAMEMBERT, *muttering, as he writes, aside.* "...will be easy to recognize, thanks to his obviously moronic appearance. Signed: An anonymous citizen..." (*He pauses and reflects for a moment, then continues.*) "...who prefers to remain nameless." (*Putting down his pen.*) There! (*Folding the letter, putting it in his pocket, still aside.*) That should take care of you, my friend!

PÉPITA, *suddenly.* Oh! My goodness!

CAMEMBERT, *with a start, turning toward her.* What's the matter?

PÉPITA. She died!

CAMEMBERT. She did?... Who?

PÉPITA. That woman in Versailles... The one who was stabbed last night with the pruning-shears...

CAMEMBERT, *turning back.* Oh, that...

He begins to address an envelope.

PÉPITA. Isn't that just the most awful...

CAMEMBERT, *offhand*. I thought it was something important... The way you screamed...

PÉPITA. Octave! What a heartless thing to say! She died, for heaven's sake!

CAMEMBERT. So? It happens all the time. Here today, gone tomorrow... All in a day's work...

PÉPITA, *incredulous*. With pruning-shears?

CAMEMBERT. Besides... (*With a pseudodramatic air*.) I scoff at death... Like our ancestors the Gauls!

PÉPITA. Oh, of course you do!

CAMEMBERT, *turning toward her*. I mean, it's not as if *I* died, or something like that... That would be different... Then I might care...

PÉPITA. Yes, I suppose you might!

CAMEMBERT, *turning back*. But as long as it's someone else...

He finishes addressing the envelope and puts down the pen.

PÉPITA. Really! How can you be so... so careless?

CAMEMBERT, *turning toward her, quizzically*. I beg your pardon?

PÉPITA. So careless!... You have absolutely no heart! No heart at all!

CAMEMBERT, *understanding*. The word, my love, is "callous." And I'm not...

PÉPITA. Don't tell me! I know what I'm talking about!... Someone is murdered in cold blood, but do you care? No! You're careless!... It's perfectly logical...

CAMEMBERT, *rather condescending*. Excuse me, but people don't use the word that way.

PÉPITA. Well, whose fault is that? They should!

CAMEMBERT, *resigned*. Very well, my love. Whatever you say... I'm careless...

He turns back, looks at the envelope, nods with satisfaction, and puts it down on the table.

PÉPITA. You certainly are! (*Contemptuously, aside*.) Ignorant... And to think, I'm married to that... (*With a shudder*.) Oh!... Me, La Passionnelle... Toast of the Paris stage... Married to a... a... (*With obvious disdain*.) a witch-doctor!

She returns to her newspaper.

CAMEMBERT, *aside*. That woman amazes me sometimes... The things she comes up with...

PÉPITA, *shaking her head*. Tsk tsk tsk! (*Reading.*) "After a night of excruciating agony, the victim, who failed to regain consciousness..."

CAMEMBERT. They should have given her an enema.

PÉPITA, *in disbelief*. They what?

CAMEMBERT. If they asked me, I'd have given her an enema.

PÉPITA. An enema?... She was unconscious! (*Aside.*) Idiot!

CAMEMBERT. Exactly! A camomile enema... Ten parts camomile, one part sweet basil... With a pinch of thyme... It does wonders...

PÉPITA. Well, they didn't ask you!

CAMEMBERT. Besides, if she was so unconscious, how do they know about her "excruciating agony," or whatever...

PÉPITA. Oh! You're impossible! You're simply the most careless...

CAMEMBERT. Callous, my love!

PÉPITA, *stubbornly*. Careless, careless, careless!

She returns to the newspaper and continues reading for a few moments in silence.

CAMEMBERT. We medical men always say...

PÉPITA, *with a sneer*. What?

CAMEMBERT. I said: "We medical men always—"

PÉPITA, *cutting him off*. What "medical men"? You sell herbs, remember?

CAMEMBERT. I beg your pardon! I do much more than "sell herbs," as you so quaintly put it. I dispense them... I prescribe them...

PÉPITA. Of course! You prescribe them!... I can just hear you: "Take your thyme, young lady... Take your thyme..."

CAMEMBERT, *with a sarcastic little laugh*. Ha ha ha! Make all the jokes you like... I happen to be a practitioner of one of the oldest and—

PÉPITA, *interrupting and continuing along with him*. ...and noblest of the healing arts! I know!

CAMEMBERT. Well, please don't forget it!

PÉPITA, *pointedly*. How can I?

She turns around with a shrug and continues reading.

CAMEMBERT, *aside*. That woman...

PÉPITA. Tsk tsk tsk!... (*Reading.*) "...the victim, who failed to regain consciousness, finally gasped her last. Following her demise, she was laid to rest this morning..." (*Shaking her head.*) Tsk tsk tsk! Isn't that awful!

CAMEMBERT. Well, it's better than if they buried her last night, don't you think? During her "excruciating agony," I mean...

PÉPITA, *speechless*. Oh...

CAMEMBERT. Besides, everyone has to go sometime, my love.

PÉPITA, *ignoring him, reading.* "The police have yet to apprehend the perpetrator of this vicious crime..." Oh, my goodness!... You mean he's still on the loose? That maniac? Roaming the streets... with his pruning-shears...

CAMEMBERT, *casually.* It takes all kinds...

PÉPITA. And the police just sit there while he goes around stabbing people...

CAMEMBERT. Don't worry! That was this morning... By now he's probably behind bars.

PÉPITA. Well, I certainly hope so!

CAMEMBERT. You'll see...

PÉPITA. Maybe there'll be something in the evening paper.

CAMEMBERT. I'm sure...

PÉPITA. When Fernand... (*Catching herself.*) When Monsieur La Mole comes I'll have him run and get one.

CAMEMBERT, *with a touch of irony.* Oh?... You mean La Mole is paying us a visit? How nice...

PÉPITA. Why, yes... I thought you knew...

CAMEMBERT. Of course I knew! Why shouldn't he?... He's only been here every day for the last six months!

PÉPITA. Really, Octave... I don't know what you have against the poor boy. He's terribly entertaining... And perfectly harmless...

CAMEMBERT, *dryly.* Yes, I'm sure... (PÉPITA *gives a shrug and returns to her paper.*) Perfectly... (*Standing up, aside, to the audience.*) The only problem is, he's after my wife! It's getting to be a nuisance... The minute he shows up, she sends me off to give the baby his bottle!... For the last six months!... He's beginning to call me "Mamma"!... Lucky for me I'm not one of your blind husbands! They can't pull the wool over my eyes for long! I know what they're up to! I figured it out last night... I was reading a play... *Othello*... By some Englishman or other... Pretty good French though... For a foreigner, I mean... Anyway, I'm reading the play, and all of a sudden I realize what's been going on! Plain as day!... Well, first I said to myself: "Octave, I think it's time for the pillow!" (*He pantomimes choking himself.*) But then I thought: "No... That's too English... I need something more Gallic... Something with a little more flair..." So I thought for a while, and it came to me! Why not write to the police... (*He takes the letter from his pocket, waving it.*) To the chief... (*Reading.*) "To whom it may concern..." (*Speaking.*) After all, we've never met... (*Reading.*) "If you want to capture a vicious public enemy, come to the home of Monsieur Octave Camembert, seven

Rue Jacquasse, this evening at five o'clock. He will be easy to recognize, thanks to his obviously moronic appearance..." (*Speaking.*) So much for you, Monsieur La Mole! (*Folding the letter with evident satisfaction, putting it in the envelope and sealing it.*) Now to find someone to deliver it for me. (*Taking out his watch.*) It's almost four... That gives us an hour... Ah! He who laughs last...

The doorbell rings.

PÉPITA, *without getting up, calling.* Suzette!

SUZETTE'S VOICE, *offstage.* Yes, madame! I'm going...

After a few moments, the hall door opens and LA MOLE *appears.*

LA MOLE, *entering.* Peek-a-boo!

PÉPITA. Ah! Monsieur La Mole... How nice to see you!

She holds out her hand, still seated.

LA MOLE, *kissing it.* Madame...

PÉPITA. I was just mentioning your name.

LA MOLE. You were?

PÉPITA. Now be a dear, won't you? Run and get me the evening paper before they're all gone.

LA MOLE. The evening—

PÉPITA, *interrupting, with an afterthought.* Oh, and... (*Getting up.*) On your way, would you stop by the police station?

CAMEMBERT *knits his brow and cocks his head, in a quizzical gesture.*

LA MOLE. Of course! I'd be delighted!... I'll be back before you know it! (*Aside.*) Her word is my command!

He begins to leave, then stops abruptly at the hall door.

PÉPITA. Well?

LA MOLE, *puzzled.* The police station?

PÉPITA. Yes... About my brooch... You remember... You said you'd ask if anyone found it.

LA MOLE. The one you lost?

CAMEMBERT, *to* PÉPITA. You mean the little dog? With the diamonds for eyes?

PÉPITA. Yes...

CAMEMBERT. You lost it?

LA MOLE. The one you were so attached to... For sentimental reasons...

PÉPITA. That's right.

CAMEMBERT, *to* PÉPITA, *suspiciously*. Sentimental reasons? What sentimental reasons?

PÉPITA, *to* CAMEMBERT. Oh... You know, Octave... It was a... a souvenir... a memento...

CAMEMBERT. Aha... Of anyone in particular?

PÉPITA, *caught short*. Why, yes... Of... of my father. He wore it for years. He was never without it. That's why it meant so much to me.

CAMEMBERT. Of course! (*Sarcastically.*) An heirloom... It's practically sacred!

PÉPITA. Of course! Especially from a father...

CAMEMBERT. And your father wore diamond brooches, did he?

PÉPITA, *stammering*. Why yes, he... he... At banquets... receptions... All those official things... You know...

CAMEMBERT. Oh?

PÉPITA. He never did have a decoration, after all... And nowadays anyone without a decoration... (CAMEMBERT *absentmindedly fingers his empty lapel*.) Well, he didn't want to be taken for a domestic...

CAMEMBERT. No...

PÉPITA. So, with a little ribbon... You know... They thought it was something foreign... From Turkey, or some place like that...

LA MOLE, *who has been listening attentively*. Fascinating!

CAMEMBERT. Yes, isn't it!

During the following exchange, PÉPITA *goes over to the fireplace and pretends, casually, to be tidying up.*

LA MOLE. Well, I'm on my way...

CAMEMBERT, *catching him by the coattails, unobtrusively, to* LA MOLE. Just a minute, monsieur... (*Giving him the envelope.*) While you're at the police station... Give this to the officer in charge, if you don't mind...

LA MOLE, *taking it*. With pleasure, monsieur.

CAMEMBERT. Much obliged! (*Aside, to the audience, with a chuckle.*) Poetic justice! If he only knew... (*To* LA MOLE.) And don't be long!... I mean, no need to hurry... It's a little after four. You've got almost an hour...

LA MOLE. I do?

CAMEMBERT, *with forced congeniality*. Just don't forget to come back!

LA MOLE. No, no...

CAMEMBERT. The sooner the better...

LA MOLE. Thank you...

CAMEMBERT. We'll see you before five... Right? Before five? You won't forget...

La Mole. Yes... Of course... (*Bowing.*) Madame... Monsieur...

He exits, up center.

Pépita. Charming young man!

Camembert. Yes, isn't he! (*Aside.*) We'll see how charming he is in an hour!

He moves toward the door, down left. The doorbell rings.

Pépita. Now who can that be?

Camembert, *at the door, aside.* Some other charming young man, no doubt!

The hall door opens and Suzette *appears.*

Suzette. It's a gentleman who asks if he can see madame. He says his name is Monsieur Dupont.

Pépita. Dupont?... I don't know any Monsieur Dupont. (*To* Camembert.) Do you?

Camembert. No, but I'm sure he's charming!

Pépita, *to* Suzette. Well... Show him in and ask him to wait. I'm going to my room. I'll just be a moment.

Suzette. Very good, madame.

Pépita *exits, down left.*

Camembert. And I'm going to mine... If anybody cares...

He follows Pépita *out the door.* Suzette *exits, up center, leaving the door open.*

Suzette's Voice, *offstage.* This way, monsieur...

She enters, followed by Dupont, *hat in hand. He is carrying an umbrella on one arm, and, under the other, a small basket with a little dog inside, covered by his draped overcoat.*

Dupont. Thank you, mademoiselle.

Suzette. If monsieur will wait here, madame will be with him shortly.

Dupont. You're sure you told her "Monsieur Dupont"?

Suzette. Certainly, monsieur.

Dupont. Fine... Thank you...

Suzette. Don't mention it, monsieur.

She moves upstage, about to exit.

Dupont, *calling her back.* Oh... (*Awkwardly reaching into his pocket and handing her a coin, aside.*) Paris, after all...

SUZETTE, *looking at the coin, puzzled*. Monsieur?

DUPONT *smiles at her, patronizingly. She shrugs and exits.*

DUPONT. That's right... Monsieur Dupont... (*To the audience.*) Of course, when I say: "That's right..." Well, I don't mean that's really my name, you understand. My real name is Bourgeois... Philibert Bourgeois... Of the Marseille Bourgeois... Professor of Latin and Greek... But I didn't just pick Dupont out of a hat! It's my mother-in-law's name. I use it all the time when I'm... how shall I put it?... (*With a wink.*) when I'm out on a spree... I mean, no need to give my own name a bad name... (*He pauses and gives a silly little laugh, realizing his unintentional bon mot.*) So to speak!... Like now, for instance... Talk about your sprees! Alone in Paris... And my wife in Marseille... Well, I couldn't let a chance like that go to waste. So I said to myself: "Philibert Bourgeois, Monsieur Dupont is going to visit an actress!"... You see, I have an absolute passion for the theater... (*Realizing that he is stretching the truth.*) Well, that is... at least for actresses!... It's a vice... My only one... Really... Anyway, that's how I happen to be here... (*Sighing.*) Me... Here... Waiting for La Passionnelle... That ravishing creature! That *bellissima puella*! That magnificent star of the Folies Erotiques... Me, Philibert Bourgeois... Just like a real Parisian! (*He pauses.*) Of course, it wasn't that easy. I had to think of a good excuse. That's where this comes in... (*He holds up the basket, lifts his coat, and shows the dog, nuzzling it affectionately.*) Bow wow!... Woof, woof!... (*To the audience.*) It's a long story, but... Well, last night I was at the theater... The Folies Erotiques, of course... And right behind me there are these two young fops... Really, that's the only word... Anyway, who are they talking about?... Right! La Passionnelle!... And one of them says: "Have you heard the frightful news? She lost that gorgeous little dog of hers!" And the other one says: "No! Not her utterly precious Petit Bijou!... With the eyes that practically glow in the dark!" And the first one says: "That's right, Jean-Loup..." I remember his name was Jean-Loup because it rhymed with Petit Bijou... And then Jean-Loup says: "You mean that utterly exquisite little bauble? The one Prince Slopescu gave her just last Christmas?"... Well, that's all I had to hear. Suddenly I got an absolutely brilliant idea. It came to me in a flash. I said to myself: "*Optime*, Philibert Bourgeois! Here's your golden opportunity. All you have to do is find her dog..." Well, I'm not too sure exactly what a bauble looks like... A cross between a boxer and a beagle, I suppose... But I think I'd probably know one if I saw one... So this morning I got up bright and early, and followed every dog I saw... (*Holding up his umbrella.*) With this, because it was raining... cats and dogs... (*With another silly little laugh.*) So to speak!... Anyway, would you believe it? All of a sudden, *in medias res*, I turn a corner, and I see this darling puppy sniffing around at the cutest little mound of... of... well, whatever... And I said to myself: "Philibert Bourgeois, something tells me that's a bauble! In fact, something tells me it's hers! Let's find out..." So I called to him: "Here, Bijou, Bijou... Here, Petit Bijou..." And I held out my hand with a cube of sugar... Well, don't you think he came running up to me, wagging his little tail, licking my hand... (*Nodding emphatically.*) That proved it! I was right!... So here I am, bringing him back... (*With a sigh.*) To La Passionnelle!... I can't wait to see the look on her face when she... (*He stops suddenly, pricking up his ears.*) Oh my! Someone's coming... Maybe it's... (*Nervously.*) Yes, it must be... (*Controlling his emotion.*) Come, come, Philibert! This is no time to panic! Remember, you're a Frenchman! *Noblesse oblige!*... And whatever you do, don't let on you're a professor!... (*Striking a pose.*) *Per aspera ad astra!*

CAMEMBERT *enters, down left.*

CAMEMBERT, *clearing his throat.* Ahem!

DUPONT, *surprised, aside.* Oh my! That's not...

CAMEMBERT. Monsieur Dupont?

DUPONT, *nodding.* Monsieur...

CAMEMBERT, *bowing.* Delighted to make your acquaintance...

DUPONT, *bowing.* The pleasure is all mine, I assure you! (*Aside.*) Who on earth...

CAMEMBERT. Please, won't you sit down?

He offers him the chair to the right of the table, midstage left.

DUPONT. Oh, after you, monsieur... After you...

CAMEMBERT. No, no... I insist...

He holds out the chair.

DUPONT. Thank you, my good man!

He crosses over and sits down on the chair on the other side of the table, leaving CAMEMBERT *awkwardly holding the first one.*

CAMEMBERT. Don't mention it, I'm sure!

He puts down the chair and sits on it himself. There is a long moment of silence, during which both men eye each other, smile, nod, clear their throats, etc.

DUPONT, *finally breaking the silence.* Excuse me, monsieur... If you don't mind my asking...

CAMEMBERT. Monsieur?

DUPONT, *as tactfully as possible*. Do I assume correctly that you are the... (*With a knowing wink*.) the aunt of the household?

CAMEMBERT. The what?

DUPONT. The aunt... Actresses always have an... (*Emphasizing*.) old aunt...

CAMEMBERT. They do?

DUPONT. For appearances... You know... Or in your case, an old uncle...

CAMEMBERT, *aside*. Old uncle?

DUPONT. Some perfectly respectable, elderly individual...

CAMEMBERT. I beg your pardon!

DUPONT. Somewhat doddering... With a chest full of ribbons, and medals, and decorations... (*Stopping to scrutinize* CAMEMBERT's *lapel*.) I say, you are decorated, aren't you?

CAMEMBERT. I... Well, no... Not quite... That is, my wife knows a Rumanian prince, and he's promised...

DUPONT, *nodding*. Aha... I see... (*Puzzled*.) Well, if you're not the uncle, what on earth are you? What do you do here?

CAMEMBERT, *taken aback*. What do I... (*In no uncertain terms*.) I, monsieur, am Octave Camembert!

DUPONT, *jumping to his feet*. Camembert?... (*Moving upstage, as if to exit*.) You mean... But I thought Mademoiselle... I thought La Passionnelle lived here... I thought—

CAMEMBERT. *getting up and following him, interrupting*. She does! Of course she does!... She's my wife!

DUPONT, *stopping at the hall door*. Your... You mean, you're Monsieur Passionnelle?

CAMEMBERT. No, no! I just told you... I'm Octave Camembert!

DUPONT. But... I don't understand... You say your name is Camembert, and she's your wife. But her name is Passionnelle...

CAMEMBERT. So?

DUPONT. Well, I mean... I thought... A husband and wife... When my wife married me she became Madame Bourgeois, because my... (*Clearing his throat, realizing his blunder*.) Because my name is Dupont... (*Aside*.) I hope he didn't hear that!

CAMEMBERT. Really, monsieur... It's all perfectly simple... And quite interesting, if I do say so... I'll be happy to explain, if you have a minute.

He motions him back downstage.

DUPONT, *complying*. Of course... Of course...

CAMEMBERT. It's a chapter in my life that I'm sure you'd like to hear.

DUPONT. Yes, yes... I'm sure...

CAMEMBERT. Please, won't you sit down?

This time he offers him the chair to the left of the table, midstage left.

DUPONT. Oh, after you, monsieur... After you...

CAMEMBERT. No, no... I insist...

He holds out the chair.

DUPONT. Thank you, my good man!

This time he sits down on the chair to the right of the table. CAMEMBERT *is left holding his chair, as before.*

CAMEMBERT, *pausing awkwardly for a moment.* Don't mention it, I'm sure! (*Sitting down on the chair himself, aside.*) I wish he'd make up his mind!

DUPONT. You were saying, monsieur...?

CAMEMBERT. Yes... about my wife... Well, it all began because I'm a medical man.

DUPONT, *impressed.* Oh? Are you a doctor?

CAMEMBERT, *hesitating.* No... not exactly... That is, in a way...

DUPONT, *quizzically.* Monsieur?

CAMEMBERT. I'm a practitioner of one of the oldest and noblest of the healing arts... I deal in herbs...

DUPONT, *aside, disdainfully.* Indeed!

CAMEMBERT. At any rate, that's how I met her.

DUPONT. La Passionnelle?

CAMEMBERT, *nodding.* La Passionnelle... One morning she woke up feeling out of sorts... Sick to her stomach, dizzy spells... that sort of thing... And someone had the good sense to send for me...

DUPONT. Aha...

CAMEMBERT. Well, I fixed her up in no time...

DUPONT. Oh? What did you give her?

CAMEMBERT. Nothing at all. I told her to stay in bed and get plenty of rest. It always works.

DUPONT, *with a touch of sarcasm.* If you don't overdo it!

CAMEMBERT. Next day she was fit as a fiddle.

DUPONT, *aside.* I'm sure!

CAMEMBERT. But the interesting part is that, two weeks later, I married her! And five months after that, monsieur, I was a proud father!

DUPONT. No!

CAMEMBERT. A beautiful baby boy! Four months premature, but the picture of health... A perfect specimen, from head to toe...

DUPONT, *dubiously*. Four months...

CAMEMBERT. Something of a medical miracle...

DUPONT. I daresay! In the words of Cicero, *mirabile dictu!*

CAMEMBERT. Cicero the tailor?

DUPONT. Cicero the... No, no...

CAMEMBERT. I was going to report it to the Academy of Science, but my wife didn't think I should bother.

DUPONT, *nodding*. Aha...

CAMEMBERT. I'd love to hear those bigwigs try to explain it!

DUPONT, *shaking his head*. Four months...

CAMEMBERT. Anyway, monsieur, that's how Mademoiselle Pépita Passionnelle became Madame Octave Camembert! I told you it was interesting...

DUPONT, *unenthusiastically*. I should say.

CAMEMBERT. Of course, she keeps her stage name for professional reasons.

DUPONT. Of course...

CAMEMBERT. And frankly, that's just fine with me. I'd hate to see Camembert spread all over the billboards!

DUPONT. Yes, I should think...

CAMEMBERT. After all...

There is another moment of embarrassed silence, with more polite smiles, clearing of throats, etc.

DUPONT, *finally breaking the silence*. Excuse me, monsieur... Are you sure Mademoiselle... Madame Camembert knows I'm here?

CAMEMBERT. Certainly, monsieur. She won't be a minute.

There is another pause.

DUPONT, *growing a little fidgety*. I say, do you find it rather chilly in here?

CAMEMBERT. No... not particularly...

DUPONT, *standing up*. I don't know why it is, but the minute I take off my coat I feel cold...

CAMEMBERT, *very matter-of-fact*. Have you ever tried a camomile enema, monsieur? They do wonders...

DUPONT, *with a sidelong glance*. I'm sure!... (*With both hands full, he awkwardly tries to put his coat over his shoulders like a cape.*) If you don't mind, monsieur...

As he continues manipulating everything in his hands, he uncovers the dog in the basket.

CAMEMBERT, *noticing it, jumping up, surprised.* My goodness! What's that?

DUPONT. Shhh, shhh!... Please, monsieur... It's a surprise...

CAMEMBERT. It is?

DUPONT. Please... Shhh! Not a word...

The door, down left, opens and PÉPITA *enters.*

CAMEMBERT, *going to join her.* Ah! Pépita...

DUPONT *steps back and hides the basket behind his back as best he can.*

PÉPITA *to* DUPONT. I'm sorry to keep you waiting, monsieur. I hope you'll excuse me.

DUPONT, *bumbling.* Not at all, madame... The pleasure is all—

PÉPITA, *motioning toward the chair in front of the fireplace.* Please, won't you sit down?

DUPONT. Oh, after you, madame... After you...

He backs around toward the fireplace, still hiding the basket, and, awkwardly, with his other hand, offers her the chair.

PÉPITA, *moving toward him, motioning.* No, no... I insist...

DUPONT, *solicitously.* No, please... (*Emphasizing.*) *I* insist...

PÉPITA. Thank you, monsieur...

She crosses left and casually sits on the chair to the left of the table.
DUPONT, *still in front of the fireplace, offering the empty chair, looks at it for a moment in surprise.*

CAMEMBERT, *quickly crossing right, sitting down on the chair, to* DUPONT. Thank you, monsieur! The pleasure is all mine!

DUPONT, *looking at* PÉPITA *and* CAMEMBERT *in turn, with a shrug.* Hmm!

He crosses left and sits, tentatively, on the chair across the table from PÉPITA.

PÉPITA, *to* DUPONT. Now then... To what do I owe the honor...

DUPONT. It's really very simple, madame... (*Obviously intimidated by the presence of his idol, stammering.*) I... I...

PÉPITA. Monsieur?

DUPONT. I... I have something for you... something very special... something that I know is going to make you very happy...

PÉPITA, *trying to be obliging.* You do?... Well, let me guess...

DUPONT. Madame?

PÉPITA. I just love surprises!... (*After a moment of pretended reflection, rather patronizingly.*) I know!... Now tell me if I'm right... You're terribly talented...

DUPONT, *fatuously*. Well...

PÉPITA. And clever... and young...

DUPONT, *surprised, aside*. Young?

PÉPITA. And witty...

DUPONT, *aside*. I'm as young as anyone else my age...

PÉPITA. And you've brought me a play!... Now that's it, isn't it? (*Even more patronizingly*.) You've brought me a play that you've written just for me!

DUPONT I...

PÉPITA. And you know that no one else can possibly do it justice! Right?

DUPONT. Well... No...

PÉPITA. No?

DUPONT. Not exactly, madame... I... (*He stands up and holds out the basket*.) I've brought you this...

PÉPITA, *startled, jumping to her feet*. A dog? What in the name of—

DUPONT, *interrupting*. It's not very fancy... I tried wrapping him up in a box of chocolates, but... well, he ate them all and... (*Clearing his throat*.) and messed in the box... I thought this was better...

PÉPITA, *agape*. A dog, monsieur?

DUPONT, *showing her, emphasizing*. *Your* dog, madame....

PÉPITA. My—

DUPONT. Your Petit Bijou... The one you lost...

PÉPITA. The one I—

CAMEMBERT, *breaking out in a laugh*. Ha ha ha! Her dog!... That's a good one!

PÉPITA. *to* DUPONT. But monsieur...

CAMEMBERT, *laughing even harder*. Now I've heard everything!... Her dog!...

PÉPITA, *to* DUPONT. I'm afraid there's some mistake.

DUPONT. Mistake?

CAMEMBERT, *doubled up*. I'll say!... Her dog!...

PÉPITA, *to* DUPONT. That's not my dog!

DUPONT, *taken aback*. It's not?

PÉPITA. No, monsieur...

DUPONT. But... but I thought you lost one...

PÉPITA. I did!... But mine is a brooch, monsieur... A little brooch...

CAMEMBERT, *laughing*. Her dog!...

DUPONT. A brooch?... I thought it was a bauble... (*Holding out the basket*.) See? This one's a bauble... (*Sheepishly*.) At least, I think it is...

PÉPITA. I'm afraid you don't understand, monsieur. Mine is just a head...

DUPONT, *startled*. Just a... You mean... Good God! How does it walk, and... and everything?

PÉPITA. I mean, monsieur, that it's a brooch... a pin... a piece of jewelry...

CAMEMBERT, *still laughing*. With two diamonds for eyes!

DUPONT. Diamonds?... A pin?... Oh my!...

CAMEMBERT, *beginning to control himself*. It's worth a small fortune!

DUPONT, *abashed*. Yes... I imagine... A dog's head, with diamonds... You don't find those running around the streets...

PÉPITA. Hardly, monsieur!

DUPONT. And here I thought... (*To* PÉPITA.) I say, do you find it rather warm in here?

PÉPITA. No... not particularly...

DUPONT *puts the basket and his hat down on the table, and leans his umbrella against his chair.*

DUPONT, *slipping off his coat, draping it over the basket, covering the dog*. I don't know why it is, but the minute I put on my coat...

CAMEMBERT, *still chuckling*. Her dog!...

PÉPITA, *to* DUPONT. Well, monsieur... I certainly appreciate your trying to help. But I'm afraid you can see that your dog and mine... well...

DUPONT. Yes... There's not much comparison, is there, madame?

PÉPITA. I'm afraid not, monsieur.

DUPONT, *trying to salvage his self-respect*. But after all, it's the thought that counts. Don't you agree?

PÉPITA. Oh, no doubt...

DUPONT. *Errare humanum est*, as they say...

PÉPITA. Beg pardon?

DUPONT. *Errare humanum est.*

PÉPITA. Are you Spanish, monsieur?

DUPONT. No... no...

PÉPITA. Because my mother was Spanish, and I thought... What you just said... "Errare..."

DUPONT. *Errare humanum est*... Freely translated, "To err is human..."

CAMEMBERT, *interjecting*. "But to forgive in time saves nine."

DUPONT, *to* CAMEMBERT. Monsieur?

CAMEMBERT. It reminds me of something that happened to me once... I was fishing in the Seine... Way, way upstream... And the fish just weren't biting... Not a nibble all day...

PÉPITA. Octave...

CAMEMBERT. Then, all of a sudden, I felt something on my line, and I said to myself: "It's got to be a herring!"

PÉPITA, *beginning to lose patience*. Really, Octave...

CAMEMBERT. So I pulled it in...

　　He pauses briefly.

DUPONT. And...?

CAMEMBERT. And it wasn't a herring at all, monsieur! It was just an old shoe!

　　He pauses again.

DUPONT. Excuse me, monsieur, but... I'm not sure I see the connection...

CAMEMBERT. Who said there was a connection? I said: "It reminds me of something that happened to me..."

DUPONT, *puzzled by his logic, but too polite to protest*. Aha...

　　PÉPITA *shakes her head, out of patience.*

CAMEMBERT, *aside*. So there!

DUPONT, *changing the subject as gently as possible, apologetically, to* PÉPITA. At any rate, madame... I'm sorry to have troubled you...

PÉPITA. Not at all, monsieur...

DUPONT. I wish I had found your Petit Bijou...

PÉPITA. I wish you had too, monsieur.

CAMEMBERT, *sarcastically*. After all, an heirloom...

DUPONT, *with a sigh, as if getting ready to leave*. Well...

CAMEMBERT, *to* DUPONT. Too bad! This way you can't claim the reward!

DUPONT, *the picture of injured dignity, to* CAMEMBERT. I beg your pardon...

PÉPITA, *to* CAMEMBERT. Really, Octave...

CAMEMBERT, *to* PÉPITA. Well, he can't! (*To* DUPONT.) I mean, you didn't find it, did you? Good intentions be damned!

DUPONT, *at a loss for words*. I... I...

PÉPITA. Octave!

CAMEMBERT. They're all well and good, but they don't pay the rent!

DUPONT, *stammering*. That... that was hardly why I...

PÉPITA, *to* DUPONT. Of course it wasn't, monsieur! (*To* CAMEMBERT, *peremptorily*.) The baby's crying! Go give him his bottle!

CAMEMBERT. Oh?... (*Getting up*.) Right away, my love... Right away...

(*Crossing down left.*) The bottle!... (*Looking at his watch, aside.*) Well, he who laughs last...

He exits, down left.

PÉPITA, *to* DUPONT. Please don't mind my husband, monsieur.
DUPONT. Not at all...
PÉPITA. You mustn't take him seriously. That's just his sense of humor.
DUPONT, *nodding*. Aha...

The doorbell rings.

PÉPITA. He's really very pleasant... (*Dryly.*) And terribly amusing...
DUPONT. Yes... I'm sure... You'd never think so, but I'm sure he must be.
LA MOLE'S VOICE, *offstage*. Don't bother, Suzette. I can show myself in.

The hall door opens and LA MOLE *appears.*

LA MOLE. Peek-a-boo! (*Waving a newspaper.*) I'm... (*Suddenly noticing* DUPONT.) Oh! Excuse me... I didn't know...
PÉPITA, *moving upstage to meet him*. Monsieur...
DUPONT, *still standing by his chair, aside*. Who on earth...
PÉPITA, *to* LA MOLE, *introducing*. I'd like you to meet Monsieur Dupont. (*To* DUPONT.) Monsieur Dupont... Monsieur La Mole...
LA MOLE, *bowing*. Delighted, monsieur!
DUPONT, *bowing*. The pleasure is all mine!
LA MOLE, *coming downstage*. My father knew a Dupont once... his podiatrist... He said there was nobody like him for bunions...
DUPONT. Oh?
LA MOLE. An absolute artist... I don't suppose you're the same one...
DUPONT, *somewhat ruffled*. No... no, monsieur... I'm afraid that's not one of my talents...
LA MOLE. Well anyway, that Dupont must be dead and buried by now! Even then he had one foot in the grave... (*Pointing to his head.*) And a little soft up here, if you know what I mean...
DUPONT, *aside*. Much obliged, I'm sure!
LA MOLE. Too bad, monsieur... We could have talked about old times...

He and PÉPITA *move down right.*

DUPONT. Yes... Quite... (*Aside.*) And his father's feet!
PÉPITA, *to* LA MOLE. Any luck?
LA MOLE. About the brooch?

PÉPITA. Yes... Did anyone turn it in?

LA MOLE. Not yet...

PÉPITA, *disappointed*. Oh...

LA MOLE. But they promised to let you know...

PÉPITA, *to* DUPONT. Excuse us, monsieur. We're being terribly impolite.

DUPONT. Not at all, madame... Please... I really should be going...

PÉPITA, *not objecting too strenuously*. Well, if you're sure you can't stay...

DUPONT. But I must say, I'm delighted to have had the opportunity...

PÉPITA. My pleasure, monsieur...

DUPONT. No, no, madame... The pleasure is—

PÉPITA, *going to the hall door, ready to show him out, interrupting*. And I do want to thank you for trying to help.

DUPONT, *picking up the basket, still covered with his coat, embarrassed*. Yes... Well...

PÉPITA. It was terribly sweet...

DUPONT, *mumbling inaudibly, takes his hat but forgets his umbrella, and goes to the hall door, casting a glance at* LA MOLE *in passing*.

LA MOLE, *bowing*. Monsieur...

DUPONT, *nodding*. Monsieur... (*Aside*.) Podiatrist my foot! (*At the door, to* PÉPITA.) *Ave atque vale*, madame!

PÉPITA, *nodding*. Monsieur...

DUPONT *exits*.

LA MOLE. Who the devil was that?

PÉPITA. Oh... Nobody, really... Nobody important...

LA MOLE. That much was obvious!

PÉPITA. A little strange, but harmless...

LA MOLE. Yes, I'm sure...

PÉPITA, *joining him downstage*. Oh, good! You brought the paper... (*She takes it from him and opens it*.) I wonder if it tells...

LA MOLE. Tells what?

PÉPITA, *scanning the paper*. About last night... That woman in Versailles... The one with the pruning-shears... (*Spotting the article*.) Ah! Here it is... (*Reading*.) "Versailles murderer identified..." (*With a sigh of relief*.) Well, thank heaven for that!... He was right, for a change!

LA MOLE. Who?

PÉPITA. Camembert... He said he was sure the police would catch him. (*She continues reading*.) "Enraged when he lost his ex—"

(*She pronounces "his sex."*)

LA MOLE. Poor chap! I don't blame him!

PÉPITA. Beg pardon?

LA MOLE. Lost his sex, did he? I'd be enraged too!

PÉPITA. Lost his... Please, be serious! (*Continuing.*) "Enraged when he lost his ex-mistress to his gardener..."

LA MOLE, *aside*. I should think so!

PÉPITA. "...the murderer brutally stabbed her thirteen times..."

LA MOLE. Well, at least he's not superstitious!

PÉPITA. Please! You're as careless as Camembert!

LA MOLE. I'm what?

PÉPITA. As careless... Oh, never mind! (*She continues reading.*) "Although he eluded the police and remains at large..." (*Taken aback.*) What?... Oh no! I thought it said they caught him! (*Reading.*) "...the authorities have ascertained that his name is Dupont, and that he..." (*Suddenly stopping, agape.*) Dupont?... My God! You don't suppose...

LA MOLE, *pointing to the hall door*. Him? Don't be silly!

PÉPITA. Why not?

LA MOLE. The harmless one?

PÉPITA. It's possible...

LA MOLE. Do you know how many Duponts there are in Paris?

PÉPITA. I know, but still... You heard what it said. He... (*Reading, with emphasis.*) "...remains at large..." (*Waving the paper.*) They don't know where he is! He could be anywhere... Even here...

LA MOLE. Not very likely!

PÉPITA. These criminals are so clever... Who would ever think of looking for him here? (*Growing more and more apprehensive.*) I'm sure... It's so obvious...

LA MOLE. Come now, you don't really—

PÉPITA. Listen!... (*Continuing to read.*) "The police have furnished the following description: Dupont is a male..."

LA MOLE, *sarcastically*. No!

PÉPITA. "...forty-five years old, of average height..." (*To* LA MOLE.) How tall is "average?"

LA MOLE. Oh... About so...

He holds up his hand, palm down, to the appropriate height.

PÉPITA, *excited*. That's just how tall he was!... Exactly!... You see?

LA MOLE. Naturally! Because he's average...

PÉPITA, *reading*. "...of average height, about five foot six..."

LA MOLE, *nodding*. Aha...

PÉPITA, *continuing*. "...with straight, dark brown hair..." (*Putting down the paper*.) There! I knew it!

LA MOLE. Knew what? He was practically white!

PÉPITA. Of course! He probably dyed it! You wouldn't expect him not to disguise himself, would you?

LA MOLE. Well...

PÉPITA. Or he's wearing a wig!... Or... or he turned white overnight...

LA MOLE. What?

PÉPITA. From worry! It happens, you know...

LA MOLE. Really...

PÉPITA. And if not, his hair would be dark brown! Just like the description!

LA MOLE, *beginning to have some doubts*. Well... it could be, I suppose...

PÉPITA. Of course it would!

LA MOLE, *pointing to the paper*. What else does it say?

PÉPITA, *finding her place, reading*. "...with straight, dark brown hair, a small brown mustache—"

LA MOLE, *interrupting*. There! Ours didn't have a mustache! I'm sure—

PÉPITA, *triumphantly*. That proves it! He shaved it off! Don't you see...

LA MOLE, *beginning to relent again*. Well...

PÉPITA, *with a shudder*. Oh! When I think...

LA MOLE, *pointing to the paper*. Anything else?

PÉPITA, *reading*. "...a small brown mustache, brown eyes..." (*To* LA MOLE.) Oh dear! I don't remember his eyes... Do you?

LA MOLE. No... I didn't get a good look...

PÉPITA. Neither did I... (*Categorically*.) But they must have been brown!... (*Reading*.) "...average nose, average mouth..."

LA MOLE. Big help!

PÉPITA, *continuing*. "...full set of teeth, except for his upper left wisdom tooth, which is missing..." (*To* LA MOLE.) Ah! Keep that in mind! (*Reading*.) "He has no scars..." (*To* LA MOLE.) See? He didn't have any scars, did he?

LA MOLE, *reflecting*. No... Not that I—

PÉPITA, *excited*. Now do you believe me?

LA MOLE. Well...

PÉPITA, *reading*. "...no scars or other distinguishing features, except for a small strawberry mark below his right nipple..."

LA MOLE. Oh?

PÉPITA. Remember that... Strawberry... (*Reading.*) "It is also believed that he generally wears a red flannel undershirt..."

LA MOLE, *nodding, making a mental note.* Red flannel...

PÉPITA, *sighing.* Oh! When I think... (*Visibly shaken at the thought.*) That murderer... Here! In my house!... That maniac... Alone with me...

LA MOLE. Now, now... We're not absolutely sure... We only think...

The doorbell rings.

PÉPITA, *moving left, to the table.* Maybe *you're* not sure... I don't know how much more proof you need!

LA MOLE, *cocking his head.* Wasn't that the doorbell?

PÉPITA. Oh, I don't care! I'm not at home!... I'm just too upset... (*Throwing the newspaper down on the table, suddenly noticing* DUPONT's *umbrella, pointing.*) Oh, my God! Look!

LA MOLE. His umbrella!

PÉPITA. Do you suppose it has any clues?

LA MOLE. It might...

PÉPITA. Well, there's only one way to find out!...

She invites him, with a gesture, to pick up the umbrella. He does so, and inspects it.

LA MOLE. It looks perfectly... average!

PÉPITA. Open it! Maybe there's something inside...

He complies.

SUZETTE's VOICE, *offstage.* But monsieur...

DUPONT's VOICE, *offstage.* Quite all right, I know the way...

SUZETTE's VOICE. But...

The hall door opens and DUPONT *appears, wearing his coat, hat in hand.*

DUPONT, *aside.* One tip is enough! (*Aloud, entering.*) It's only me...

PÉPITA *and* LA MOLE *wheel around, appalled.* LA MOLE *is holding the umbrella over their heads.* PÉPITA, *terrified, flings her arms around* LA MOLE's *neck and jumps up into his arms.*

PÉPITA,
LA MOLE, } *together.* { You!
{ Him!

DUPONT, *sheepishly*. The pleasure is all... (*Noticing the open umbrella.*) I say... (*Looking up at the ceiling and holding his hat over his head for protection.*) Is there a leak?

LA MOLE, *babbling*. Yes... That is...

PÉPITA. No, no... We were going for a walk, and...

LA MOLE, *dropping her to her feet*. And you know what a rainy month this has been...

DUPONT. I know! Cats and dogs... (*To* PÉPITA, *doffing his hat.*) If you'll pardon the expression...

PÉPITA. Not at all... Not at all...

LA MOLE. So it's always a good idea to take one's umbrella...

DUPONT. "One's" umbrella, indeed!... (*Timidly.*) If you don't mind, monsieur... *My* umbrella... That's why I came back...

LA MOLE. Of course... I was just saying...

He is about to pass the open umbrella to DUPONT.

PÉPITA, *intercepting it, to* DUPONT. No, no, no, monsieur! What do you think we are? We wouldn't dream of letting you go out in weather like this!

DUPONT. You wouldn't?

PÉPITA. Certainly not! (*To* LA MOLE.) Would we?

She closes the umbrella, crosses to the fireplace, and hangs it from the mantelpiece. At the same time she notices the yardstick, picks it up and fingers it for a few moments during the following exchange, as if conceiving a plan.

LA MOLE, *to* DUPONT. Please, won't you have a seat?

He holds out the chair to the right of the table.

DUPONT. Oh, after you, monsieur... After you...

LA MOLE. No, no... I insist...

He holds out the chair.

DUPONT. Thank you, my good man!

He goes upstage, takes the chair to the right of the hall door, brings it center and sits down. LA MOLE *is left holding the other chair for a moment.*

LA MOLE, *finally replacing it at the table*. Hmmm!

PÉPITA, *crossing, to* DUPONT. There, monsieur! Just make yourself comfortable!

DUPONT, *realizing that he sat down before* PÉPITA, *jumping up.* Oh! Excuse me, madame... I didn't realize... (*Motioning toward the chair by the fireplace.*) Please...

PÉPITA, *joining* LA MOLE, *far left, to* DUPONT, *motioning.* Please, monsieur! You sit right down! We don't stand on ceremony!

DUPONT, *reluctantly complying.* Well... if you're sure...

PÉPITA, *to* LA MOLE, *whispering.* You see? I told you! Look at his eyes!

LA MOLE, *scrutinizing* DUPONT *from a distance, to* PÉPITA, *whispering.* They're brown!... And his nose...

PÉPITA, *nodding, to* LA MOLE, *whispering.* Very average... And his mouth...

LA MOLE. *nodding, to* PÉPITA, *whispering.* Average... average...

DUPONT, *reacting to their whispering, self-consciously fingering his necktie, aside.* Is there something wrong with the way I look? (*Clearing his throat, rather loudly.*) Ahem!

PÉPITA,
LA MOLE, } *together, with a start.* { Oh!
Monsieur!

DUPONT, *to* PÉPITA. By the way, madame... I thought you might like to know... I disposed of... (*Embarrassed.*) of our friend...

LA MOLE, *aside.* Good God! He admits it!

PÉPITA, *to* DUPONT. I know... (*Confused.*) I mean... "Our friend," monsieur? What friend?

DUPONT, *with a knowing wink.* You know... Bow wow! Bow wow!... Woof woof woof!...

LA MOLE, *aside.* He's out of his mind!

PÉPITA, *to* DUPONT, *suddenly understanding.* Oh!... I see... That...

DUPONT. Yes... The bauble... I disposed of it...

LA MOLE, *aside.* The what?

PÉPITA. You didn't!

DUPONT. Why not?

PÉPITA. You... you mean you strangled it?

DUPONT. Strangled...? Heavens no!

PÉPITA, *shuddering.* Cut off its head? Shot it? Poisoned it?...

DUPONT. Of course not, madame!

PÉPITA. You drowned it?

DUPONT. No, no, no!...

PÉPITA. Well what else is there? You just said you killed it...

DUPONT, *puzzled*. I did? (*To* LA MOLE.) Did I say I killed it, monsieur?

LA MOLE, *confused*. Killed what?

DUPONT. The bauble! Why does she think I killed it?

LA MOLE, *shaking his head*. Don't ask me!

DUPONT, *to* PÉPITA. Why on earth should I kill it?... I gave it away... (*Pointing downstairs*.) To your concierge...

PÉPITA. Oh...

DUPONT. That is, actually I gave it to her daughter... I said... (*Chuckling*.) It was terribly amusing... I said: "Mademoiselle, I come bearing gifts. But don't worry, I'm not Greek!"... (*He pauses, smiling, waiting in vain for a reaction*.) You know... "*Timeo Danaos et dona ferentes...*"

PÉPITA, *at a loss*. Yes... I'm sure...

LA MOLE, *aside*. Out of his damn mind!

DUPONT. Then I said: "Please present it to your mother, with the compliments of Monsieur Philibert Bour— (*Correcting himself*.) Philibert Dupont!"

PÉPITA. Yes...

DUPONT. Well, she couldn't have been more pleased! She said: "Oh, thank you, monsieur! Mamma has simply been dying for a cat! I know she'll be delighted!"

He breaks out laughing. PÉPITA *and* LA MOLE *join in, politely, exchanging glances.*

PÉPITA *to* DUPONT. Yes... That was nice of you... (*To* LA MOLE.) Wasn't it nice of him?

LA MOLE, *with no conviction and less comprehension*. Oh yes... Terribly...

DUPONT, *getting up, moving left and placing his hat on the table, to* PÉPITA. Excuse me, madame... May I take off my coat?

PÉPITA. Of course, monsieur... Please...

DUPONT. Thank you...

He takes off his coat, facing left, and begins folding it with great care, as if preparing, during the ensuing dialogue, to lay it on the chair to the right of the table.

PÉPITA, *while* DUPONT's *back is turned, to* LA MOLE, *whispering*. Quick! Here's our chance...

She crosses quickly to the fireplace, picks up the yardstick, and brings it back to LA MOLE.

LA MOLE, *to* PÉPITA, *whispering*. What...?

Their following exchange continues in whispers.

PÉPITA. To measure him, for heaven's sake! (*Holding up her hand, palm down, to indicate his height.*) You know... Five foot six...

LA MOLE. Damn! If you think it's going to be easy...

PÉPITA. Never mind! Do your best...

DUPONT, *still with his back turned, as* LA MOLE *tries to measure his height.* I don't know why it is, but... (*He turns around, interrupting* LA MOLE's *attempt, as the latter, affecting a nonchalant air, begins swinging the yardstick around his head.*) What on earth... (DUPONT, *still holding his neatly folded coat, moves around the table, as if to place it on the other chair, left, followed by* LA MOLE, *who persists in his efforts to measure him.*) I don't know why it is, but... (*He turns again, once more catching* LA MOLE *in the act.*) Again? (LA MOLE *pretends to be measuring the length and breadth of the table, and in so doing sends* DUPONT's *hat flying with the yardstick.*) Please, monsieur! My hat... (*He picks it up, brushes it off, moves up left, and places it on the console table against the rear wall, then lays his coat on the remaining upstage chair, to the left of the door, closely shadowed by* LA MOLE *and his yardstick.*) I don't know why it is... (*Bending over the chair at a ninety-degree angle, back to audience, neatly arranging his coat.*) but the minute I put on my coat...

During the preceding, LA MOLE *has been trying to take his measurements in stages, from the feet up, apparently with no success.*

LA MOLE, *frustrated, aside.* Damn!

DUPONT, *suddenly straightening up, almost knocking the yardstick out of* LA MOLE's *hands.* Monsieur?

During the following exchange, LA MOLE *casually pretends to be measuring the wall, the door, etc., gradually working his way toward* PÉPITA, *who is standing by the fireplace.*

LA MOLE, *innocently.* Hmmm?

DUPONT. Did you say something?

LA MOLE. Me?

DUPONT. I thought you said "Damn!"

LA MOLE. Oh, did I? Sorry... (*Pointing to the walls, etc., that he is ostensibly engaged in measuring, with a professional air.*) This is harder than it looks...

DUPONT, *nodding, puzzled.* Aha... (*Aside.*) What is he? An architect or something? (*To* LA MOLE.) *Labor omnia vincit,* my good man!

LA MOLE, *nodding, pretending to understand*. So they say...

He turns to PÉPITA *and shrugs, as* DUPONT *moves down center. The two once again discuss their strategy in whispers.*

PÉPITA. Well?

LA MOLE. Impossible! He keeps moving!

PÉPITA. But we've got to find out!

DUPONT, *noticing their tête-à-tête, aside*. Always whispering, those two!... Damned impolite, if you ask me...

LA MOLE, *to* PÉPITA, *still in a whisper*. Well... Talk to him... Get his attention... Maybe you can make him stand still for a minute!

DUPONT, *inspecting his appearance, aside*. It *must* be something about the way I look...

PÉPITA, *going over to* DUPONT, *who is standing by the chair, center stage, facing the audience*. Really, monsieur, that was terribly thoughtful of you!

LA MOLE *ambles behind them, as inconspicuously as possible.*

DUPONT, *quizzically*. Madame?

PÉPITA. Giving that darling little dog to my concierge...

LA MOLE *is about to try measuring him again.*

DUPONT, *sitting down*. Well, under the circumstances... (*Embarrassed*.) As long as it wasn't yours...

LA MOLE *is left standing behind him, yardstick still poised, as* DUPONT *turns and looks at him for a moment in bewilderment.* PÉPITA, *clearly frustrated, moves off to the left. To cover his embarrassment,* LA MOLE *begins thrusting in the air with the yardstick, as if he were fencing with an imaginary opponent, gradually edging left to join* PÉPITA.

LA MOLE, *to* PÉPITA, *whispering*. It's no use! It won't work!

DUPONT, *aside*. Queer chap! Even for an architect! (*To* PÉPITA, *who is obviously not listening*.) I mean, all things considered...

PÉPITA, *to* LA MOLE, *whispering*. But there must be a way! Think of something!

LA MOLE, *to* PÉPITA, *whispering*. I'm thinking...

DUPONT, *trying, unsuccessfully, to get* PÉPITA's *attention*. All things considered...

PÉPITA, *struck by an idea, to* LA MOLE, *still in a whisper*. I know! Start yawning!

LA MOLE, *forgetting himself, aloud*. What did you say?

DUPONT. I said: "All things considered..."

LA MOLE, *to* DUPONT. Who asked you?

DUPONT, *taken aback.* I beg your pardon... I thought...

PÉPITA, *to* LA MOLE, *whispering.* I said: "Start yawning!" Don't you understand?

DUPONT, *to* LA MOLE, *who is ignoring him completely.* You said: "What did you say?" And...

LA MOLE, *to* PÉPITA, *whispering.* Why? I'm not tired!

DUPONT. ...and I thought you meant me, so...

PÉPITA, *to* LA MOLE, *whispering.* The wisdom tooth! Understand?

DUPONT. ...naturally, I told you...

LA MOLE, *understanding, to* PÉPITA, *still in a whisper.* Aha! The wisdom tooth!

DUPONT, *to* PÉPITA. You see, all things considered, madame... (*Aside.*) I must say, they don't seem too interested...

PÉPITA *and* LA MOLE *take the two chairs from the table, left, and place them on either side of* DUPONT, *still seated center stage. They then proceed to sit down,* PÉPITA *to his right and* LA MOLE *to his left.*

PÉPITA, *after a moment, yawning.* Aaaah!

LA MOLE *draws his chair as close as possible to* DUPONT'*s, virtually on top of him.*

LA MOLE, *yawning.* Aaaah!

DUPONT, *pulling his chair downstage a few feet, turning to* PÉPITA. I say... All things considered, madame...

PÉPITA, *pulling her chair downstage, as close as possible to his, yawning.* Aaaah!

DUPONT, *edging a few feet farther.* ...I really couldn't keep it myself...

LA MOLE, *pulling abreast of him, yawning.* Aaaah!

PÉPITA, *likewise pulling abreast, yawning more loudly.* Aaaaah!

By now the three chairs, in a tight row, are as far downstage as possible.

DUPONT, *turning to* LA MOLE. I mean, as much as I would have liked to...

LA MOLE, *replying with a huge, almost violent yawn.* Aaaaaah!

DUPONT, *turning to* PÉPITA. A man in my position...

PÉPITA, *replying with an even more exaggerated yawn, right in his face.* Aaaaaaah!

DUPONT, *turning to* LA MOLE. A man in my position...

LA MOLE, *louder still*. Aaaaaaaah!

DUPONT, *with more than a touch of sarcasm, to* LA MOLE. I can see that you're utterly fascinated, monsieur!

LA MOLE, *matter-of-fact, yawning as he speaks*. Not at all! But that's all right... Don't stop now!

DUPONT. Much too kind... As I was saying... A man in my position... (*He turns back and forth between* PÉPITA *and* LA MOLE, *who continue to yawn in his face, more and more aggressively*.) My goodness... (*Beginning to yawn himself*.) It's contagious! (*Opening his mouth in a gaping yawn*.) Aaaaah! (PÉPITA *and* LA MOLE *lunge toward him simultaneously, trying to inspect his upper teeth, but he immediately and very discreetly covers his mouth with his hand*.) I beg your pardon!

PÉPITA *stamps her foot and turns aside in obvious frustration*.

LA MOLE. Damn!

DUPONT. Monsieur?

LA MOLE, *innocently*. Hmmm?

DUPONT. I think you said it again.

LA MOLE. Said what?

DUPONT. "Damn!," monsieur. You just said it again...

LA MOLE. Oh, did I?... Sorry!

DUPONT, *getting up and taking his chair back upstage, replacing it to the right of the hall door, aside*. I suppose they're insulted... But after all, they started it...

PÉPITA *and* LA MOLE, *exchange frustrated glances, replace the two chairs at the table and move down left, whispering to each other*.

LA MOLE. Now what?

PÉPITA. I don't know...

LA MOLE. We could always try the birthmark... the strawberry...

PÉPITA. Below his right nipple...?

DUPONT, *still upstage, aside*. I mean, if I bother them that much, why did they ask me to stay?

He picks up his coat from the chair to the left of the hall door.

LA MOLE, *to* PÉPITA, *still whispering*. Yes... And the red flannel undershirt...

Pépita, *to* La Mole, *whispering*. I suppose it's worth a try. But it won't be easy...

Dupont *puts his coat around his shoulders*.

Dupont, *about to take his hat from the console table, nodding to* Pépita *and* La Mole. Madame... Monsieur...

Pépita, *rushing toward him*. Oh, please, monsieur! You're not leaving so soon!

Dupont, *bewildered*. I'm not?

La Mole, *joining* Pépita. Of course not!

Pépita, *to* Dupont. You just got here!

She and La Mole *gradually lead him back downstage during the following dialogue*.

Dupont. I know, madame... It's just that, I thought... I don't know why it is, but the minute I take off my coat I feel cold.

Pépita, *very solicitously*. Maybe it's your stomach... You must let me get you something to eat...

Dupont. Eat?... No, no... Really, madame... Not between meals...

Pépita. Oh, but you must! I'll be terribly hurt!... (*Wheedling*.) You wouldn't want me to be hurt, monsieur, would you?

Dupont. No... certainly not... but...

Pépita. Just something simple... Perhaps a little fruit...

Dupont, *weakening*. Well... If you insist...

La Mole. Some strawberries! They're delicious!

Pépita. Yes! Strawberries...

Dupont. Strawberries?

Pépita, *to* Dupont, *pointedly*. I'm sure you like strawberries...

Dupont. Like them? I love them!... How did you—

Pépita, *interrupting*. You do?

Dupont. Why yes! But I can't eat them. I'm afraid they don't agree with me...

La Mole. Oh?

Dupont. No... I have a devil of a time digesting them...

La Mole, *affecting deep interest*. Aha...

Dupont. Yes... Ever since I can remember... Why, one day I ate a handful... maybe four or five... and I had strawberry on my stomach for weeks and weeks... (Pépita *and* La Mole *exchange knowing glances*.) Even now, just thinking about them...

PÉPITA *and* LA MOLE *turn aside and begin whispering again.*

PÉPITA. On his stomach!

LA MOLE. Close enough!

PÉPITA. That settles it!

DUPONT, *aside.* Again?... What on earth do they keep whispering about? (*Self-consciously.*) I can't be that odd!

PÉPITA, *aside.* There's only one way... (*To* DUPONT.) Now that you mention it, monsieur... It is rather chilly in here...

LA MOLE, *aside.* Chilly?

DUPONT, *surprised at the sudden change of subject, to* PÉPITA. Madame?

PÉPITA. I can see why you put your coat on, monsieur...

DUPONT. As a matter of fact... I was just about to say...

PÉPITA, *to* LA MOLE, *winking broadly.* Don't you feel chilly?

LA MOLE, *a little puzzled, but playing along.* Why, yes... Yes... Quite...

DUPONT. I was just about to say I felt rather warm... (*He begins to take off his coat again.*) If you don't mind, madame... (PÉPITA *affects a look of surprise.*) I don't know why it is, but the minute I put on my coat—

PÉPITA, *interrupting.* You feel warm!

DUPONT. Why, yes... How did you...

PÉPITA, *to* LA MOLE. Imagine! It's so chilly in here, and monsieur feels warm!

DUPONT *moves upstage and puts the coat back on the chair to the left of the hall door.*

LA MOLE, *still not quite sure what strategy* PÉPITA *is developing.* Imagine!... (*To* PÉPITA, *whispering.*) So what?

PÉPITA, *replying in a whisper.* You'll see! (*Aloud, to* DUPONT.) I wonder... (*Pretending to be searching for an explanation.*) Could it be that... (*Suddenly finding it.*) Of course! That's it!... I'll bet you wear flannel!

LA MOLE, *comprehending, aside.* Aha!

DUPONT, *to* PÉPITA. Indeed! I wouldn't be without it!... The weather here in Paris...

PÉPITA. You're so right, monsieur! (*To* LA MOLE.) Isn't he? (*Continuing, as* LA MOLE *nods vigorous approval, to* DUPONT.) You took the words right out of my mouth!

DUPONT, *aside.* I did?

PÉPITA. And besides, nowadays it comes in such fashionable styles...

DUPONT, *quizzically.* Flannel?

PÉPITA. And such becoming colors...

LA MOLE, *joining in*. Whites...

PÉPITA. Blues...

LA MOLE. Greens...

PÉPITA. Yellows...

LA MOLE. Polka dots...

DUPONT, *aside*. Really?

PÉPITA. Stripes...

LA MOLE, *getting carried away*. Even blue, white and red... For when you're feeling patriotic...

DUPONT, *aside*. I say! Maybe in Paris... (*To* LA MOLE, *trying to be agreeable*.) No doubt, monsieur!

PÉPITA, *to* DUPONT. Nothing like being patriotic, now is there?

DUPONT. No... Certainly... *Pro patria*, after all...

PÉPITA, *as if in complete agreement*. Quite!

DUPONT, *still upstage, aside*. I thought she was getting me something to eat?

PÉPITA, *to* DUPONT, *hesitating*. If... if you don't mind my asking, monsieur... Please don't think I'm being... well, indiscreet... But I'm terribly curious... (DUPONT *gives her a puzzled look*.) What color is yours, monsieur?

DUPONT, *not sure he has understood*. Please?

PÉPITA. Your underwear, I mean... Especially your undershirts...

DUPONT, *startled*. My... I beg your pardon!

LA MOLE, *moving toward him, almost menacingly*. Quick! Don't think...

DUPONT, *to* PÉPITA, *who has joined them upstage*. I don't see what business that is—

LA MOLE. Quick! Quick! What color...?

DUPONT, *to* LA MOLE. They're gray, if you must know! (*Aside*.) I don't for the life of me see what business...

He continues grumbling to himself, as PÉPITA and LA MOLE move down center, whispering to each other.

PÉPITA. See? He's lying! That proves it!

LA MOLE. Naturally! You don't expect him to admit that they're red!

PÉPITA. And incriminate himself? Of course not!

LA MOLE. Just look at his face... It's got "murderer" written all over it...

DUPONT, *upstage, back to audience, picks up his coat, as* PÉPITA *and* LA MOLE *continue observing him obliquely and whispering*.

PÉPITA. The criminal type if I ever saw it!

LA MOLE. Like the kind they ship off to Devil's Island!

DUPONT, *putting his coat around his shoulders, still grumbling, aside.* These Parisians! I never...

PÉPITA, *to* LA MOLE, *still whispering.* See? He can't keep his coat off! It's always too cold for him!

LA MOLE, *to* PÉPITA, *likewise.* And he has to wear flannel!... That means he must be used to a warm climate!

DUPONT, *about to pick up his hat from the console table, aside.* Actress or not, I don't see any point in staying...

PÉPITA, *to* LA MOLE, *categorically.* Devil's Island!

LA MOLE, *nodding.* Exactly!

DUPONT, *to* PÉPITA. Excuse me, madame... I can see I'm intruding...

PÉPITA, *protesting.* Not at all, monsieur! On the contrary... Intruding?

LA MOLE, *to* DUPONT, *trying to be tactful.* Intruding? Don't be silly! We don't even know you're here!

DUPONT, *aside.* Much obliged! (*To* PÉPITA.) Madame... I must say, it's been a pleasure... A rare pleasure indeed! (*Bowing, about to leave.*) Please give my best to Monsieur Pass... (*Correcting.*) Monsieur Camembert.

PÉPITA, *joining him upstage.* Now, now... You naughty boy! You're not going to leave us... We simply won't hear of it! (*To* LA MOLE.) Will we?

DUPONT, *protesting.* But madame, I...

PÉPITA, *putting her index finger to her mouth.* Tsk tsk tsk! Now, now... Not another word!... I know! A dish of yogurt!

DUPONT, *quizzically.* Please?

PÉPITA. That's what you'll have! A lovely dish of yogurt...

DUPONT. But...

LA MOLE, *aside.* With strawberries...

PÉPITA, *leading* DUPONT *downstage, far left, toward one of the armchairs.* You just make yourself right at home while I run and get some...

DUPONT. But really, madame...

PÉPITA. I'm sure you and Monsieur La Mole must have all kinds of interesting things to talk about...

DUPONT. Yes... (*Aside.*) Striped underwear and bunions!

PÉPITA. I'll be back before you know it! (*Crossing in front of* LA MOLE, *whispering.*) You keep him here! I'm going for the police!

LA MOLE, *terrified, whispering, as she passes quickly in front of him.* You're not going to leave me alone with—

PÉPITA, *at the hall door, to* DUPONT, *sweetly.* Now don't you go running away!

She blows him a kiss and exits.

LA MOLE, *after she has left, aside.* Oh my! She did! (*Moving down right, observing* DUPONT, *askance, at a distance, still aside.*) Now what do I do?

DUPONT, *far left, aside.* What on earth did she leave me with *him* for?... Young fop!

LA MOLE, *aside.* Act brave, I suppose... Tough...

DUPONT, *aside.* Really, that's the only word...

LA MOLE, *aside.* Don't let on...

He effects an air of bravado and begins humming the "Marseillaise."

DUPONT, *aside.* Fop, fop, fop!... No manners... No savoir-faire... (LA MOLE *continues humming, sneaking a glance at* DUPONT *from time to time.*) Forever whispering behind my back... Making fun of the way I dress...

LA MOLE, *still eyeing him, aside.* After all, a murderer... a real one!...

He continues humming.

DUPONT, *growing more and more outraged, aside.* Trifle with me, will he?... I think it's time I taught him a lesson!... *Hic et nunc!*...

LA MOLE, *aside.* It's the first time I ever saw one... In the flesh, I mean...

He continues humming.

DUPONT, *aside.* Show him what men from Marseille are made of! (*Getting up and approaching* LA MOLE, *menacingly, clearing his throat.*) Ahem!

LA MOLE, *startled, recoiling.* Monsieur?

DUPONT, *peremptorily.* I'll thank you to explain yourself!

LA MOLE, *at a loss.* Explain...?

He continues to recoil with each of DUPONT's *ensuing verbal attacks.*

DUPONT. I'll have you know I don't enjoy being stared at...

LA MOLE. Why, monsieur...

DUPONT. ...or whispered about...

LA MOLE. I... I...

DUPONT. ...as if I came from the end of the world...

LA MOLE. But... I never...

DUPONT. ...or had two heads or something!

LA MOLE. Really, I...

DUPONT. And I simply won't have it! You understand? (*Emphatically.*) I won't have it!

LA MOLE, *feebly protesting.* But...

DUPONT. You and your ilk!

LA MOLE, *puzzled, aside.* My ilk?

DUPONT. You're all alike! Every one of you!

By now LA MOLE *is backed up against the wall, far right, next to the fireplace, with* DUPONT *hovering over him.*

LA MOLE, *aside, as* DUPONT, *arms akimbo, pauses momentarily to revel in his unaccustomed self-assertiveness.* We are?... (*Suddenly thinking he understands the allusion, aside.*) Oh my! He must mean... He can tell I'm not one of his kind... Not one of the crime fraternity!

DUPONT, *aside.* Parisians! (*With a disdainful shrug.*) Hmmph!

LA MOLE *aside.* Maybe... If I can make him think... Convince him that I'm really... (*As courageously as possible, to* DUPONT.) Monsieur... There's something I think you should know... (*Putting his index finger to his mouth, and shuffling toward* DUPONT, *who gradually retreats.*) Shhh! Shhh! Shhh! Shhh! Shhh! Shhh! Shhh! Shhh!

DUPONT, *as* LA MOLE *continues, aside.* Good heavens! The man must think he's a train!

LA MOLE, *confidentially.* I wouldn't tell everyone, but... Monsieur, I'm not what you take me for!

DUPONT. Oh? (*Aside.*) Funny! He certainly *looks* like a Parisian!

LA MOLE, *affecting an air of pride.* I'm a... a... (*Offering* DUPONT *his hand.*) We're kindred spirits, monsieur!

DUPONT, *about to take his hand, as if by reflex.* Delighted, I'm sure! The pleasure is all—

LA MOLE, *interrupting.* I'm a murderer!

DUPONT, *recoiling.* What?

LA MOLE. Oh, I know... You'd never think... just to look at me, I mean...

DUPONT. I...

During the following exchange, DUPONT *keeps backing up before* LA MOLE's *gradual advances.*

LA MOLE. Not one of your everyday, honest, dull citizens!... Disgusting!... (*Pretending to spit, contemptuously.*) Ptui!

DUPONT. I...

LA MOLE. And don't think I'm just some upstart... some amateur... A nice little murder now and then, here and there... Oh no!...

DUPONT. I... I...

LA MOLE. I'm a professional, monsieur... Your kind!

DUPONT, *hardly taking in everything that is being said.* I... I...

LA MOLE. Only worse... I mean, better... (*Confused.*) No, no... Worse... Worse...

DUPONT. I... I...

LA MOLE, *getting carried away.* I've killed my mother, monsieur... My father... My sister... My brother...

DUPONT. Ay ay ay!

LA MOLE. All my aunts and uncles... My cousins... (*Aside.*) Good God! If he doesn't stop me I won't have anyone left!

DUPONT, *aside.* What kind of a maniac... It's some sort of trap...

At this point the two men are stage left, DUPONT *cringing behind the table,* LA MOLE *in front of it.*

LA MOLE. My concierge, monsieur... I've killed my concierge... (DUPONT *moves out from behind the table and quickly crosses right, seizing the chair in front of the fireplace, ready to defend himself with it if need be.*) That's why I've always looked up to your work, monsieur... Your style... Your technique...

DUPONT, *aside.* My what?

LA MOLE, *following him.* You're... you're my ideal, my inspiration, my... Monsieur... (*Holding out his hand in a sweeping gesture toward* DUPONT, *while turning his head dramatically in the other direction.*) It's an honor and a privilege to shake the hand of a master!

He grasps the leg of the chair, which DUPONT *is holding out in front of him, and begins shaking it vigorously.*

DUPONT, *pulling back the chair, recoiling, aside.* Me?

LA MOLE. Because, when it comes to being a master criminal, monsieur... you're a... you're a... (*Bumbling.*) a master!

DUPONT, *nonplussed.* I... Thank you, I'm sure... I mean... you're much too kind... (*Aside.*) What on earth makes him think...

LA MOLE. Not at all, monsieur! Ask anyone! You're a genius!

DUPONT, *utterly at a loss.* I... Yes... So they tell me... But then... (*Aside.*) Better play along if I want to get out alive... (*To* LA MOLE, *categorically.*) Quite right, monsieur! I can't deny it!

He plants the chair firmly on the floor, in a gesture of bravado, accidentally catching LA MOLE's *foot.*

LA MOLE, *in pain.* Ayyyy!

DUPONT, *losing his aplomb for a moment.* Oh! Sorry! I...

LA MOLE, *hobbling.* No, no!... Please! Think nothing of it!

DUPONT, *back in character, continuing where he left off.* Yes, monsieur! You're quite right!... (*Feigning great enthusiasm.*) Crime!... Crime, my friend!... What would a criminal's life be without it?

LA MOLE. What indeed!

DUPONT, *playing his part to the hilt.* Crime!... Ah! Crime is my life! I live and breathe crime!... *Malefacio ergo sum!*

LA MOLE. You see? I told you we were kindred spirits!

DUPONT. Brothers under the skin!

LA MOLE. Brothers... Brothers in crime!

DUPONT. *Fratres in crimine!* (*Holding out his hand.*) *Frater!... Frater mihi!...*

LA MOLE, *aside.* That must be their password! (*To* DUPONT.) Yes... (*Mumbling.*) Fra... Frafra mimi...

They shake hands.

DUPONT. What a joy to shake a hand dripping with so much blood!

LA MOLE. A hand literally steeped in gore... What a pleasure!

DUPONT, *as if by reflex.* The pleasure is—

LA MOLE, *interrupting, still shaking his hand energetically.* ...is all mine, monsieur! All mine!...

DUPONT, *momentarily taken aback.* Oh?

LA MOLE. All mine!... (*Still holding* DUPONT's *hand, looking at it admiringly.*) A hand with so many crimes to its credit...

DUPONT, *correcting.* Both hands... Both...

LA MOLE. So many wonderful, gruesome crimes...

DUPONT. Yes, I must say... I have had a rather distinguished career!

LA MOLE. Distinguished?... Illustrious! Brilliant!

DUPONT. And long, monsieur! (*Emphasizing.*) Long!

LA MOLE. Well... That's true, but... (*Beginning to retrench.*) No longer than mine, after all...

DUPONT. Oh?

LA MOLE. I started very young!

DUPONT. So did I! Believe me...

LA MOLE. No, no... When I say "young"... I mean young... Really young...

DUPONT, *becoming slightly peeved.* So do I, I assure you...

La Mole. I mean, I was still in the cradle, monsieur... Still in diapers...

Dupont, *caught short*. Oh... That young?

La Mole. One day my wetnurse was feeding me, monsieur...

Dupont. Feeding...? You mean...?

He pantomimes a woman nursing a baby. La Mole *nods*.

La Mole, *continuing*. Well, there I was... how shall I put it?... dining to my heart's content... when a certain young soldier came along, monsieur... Someone I thought she was a little too fond of... And all of a sudden I flew into a rage...

Dupont. Jealousy?

La Mole. In a word!... And I gave her nipple such a bite that it killed her!... Dead on the spot!... And the soldier too!

Dupont, *puzzled*. The... I beg your pardon? The soldier...?

La Mole. Of a broken heart, monsieur!

Dupont. Aha... (*Aside.*) Bloody butcher! (*To* La Mole.) Yes, that *was* young!

La Mole, *modestly*. Well...

Dupont. But I was even younger!

La Mole, *incredulous*. No!

Dupont. I wasn't even born!

La Mole, *startled*. You—

Dupont. There I was in my mother's womb... (La Mole's *jaw drops in disbelief.*) I take one look around, and I see there are two of me... I'm going to be twins... Well, I turn to my brother and I tell him: "Listen! There just isn't enough room in here for the two of us! One of us has got to go, and it's not going to be me!..."

He pauses.

La Mole. So?

Dupont. So I blew his brains out! (*Aside, sighing.*) Whew!

La Mole. Amazing!

Dupont. I know...

La Mole, *holding out his hand*. Frafra... Mimi...

They shake hands, then stand for a moment, feigning the greatest of mutual admiration.

Dupont, *after the brief pause*. Tell me... now that we know each other... What brings you here?

LA MOLE. Here? (*Giving himself time to think*.) You mean, here?... In this house?

DUPONT. Yes... Business, I suppose... Some vicious new crime up your sleeve? Some new murder?

LA MOLE. Of course! (*Very matter-of-fact, gesturing toward the hall door, through which* PÉPITA *left minutes before*.) I'm going to kill her husband.

DUPONT. No!

LA MOLE. Slice up that Camembert into a thousand little pieces...

DUPONT, *shaking his head, momentarily forgetting himself*. Tsk tsk tsk! Poor thing!

LA MOLE. What? Don't tell me you pity him!

DUPONT, *realizing his faux pas*. Pity? What's that? Never heard of the word! What's pity?

LA MOLE, *sarcastically*. A palace in Venice!

DUPONT, *trying to correct him*. In Rome...

LA MOLE. Wherever...

DUPONT. Quite!... Pity? Don't make me laugh!... Why, what say we kill him together, poor fool?

LA MOLE. Wonderful idea! Five hundred pieces each... With... (*Emphatically, with obvious innuendo*.) pruning-shears?

DUPONT, *grimacing, aside*. Good God! (*To* LA MOLE.) If you like...

LA MOLE. Fine!

DUPONT, *as casually as possible*. That settles it... He's dead... (*Aside*.) Just like that! I'm a murderer!... (*To* LA MOLE, *after a brief pause*.) By the way, you didn't tell me... Why are we going to kill him?

LA MOLE. I love his wife. Why else?

DUPONT. La Passionnelle?... You... you love her?

LA MOLE. Love her? (*Emotionally*.) I'm wild about her... crazy about her... mad about her...

DUPONT. That much?

LA MOLE. And more, monsieur! More!... More!... How can I explain it?

DUPONT. Ah!... (*Waxing poetic, declaiming*.) "How do I love thee? Let me count the ways..."

LA MOLE, *with a sidelong glance*. Ha! You sound like a professor!

DUPONT, *forgetting himself, proudly*. Well I should hope so! I am...

LA MOLE, *startled*. You are?

DUPONT, *quickly covering his blunder*. I... I... Yes, in a crime school!

LA MOLE, *not sure he has heard correctly*. In a...

DUPONT. A school for young criminals... You know... murderers, burglars... The cream of the crop... We get them when they're young and give them a good start!

LA MOLE, *nodding.* Aha...

DUPONT, *going over to the armchair, far right, with a sigh, aside.* Whew! Almost gave myself away! That would have been pretty!

He falls in a heap in the armchair.

LA MOLE, *going over to the other armchair, far left, aside.* Crime school? Good heavens! What will they think of next?

He sits down. Both men sit fanning themselves, visibly shaken by their long charade. After a few moments, the hall door opens and CAMEMBERT *tiptoes in gingerly, unseen by them. He quietly closes the door and locks it.*

CAMEMBERT, *putting the key in his pocket, aside.* There!... Now let's see you try to escape, my friend! *(He looks at his watch.)* They're downstairs... Right on time!... And I'll just stand back and watch them haul you off!... *(Tiptoeing to the door, down left, still aside.)* Ah! Revenge is sweet!... He who laughs last...

He exits quietly, but stands peeking out from behind the door, left ajar.

DUPONT, *with a sigh of relief, aside.* Talk about close calls!

LA MOLE, *likewise.* Lucky I kept my wits about me!

After a moment, a commotion is heard in the hall, offstage.

SUZETTE'S VOICE. But monsieur...

BLOARDE'S VOICE. No, damn it! No mistake!... Right place! Right place!

DUPONT and LA MOLE *wheel around in their chairs.*

DUPONT, } *together.* { What was that?
LA MOLE, }   { Now what?

There are several sharp raps at the hall door, repeated from time to time throughout the following dialogue.

BLOARDE'S VOICE. Open up! Open up!... In the name of the law!

DUPONT and LA MOLE *jump up in unison.*

LA MOLE, } *together.* { Oh my!
DUPONT, }   { The police!

BLOARDE'S VOICE, *more insistent*. Open up!... Know you're in there!

DUPONT *and* LA MOLE *rush to apprehend each other, meeting center stage.*

LA MOLE, *to* DUPONT. Stay right where you are!

DUPONT, *to* LA MOLE. Don't you move! Understand?

They look at each other for an instant in near panic, then each man turns and makes a dash for one of the upstage doors, DUPONT *up left,* LA MOLE *up right, exiting and slamming the doors behind them.*

BLOARDE'S VOICE. Open up, goddammit!

The door, up right, opens and LA MOLE *pokes his head out.*

LA MOLE, *terrified*. Good God! It's a closet!

He pulls his head back and slams the door shut.

BLOARDE'S VOICE. No use!... Can't escape!...

The door, up left, opens and DUPONT *pokes his head out.*

DUPONT. A closet! I'm trapped!

He pulls his head back and slams the door shut.

BLOARDE'S VOICE. Building surrounded!... Open up, goddammit!

CAMEMBERT *opens his door, down left, and strides out, confidently, moving upstage.*

CAMEMBERT. Coming... coming... (*He opens the hall door, ready to relish his victory.*) Yes... He who laughs last... (BLOARDE *enters, followed by the* FIRST POLICEMAN, *as* CAMEMBERT *rubs his hands together, still musing.*) Right, Monsieur Othello?

BLOARDE, *dressed in civilian clothes and wearing a grocer's apron, to* CAMEMBERT. Wrong!... Monsieur Bloarde!... Hands up! You're under arrest!

CAMEMBERT, *stunned*. I'm what?

BLOARDE. You heard me! (*To the* FIRST POLICEMAN.) Get him out of here!

CAMEMBERT, *eluding him, moving downstage*. Who the devil are you?

BLOARDE. Me?... Old friend of the chief's... Playing cards just now... Tells me: "Bloarde, do me a favor... Can't move with my goddamn gout... Go make an arrest..."

CAMEMBERT. You?

BLOARDE. Just deputized me... Used to be in the army together... Alsace... Infantry... (*Pointing an imaginary gun.*) Bang bang bang!

CAMEMBERT. But you're... (*Pointing to his outfit.*) You're a...

BLOARDE. A grocer... Shop next to the station... Nothing but the best... (*Taking a circular out of his pocket and handing it to* CAMEMBERT.) Here... This week's specials... Where do you buy your coffee?

CAMEMBERT. My... I don't... I can't drink it...

BLOARDE. Don't drink coffee? (*To the* FIRST POLICEMAN.) Take that down! (*To* CAMEMBERT.) Could be serious!

The FIRST POLICEMAN *takes out his notepad and pencil, and writes.*

CAMEMBERT. It gives me heartburn!

BLOARDE, *to the* FIRST POLICEMAN. All right... Heard enough... Get him out of here!

CAMEMBERT, *moving toward the fireplace, avoiding him, to* BLOARDE. You've got to be joking!

BLOARDE. Never joke on the job... (*Pointing the imaginary gun.*) Bang bang bang!

CAMEMBERT. But I'm telling you...

BLOARDE, *to the* FIRST POLICEMAN. Resisting arrest... Take that down!

The FIRST POLICEMAN *complies, as before.*

CAMEMBERT, *at the fireplace.* You've got the wrong man! It's not me! I'm not the one!

BLOARDE, *sardonically.* Ha ha ha! Good try!... Won't work... (*Brandishing* CAMEMBERT'*s letter.*) See?... Description... (*Reading.*) "...easy to recognize, thanks to his obviously moronic appearance..."

CAMEMBERT, *with something of a pout.* Well...?

BLOARDE, *pointing to the mirror above the fireplace.* Take a look, goddammit!... Mirror, right behind you... Think I'm blind maybe?

CAMEMBERT, *abashed.* I... I beg your... I...

BLOARDE, *waving the letter.* Think we're born yesterday?... Don't know how to read?

CAMEMBERT, *growing desperate.* But I'm telling you... I vote! I pay my taxes! I—

BLOARDE, *with a wave of the hand, cutting him off.* Politics... Unimportant... Can't talk politics... Not allowed...

CAMEMBERT. But listen! I'm telling you... For God's sake—

BLOARDE, *cutting him off again with the same gesture.* No religion! No religion!... Can't talk religion... Not allowed...

CAMEMBERT, *finally putting his foot down*. Now just one minute! If you want to know the truth, I—

BLOARDE, *interrupting, to the* FIRST POLICEMAN. Take this down! Confession...

CAMEMBERT, *furious*. Confess... It's nothing of the kind!

BLOARDE, *to the* FIRST POLICEMAN. Take that down! Still denies it!

CAMEMBERT, *confused*. No, I don't...

BLOARDE, *hands on hips*. Well, which is it?

CAMEMBERT. I mean... there's nothing to deny! I'm telling you... (*Emphasizing.*) You've got the wrong man! (*Pointing to the door, up right.*) The one you want is in there! In the closet!

BLOARDE. What?... Should have said so sooner! Save a lot of time...

CAMEMBERT, *exasperated*. I should have said... What do you think I've been trying to—

BLOARDE. Shhh! Shhh! Shhh!

CAMEMBERT, *grumbling*. He wants me to talk and he tells me to "shhh!"

BLOARDE, *going to the door, up right*. See about that!

CAMEMBERT, *under his breath*. Of all the damn...

BLOARDE, *pounding on the door*. Open up! Open up!... In the name of the law!

The door opens a crack.

LA MOLE, *peeking out*. Wrong door!... (*Pointing across, up left.*) That one!... That one!...

BLOARDE. Beg pardon!

He begins to cross left.

CAMEMBERT, *still down right, appalled at seeing his plan going awry*. Oh!

BLOARDE, *stopping, returning to* LA MOLE, *handing him a circular from his pocket*. Here!... Chez Bloarde... This week's specials...

LA MOLE *takes the circular and looks at it in bewilderment as* BLOARDE *crosses left.*

CAMEMBERT, *trying, unsuccessfully, to protest*. But... but...

BLOARDE, *pounding on the other door*. Open up!... In the name of the law!

The door opens a crack.

DUPONT, *peeking out*. Not here! Not here!... (*Pointing across, up right.*) Try that one...

BLOARDE, *to* DUPONT. What?... Just did!... Don't be funny! (*Pointing.*) This one... That one...

CAMEMBERT, *pointing to* LA MOLE. But I'm telling you...

BLOARDE. That one... This one... Some kind of a goddamn game or something?

CAMEMBERT, *still pointing to* LA MOLE. He's the one!

LA MOLE, *noticing* DUPONT, *pointing*. There he is!

DUPONT, *noticing* LA MOLE, *pointing*. There! Grab him!

The three continue accusing one another with appropriate exclamations—"It's him!" "Him, not me..." etc.—in a scene of mounting confusion, as BLOARDE *tries to restore order.*

BLOARDE, *finally making himself heard above the din, in a military voice*. Ten-shun!... Ten-shun!... (*As the clamor gradually subsides, to the* FIRST POLICEMAN, *with a sweeping gesture.*) Arrest the whole bunch, goddammit!

CAMEMBERT. What?

LA MOLE *and* DUPONT, *together*. Why?

BLOARDE. None of your goddamn business! (*To the* FIRST POLICEMAN.) Take 'em in!

As the FIRST POLICEMAN *begins to carry out the order, the uproar starts up again, with exclamations like "But I'm telling you..." "For heaven's sake..." etc. At that moment the hall door opens and* PÉPITA *appears, wearing her hat and coat.*

PÉPITA, *entering, followed by the* SECOND POLICEMAN, *who stands at the door*. What in the name of...

LA MOLE. Thank heavens! Madame... Stop them...

CAMEMBERT, DUPONT, *together*. Pépita... Pépita... Please... Madame...

PÉPITA. What's going on?

CAMEMBERT, DUPONT, *together, pointing to* BLOARDE. He wants to arrest me... Tell him who I am...

PÉPITA, *pointing to* BLOARDE, *in evident disbelief*. Him?

LA MOLE, *pointing to* BLOARDE. He thinks I'm the murderer! Tell him! Tell him!

PÉPITA, *to* LA MOLE. Murderer? (*Laughing.*) You...? (*To* BLOARDE, *pointing to* DUPONT, *categorically.*) There's your murderer, monsieur!

DUPONT, *nonplussed*. Me?

CAMEMBERT, *puzzled*. What?

LA MOLE. That's right!... He admitted it!... He... he teaches in a crime school!

DUPONT. But... (*Pointing to* LA MOLE.) He killed his concierge!... He bit his nurse's nipple!... He... (*Pointing to* CAMEMBERT.) He came to kill *him*!... In a thousand little pieces!... (*Babbling.*) Five hundred each...

PÉPITA, *nodding, sarcastically*. Of course, monsieur! Of course!

BLOARDE, *to* DUPONT, *losing patience*. All right, you!... Name? Name?

DUPONT, *in despair. O tempora, o mores!*

BLOARDE. What kind of a... What are you, goddammit? Some kind of a damn foreigner?... Last name! Last name!

DUPONT, *dejected at his unmasking, resigned*. Bourgeois, monsieur... I'm Bourgeois...

BLOARDE. Aren't we all!

LA MOLE. He's lying!

BLOARDE. Except the wife's brother... (*Tapping his forehead.*) Thinks he's Napoleon...

DUPONT. No, no, no!... That's my name!... Bourgeois... Philibert Bourgeois...

PÉPITA. It's not!

BLOARDE, *to* DUPONT. From?

DUPONT, *not understanding*. From, monsieur...?

BLOARDE, *sarcastically*. Live somewhere, don't you?

DUPONT, *as if it should be obvious*. Why... In France...

BLOARDE, *even more sarcastically*. Ha ha ha! Funny!... Big place, France!

DUPONT, *trying to be agreeable, nodding. Gallia est omnis divisa in partis tres...*

BLOARDE. Same to you!... What city, goddammit?

DUPONT. Marseille, monsieur... Philibert Bourgeois... Of the Marseille Bourgeois... Professor of Latin and Greek...

LA MOLE. That's a lie!

PÉPITA. He's Dupont... the murderer... the one who killed that woman in Versailles!

BLOARDE, *pointing to* DUPONT. Him?... Can't be!... Caught that one half an hour ago... Pruning the bushes behind the station...

LA MOLE,
PÉPITA, } *appalled, together*. {What?
No!

DUPONT, *to* LA MOLE *and* PÉPITA. See? (*To* BLOARDE, *taking out his wallet.*) Besides, I can prove it... (*Reluctantly.*) If I really have to... (*Handing his papers to* BLOARDE.) Dupont is just a... It's just a name I use... (*Sheepishly.*) Sometimes...

BLOARDE, *examining his papers.* Hmmm!... Looks all right to me...

LA MOLE, *to* DUPONT. But... but all those things you told me... Crime is your life... Remember?

DUPONT. I... (*Embarrassed.*) I made it all up...

LA MOLE. What?

DUPONT. You frightened me into it!

LA MOLE. No! You mean, you're not... You never... Not even one?

DUPONT. Not a one! And you?

LA MOLE, *no less embarrassed.* Same here...

Both men look at each other for a moment, with sighs of relief and amazement, as BLOARDE *looks on, scratching his head.*

DUPONT. Of all things...

LA MOLE. Who would think...

DUPONT, *holding out his hand, smiling.* Monsieur...

LA MOLE, *taking it.* Monsieur... It's a pleasure!

DUPONT. The pleasure is all mine!

LA MOLE, *smiling, as they shake hands.* Frafra... Right?... Frafra mimi...

BLOARDE, *still very confused.* "Frafra?" "Froufrou?"... What the hell...

DUPONT, *laughing, to* LA MOLE. Right! Brothers in crime...

LA MOLE, *correcting.* Stepbrothers, monsieur!

BLOARDE, *pointing to* CAMEMBERT, *who has remained very self-effacing.* And what about that one?

PÉPITA, *enthusiastically.* Oh... He's only my husband...

BLOARDE. Then who's the goddam criminal, goddammit?

CAMEMBERT, *as innocently as possible.* Criminal? What criminal?

PÉPITA, *to* BLOARDE. Well, I guess there isn't any...

BLOARDE. Then why in hell all the fuss? (CAMEMBERT *shrugs, as if to say* "Don't ask me!", *as* BLOARDE *points to the* FIRST *and* SECOND POLICE-MEN.) You two... Back to the station! Tell the chief "false alarm!" Be over in a minute to finish my hand!

FIRST *and* SECOND POLICEMEN, *saluting.* Yes, monsieur!

They exit, up center.

DUPONT, *aside.* Actresses... Paris... They can keep it! (*Aloud.*) Well... I'll be on my way...

He moves toward the hall door. During the following dialogue he suddenly realizes that he doesn't have his umbrella, and begins to look around for it.

BLOARDE. Me too! Back to the groceries... (*As he passes* PÉPITA, *he stops and gives her a circular.*) Oh... This week's specials, madame... Nothing but the best...

PÉPITA, *taking it, quizzically.* Monsieur?

BLOARDE. Don't mention it!... (*Aside.*) Business gets bad? (*Shrugging.*) Can always do this!... Good experience... (*At the hall door.*) "In the name of the law..." (*Pointing an imaginary gun.*) Bang bang! Bang bang bang!

He exits.

PÉPITA, *taking off her hat and coat, to* LA MOLE, *nodding.* Monsieur...

LA MOLE, *bowing.* Madame...

There is a brief pause during which they exchange meaningful glances.

DUPONT, *finally spying his umbrella on the mantelpiece.* Aha!

PÉPITA, *to* CAMEMBERT, *pointedly.* Octave... Didn't you hear the baby?

CAMEMBERT, *submissively.* Of course, my love... The bottle... Right away...

DUPONT, *taking the umbrella and backing upstage, bowing his way to the door, to each of them in turn.* Madame... Monsieur... Monsieur...

CAMEMBERT, *aside.* One of these days... Oh! One of these days...

He crosses resignedly toward the door, down left, as the curtain slowly falls.

CURTAIN

MIXED DOUBLES

•

C'est une femme du monde

BY

GEORGES FEYDEAU

and

MAURICE DESVALLIÈRES

CHARACTERS

Pompe-Nicole

Bordeleau

Albert

Clémentine

Aphrodite

Philomèle

A private dining room in a fashionable restaurant. Upstage center, the door leading out to the corridor. On both sides of the door, against the rear wall, a chair. Three other doors: up right, down right, and down left. Up right, against the rear wall, a sideboard with tablecloth, silverware, glasses, napkins, etc. Down right, a canape. On the side wall, up left, a large mirror. Midstage left, a table and two chairs. On the table, a pushbutton that rings an electric bell. Down left, an armchair. Other appropriate furnishings ad lib.

At rise, ALBERT is hovering about the table.

ALBERT. Now then... How many places, I wonder?... Two? Three? Four?... You never know in this business, but it's always fun to guess. (*He goes to the sideboard, gets the tablecloth, and spreads it on the table.*) Sometimes I even bet on it... With myself, that is... All kinds of money... Hundreds, thousands... What's the difference, as long as I'm at it? After all, I can't lose... Well, I mean... Of course, I can lose, every now and then... (*He goes back and gets two settings.*) But when I lose, I win, so... (*He shrugs.*) I look at it this way. Your twos are lovers, your fours are good friends, and your threes... the internal triangles, like they say... Not too many of those here... (*He gets the two chairs from upstage and places them at the table.*) No, tonight let's say four... It's better for business... They order twice as much... (*He goes to the sideboard and gets two more settings.*) Besides, the twos aren't here to eat... Oh, they're hungry all right, but not for what's on the menu!... (*He gives a knowing laugh.*) So! Four it is!... Ten thousand francs on four!

Just as he finishes, PHILOMÈLE enters, upstage, carrying a large tray of food in both hands.

PHILOMÈLE, *moving left.* The appetizers, Albert...

ALBERT. Philomèle! You gorgeous creature...

151

He goes over and gives her a kiss.

PHILOMÈLE. Oh! Albert, you... Can't you see I've got my hands full!

ALBERT, *pinching her behind, slyly.* I know! Tsk tsk tsk! (*Holding up his empty hands.*) But I don't!

He embraces her and kisses her again.

PHILOMÈLE, *handing him the tray.* Please, Albert... Not now... ALBERT *goes upstage to the sideboard and puts down the tray.*) Really! What if Monsieur Dominique came in?

ALBERT. The boss? (*With a shrug.*) Pfff!

PHILOMÈLE. You know what he always says... (*Mimicking.*) "Don't mix business with funny business!"

ALBERT, *returning downstage.* Funny business? You're my wife! What's funny about that? We can do what we please.

PHILOMÈLE. I know, but not here! Like he always says... "Here you're a cashier, mademoiselle, not a wife!"

ALBERT. That's what he thinks!

PHILOMÈLE, *continuing.* And... "A cashier belongs to her customers, not her husband!"

ALBERT. Yes, well... Let him stick his own wife on the job, why doesn't he! See who *she* belongs to!

PHILOMÈLE. Her? That ugly... She'd frighten them away without paying, for heaven's sake!

ALBERT. You can say that again!... (*Good-naturedly.*) Well, I guess you're here to stay. Just don't let me catch you with any of the customers!

PHILOMÈLE. Me? Of course not! (*Coyly.*) I wouldn't dream of letting you catch me!

ALBERT. Now, now... You know what I mean...

PHILOMÈLE. And you know you don't have to worry, Albert! Like the other night, for instance... Remember? That customer? The rich one who tried to get funny, and I slapped him?

ALBERT. And a damn good thing too! I'm only surprised Monsieur Dominique didn't fire you!

PHILOMÈLE. Fire me? Don't be silly! He gave me a raise!

ALBERT. You're joking!

PHILOMÈLE. No, I'm serious... He did... He said: "There's nothing like a slap in the face to get a man excited..."

ALBERT. What?

PHILOMÈLE, *continuing.* "And once you get them excited, they'll keep coming back for more!"

ALBERT, *taken aback.* More what?

PHILOMÈLE, *continuing.* "So keep it up, mademoiselle. It's good for business!"

ALBERT. Oh, he said that, did he!

PHILOMÈLE, *in her own voice.* But you don't have to worry, Albert. The more they come back, the more I'll slap.

ALBERT. Yes... Please see that you do!

PHILOMÈLE. Besides... (*Waxing poetic.*) You know you're the only one, Albert... the only man in my life...

ALBERT, *tenderly.* Philomèle...

PHILOMÈLE. Just like I'm the only woman in yours... Isn't that so, darling?

ALBERT, *sitting down on the canape, down right, taking her hand and drawing her toward him.* What a question!

PHILOMÈLE, *sitting on his lap.* No, I mean... Because, before... Well, I suppose you must have loved your other wives too...

ALBERT, *protesting.* Me?

He makes a gesture as if to say "Not at all!"

PHILOMÈLE. And you'll just never know how jealous that makes me.

ALBERT. It does?

PHILOMÈLE. To think... You... My Albert... (*Embracing him.*) In another woman's arms... Two other women...

ALBERT. Philomèle...

PHILOMÈLE. Not at the same time, I know... But still... Not to mention all the others...

ALBERT. Others? What others?

PHILOMÈLE. Oh, you know what I mean! The little extras, now and then...

ALBERT, *the picture of injured innocence.* Philomèle... Really...

PHILOMÈLE. In your arms... Just like this... Oh! It makes me too jealous for words, Albert!

ALBERT. But it shouldn't, silly... First of all, I didn't love them... Not the way I love you... Either of them... (*As an afterthought.*) Any of them...

PHILOMÈLE. Oh, that's what they always say!

ALBERT. And besides, what's the difference? I'm a widower... Twice! You know that! The past is dead and buried.

PHILOMÈLE. I know... I know, but—

ALBERT, *interrupting.* So just don't you worry your head about the others. That's all over and done with.

PHILOMÈLE. If you say so, Albert...

ALBERT. Of course I say so!

PHILOMÈLE. And you'll always love me? Just the way you do now?

ALBERT. Just the way... (*Suddenly categorical.*) No!

PHILOMÈLE, *with a start.* What?

ALBERT. Even more, Philomèle! Even more!

PHILOMÈLE. Oh, Albert...

She kisses him. At that moment POMPE-NICOLE *enters quickly, upstage. He is dressed in evening clothes and is wearing an overcoat.*

POMPE-NICOLE. Good evening, I... (*Noticing* PHILOMÈLE *and* ALBERT *on the canape, embracing.*) Oh, I say...

PHILOMÈLE, *jumping up.* A customer...

POMPE-NICOLE, *embarrassed.* Don't mind me... I'm just leaving...

ALBERT, *getting up.* No, no, monsieur... Please...

POMPE-NICOLE. I... (*Looking at* ALBERT.) Oh, the maître d'hôtel! I... Excuse me, I thought...

ALBERT, *to* PHILOMÈLE. You... Out...

PHILOMÈLE, *scurrying around the canape and upstage, to* POMPE-NICOLE, *nodding.* Monsieur...

ALBERT, *going to the sideboard and handing her the tray of food.* And take these with you. They're for room number six.

She runs off.

POMPE-NICOLE, *moving down left.* Please, don't let me interrupt...

ALBERT. Not at all, monsieur... We're just passing the time.

POMPE-NICOLE. Yes, yes... So I see...

ALBERT. Before the evening rush...

POMPE-NICOLE, *nodding.* Aha...

ALBERT. And besides, monsieur... This room was just furnished. Monsieur Dominique asked me to make sure personally that everything was in order. (*Mimicking.*) "Nothing is too good for our guests, Albert..." That's what he said, monsieur...

POMPE-NICOLE, *pointing to the canape.* And so you were breaking it in, so to speak!

ALBERT. Well, I wouldn't put it quite that way myself, Monsieur Pompe-Nicole, but—

POMPE-NICOLE, *interrupting.* I beg your pardon?

ALBERT. I said: "I wouldn't put it quite—"

POMPE-NICOLE. No, no... I mean... Did you say "Monsieur Pompe-Nicole"?

ALBERT. Of course, monsieur!

POMPE-NICOLE, *surprised.* You... you know me?

ALBERT, *proudly.* I know all the important people in Paris, monsieur!

POMPE-NICOLE, *rather fatuously.* Oh...

ALBERT. I'm sure monsieur remembers me. Albert...

POMPE-NICOLE, *nodding, obviously unsure.* Ah... Yes... Albert... (*Searching his memory.*) Which one? There are so many...

ALBERT. From Maxim's, monsieur... The ex-maître d'hôtel...

POMPE-NICOLE. Oh, that Albert! Of course! What was I thinking... I knew I remembered the face... (*With a laugh.*) It's not easy to forget...

ALBERT. Monsieur is too kind!

POMPE-NICOLE. But the name... You know how it is with names... Of course! Albert... Well, well... just like old times...

He shakes his hand.

ALBERT. Thank you, monsieur.

POMPE-NICOLE, *slyly.* I see we're still up to our old tricks, Albert...

ALBERT. Old tricks, monsieur?

POMPE-NICOLE. Still the lady's man, aren't we! (ALBERT *is about to object.*) As long as our wife doesn't catch us! Right?

ALBERT. Begging monsieur's pardon, but... Madame *is* my wife!

POMPE-NICOLE. She is? Oh... Sorry!

ALBERT. Quite all right, monsieur. It's a natural mistake.

POMPE-NICOLE. Yes... I thought you once told me that your wife worked in clothing.

ALBERT, *dryly.* I daresay she did, monsieur.

POMPE-NICOLE, *laughing.* No, no... I mean, selling!... Isn't that what you told me?

ALBERT. I did indeed, monsieur. But that was my number two...

POMPE-NICOLE, *pointing to the door, upstage.* Aha! And...

ALBERT. And madame is number three.

POMPE-NICOLE. Number three? My, my Albert! We're insatiable, aren't we!

ALBERT. One develops a taste, monsieur. And as long as it's only one at a time...

POMPE-NICOLE, *nodding.* Good point... (*Crossing down right.*) What happened to number two, if you don't mind my asking?

ALBERT. Not at all, monsieur... Though it's not very pleasant...

POMPE-NICOLE. Oh?

ALBERT. I'm afraid she succumbed...

POMPE-NICOLE. Tsk tsk tsk! To what? Consumption?

ALBERT. To a handsome young Romeo... (*Sighing.*) Just like number one...

POMPE-NICOLE. No!

ALBERT. Yes, monsieur. Sad but true... (*With a gesture.*) Pfff! Out of my life forever!

POMPE-NICOLE, *shaking his head.* Shame...

ALBERT. Here today, gone tomorrow... (*Reflecting.*) Or, in this case, monsieur, here yesterday, gone today...

POMPE-NICOLE. Yes...

ALBERT. Figuratively speaking...

POMPE-NICOLE. I must say, you don't have much luck with your wives, Albert!

ALBERT. Not with those two, monsieur. If an animal comparison isn't too crude, one could say I panted after them, but they didn't pant back.

POMPE-NICOLE, *unable to resist the pleasantry, chuckling.* Well, one pair of pants in a family is enough!

ALBERT, *with a reproachful look.* Monsieur...

POMPE-NICOLE. Sorry...

He sits down on the canape.

ALBERT. Divorce is nothing to laugh about.

POMPE-NICOLE. Divorce?

ALBERT. Yes, monsieur.

POMPE-NICOLE. Number two?

ALBERT. Number two and number one! It's the story of my life. If monsieur would like to hear...

He sits down on the canape next to him.

POMPE-NICOLE, *with a glower of surprise.* Albert!

ALBERT, *jumping up.* Begging monsieur's pardon... I get carried away!

POMPE-NICOLE, *smiling.* Yes... Like your wives!

ALBERT. In a manner of speaking... (*Continuing his story.*) It's really quite interesting... As divorces go, that is... Not the usual kind...

POMPE-NICOLE. Oh? What other kind is there?

ALBERT. "Divorce in obsession," monsieur... That's what the judge called it... Both times...

POMPE-NICOLE, *quizzically.* "In obsession"?

ALBERT. Yes, monsieur.

POMPE-NICOLE, *after thinking for a moment.* Ah! "In absentia"... You mean, your wives weren't there?

ALBERT. Exactly!

POMPE-NICOLE. Neither one?

ALBERT. Neither one!

POMPE-NICOLE. My, my! That means each one still thinks... (*Laughing.*) They have no idea...

ALBERT, *pointing to the door, upstage.* Or number three either!

POMPE-NICOLE. Oh?

ALBERT. She thinks I was a widower.

POMPE-NICOLE. What? Twice?

ALBERT. That's what I told her. It seemed so much simpler. Monsieur knows women... Divorce, and all that...

POMPE-NICOLE. Of course, Albert! (*With a smile.*) Not to mention our pride!

ALBERT. Well... At any rate, that's what she thinks. I wouldn't tell just anyone, but monsieur is an old friend...

POMPE-NICOLE, *with a touch of sarcasm.* You flatter me...

ALBERT. And I'm sure he can keep a secret.

POMPE-NICOLE. Albert, my lips are sealed!

ALBERT. Much obliged, monsieur. I was sure they would be.

POMPE-NICOLE, *getting up.* I must say, Albert... old friend... your life story is fascinating... Numbers one, two, three... Divorce... Widowhood...

ALBERT, *correcting.* "Er," monsieur... "Er"...

POMPE-NICOLE, *puzzled.* Beg pardon?

ALBERT, *emphasizing.* Widowerhood, monsieur...

POMPE-NICOLE. Whatever... (*Continuing.*) But that's really not why I'm here, Albert.

ALBERT. No, no, monsieur... I understand...

POMPE-NICOLE. No offense...

ALBERT. Not at all, monsieur... I'm afraid sometimes I do let myself go. But I'm glad monsieur stopped me when he did. (*Laughing.*) If not, I might have tried to tell him all my troubles... (*He pauses.*) Like the time number one—

POMPE-NICOLE, *raising his voice, interrupting.* If you don't mind, Albert...

ALBERT. Monsieur?

POMPE-NICOLE. I'm going to need a room... a private room... for this evening...

ALBERT. Oh, certainly, monsieur!

POMPE-NICOLE. Do you have one?

ALBERT. For Monsieur Pompe-Nicole? Of course! All the rooms monsieur wants!... (*Reflecting for a moment.*) Except number six...

POMPE-NICOLE. Thank you! One should be enough!

ALBERT. Will this one do, monsieur?

POMPE-NICOLE. Admirably! Admirably! (*Testing the springs of the canape.*) Especially now that it's been properly broken in!

ALBERT. Fine! I'll put monsieur down... (*He takes a pad and pencil from his pocket and writes a note.*) Will there be anything else?

POMPE-NICOLE. Yes... About the menu...

ALBERT, *holding up his hand.* Tsk tsk tsk! Please... Monsieur can leave everything to me. I know his taste.

POMPE-NICOLE. You do?

ALBERT. A maître d'hôtel never forgets, monsieur!

POMPE-NICOLE. Well... If you're sure...

ALBERT. And how many will there be in monsieur's party, if I may ask?

POMPE-NICOLE, *moving far left.* How many? How many do you think? One plus one... That makes two...

ALBERT, *writing.* Merely checking... (*He puts the pad and pencil in his pocket, removes two settings from the table—silverware, glasses, napkins— places them on the sideboard, and replaces two of the chairs, upstage. Aside.*) Damn! I lose again! That's another ten thousand I owe myself! (*Shrugging.*) Oh well...

BORDELEAU *enters, upstage. He is dressed in evening clothes and is wearing an overcoat.*

BORDELEAU, *calling.* Garçon! Garçon!

ALBERT, *at the sideboard.* Monsieur?

BORDELEAU. Are you the waiter?

ALBERT. I'm the maître d'hôtel, monsieur!

POMPE-NICOLE, *down left.* I say, that's not... (*Calling.*) Bordeleau, of all people!

BORDELEAU, *moving downstage.* Pompe-Nicole! Is that you?

ALBERT, *moving down right, pointing.* Monsieur knows... monsieur?

POMPE-NICOLE, *ignoring* ALBERT. What a nice surprise! What brings you here?

BORDELEAU. Same thing that brings you here, I imagine! (*Slyly.*) Night out? Dinner for two?

Pompe-Nicole, *nodding.* Night out...

Albert, *nodding, ingenuously.* Dinner for two...

Bordeleau, *to* Albert, *with a look of surprise.* Yes... Quite... (*To* Pompe-Nicole.) It's been ages, old boy...

Pompe-Nicole. Two years!

Bordeleau. No! It can't be! Two years?

Pompe-Nicole. If not more!

Bordeleau. My, my! How time flies!

Pompe-Nicole. You can say that again!

Albert. My, my! How time flies!

Bordeleau, *giving* Albert *a sidelong glance.* Yes... Quite... (*To* Pompe-Nicole.) Delighted to see you looking so well...

Pompe-Nicole. You too, I must say!

Bordeleau. And happy...

Pompe-Nicole. Why not? I have no complaints.

Bordeleau. And the ladies, Pompe-Nicole? No complaints on that score?

Pompe-Nicole. Not at all! Not at all!... If I did... (*With a gesture.*) I wouldn't be here!

Bordeleau, *laughing.* Touché, old boy!

Pompe-Nicole, *laughing.* Or you either!

Bordeleau, *modestly.* Well... No doubt she's something special?

Pompe-Nicole. As I say, no complaints! And you?

Bordeleau. Oh, you know me. If it's not one, it's another!

Pompe-Nicole. Still the same old Bordeleau!

Bordeleau. Always something on the string!

Pompe-Nicole. And married, they tell me! Didn't I hear—

Bordeleau. Me? Married?... Heavens, no!

Albert, *who has been following the exchange intently.* No knots in the string!

Bordeleau, *nodding.* No knots... (*Catching himself, with a glance at* Albert.) Yes... Quite... (*To* Pompe-Nicole.) Our maître d'hôtel isn't bashful, is he!

Pompe-Nicole. Oh, don!t mind Albert! He's a friend of the family!

Albert, *to* Pompe-Nicole. Much obliged!

Pompe-Nicole, *to* Bordeleau, *introducing.* Albert... late of Maxim's... (*To* Albert.) Monsieur Bordeleau...

Albert, *to* Bordeleau. Delighted, monsieur...

Bordeleau, *to* Albert, *emphasizing.* Bordeleau... Borde*leau*... Mind the accent.

ALBERT. Yes, monsieur.

BORDELEAU. Not everybody does.

ALBERT. I imagine, monsieur...

BORDELEAU. At any rate... I'm glad you're here, Albert. I'm going to need a room.

ALBERT. I assumed as much, monsieur.

BORDELEAU. Yes... Something with atmosphere... Mysterious... Provocative...

ALBERT. Intimate...

BORDELEAU. Exactly!

ALBERT. Something to break the ice, if I may say...

BORDELEAU. Well...

ALBERT. I have just the perfect room for monsieur. (*Pointing toward the door, up right.*) Number five... A lovenest... Suggestive, but not overwhelming...

BORDELEAU. Fine! Fine!

ALBERT. I'll go set the table.

He begins to move off, up right.

BORDELEAU, *calling him back.* Just a minute!... The menu...

POMPE-NICOLE, *holding up his hand.* Tsk tsk tsk! Don't bother... He knows our taste.

BORDELEAU. He does?

POMPE-NICOLE. Well... Mine...

BORDELEAU, *objecting.* Yes, but—

ALBERT, *to* BORDELEAU. Please! I assure monsieur he can leave everything to me. (*Moving up right, aside.*) And I bet on four for that room too!... Damn! Another ten thousand... At this rate I'll break myself in no time! (*Stopping as he reaches the door, to* BORDELEAU, *with a little bow.*) Monsieur... (*To* POMPE-NICOLE, *likewise.*) Monsieur...

He exits.

POMPE-NICOLE. Well, well, well... Old Bordeleau... What a pleasant surprise!

BORDELEAU. Pompe-Nicole... I can't believe it!

POMPE-NICOLE. And here, of all places... What a coincidence!

The two of them begin crossing right, talking as they go.

BORDELEAU. Poetic justice, old boy... Only poetic justice...

POMPE-NICOLE. Oh? How's that?

BORDELEAU. Come, come now... You remember... The first time we met you were out on a lark...

POMPE-NICOLE, *smiling at the recollection.* How well I remember...

BORDELEAU. Now you're out on another!

He sits down on the canape.

POMPE-NICOLE. "Lark" is right, Bordeleau! If my mistress ever found out...

He sits down next to him.

BORDELEAU. Your mistress?

POMPE-NICOLE. My "unlawfully wedded wife," if you prefer!

BORDELEAU. Or "semi-spouse"!

POMPE-NICOLE. Nicely put!

They laugh.

BORDELEAU. You mean... you're cheating on your mistress, Pompe-Nicole?

POMPE-NICOLE, *with exaggerated concern.* Shhh! I told you... If she ever found out...

BORDELEAU. Talk about coincidences, old boy... So am I!

POMPE-NICOLE. No!

BORDELEAU. Quite!... After all, I look at it this way. A mistress deserves to be treated like a wife. You agree?

POMPE-NICOLE. Absolutely!

BORDELEAU. And that means she deserves to have me cheat now and then! It's the least I can do!

POMPE-NICOLE. The very least!

BORDELEAU. And besides, when you make a catch like the one I've just made...

POMPE-NICOLE. It's almost a crime not to pull her in! Right?

BORDELEAU. Exactly! You took the words out of my mouth!

POMPE-NICOLE. Pretty?

BORDELEAU. Ravishing!

POMPE-NICOLE. Especially at night?

BORDELEAU. As a matter of fact...

POMPE-NICOLE, *cynically.* On a streetcorner... Under a lamppost...

BORDELEAU, *getting up.* Now, now, Pompe-Nicole... I know what you're thinking! But that's not my cup of tea...

POMPE-NICOLE. It's not?

BORDELEAU. She's high class, this one... Society... Upper crust...

POMPE-NICOLE. No! Really?

BORDELEAU. Believe me, old boy, that's the only kind!

POMPE-NICOLE, *getting up.* Oh, you don't have to tell me! I couldn't agree more! I always say: "Give me a society lady!" Nothing like them... the excitement... the intrigue...

BORDELEAU. The danger!

POMPE-NICOLE, *agreeing.* The danger!... Meeting on the sly... little back-street hotels... curtains drawn, lights down low... And the husband, poor fool...

BORDELEAU. I know, I know...

POMPE-NICOLE. The thought that any second he could be outside the door... break it down... come storming in, in a jealous rage... find you...

BORDELEAU. With the police!

POMPE-NICOLE. With the police!

BORDELEAU. Ah!

POMPE-NICOLE. Talk about danger... (*He pauses, sighing.*) That's what I call an affair! A real affair! Yes... Give me a society lady, Bordeleau! That's love with a kick to it!

BORDELEAU. My sentiments exactly!

POMPE-NICOLE. Not like the other kind...

BORDELEAU. Under the lamppost...

POMPE-NICOLE. The ordinary, everyday, dull, boring kind... No risk, no danger...

BORDELEAU. None!

POMPE-NICOLE. Anything for a price... You pay, you play...

BORDELEAU. Boring!

POMPE-NICOLE. One, two, three!... Next!

BORDELEAU, *shaking his head.* Dull, dull, dull!

POMPE-NICOLE. No, no, Bordeleau... "A society lady or nothing!" That's my motto!

He pauses.

BORDELEAU. In other words, old boy, what you're trying to tell me is that... (*Emphasizing.*) you've caught one too!

POMPE-NICOLE, *emphasizing.* Quite, old boy! I've caught one too!

BORDELEAU, *smiling.* Which means that we've both caught...

POMPE-NICOLE *and* BORDELEAU, *together.* Society ladies!

They shake hands, laughing.

BORDELEAU. Talk about coincidences!... What is she like?

POMPE-NICOLE. Mine?

BORDELEAU. Tell me about her.

POMPE-NICOLE. Well, first of all, she's a widow... a beautiful young widow... Her husband was a colonel in the cavalry, poor chap...

BORDELEAU. Dead?

POMPE-NICOLE. Of course...

BORDELEAU. Tsk tsk tsk!

POMPE-NICOLE. Died in the saddle, as they say... First campaign...

BORDELEAU. No!

POMPE-NICOLE. Hardly had time to get off a volley...

BORDELEAU. And the widow?... No... how shall I say?... no "skirmishes" since?

POMPE-NICOLE. Not a one, poor thing! I'm her first... That is, I will be...

BORDELEAU. Lucky devil!

POMPE-NICOLE. Yes... It seems she lives with a rich old aunt. I met her yesterday on her way back home. You remember what a terrible day it was yesterday... The rain, the wind...

BORDELEAU. All day... I remember...

POMPE-NICOLE. No day to be caught without an umbrella... Well, to make a long story short, Bordeleau... There I was, standing in the rain... Dripping... Absolutely dripping... All of a sudden, next thing I know, this perfectly charming young lady is standing beside me, saying: "Wouldn't you like to share my umbrella, monsieur?"

BORDELEAU. Just like that?

POMPE-NICOLE. Just like that! But as sweet as could be... Innocent... Uncomplicated... No ulterior motives, no suspicion... Nothing like the kind you usually run into... the kind that know exactly what you're after, Bordeleau, and exactly what they're probably going to wind up doing...

BORDELEAU. I know the kind you mean!

POMPE-NICOLE. But a society lady, like my widow... well... Anyway, somehow I managed to convince her to come join me here tonight. And if you think it was easy...

BORDELEAU. I can imagine!

POMPE-NICOLE. And yours?

BORDELEAU. No easier, believe me! For one thing, she's married!

POMPE-NICOLE, *enthusiastically.* Oh? The plot thickens!

BORDELEAU. And a husband that watches her like a hawk!... (*Offhand.*) He's in Canada...

POMPE-NICOLE, *surprised.* He's in... (*With a chuckle.*) He must have good eyes!

BORDELEAU. He left her with her mother, old boy! That's no laughing matter! She's the world's worst prude!

POMPE-NICOLE. Oh?

BORDELEAU. The only consolation is, she's deaf as a post!

POMPE-NICOLE. Well, at least that's something. Be thankful for small favors!

BORDELEAU. The two of them were at the Folies Bergère the other night. That's how I met her.

POMPE-NICOLE. The Folies Bergère?... The world's worst prude?

BORDELEAU. I know, I know... But I told you, she's deaf. My sweet young thing told her they were going to the Opera!

POMPE-NICOLE. No! You must be joking!

BORDELEAU. I'm serious, old boy! Really! She told her they were going to see *Carmen*!

POMPE-NICOLE. She didn't!... And the old woman believed her?

BORDELEAU, *laughing.* Did she?... You should have seen her, standing around during the intermission, humming and singing under her breath... "Toreador, en ga-a-a-arde..." It was priceless!

POMPE-NICOLE. I'm sure! And very appropriate! (*Pointing his finger, mimicking.*) "En garde, young man! En garde!... Don't you go getting any ideas about my daughter!"

BORDELEAU. Oh, the daughter knew how to take care of herself, thank you! Typical society lady, Pompe-Nicole... Sophisticated, and all that, but perfectly natural... No airs, no affectation...

POMPE-NICOLE, *nodding.* Typical... typical...

BORDELEAU. Every so often she would turn to me and smile. Then she asked if she could borrow my program... Then my glasses... Soon she was telling me all about the show. It was the eighth time she saw it...

POMPE-NICOLE, *laughing.* No! Her mother must be crazy about *Carmen*!

BORDELEAU, *laughing.* Yes, I'm sure!

POMPE-NICOLE. Then what?

BORDELEAU. Well, after a while she was telling me her whole life story! Her marriage... her husband in Canada... her mother, and how she's a deaf old prude...

POMPE-NICOLE. And you?

BORDELEAU. Me? What do you think? I told her that I knew a charming little restaurant where married women whose husbands are in Canada come all the time, but who leave their deaf old prude mothers at home!

POMPE-NICOLE. You told her... Just like that?

BORDELEAU. Not in so many words, old boy. I couldn't come right out...
You know these society ladies!

POMPE-NICOLE. I should say!

BORDELEAU. It's so easy to frighten them off!

POMPE-NICOLE, *agreeing.* One wrong word!

BORDELEAU. Well, not me, Pompe-Nicole! (*Tapping his forehead.*) Experience... Tact... And to prove it, she's coming here tonight!... Without the old prude!

POMPE-NICOLE, *smiling.* Let's hope so!

BORDELEAU. You don't know what a struggle it was to convince her! Poor child... She couldn't bear the thought of lying to her mother. She never did before...

POMPE-NICOLE. Oh?

BORDELEAU. Not a big lie, that is...

POMPE-NICOLE. No... not like the Folies Bergère, or that sort of thing...

BORDELEAU. Right...

POMPE-NICOLE. Well, there's a first time for everything.

BORDELEAU. That's what I told her.

POMPE-NICOLE. Anyway, all's well that ends well! Here you are...

BORDELEAU. Oh, it wasn't that easy! That still left the problem with my other one... My mistress...

POMPE-NICOLE. Your "semi-spouse," as you so aptly put it!

BORDELEAU. Exactly! My "semi"...

POMPE-NICOLE. Why? What was the problem?

BORDELEAU. Jealousy, old boy! Jealousy! She wouldn't be too happy if she knew I was... how shall I say?...

POMPE-NICOLE. Cheating?

BORDELEAU. In a word... She thinks I'm as faithful as she is!

POMPE-NICOLE. Oh?

BORDELEAU, *mimicking.* "What's good for the goose is good for the gander!" That's all she keeps telling me!

POMPE-NICOLE. And the "goose," I assume, is...

BORDELEAU. Faithful to the core, Pompe-Nicole! To the core!... I couldn't pry her loose if I tried!

POMPE-NICOLE. Poor Bordeleau! I sympathize, believe me! Mine is exactly the same! Maybe worse! I can't make a move...

BORDELEAU. Then you know what I mean. The problem was how to escape for the night...

POMPE-NICOLE. I know, I know...

BORDELEAU. Well, there must be a god who looks after lovers...

POMPE-NICOLE, *chuckling.* The same one who looks after fools and little children!

BORDELEAU. I suppose... Because there I was, old boy, wracking my brain to come up with some excuse... anything... when all of a sudden, out of a clear blue sky, she comes running up to me, in tears, waving a telegram... Something about her dear old aunt, who's sick and dying... And she's got to rush off... And I mustn't wait up because she'll certainly spend the night... In fact, maybe two or three...

POMPE-NICOLE, *surprised.* No! Her sick old aunt?

BORDELEAU. Right...

POMPE-NICOLE. Mine too!

BORDELEAU, *quizzically.* Your sick old aunt?

POMPE-NICOLE. No, no! My... my "semi"... my mistress... *Her* sick old aunt!

BORDELEAU. What?

POMPE-NICOLE. Yes! She has one too!

BORDELEAU. An old aunt?

POMPE-NICOLE. Yes!

BORDELEAU. And sick?

POMPE-NICOLE. Dying! Dying!... That's why I'm here. The same as you... The tears, the telegram... "Aunt sick... Not expected to live... Come at once..."

BORDELEAU. Talk about coincidences!

POMPE-NICOLE. Well, I wasn't going to let a free night go to waste! So, while she's watching her aunt die in Versailles, I'll be here with my—

BORDELEAU, *interrupting.* Versailles?

POMPE-NICOLE. Yes... Her aunt lives in Versailles.

BORDELEAU. No! So does mine!

POMPE-NICOLE. Your aunt?

BORDELEAU. No, no, no! Hers! My... You know...

POMPE-NICOLE. She doesn't!

BORDELEAU. She does!

POMPE-NICOLE. Of all things!

BORDELEAU, *laughing.* Do you suppose they both have the same aunt?

POMPE-NICOLE, *laughing.* Now that *would* be a coincidence!

BORDELEAU. Maybe they're cousins!... What would that make us?

POMPE-NICOLE. Well... Cousins-in-law, I imagine...

BORDELEAU. In law?

POMPE-NICOLE. Or out of it!

BORDELEAU. No, no... "Semi-cousins," old boy!

POMPE-NICOLE. "Semi-cousins"! Exactly!

They shake hands, laughing. After a few moments, BORDELEAU *takes out his pocket watch and looks at it in surprise.*

BORDELEAU. My goodness! Five past seven, and here I am, talking, talking, talking! She must be waiting outside... I told her seven o'clock.

POMPE-NICOLE, *looking at his own watch.* You're right! Five past... I told mine seven sharp. She should be here any minute.

ALBERT *enters, up right.*

ALBERT, *to* BORDELEAU. Monsieur's private room is ready, monsieur.

BORDELEAU. Ah... Thank you, Albert.

POMPE-NICOLE, *to* ALBERT. I say, Albert... You wouldn't know if a lady has been asking for me, would you?

ALBERT, *moving left.* Not that I know of, Monsieur Pompe-Nicole...

He begins tidying up the table, arranging the silverware, the glasses, etc.

BORDELEAU, *to* POMPE-NICOLE. Well, I'll be going... Nice seeing you, old boy! We must get together... Good luck, and all that!

POMPE-NICOLE, *laughing.* Yes... And the same to you, I'm sure!

BORDELEAU, *laughing.* From one "semi-cousin" to another!

POMPE-NICOLE. Right!... (*Struck by an idea, as* BORDELEAU *moves upstage, toward the door.*) Wait a minute, Bordeleau!...

BORDELEAU, *at the door, stopping.* Yes?

POMPE-NICOLE. What's the matter with me? Why didn't I think of it before?

BORDELEAU. Please?

POMPE-NICOLE. I've just had a perfectly brilliant idea!

BORDELEAU. Oh?

POMPE-NICOLE. Why don't you join us? The two of you...

BORDELEAU. You mean, me and my...

POMPE-NICOLE. Yes... Why not? The four of us can have a delightful evening.

ALBERT, *at the table, to* BORDELEAU. Twice as delightful as two, monsieur...

BORDELEAU, *with a glance in* ALBERT's *direction.* Yes... Quite...

POMPE-NICOLE, *to* BORDELEAU. Don't you think...

BORDELEAU. Well... I don't know...

POMPE-NICOLE. Besides, it makes things much easier all around... More relaxed... No strain...

BORDELEAU. It does?

POMPE-NICOLE. Look at it this way. Say all of a sudden she begins to have second thoughts. Conscience... Guilt... That sort of thing...

BORDELEAU. So?

POMPE-NICOLE. Well, if you're alone with yours, or I'm alone with mine, you know what's going to happen. (*Mimicking.*) "No, really, I shouldn't... I don't know why I let you talk me into this. I'm going to hate myself in the morning..." You've heard it all before!

BORDELEAU. Once or twice!

POMPE-NICOLE. At least!... But with four it's a different story. They'd never dream of backing down!

BORDELEAU. They wouldn't?

POMPE-NICOLE. Of course not! Pride, Bordeleau! Pride!... It's a sure thing... Never fails... Now then, what do you say? Shall we?

BORDELEAU. Well, I suppose... Only, what about the ladies? Maybe they won't want to...

POMPE-NICOLE. That's true. With society ladies you can never be sure. They're not like the others...

BORDELEAU. You mean, under the lamppost...

POMPE-NICOLE. Right...

BORDELEAU. Maybe they'd be embarrassed.

POMPE-NICOLE. Well, there's only one way to find out. I'll ask mine...

BORDELEAU. And I'll ask mine... And if they say yes...

POMPE-NICOLE. They will! They will! Mine is happy to oblige!

BORDELEAU. And mine is easy to convince!

POMPE-NICOLE. Good! Then it's settled. We meet here... the four of us... unless something comes up...

ALBERT, *still at the table, to* BORDELEAU. I think monsieur has made a very wise decision.

BORDELEAU, *smiling, to* ALBERT. Thank you, Albert.

ALBERT. Yes... It's always been my experience, monsieur—

BORDELEAU. I know... Thank you...

ALBERT. With four it's so much more pleasant...

BORDELEAU, *laughing.* I know! And believe me, tonight I'm in the mood!

ALBERT. So I see, monsieur!

BORDELEAU, *still at the door.* Wine, women and song, Albert! Dancing-girls! Dancing-girls!... Bring on the dancing-girls!

ALBERT. I'm sorry, monsieur, but the house doesn't provide—

POMPE-NICOLE, *still down right, laughing.* Figuratively speaking, Albert...

ALBERT. Aha...

He moves toward the door, upstage.

BORDELEAU. Tonight I could kiss them all! (PHILOMÈLE *enters, upstage, carrying a wine-cooler.*) Like this one!

He plants a kiss on her cheek.

PHILOMÈLE, *taken by surprise.* Oh!

She gives him a resounding slap.

BORDELEAU. Ayyy!

ALBERT, *simply, to* BORDELEAU, *introducing.* Monsieur, my wife...

BORDELEAU, *rubbing his cheek, to* ALBERT. I beg your pardon! (*To* PHILO-MÈLE, *with a bow.*) Delighted, madame... (*To* POMPE-NICOLE.) Back soon, old boy...

He exits.

POMPE-NICOLE, *to* ALBERT. Your wife has quite a temper!

He crosses left.

PHILOMÈLE, *going to the sideboard and putting down the wine-cooler.* The nerve!

ALBERT, *replying to* POMPE-NICOLE. Yes, monsieur. Quite!

PHILOMÈLE, *to* ALBERT. Who does he think he is? A woman walks in the door, and he kisses her! Just like that!

ALBERT, *to* PHILOMÈLE. I'm sure he didn't mean any harm. He was only—

PHILOMÈLE. Maybe not! But if you walked in the door, and some strange woman kissed you, what would you do?

ALBERT, *hesitating.* Well...

PHILOMÈLE. You'd do just what I did, now wouldn't you? Admit it!

ALBERT, *without much conviction.* Of course... Of course...

PHILOMÈLE, *to* POMPE-NICOLE. See, monsieur? If every couple did like Albert and me, the world would be a better place!

POMPE-NICOLE. No doubt, madame...

PHILOMÈLE. And people wouldn't talk about divorce all the time!

POMPE-NICOLE. Very true...

ALBERT, *suddenly eager to change the subject, to* POMPE-NICOLE. Did monsieur say he wanted me to set two more places?

POMPE-NICOLE. Yes, Albert... Please...

ALBERT. Right away, monsieur! (*To* PHILOMÈLE.) Philomèle... Two more
 places...

PHILOMÈLE, *repeating.* Two more places...

ALBERT *gets the two chairs, upstage, and sets them in place. At the same
time,* PHILOMÈLE, *at the sideboard, retrieves the two settings previously
removed by* ALBERT, *and replaces them on the table.*

ALBERT, *surveying the room to make sure everything is in order, aside.*
 Well, well! Four after all! That's ten thousand I win!... In this room,
 that is... Because in there... (*He looks off, up right.*) Zero!... Well, at
 least I break even!

PHILOMÈLE, *as she finishes arranging the two settings, to* POMPE-NICOLE.
 There, monsieur! Everything is ready.

POMPE-NICOLE, *still down left.* Fine! (*To* ALBERT.) And the menu, Albert?
 Did you order the menu?

ALBERT. Presently, monsieur... I'm on my way to the kitchen... (*To* PHILO-
 MÈLE.) Come Philomèle... Back to work!

POMPE-NICOLE, *laughing, to* ALBERT. You're not afraid to leave her alone
 with me, are you?

ALBERT. One never knows, monsieur!

POMPE-NICOLE. Why, thank you, Albert! I'm flattered!

ALBERT. My pleasure, monsieur!

He and PHILOMÈLE *exit, upstage. After they have left,* POMPE-NICOLE
*moves about the room, examining the table, stopping at the canape to test
the springs, etc. Finally he stops up left, in front of the mirror, looks at
himself, takes out a comb and arranges his hair, and stands admiring his
reflection.*

POMPE-NICOLE. There... Perfect... (*Smiling at himself.*) I must say, you
 look dashing tonight, Pompe-Nicole... If you do say so yourself!... (*Taking
 out his watch.*) Good heavens! Seven fifteen already! What on earth can be
 keeping her?... Just like a society lady!... Always late!

PHILOMÈLE *enters, upstage, showing in* CLÉMENTINE. *The latter is
wearing a coat and hat.*

PHILOMÈLE. This way, madame...

She exits.

POMPE-NICOLE. Ah! Speak of the devil... (*To* CLÉMENTINE, *going to meet
 her.*) Madame... I can't tell you how delighted... how honored...

CLÉMENTINE, *moving downstage with him, fanning herself with her gloves, nervously.* Oh, monsieur...

POMPE-NICOLE, *with good-natured reproach.* No, no, my dear... Please!... (*Wagging his finger.*) Tsk tsk tsk! Not "monsieur"...

CLÉMENTINE. But I... I hardly know you!

POMPE-NICOLE. Well, I'm sure we can take care of that... (*Slyly.*) That's why we're here...

CLÉMENTINE. Oh, monsieur, I... I don't know what to say! This is all so new to me... Really, I—

POMPE-NICOLE. Besides... Appearances, after all... We don't want the help to get any ideas!

CLÉMENTINE. Oh no!

POMPE-NICOLE. As far as they're concerned, we're just another man and wife.

CLÉMENTINE. We're what?

POMPE-NICOLE. For your sake, my dear... You know how tongues can wag!

CLÉMENTINE. Oh, I know! I know!... (*Fanning herself, nervously.*) That's exactly what I mean!... I just don't know what ever got into me, monsieur... Coming here this way... It's... It's all so new...

POMPE-NICOLE. Now, now... There's nothing to worry about, my sweet...

CLÉMENTINE. Why, the whole way I just knew that everyone in the street was looking! I sat in a corner and pulled down the shade. I... I didn't even want the driver to see me!

POMPE-NICOLE. Poor child!

CLÉMENTINE. And it seemed to take absolutely forever!

POMPE-NICOLE. So I noticed...

CLÉMENTINE. I kept telling him: "Faster, faster!"... That's why I got here so early...

POMPE-NICOLE, *surprised.* Early? Seven fifteen? I thought we said seven...

CLÉMENTINE. Seven fifteen? No, it can't be...

POMPE-NICOLE, *looking at his watch.* Well...

CLÉMENTINE. Oh! I'm sorry, monsieur! I... Oh, what can I say?... It's just that I'm so upset... I... I... Really...

POMPE-NICOLE. Now, now, now... No harm done... You're here, and that's all that matters.

CLÉMENTINE. Yes, I'm here... (*As if suddenly realizing the fact.*) Oh, my God! You're right! I'm here... With... with a man!

POMPE-NICOLE. Yes...

CLÉMENTINE. I'm here, monsieur! Alone... With you!

POMPE-NICOLE, *with a shrug.* That's the general idea...

CLÉMENTINE. Oh! If my aunt ever caught me here, she'd kill me! I just know it! She'd absolutely kill me!

POMPE-NICOLE. Don't worry... I'm sure you'd find something to tell her!

CLÉMENTINE. Well, maybe... But... (*Very grave, pointing toward the ceiling.*) What about him, monsieur?

POMPE-NICOLE. I beg your pardon?

CLÉMENTINE, *pointing.* What do I tell *him*?

POMPE-NICOLE. Who? The upstairs neighbor?

CLÉMENTINE. Him!... My poor husband... looking down from... (*Dramatically.*) above!

POMPE-NICOLE. Come, come now... This is really no time to be talking about your husband!

CLÉMENTINE, *fanning herself.* Of course! Of course! You're absolutely right... (*She sits down on the canape.*) Just promise you won't take advantage of me, monsieur... I mean, this is all so new...

POMPE-NICOLE. Now, now...

CLÉMENTINE. Please... Promise you won't let me do anything he'll be sorry for...

POMPE-NICOLE, *pointing toward the ceiling.* Him?... I promise! There!

He sits down next to her.

CLÉMENTINE, *coquettishly.* Thank you, monsieur.

POMPE-NICOLE. And please... I wish you would call me Pompe-Nicole!

CLÉMENTINE. What?

POMPE-NICOLE. I said: "I wish you would call me Pompe-Nicole!"

CLÉMENTINE. You do?... (*Ingenuously.*) Why?

POMPE-NICOLE. Why?... Because that's my name! Why else?

CLÉMENTINE. It is, monsieur? (*Repressing a laugh.*) Pumpernickel?... (*Sympathetically.*) Tsk tsk tsk! Can't you change it?

POMPE-NICOLE. No, no... (*Aside.*) Delightful child! (*To* CLÉMENTINE.) Pompe-Nicole... Boniface Pompe-Nicole... With a hyphen... Pompe hyphen Nicole...

CLÉMENTINE. All that?... What a long name! How do people ever remember it?

POMPE-NICOLE. Long?... (*Realizing her misunderstanding.*) No, no, my sweet... The hyphen is silent.

CLÉMENTINE. Oh... Of course! What was I thinking?

POMPE-NICOLE. Besides, what's in a name? We're not here to worry about such things! Not tonight!... Eat, drink, and be merry...

CLÉMENTINE. Well, if you say so...

POMPE-NICOLE. Good company, good food, good wine... (*Pointing to the wine-cooler on the sideboard.*) Champagne... Have you ever had champagne?

CLÉMENTINE. Have I ever... (*Forgetting herself momentarily.*) Damn right!

POMPE-NICOLE, *shocked.* What?

CLÉMENTINE, *covering her gaffe.* Last night! Last night!... You asked if I ever had champagne, Boniface, and I—

POMPE-NICOLE, *surprised.* Boniface?

CLÉMENTINE. Oh!... Excuse me, monsieur! It... it just slipped out...

POMPE-NICOLE. Not at all...

CLÉMENTINE. There I go, taking liberties... Oh! What ever will you think of me? It's just that I'm so... This is all so new...

POMPE-NICOLE. No... Please... Take liberties! Take all the liberties you want! I insist...

CLÉMENTINE. It's just... This isn't like me at all. I... I'm really not myself. I... I'm usually so shy. But somehow, tonight... Here, with you... I don't know what it is... There's something... something about you... I... I hardly know you, but there's something about you... I just can't help it, no matter how I try...

POMPE-NICOLE, *passionately.* Don't try! Don't try!

CLÉMENTINE, *staring at him.* Look at me... Look me in the eye...

POMPE-NICOLE. Yes... Yes...

CLÉMENTINE, *motioning him to move his head slightly.* No, no... Straight... Look me straight in the eye...

POMPE-NICOLE, *complying.* Yes...

She studies him for a moment.

CLÉMENTINE. That's it! I've got it! (*Matter-of-fact.*) It's the nose...

POMPE-NICOLE, *taken aback.* What?

CLÉMENTINE. Your nose... You've got his nose...

POMPE-NICOLE. Whose nose?

CLÉMENTINE, *pointing to the ceiling.* His... I knew there was something...

POMPE-NICOLE, *jumping to his feet.* Your husband?... (*Exasperated.*) No, no, no!... Thank you! Thank you just the same!

CLÉMENTINE, *getting up.* But he had a lovely nose...

POMPE-NICOLE. I'm sure!

CLÉMENTINE. Really, he did...

POMPE-NICOLE. I don't care what kind of a nose he had! We said we weren't going to talk about him! Now please...

CLÉMENTINE. You're absolutely right! I'm just so... This is all so new...

POMPE-NICOLE. You're here, and I'm here... The two of us... You and me... That's all that matters.

CLÉMENTINE. And there's no turning back.

POMPE-NICOLE, *shaking his head.* No turning back!

CLÉMENTINE. "He died in a cast," as they say.

POMPE-NICOLE, *puzzled.* "He died...?" (*Suddenly understanding.*) Aha! Yes... The die is cast! Exactly!... We're at the Rubicon!

CLÉMENTINE, *surprised.* We are? (*Looking around.*) I thought it was Chez Dominique...

POMPE-NICOLE. No, no... The Rubicon... It's an expression...

CLÉMENTINE. Of course! What was I thinking?

POMPE-NICOLE, *aside.* Delightful child! (*To* CLÉMENTINE.) Yes... Just the two of us...

CLÉMENTINE. Just the two of us...

POMPE-NICOLE. You and me...

CLÉMENTINE, *trying to appear sophisticated.* At the Rubicon...

POMPE-NICOLE. Though, of course, when I say "you and me"... (*About to broach a subject, delicately.*) There could be more...

CLÉMENTINE. More?

POMPE-NICOLE. Yes... Two more, for example...

CLÉMENTINE. Two more people?

POMPE-NICOLE. Why, yes... In fact, now that you mention it... I've got an idea... A simply splendid idea...

CLÉMENTINE. Oh? What is it? I love ideas!

POMPE-NICOLE. Well... First, there's something I think I should tell you. You see, I'm an epicure...

CLÉMENTINE. Oh, that's all right. I'm a Catholic myself, but it really doesn't matter...

POMPE-NICOLE. No, no, my love... An epicure... A dilettante...

CLÉMENTINE, *as if she understands.* Oh, that...

POMPE-NICOLE. A man of refinement and taste...

CLÉMENTINE. I should hope...

POMPE-NICOLE. Yes... Unusual taste... I... How shall I put it?... I enjoy my pleasures, like the rest of us...

CLÉMENTINE, *nodding.* Of course...

POMPE-NICOLE. But for me, the more exquisite the pleasure, the longer it should last... The more it should be savored... Sipped slowly, slowly, like a fine old wine... Even left in the bottle as long as you can, until you can't resist it... Until...

He sighs.

CLÉMENTINE, *puzzled by his poetic outburst.* Monsieur?

POMPE-NICOLE, *continuing.* Oh, I know what you're going to say. You're going to tell me it's depraved...

CLÉMENTINE, *aside.* I am?

POMPE-NICOLE. Decadent... perverted... I know... But it's not! Not at all! It's just that I'm... I'm past the age of instant pleasure... transient satisfaction... fleeting delight...

CLÉMENTINE. Aha...

POMPE-NICOLE. Yes... There comes a time when a man stops being a... a glutton, and becomes a gourmet!

CLÉMENTINE, *aside.* There is?

POMPE-NICOLE. And I'm there, my love! I'm there... I'm no longer a child...

CLÉMENTINE. No...

POMPE-NICOLE. I know true pleasure for what it really is! I know that it has to be resisted... countered... tempered with displeasure... even with pain...

CLÉMENTINE, *shocked.* Oh no! You're not one of *them!* Don't tell me...

POMPE-NICOLE. Them?... Who?

CLÉMENTINE. The ones with whips and things... I mean... (*Aside.*) I've met that kind before, but I didn't know they were pedicures...

POMPE-NICOLE, *laughing.* No, no, my love! No whips...

CLÉMENTINE, *reassured.* Well, I hope not...

POMPE-NICOLE. Only the excruciating pleasure of delay...

CLÉMENTINE, *with a start.* The what?

POMPE-NICOLE. Delay, delay... Postponement, my love... Procrastination, if you prefer...

CLÉMENTINE, *with a dubious nod.* Aha...

POMPE-NICOLE. Here we are... The two of us... No obstacles in our path... (*Poetizing more and more.*) Nothing to prevent us from simply reaching out and plucking the inevitable fruits of our... adventure.

CLÉMENTINE, *aside.* Plucking the fruits?

POMPE-NICOLE. Which brings me to my idea, if I may...

CLÉMENTINE. Yes... Please...

POMPE-NICOLE. Those obstacles, my love... Why not make them for our-selves? Why not strew our path with pitfalls?

CLÉMENTINE, *pretending to understand.* If you like...

POMPE-NICOLE, *beginning to get carried away.* Why not heighten the delights of our intimate rendezvous... our dinner for two... with an alien presence? (CLÉMENTINE *gives him a quizzical look.*) Why not surround ourselves with strangers?

CLÉMENTINE. Strangers?

POMPE-NICOLE. Yes! Yes!... With just one thought in mind... To be rid of them! Don't you see? To long... to yearn for that glorious moment! Finally!... Just you and me... Just the two of us... Alone!

CLÉMENTINE, *aside.* You suppose he wants to go eat in a cafeteria?

POMPE-NICOLE, *continuing.* I don't care what your philosophers say... "No pleasure with discomfort!" A true hedonist, like myself—

CLÉMENTINE. A what?

POMPE-NICOLE. A hedonist, my love...

CLÉMENTINE. Oh? I thought you were a pedicure...

POMPE-NICOLE. A pedi... No, no...

CLÉMENTINE, *aside.* I wish he'd make up his mind!

POMPE-NICOLE, *continuing his train of thought.* A true hedonist like myself says: "No pleasure *without* discomfort!" Understand?

CLÉMENTINE, *blandly.* Of course...

POMPE-NICOLE. That's why I thought... You and me, and...

CLÉMENTINE. And some strangers...

POMPE-NICOLE. Yes... Exactly!

CLÉMENTINE. I see...

POMPE-NICOLE. Well, they're not really strangers. That is, one of them is an old friend. A perfectly charming gentleman... Witty, sophisticated... I met him a little while ago. He's here, with a lady...

CLÉMENTINE. Oh?

POMPE-NICOLE. And I thought that, since they're alone, and since we're alone... Why not get together, all four of us?

CLÉMENTINE, *crossing left.* Well, I don't know... After all... (*Hesitating.*) Who's the lady?

POMPE-NICOLE. No problem, believe me!... Fine family... Society... You know, our kind!

CLÉMENTINE. Aha...

POMPE-NICOLE. Otherwise I never would have dreamed of suggesting...

CLÉMENTINE. Well, if you're sure...

POMPE-NICOLE. Oh, I'm sure! I'm sure!

CLÉMENTINE. All right, I suppose so... (*Aside.*) A society lady... That ought to be fun!

POMPE-NICOLE. Good! I know you won't be sorry.

CLÉMENTINE. And you say your friend is rich?

POMPE-NICOLE. Did I? I don't remember...

CLÉMENTINE. I thought you did.

POMPE-NICOLE. Well anyway, he is! A millionaire, they tell me...

CLÉMENTINE, *aside.* All the better! (*To* POMPE-NICOLE.) How nice for him...

POMPE-NICOLE. So, the four of us then?

CLÉMENTINE. The four of us!... (*She moves upstage toward the door.*) Just let me take off my coat and freshen up a bit...

POMPE-NICOLE. Good idea! I think I'll do the same. (*He goes over to the table.*) Wait a moment, I'll ring...

He rings the bell on the table. A moment later, PHILOMÈLE *appears at the door, upstage.*

PHILOMÈLE. Monsieur rang?

POMPE-NICOLE. Yes, mademoiselle. Madame and I would like to leave our coats.

PHILOMÈLE, *pointing to the door, down left.* Through that door, monsieur... (*Pointing to the door, down right.*) Or that one... Monsieur and madame can take their pick...

POMPE-NICOLE. Thank you... (*At the door, down left, stepping aside to let* CLÉMENTINE *pass in front of him.*) After you, my love...

CLÉMENTINE *exits, with* POMPE-NICOLE *close behind.* PHILOMÈLE *moves downstage, looks around to make sure everything is in order, finally stopping at the table and giving a few finishing touches.* BORDELEAU *enters, upstage, followed by* APHRODITE. *He is no longer wearing his overcoat, but she is wearing a coat and extravagant hat.*

BORDELEAU. This way... In here...

APHRODITE, *moving down left, looking around.* You mean, this is it? This is the private room?

BORDELEAU, *down right.* This is it...

APHRODITE. But... where's the bed?

BORDELEAU, *surprised.* The bed?

APHRODITE. Yes, I thought... A private room... You know, like in a hotel...
Or a hospital...

BORDELEAU, *smiling.* No, no... Private dining room... (*Emphasizing.*)
Dining room...

APHRODITE, *simply.* Oh...

BORDELEAU, *aside.* Innocent child!

PHILOMÈLE. If monsieur and madame won't be needing me...

BORDELEAU, *to* PHILOMÈLE. No... No, thank you...

PHILOMÈLE, *nodding to each, in turn.* Madame... Monsieur...

> *She exits, upstage.*

BORDELEAU. Anyway, as I was saying... You don't mind if they join us?

APHRODITE. No... Not if you're sure they're our kind of people...

BORDELEAU. Oh, absolutely! I told you... He's an old friend...

APHRODITE. And she?

BORDELEAU. No question...

APHRODITE. And your friend... You're sure he's discreet?

BORDELEAU. "Discreet" isn't the word! He's a bottomless pit!

APHRODITE, *joining him, far right.* Because I know I'd just die if anyone
found out! Especially my mother!... Oh! If she had the slightest idea...
She'd kill me! Really! She'd simply kill me!

BORDELEAU. Now, now, now... Don't even think about it! You can tell
her you went to see *Carmen*...

APHRODITE. But...

BORDELEAU. You'll see, we're going to have a lovely time. Just take off your
hat and coat, and make yourself comfortable.

APHRODITE. Well, I suppose...

> *She begins to move toward the upstage door.*

BORDELEAU, *pointing to the door, down right.* Here, this way... It's faster.

> *She returns down right.*

APHRODITE, *stopping at the door.* Really, monsieur... I don't know why I
let you talk me into this. I'm going to hate myself in the morning.

BORDELEAU. Not at all! I promise... Believe me, everyone does it...

APHRODITE. I know... I know, but...

BORDELEAU. Take your time. There's no hurry. I'll be checking the menu.

APHRODITE, *shaking her head.* I just know I'll be sorry...

> *She exits.*

BORDELEAU, *moving upstage.* Now to find Albert...

POMPE-NICOLE *enters, down left, without his overcoat.*

POMPE-NICOLE. Ah! Bordeleau! You're back!

BORDELEAU. In the flesh!

POMPE-NICOLE. And your... your "catch"?

BORDELEAU, *pointing to the door, down right.* Getting ready...

POMPE-NICOLE. Aha... (*Pointing down left.*) Mine too...

BORDELEAU. In the meantime, I thought I'd go check the menu.

POMPE-NICOLE. Good idea...

BORDELEAU. Won't you join me?

POMPE-NICOLE. With pleasure! (*With a gesture.*) After you...

BORDELEAU *exits, upstage.* POMPE-NICOLE *follows, but just as he is about to leave,* CLÉMENTINE *enters, down left, without her hat and coat.*

CLÉMENTINE. Ready?

POMPE-NICOLE, *stopping at the door.* Ah! There you are! I was just going to check the menu.

CLÉMENTINE. Oh?

POMPE-NICOLE. If you don't mind... I won't be long...

CLÉMENTINE, *joining him at the upstage door.* Please, monsieur...

POMPE-NICOLE, *with a note of good-natured reproach.* Tsk tsk tsk! Still "monsieur"?

CLÉMENTINE. Sorry!... Pump... Pimp...

POMPE-NICOLE. Pompe... Pompe-Nicole!

CLÉMENTINE. Pompe-Nicole!

POMPE-NICOLE, *aside.* Delightful child!

He exits, upstage.

CLÉMENTINE, *moving downstage.* Well, what do you know! A society lady!... Little old me, with the likes of a real society lady!... (*She moves up left, to the mirror, and primps as she talks.*) If poor Bordeleau could only see me now!... (*Laughing.*) Really! How stupid can some men be! My sick old aunt!... God! That's as old as the hills, but they fall for it every time!

She continues primping. After a moment, APHRODITE *enters, down right, without her hat and coat.*

APHRODITE, *to herself.* Poor Pompe-Nicole! If he knew, he'd be fit to be... (*Suddenly catching sight of* CLÉMENTINE, *aloud.*) Oh!

CLÉMENTINE, *startled, turning around.* What?

APHRODITE, *aside.* There she is!

CLÉMENTINE, *aside.* That must be her! (*To* APHRODITE, *with a ceremonious bow.*) Madame...

APHRODITE, *outdoing her.* Madame...

They exchange forced smiles for a few moments in embarrassed silence. Finally each one sits down; APHRODITE *on the canape,* CLÉMENTINE *in the armchair, down left.*

CLÉMENTINE, *aside.* Better be careful what I say... (*Aloud, with exaggerated affectation.*) I must say, madame, I'm utterly ecstatic that circumstances have seen fit to conspire in this manner to bring us together!

APHRODITE, *aside.* My my! These society ladies know how to talk! (*Aloud.*) Oh, madame! Please! The static is all mine, I assure you!

CLÉMENTINE. I'm delighted beyond words!

APHRODITE. No, no, no! If anyone is delighted, madame, it's me... (*Correcting herself.*) It's I... (*Very casually.*) They're both correct, you know...

CLÉMENTINE. Heavens! Our kind can say what we like, my dear! After all, we make the rules!

APHRODITE. You couldn't be righter!

There is a brief pause during which they exchange more forced smiles.

CLÉMENTINE. Truly, I never expected to have the pleasure...

APHRODITE. Oh! Believe me, madame! The pleasure exceeds my wildest expectorations!

CLÉMENTINE. Much too kind...

APHRODITE. Not at all...

Another pause, and more smiles.

CLÉMENTINE. I trust you're enjoying the season to the fullest?

APHRODITE. The season?... Why, yes... Though actually it's been a trifle damp, don't you think?

CLÉMENTINE. No, no... The social season, my dear...

APHRODITE. Oh, the social—

CLÉMENTINE. I'm utterly chagrined to think that our paths have failed to cross heretofore and notwithstanding.

APHRODITE. Indeed, indeed!... Well, you know how it is... One party after another...

CLÉMENTINE. I know! Isn't it the truth!

APHRODITE. After a while one learns to pick and choose...

CLÉMENTINE. Oh, one has to! One has to!

APHRODITE. To disseminate...

CLÉMENTINE. Utterly!

APHRODITE. I'm afraid this winter I'm not much of a gadfly.

CLÉMENTINE. I know precisely what you mean, my dear! A few parties...
A few balls every now and again... But only when the right people give
them, of course!

APHRODITE. Of course!

They pause again, all smiles.

CLÉMENTINE. And the races?

APHRODITE. The races?

CLÉMENTINE. Yes... I imagine you must frequent the noble quadrupeds...

APHRODITE, *misunderstanding.* Oh, I should say I do! The nobler the better!

CLÉMENTINE. And you wager?

APHRODITE. I what?

CLÉMENTINE. On the horses... Do you wager?

APHRODITE. Oh, the horses... Yes, yes... All the time... I'm an absolutely
invertebrate wagerer! (*She gets up and crosses left.*) Except... (*Beginning
to forget herself.*) You know, I've got the rottenest luck!

CLÉMENTINE, *getting up, likewise beginning to lose her aplomb.* Luck?
Don't talk! It can't be any worse than mine, darling! Would you believe...
Last Sunday I got this terrific tip...

APHRODITE. From who?

CLÉMENTINE. Some tout at the track... (*Catching herself momentarily.*) I
mean, one of the grooms... In the marquis' stables...

APHRODITE. Oh?

CLÉMENTINE. My friend, the Marquis Desgranges... You know him, of
course...

APHRODITE. Of course! Of course!

CLÉMENTINE. Well... (*Lapsing again.*) I go to my bookie... My regular...
Bilkmann...

APHRODITE. Bilkmann?... Not Froufrou's friend, Bilkmann?

CLÉMENTINE. Friend?... Darling, they're lovers!

APHRODITE. No! Since when?

CLÉMENTINE. Since... Don't make me laugh!

APHRODITE. Lovers?... I never knew...

CLÉMENTINE. Anyway, I go to Bilkmann and I tell him: "Here's everything
I've got. Stick the whole wad on My Bellybutton in the third."

APHRODITE. And he didn't win?

CLÉMENTINE. Oh, he won all right! He won a bundle! But not me!

APHRODITE. How come?

CLÉMENTINE. When I go to collect, no Bilkmann! That's how come!

APHRODITE. No!

CLÉMENTINE. Disappeared... Took a powder... Him and my money!

APHRODITE, *scandalized*. That louse!

CLÉMENTINE. So don't talk luck to me, darling! If I ever get my hands on that scum...

APHRODITE. They're all alike, those bookies! Crooks, every one of them...

CLÉMENTINE. Who are you telling!

APHRODITE. You wonder how people like that were brought up!

CLÉMENTINE, *reassuming her pose*. Well, what do you expect, my dear? They live in a different world than you and I! They're simply not our kind!

APHRODITE, *likewise*. Thank goodness!

They pause.

CLÉMENTINE, *finally breaking the uncomfortable silence*. Tell me, my dear... Your hair... It's utterly divine! Who does it, if you don't mind my asking? Du Chignon?

APHRODITE, *with a note of scorn*. Du Chignon? Heavens, no... Le Coiffenard, of course!

CLÉMENTINE, *admiringly*. Le Coiffenard himself?

APHRODITE. Oh, absolutely! I wouldn't let anybody else touch my hair! You know what butchers they all are nowadays! No taste, no style...

CLÉMENTINE, *self-consciously fingering her own coiffure, somewhat abashed*. Well, not all of them...

APHRODITE. Besides, he knows my taste in hats. I never have to tell him: "A little more in front... More this... More that..." He has an extinctive feeling for that sort of thing...

CLÉMENTINE. Yes, no doubt...

APHRODITE. Because, you know... It's like the old Chinese adverb says... "A hat is only as pretty as the hair it sits on!"

CLÉMENTINE. I know! That's so true!

APHRODITE. Like the one I wore tonight... An original Fifi Latour...

CLÉMENTINE, *impressed*. No! Really?

APHRODITE. An exclusive! You've got to see it to believe it!

CLÉMENTINE. Oh, I'd love to! Can I... (*Correcting herself.*) May I?... (*Casually.*) They're both correct...

APHRODITE. Please! I insist... Wait here... I'll be right back!

She exits quickly, down right.

CLÉMENTINE, *watching as she leaves, sighing.* Now that's what you call a society lady! Talk about class!... And chic?... (*With a gesture of admiration.*) Pfff!

POMPE-NICOLE *enters, upstage.*

POMPE-NICOLE, *moving down left, to* CLÉMENTINE. Well, everything is ready! The menu... The champagne... (*Rubbing his hands.*) Perfect! You're going to love it!

CLÉMENTINE. Oh, I'm sure...

POMPE-NICOLE. Now then, I'd like you to meet my friend... My dear friend, Monsieur... (*He turns around as if to introduce them.*) Where did he go? He was right behind me... (*Moving upstage, at the door, calling.*) Come in... Come in... (*Jovially.*) Don't be bashful!

BORDELEAU *enters.*

BORDELEAU, *at the door, laughing.* Me? Bashful?

He and POMPE-NICOLE *stride downstage.*

POMPE-NICOLE, *to* CLÉMENTINE, *who is demurely looking in the opposite direction.* My love, I'd like you to meet—

CLÉMENTINE, *turning, with a start.* Bordeleau!

BORDELEAU, *agape.* Clémentine!

POMPE-NICOLE, *surprised.* You... you know each other?

BORDELEAU, *ignoring* POMPE-NICOLE, *to* CLÉMENTINE, *angrily.* What are you doing here?

CLÉMENTINE, *furious.* What am *I* doing... What am *I*... Oh no! Really! That's the limit!... What am *I*—

BORDELEAU. So! This is how you take care of your sick old aunt!

POMPE-NICOLE, *startled.* What?

BORDELEAU. I should have known!

CLÉMENTINE, *nose to nose with* BORDELEAU. *You* should have known? Don't make me laugh! I suppose you're going to tell me you're not here with some woman!

BORDELEAU. Never mind who I'm here with! You're a fine one to talk! You're... (*Pointing an accusing finger at* POMPE-NICOLE.) You're here with him, damn it!

POMPE-NICOLE, *beating a hasty retreat, down right, behind the canape.* Not at all! Not at all! Don't jump to conclusions!

BORDELEAU, *to* POMPE-NICOLE, *angrily.* "Conclusions" my foot! What kind of a fool do you take me for? You... You...

POMPE-NICOLE. Please... I assure you...

BORDELEAU. Poaching on my preserves...

POMPE-NICOLE. What?

BORDELEAU. Fishing in my waters... You! (*Pointing to* CLÉMENTINE.) Here, with her!

POMPE-NICOLE. Poaching...? Fishing...? Really, I—

BORDELEAU. Well, you'll hear from me, monsieur! My seconds will visit you in the morning!

POMPE-NICOLE. Your seconds? Your... No, really—

APHRODITE *enters suddenly, down right, holding her hat on her head.*

APHRODITE. There! Isn't it stunning?... (*Noticing* POMPE-NICOLE, *with a start.*) Oh!

She stops short in front of the canape.

POMPE-NICOLE. Aphrodite!

APHRODITE. Pompe-Nicole!

BORDELEAU *and* CLÉMENTINE, *looking at each other in amazement.* What?

POMPE-NICOLE, *to* APHRODITE. What are you doing here? You're supposed to be in Versailles?

APHRODITE, *bumbling.* I... I... (*Regaining her composure.*) Me?... (*Furious.*) Oh! You swine!... You're... (*Pointing to* CLÉMENTINE.) You're here with her, aren't you?

POMPE-NICOLE. I... I... (*Suddenly realizing the awful truth.*) Oh no! I don't believe it! You... (*Pointing to* BORDELEAU.) And him... You mean... Oh! (*Glowering, to* APHRODITE.) You... (*To* BORDELEAU.) You...

APHRODITE, *still in front of the canape, glowering, to* POMPE-NICOLE. You... (*To* CLÉMENTINE.) You...

POMPE-NICOLE, *crossing left, to* BORDELEAU. You'll hear from me, monsieur!

BORDELEAU. Fine! The sooner the better!

They move upstage, gesticulating and exchanging threats.

APHRODITE, *crossing left, to* CLÉMENTINE, *still downstage.* You... you... (*Menacingly.*) I'll teach you to steal my man...

CLÉMENTINE. Me? Steal *your* man... You... you bag!

APHRODITE. You tramp!

CLÉMENTINE. You slut!

They continue to have at one another—verbally and physically—adding to the uproar of the continuing argument between POMPE-NICOLE *and* BORDELEAU. *As the commotion reaches its peak,* ALBERT *and* PHILOMÈLE *come running in, upstage. He is carrying a soup tureen, and she, a bottle of champagne.*

ALBERT. What in the name of...

PHILOMÈLE. What's the matter?

ALBERT *hurriedly sets the tureen down on the sideboard.* PHILOMÈLE *puts the champagne in the wine-cooler.*

ALBERT, *to* POMPE-NICOLE *and* BORDELEAU. Please... Gentlemen... (*Moving downstage to* CLÉMENTINE *and* APHRODITE, *trying to separate them.*) Ladies... Please... (*To* CLÉMENTINE.) Madame... (*Suddenly recognizing her.*) Clémentine!

CLÉMENTINE, *startled.* Albert!

She runs off, upstage.

PHILOMÈLE, *up left.* What on earth...

ALBERT. How the devil... (*Turning around, finding himself face to face with* APHRODITE.) Aphrodite!

APHRODITE, *no less startled.* Albert!

She too runs off, upstage.

ALBERT, *in a panic.* Good God! Let me out of here!

He dashes out, down right.

PHILOMÈLE, *following him.* Albert! What's the matter?... Albert!... Albert!...

She exits, still calling after him, as POMPE-NICOLE *and* BORDELEAU *watch in utter confusion.*

POMPE-NICOLE, *hands on hips.* Now what was all that about?

BORDELEAU. Damned if I know!

They look at each other for a moment, in silence, then both burst out laughing.

POMPE-NICOLE, *holding out his arms.* Bordeleau...

BORDELEAU, *likewise.* Pompe-Nicole...

They embrace, still laughing.

POMPE-NICOLE, *moving down left.* To think, we were ready to fight a duel over those two!

BORDELEAU, *following him.* Over a pair like that!

POMPE-NICOLE. Our society ladies!

BORDELEAU, *laughing.* Well, just between you and me, old boy, mine isn't really very high society!

POMPE-NICOLE, *laughing.* No... Neither is mine!

BORDELEAU. In fact, no society at all!

POMPE-NICOLE, *with a broad wink.* You mean... under the lamppost?

BORDELEAU. Under the lamppost... And yours?

POMPE-NICOLE. The same!... (*Wryly.*) Well, probably not the same lamppost!

BORDELEAU. No, I don't suppose...

They look at each other and burst out laughing again.

POMPE-NICOLE, *holding out his arms.* Bordeleau...

BORDELEAU, *likewise.* Pompe-Nicole...

They embrace. After a moment, ALBERT *enters, down right, with* PHILO-MÈLE *on his heels.*

ALBERT, *to* POMPE-NICOLE. Monsieur... (*To* BORDELEAU.) Monsieur... I'm afraid the ladies have left...

BORDELEAU. Yes! So it seems!

POMPE-NICOLE. What happened, Albert? What got into you all of a sudden?

PHILOMÈLE, *to* POMPE-NICOLE. Maybe monsieur can get him to talk! I can't get a word out of him!

POMPE-NICOLE, *to* ALBERT. Do you know Aphrodite?

BORDELEAU, *to* ALBERT. Do you know Clémentine?

ALBERT. Know them? (*Sighing.*) I'm afraid so... They're... (*He glances back and forth at a confused and anxious* PHILOMÈLE.) They were... They're... (*Resigning himself.*) They used to be my wives!

POMPE-NICOLE. No!

PHILOMÈLE, *with a start.* Your wives?

POMPE-NICOLE, *laughing, to* ALBERT, *as a puzzled* BORDELEAU *looks on.* You mean, those two...

PHILOMÈLE, *to* ALBERT. Your... But I thought...

BORDELEAU, *to* POMPE-NICOLE. Will somebody please tell me—

POMPE-NICOLE, *to* BORDELEAU. I'll explain... I'll explain...

He takes him aside and they move upstage. During the ensuing dialogue, he explains ALBERT's *marital situation, sotto voce.*

PHILOMÈLE, *to* ALBERT, *still downstage.* How can they be? They're dead!

ALBERT, *abashed.* Not quite, my love...

PHILOMÈLE. But they must be! You're a widower!... Twice!... You told me! You're a... (*Stopping abruptly, struck by a sudden doubt.*) Aren't you?

ALBERT, *apologetically.* I'm afraid not...

PHILOMÈLE. Not even once?

ALBERT. Not even...

PHILOMÈLE. Then... (*Realizing the truth.*) Oh! That means... that means you must be divorced?

ALBERT. In a word...

PHILOMÈLE. Divorced? You?... (ALBERT *nods sheepishly.*) Both times?

ALBERT. Both times...

PHILOMÈLE, *suddenly enthusiastic.* Albert, daring! That's wonderful! You're divorced! I'm so happy!

She throws her arms around him.

ALBERT, *startled.* What?

PHILOMÈLE. Of course! What a wonderful surprise! Why didn't you tell me?

ALBERT. Why didn't I... Well, I assumed... I thought... I mean, you're so jealous and all... I... I said to myself: "She can't be jealous of my past if she thinks it's dead and buried!"

PHILOMÈLE. Don't be silly! That's not how I felt at all!

ALBERT. It's not?

PHILOMÈLE. No!... I said to myself: "If he's a widower, that means they're dead..."

ALBERT, *nodding.* True...

PHILOMÈLE, *continuing.* "And if they're dead, who knows? Maybe he still loves them!" But as long as you're divorced... Well, that means that's what you wanted... It's better than if they were dead! Don't you see?... You got rid of them... Both of them... So why should I be jealous?

ALBERT. Now why didn't I think of that?

PHILOMÈLE, *with a laugh.* Because you're not a woman, darling!

She gives him a kiss and exits, briskly, upstage.

BORDELEAU, *to* POMPE-NICOLE. I say, Pompe-Nicole... With all the excitement, we almost forgot...

POMPE-NICOLE. Forgot?

BORDELEAU. To eat, old boy! To eat... (*Motioning* POMPE-NICOLE *to the table.*) After you...

POMPE-NICOLE. With pleasure!

They sit down at the table, across from each other, facing the wings.

BORDELEAU, *calling.* Albert! The first course!

ALBERT, *moving upstage.* Right away, monsieur! (*He serves two bowls of soup from the tureen on the sideboard.*) Vichyssoise Dominique...

BORDELEAU *and* POMPE-NICOLE *tuck in their napkins and begin to eat.*

BORDELEAU, *smacking his lips.* Excellent!

POMPE-NICOLE. Superb!

BORDELEAU, *to* ALBERT. Your wives don't know what they're missing, Albert!

They all laugh, as ALBERT *serves the champagne.*

POMPE-NICOLE, *after a moment, rather wistfully, to* BORDELEAU. All things considered, I'd say we've been served up some wild goose, Bordeleau!

BORDELEAU. Wild geese, old boy! Wild geese...

POMPE-NICOLE. And they led us a merry chase!

BORDELEAU. Well, we'll just keep on chasing. You can bet they won't go far!

POMPE-NICOLE. Not very!... They never do!

ALBERT, *behind the table, putting down the bottle.* Pardon the indiscretion, but... (*Turning to* BORDELEAU.) Did I understand monsieur... (*Turning to* POMPE-NICOLE.) and monsieur... to say that they intend to continue pursuing my wives?

POMPE-NICOLE. Well...

BORDELEAU. Only if you're sure you don't mind, Albert...

ALBERT, *to* BORDELEAU. Me? Mind?... Not at all! As long as they know what they're letting themselves in for...

BORDELEAU, *laughing.* Oh, we do, Albert!

POMPE-NICOLE, *laughing.* We do!

ALBERT, *replacing the bottle in the wine-cooler, nodding.* Yes, I daresay... (*Moving downstage.*) I daresay... (*Watching* BORDELEAU *and* POMPE-NICOLE *eat, suddenly struck by a realization, aside.*) Oh my! Look at that! It's two after all!... Technically speaking, I know... But still... (*Sighing.*) Well, I guess that means I lose my ten thousand!... Now if only I can remember to pay myself in the morning...

CURTAIN

THE BOOR HUG

•

Les Pavés de l'ours

CHARACTERS

Flugel

Casimir Ferret

Mimi

Madame Prévallon

The salon-dining room in CASIMIR FERRET's *bachelor apartment, elegantly carpeted and furnished. Upstage center, a double door opening out on a vestibule. In front of it, a small rug. Upstage right, a door, to the study; next to it, downstage, a fireplace. On the mantle, an ashtray, a statuette of a nude Diana, and a framed photo of a woman. Over the fireplace, a picture of "Leda and the Swan." Near the study door, a small square table, with two chairs facing each other, left and right. On the table, two place settings—plates, silverware, glasses, and napkins—a bowl of salad, a carving knife and fork, and a bottle of wine. Near the fireplace, a love seat and an end table. Upstage left, a sideboard. On it, several plates, napkins, an empty serving platter, oil and vinegar cruets, salt and pepper shakers, and an atomizer. Downstage left, a door leading to the washroom. Close by, a writing desk, and an armchair facing the wall, with* CASIMIR's *suit jacket draped over the back. Near the writing desk, a wastebasket. Other furniture—lamps, pictures, bric-a-brac, etc.—ad lib.*

At rise, CASIMIR, *in his shirtsleeves, is seated at his desk, down left, writing.*

CASIMIR *reading aloud as he writes.* "Alas, Mimi dearest, there are times in a man's life when he finds he must sacrifice his happiness to his duty..." *(Rereading.)* "... sacrifice his happiness to his duty..." *(Nodding.)* Good... "But difficult though it may be..." *(He puts the tip of his pen to his lips, gazes at the ceiling for a moment, then continues.)* "... there comes a time... *(He stops.)* No, no! That's awful! *(Rereading.)* "... there are *times* in a man's life... there comes a *time*..." *(He crumples up the paper and throws it in the basket.)* Damn! Some letters are just impossible to write! *(He takes a new sheet and begins again.)* "Alas, Mimi dearest, there are times in a man's life..."

The door, up center, opens suddenly and MIMI *appears, carrying a military uniform—blue coat, red trousers—and a pair of boots.*

MIMI, *entering.* All done, darling!

CASIMIR, *with a start.* Mimi! (*He throws down the pen and jumps to his feet.*) Already?

He hides the letter behind his back.

MIMI, *holding out the uniform.* There wasn't much to do. Just a few loose buttons and a couple of seams...

CASIMIR, *nodding, awkwardly.* Aha!

MIMI, *holding out the boots.* And I even polished your boots. They were simply filthy!

CASIMIR, *turning aside and stuffing the letter into his trouser pocket as inconspicuously as possible.* Fine!... That's just fine!

MIMI, *noticing his embarrassment.* Casimir?

CASIMIR. Yes, love?

MIMI. Are you hiding something?

CASIMIR, *ingenuously.* Hiding something?... What would I be hiding?

MIMI. What you were writing... Just now, when I came in...

CASIMIR, *feigning innocence.* Oh!... Oh that!... No, no... I'm not hiding it... I... I just put it in my pocket, that's all...

MIMI. You mean, so I wouldn't see it?

CASIMIR, *bumbling.* Right... That's right...

MIMI. Because?...

CASIMIR. Because?... Because it's for you, that's why...

MIMI, *with a note of good-natured sarcasm.* Of course! Now why didn't I think of that!

CASIMIR. You understand?

MIMI. Perfectly! You say it's for me, but you don't want me to see it. (*Laughing.*) Who wouldn't understand a simple thing like that?

CASIMIR. It's... it's just that... there are certain times, Mimi, when you can't say what you want... Face to face, I mean... And so, instead, you write it...

MIMI. Good! Then let me read it!

CASIMIR, *recoiling.* Read it?... Just like that?... No, no! Certainly not! It's... it's not finished.

MIMI. Oh?

CASIMIR. No... I... I write these things in a... a burst of passion, and they have to be polished, and... and... You know, it takes time...

MIMI, *wheedling*. Casimir, you naughty boy! (*She goes over and kisses him on the forehead.*) I do believe you want to surprise me, now don't you?

CASIMIR, *noncommittal*. Well...

MIMI. Never you mind, darling. I understand...

CASIMIR. You do?

MIMI. And I promise I'll be surprised tomorrow. Really I will.

CASIMIR. Tomorrow? What's tomorrow?

MIMI. That's all right... You don't have to pretend. I won't spoil your fun. I only turn twenty-two once, after all...

CASIMIR. Twenty... Oh!... Oh, you mean your birthday...

MIMI, *putting her finger to her lips, smiling*. Shhh! Please! Not a word. I'm supposed to be surprised!

CASIMIR. Twenty-two, did you say? I... I thought that was last year...

MIMI. Well... Maybe... Sometimes I lose track... (*Laughing.*) We women aren't like you soldiers, darling. Our active service only counts half, you know! (CASIMIR *gives a nervous little laugh.*) Which reminds me... (*She puts his boots down next to the writing desk and holds out his uniform.*) I hope this is going to be all right...

CASIMIR. Oh, I'm sure...

MIMI, *handing him the coat*. I want my general to look his best when he's out on maneuvers.

CASIMIR, *laughing*. Sergeant, love! Sergeant... And we don't do many maneuvers in the Quartermaster Corps... (*He tries on the coat.*) I'll probably spend my month at a desk, like every summer...

MIMI. Well, whatever you do, you're a hero. I just know it.

CASIMIR, *smiling*. Yes... A fat hero, I'm afraid! (*Feeling the snug fit of the coat.*) Gone are the days when this would fit me like a glove!

MIMI, *handing him the trousers*. Now, now, darling... You're going to look just fine!

CASIMIR *holds the trousers up to his waist.*

CASIMIR, *shaking his head*. Oh well...

MIMI. Tsk tsk! You vain thing, you! (*She kisses him on the forehead.*) There!... I've got to run...

She moves up center, toward the door.

CASIMIR. What?... Wait a minute! What about lunch? I thought—

MIMI. I know, I know... That's why I have to run... I forgot the dessert...

CASIMIR. Aha!

MIMI, *looking at her watch.* One o'clock... They'll be sending up the squab in about fifteen minutes. I have just enough time...

CASIMIR. Squab?

MIMI. Yes... I thought, for a change... With a lovely pâté...

CASIMIR. Efficiency, thy name is Mimi!

MIMI, *smiling.* How's that?

CASIMIR. You certainly know how to run a man's life! (*Holding out the trousers.*) His clothes... his meals...

MIMI, *taking a few steps toward him.* Well, I'm glad you finally noticed. (*Laughing.*) Maybe now you'll make an honest woman of me, after all these years!

CASIMIR, *shaking his head and wagging his finger.* Tsk tsk tsk! What I mean is, I don't know why I bother to hire a servant. With a woman like you—

MIMI, *with good-natured sarcasm.* Why, thank you, I'm sure! If you think I enjoy it... It's about time you found someone to take Etienne's place. It's been weeks since you fired him.

CASIMIR. As a matter of fact... Now that you mention it, someone's coming in today.

MIMI. Oh?

CASIMIR. And believe me, I won't make the same mistake twice. I never should have hired that... that blabbermouth in the first place. He's just like all the help you get in Paris nowadays... Too smart for their own good... Can't mind their own business or keep their big mouths shut! And a pack of liars to boot!

MIMI. And this new one?

CASIMIR. Well, he's no Etienne, I can guarantee you!

MIMI. That's a start!

CASIMIR. For one thing, he's not from Paris.

MIMI. Oh?

CASIMIR. No he's from the country... Outside of Strasbourg... My friend says he's a regular diamond in the rough. Not too much up here... (*He taps his forehead.*) But that's just fine with me... He might not do everything right, but at least he won't do anything wrong.

MIMI, *laughing.* Let's hope...

CASIMIR, *taking off the coat.* I'll train him just the way I want him. Too dumb to be dishonest, for a change...

MIMI. Well, we'll see... (*Looking at her watch.*) Oh my, I've really got to run!

CASIMIR, *handing her the coat and trousers.* Here, would you leave these in my room on your way out...

MIMI, *kissing him on the forehead.* Bye bye!

She takes the uniform and dashes out, up center. CASIMIR *sits down at his writing desk, lights a cigarette, takes the letter out of his pocket, picks up his pen, and gets ready to continue where he left off.*

CASIMIR, *rereading.* "Alas, Mimi dearest, there are times in a man's life..." (*He muses briefly, then writes.*) "... when he finds he must sacrifice his happiness to his duty..." (*Nodding.*) That much was all right. It's what comes next... (*The doorbell rings.*) Now who the devil... Don't tell me he's here already!... Well... (*He puts down the pen, stands up, and moves upstage, shaking his head.*) Very nice! Here I am opening the door for my help!

He exits, leaving the door open.

FLUGEL'S VOICE, *with a thick German accent.* Casimir Ferret? Dat's right, ya? Dat's you?

CASIMIR'S VOICE. Quite! And you're—

FLUGEL'S VOICE. Ach! A real pleasure, believe me!

CASIMIR'S VOICE, *approaching.* Yes... Come right this way...

They appear at the door together. FLUGEL *elbows his way in first.*

FLUGEL, *impressed by the elegance.* Ach! So fine!...

CASIMIR, *following him in, a little flustered.* I beg your—

FLUGEL. Mein Gott! So fine!... (*Looking all around.*) A real palace you got here!

CASIMIR, *laughing in spite of himself, aside.* Simple soul! (*To* FLUGEL.) I'm glad you like it.

FLUGEL. Like? Like? Such a place!... Who vouldn't like?

CASIMIR, *smiling.* Thank you... (*Pointing to his muddy tracks.*) But at least you could have wiped your feet, don't you think?

FLUGEL. Mein feet? Vat you talking? I vash in de river, two days ago just.

CASIMIR. No, no! I mean your boots! You should have wiped them on the mat. That's what it's there for!

FLUGEL. Ach, so?... Vell, if you say...

He wipes his boots vigorously on the rug in front of the door, up center.

CASIMIR, *startled.* What are you... Not there, for heaven's sake!

FLUGEL. But you tell me—

CASIMIR. The mat!... I said "the mat!"... (*Pointing.*) Outside!... Not the rug!

FLUGEL, *shrugging*. Rug, mat... Mat, rug... Who's to know?

He turns to leave.

CASIMIR, *calling him back*. Never mind! It's too late now! The damage is done! (*Aside.*) "Diamond in the rough" is right!

He goes over to the fireplace and puts out his cigarette in the ashtray on the mantle.

FLUGEL, *following him, looking on in surprise*. Vat... Look vat you doing! Cigarette butts in a dish yet? Vat kind a ting...

CASIMIR, *shaking his head, smiling, aside*. Incredible! (*To* FLUGEL, *very patiently.*) Look... let me explain... This is not a dish...

FLUGEL, *gawking, quizzically*. Nein? It looks just like...

CASIMIR. Yes, well... it's an ashtray... "Ash," understand? What cigarettes and cigars turn into... That's what it's for...

FLUGEL. Ach, so?

CASIMIR, *going to the rug and picking up a few bits of the debris from* FLUGEL's *boots, and putting them in the ashtray*. And for any other filth that doesn't belong on my floor!

FLUGEL. Ya, ya! I see vat you mean... Dat's real glass you bet!

CASIMIR, *smiling*. Better than glass... It's the finest crystal...

FLUGEL. Nein, nein! I mean glass... real high glass, vat you do...

CASIMIR, *suddenly understanding, laughing*. Oh, oh... Well, hardly high class... Just plain neat, that's all! (*He puts the ashtray back on the mantle and crosses over to the writing desk.*) Look, my good man... I have to finish a very important letter. (*Sitting down.*) You make yourself comfortable, and I'll be with you in a few minutes.

FLUGEL. Please... No hurry... De whole day I got...

He begins walking around, inspecting the room.

CASIMIR, *turning his back, rereading*. "Alas, Mimi dearest, there are times in a man's life when he finds he must sacrifice his happiness to his duty..."

FLUGEL, *nodding, with conviction*. Ya, ya! Dat's good!

CASIMIR, *wheeling around*. I beg your pardon!

FLUGEL. Like in church it sounds... (CASIMIR *gives him an exasperated look.*) "Times in a man's life of sacred vice, for happiness und duty..." Ya, dat's pretty! Like a berry bowl a little... Sehr schön!

CASIMIR, *puzzled*. Like a what?

FLUGEL. A berry bowl... De kind vat's in de Bible all over... Pretty names vat don't mean notting... Like de "Proud Eagle's Son," und de "Good Summer Tan," und—

CASIMIR, *in a flash of comprehension, smiling.* "Parable," my friend!... You mean a "parable"!

FLUGEL. A pair vat?

CASIMIR, *enunciating.* A "pa-ra-ble"...

FLUGEL, *smiling.* Vat you talking? Vat means a shtupid ting like dat?... "Berry bowl," I'm telling you... Dat means at least someting...

CASIMIR, *resigned, nodding.* Fine! Have it your way... Just be quiet, please, and let me finish this letter... (*He turns his back, rereads the last phrase.*) "... when he finds he must sacrifice his happiness to his duty..." (*He agonizes in silence for a few moments.*) Damn!... (*Writing.*) "I've given you ample proof of my affection ..."

FLUGEL, *at the fireplace, pricking up his ears, aside.* Hoo-hah! A voman I shmell in dat letter I bet!

CASIMIR, *rereading.* "... ample proof of my affection..."

FLUGEL, *pointing to the picture of "Leda and the Swan" over the mantle, to* CASIMIR. Dis is de vun, maybe?

CASIMIR, *annoyed, looking at him over his shoulder.* What?

FLUGEL. Dis is de voman vat you give her your infection? (CASIMIR *leers.*) Dis voman in de picture, vat's plucking a goose on her lap, mitout no clothes so she vouldn't get all dirty...

CASIMIR, *half angry, half amused.* That's "Leda and the Swan," you... "Leda..." (*With a wave of the hand, resigning himself.*) Oh, forget it!

He gets back to his letter, staring off into space for inspiration. FLUGEL *meanwhile, continues inspecting the objects on the mantle for a few moments.*

FLUGEL, *pointing to the statuette of Diana.* So dis is de vun den?

CASIMIR. Now what?

FLUGEL, *picking up the statuette and holding it out.* Dis vun here?

CASIMIR, *throwing down his pen.* In the first place, that's the goddess Diana! The Roman goddess, understand? I've never met her! (*Wryly.*) And I don't expect I ever will...

FLUGEL. Vell, dese days you couldn't tell. Paris is full mit all kinds foreigners...

CASIMIR. And in the second place, I wish you would mind your own business and stop interrupting me. I've got to finish this letter, and I don't have much time. Now please... I'm having enough trouble as it is.

FLUGEL. Ach, so! You shouldn't mind me...

He sits on the love seat, down right, and makes himself comfortable.

CASIMIR, *rereading.* "I've given you ample proof of my affection..." (*Musing out loud.*) "But due to circumstances beyond my control..." No, no... "But now, pressing problems..." (*He shakes his head.*) "As God is my witness..." (*Nodding.*) Yes, that has a nice ring... (*Writing.*) "As God is my witness, there is no force on earth that could tear me from you..."

He rereads the last few sentences in silence. Meanwhile, FLUGEL *has taken out his pipe and lit it.*

FLUGEL, *puffing, with a sigh of contentment.* Ah!

CASIMIR, *writing.* "But alas, I am not the master of my fate..." (*He nods with satisfaction.*) "Our idyllic existence must come to an end..."

FLUGEL *clears his throat, goes to spit, and looks around the floor for an appropriate receptacle. Not finding one, he gets up, goes to the fireplace, picks up the ashtray, and spits into it.*

FLUGEL. Such a ting!

CASIMIR, *rereading.* "But alas, I am not the master of my fate. Our idyllic existence must come to an end..." (*Tapping the table with his pen, reflecting.*) Now why? That's the problem... (*After a few moments, struck by an inspiration.*) Ah! (*Writing.*) "Financial reverses leave me no other choice. The injudicious investment of all my worldly wealth..."

FLUGEL, *spitting again, contemplating the ashtray.* So little!

CASIMIR. "... has left me in utterly destitute straits..." (*Dramatically, as he writes.*) "Yes, dearest, I am ruined!"

FLUGEL, *overhearing, putting his pipe down on the mantle.* Vat? Ruined?... You?

CASIMIR, *throwing down his pen.* I beg your... (*Impatiently.*) Please!

FLUGEL. Because, if dat's so... If you don't got no money...

CASIMIR. I have plenty of money, if that's any concern of yours!

FLUGEL. But you said... (*Pointing to the letter.*) Vat you vas writing...

CASIMIR. I am writing a business letter. (*Emphasizing.*) *My* business, understand? Not yours!

FLUGEL, *good-naturedly.* So?... Funny business, you mean... A joke maybe, ya?

CASIMIR, *agreeing, to end the discussion.* Right, right... A joke...

FLUGEL. Ach, sehr gut! Dat's better... Because I tink, vat a shame for a nice man like you... (CASIMIR *nods.*) Und besides, mitout no money you vouldn't got notting to pay me, und so...

He shrugs.

CASIMIR. Thank you. I'm touched!

He turns back, picks up his pen, and rereads what he has written, in silence.

FLUGEL, *with a wave of the hand.* But as long you tell me dat's a joke only...

He leans up against the mantle, takes his pipe, and continues smoking.

CASIMIR, *writing.* "I have no right to ask you to share my life of woe..." (*He thinks for a moment.*) "Nor would I allow it, however you might insist..." (*Sitting back.*) Better throw that in, just to play safe! (*Writing.*) "You are young. You are beautiful. You have your whole life ahead of you. Please, dearest, try to forget me. My one wish in life is to know that you are happy!..." (*With a smile of satisfaction.*) There! (*He puts down the pen and takes out his billfold.*) Now a handful of bills, to soften the blow... (*Changing his mind.*) Hmm! No... Not if I've just lost my shirt, after all... (*Putting back the billfold.*) Maybe a little poetry instead... (*Writing.*)

> "Alas, would I might leave thee more
> Than these my bitter tears galore!"

(*He wets his finger and makes a few smudges on the letter to simulate tears.*) She'll love it! (*Waving the letter to dry, singing to the melody of "The Blue Danube".*) My bi-itter tears, tra-la, tra-la... (*Writing.*) "Forever yours, Casimir."

He gives the letter a final cursory glance.

FLUGEL, *who has been listening all the while, with obvious emotion, putting down his pipe, sobbing.* Ay ay ay!

CASIMIR, *getting up.* What's the matter with you?

FLUGEL. Dat's so sad, dat letter!

CASIMIR. It's a joke, I told you!

FLUGEL, *all choked up.* Ya, ya... I know... But I tink vat it vould be if it vasn't no joke, und I... I couldn't help...

He blows his nose, wipes his eyes with his handkerchief, and gradually regains his composure.

CASIMIR, *shrugging his shoulders.* Well, don't let it bother you. (*Aside, shaking his head.*) Simple, simple, simple! (*He folds the letter, puts it in an envelope, seals it, and writes.*) "Mademoiselle Mimi Brochet"... There! (*He gives the envelope a little kiss.*) Finito! (*After a few moments, looking around and sniffing, to* FLUGEL.) What on earth is that smell?

FLUGEL, *sniffing.* Shmell?

CASIMIR, *grimacing.* Yes... Something burning... Like... like an old shoe...

FLUGEL. Nein, nein! Dat's Dagmar!

CASIMIR. Who?

FLUGEL, *picking up the pipe, taking a puff, and holding it up to him.* Dagmar! (*He takes another puff and blows the smoke in* CASIMIR'S *direction.*) De best friend vat I got!

CASIMIR, *waving the smoke away, coughing.* Well put your friend away, damn it! We don't smoke in here!

FLUGEL. Vat you talking, Casimir? (*Holding out the ashtray.*) Vat vas you doing mit your cigarette, so?

CASIMIR, *unable to believe his ears.* I beg your... What was I—

FLUGEL. Ya, ya! Ten minutes ago even!

He clears his throat and spits into the ashtray.

CASIMIR, *with a start.* Good God! What are you doing?

FLUGEL. Shpitting... Vat does it look?

CASIMIR, *at a loss for words, pointing to the ashtray.* But, but... But, but...

FLUGEL. In de dish... Like you tell me...

CASIMIR. Like I what?

FLUGEL, *nodding.* Ya! (*Ingenuously.*) Tings vat don't belong on de floor, dey go in de dish. You tell me yourself.

CASIMIR. Yes, but... That's an ashtray! You don't spit in an ashtray, for heaven's sake!

FLUGEL. Ach, so? Den vat you supposed to shpit in already?

CASIMIR. Nothing!... You aren't... You're not supposed to spit at all!

FLUGEL, *scratching his head.* Hoo-hah?

CASIMIR. I mean, not in here... Not in the apartment...

FLUGEL, *putting the ashtray back on the mantle.* So vat I do mit, if I don't shpit it out?

CASIMIR. That's your problem... You just don't spit in here, that's all!

FLUGEL, *shaking his head, knocks the ashes from his pipe into the ashtray and puts the pipe in his pocket.*

FLUGEL, *shrugging his shoulders.* Such a ting!

CASIMIR *goes over to the writing desk, lays down the letter, and puts on the suit jacket draped over the chair.*

CASIMIR. Now then... Let's get down to business... First of all, what's your name?

FLUGEL. Flugel.

CASIMIR. And you spell it?

FLUGEL. Ya, sometimes...

CASIMIR. No... I mean, how?... How do you spell it?

FLUGEL. Just de vay like it sounds. Mit two letters... A "flu" und a "gel"...
Flugel!

CASIMIR, *smiling.* Aha! Like the horn...

FLUGEL, *quizzical.* Bitte?

CASIMIR. Like "flugelhorn," only without the "horn"...

FLUGEL. Ya, ya... De "flugel" mitout de bugle...

CASIMIR. Quite!

FLUGEL. Vat's de matter, Casimir? Dey don't never learn you to shpell
ven you vas little?

CASIMIR. I beg your... (*Controlling himself.*) Look here, Flugel. Let me
make one thing clear from the start... (*Rather pompously.*) You do not ask
impertinent questions, understand? And you speak when you're spoken
to, not before! Now I don't want to have to remind you again... (*Noticing
that* FLUGEL *is laughing.*) What on earth is so funny?

FLUGEL, *holding his sides.* Ach, Casimir... I'm sorry!... It's dat silly vay
you talk! (CASIMIR *glares at him in disbelief.*) Mit dat phony accent, so!

CASIMIR. That what?

FLUGEL, *imitating him, exaggeratedly, as best he can.* "You speak when
you're spoken to, not before..."

CASIMIR. Of all the...

FLUGEL, *joining him by the writing desk.* Vy you don't talk normal, inshtead
mit a hot potato in de cheeks?... (*With his own accent.*) "You shpeak
ven you're shpoken to, not bevore..." See how simple?

CASIMIR, *shaking his head, laughing in spite of himself.* You're... you're
incredible! Simply incredible!

FLUGEL. Ha! Even you tink it's funny! You see?

CASIMIR, *laughing.* I never...

FLUGEL, *laughing along with him.* Ach, Gott! I tink I'm going to like you,
I bet!

He gives him a good-natured poke in the stomach.

CASIMIR, *suddenly serious, recoiling.* What do you think you're... Keep
your hands to yourself! (*Aside.*) A little too rough, this diamond of mine!

FLUGEL, *taken aback.* Casimir?

CASIMIR. And I'll thank you to stop calling me "Casimir," for heaven's
sake!

From the production of *The Boor Hug* at Wesleyan University, October 1980, directed by H. Stuart Shifman (photographs by Susan Dinsmore).

FLUGEL, Vy so? Dat's not your name, maybe?

CASIMIR. Of course it is! That's precisely why!... You can call me "monsieur."

FLUGEL, *naïvely.* Ach, nein! You call me "Flugel," I call you "Casimir"... So formal mit me you don't need!

CASIMIR, *sarcastically.* Thank you, I'm sure! Perhaps I "don't need!" But I'd rather, if it's all the same with you!

FLUGEL, *shrugging.* Vatever you say, Monsieur Casimir...

CASIMIR, *with a sigh of resignation.* Now look, Flugel... I'm going to hire you. But you realize you've still got an awful lot to learn, and you'll have to promise to do your best. That's all I ask...

FLUGEL. Ya, ya! (*He spits in his hand and holds it out to* CASIMIR.) Dat's a promise!

CASIMIR, *ignoring his hand.* Good!... Now the most important thing is money. You've got to watch out not to spend too much. Is that perfectly clear?

FLUGEL, *repeating his maneuver.* Ya, ya!

CASIMIR, *waving his hand away.* Never mind... I take your word... Just be careful, that's all. It's so easy to forget when you're spending someone else's.

FLUGEL. Ach, so! Mit me you shouldn't vorry, Casimir... (*Catching himself as* CASIMIR *glowers at him.*) Monsieur Casimir...

CASIMIR, *with a resigned shake of the head.* Let's hope... (*Moving up left, to the sideboard.*) Well, Flugel, I don't see why you can't start right away... As soon as you have your livery, that is...

FLUGEL. Nein, nein... Danke schön... Mein lunch I already finish.

CASIMIR. Your what?

FLUGEL, *grimacing,* Und anyvay, dat's vun ting I vouldn't never eat...

CASIMIR, *suddenly comprehending.* No, no, no! Your livery! Your uniform! Like a kind of costume... You know...

FLUGEL. I got to vear a costume?

CASIMIR. Of course you do. This is Paris, don't forget. You're not back home.

FLUGEL. Vat kind a costume yet?

CASIMIR. Well, it's blue, with gold buttons, and... You'll see... (*Pointing toward the door, up center.*) It's in my bedroom.

FLUGEL. Und I vear it all de time?

CASIMIR. You wear it while you're working.

FLUGEL. Like a party it sounds!

He turns and moves toward the door, as if about to leave.

CASIMIR. Wait a minute... You'll put it on when I'm through. I still have a few things to tell you.

He goes back to the writing desk.

FLUGEL, *following him.* So?

CASIMIR. Yes... And they're very important. For instance, when someone rings the bell, you go and open the door... Very carefully, understand? No impolite questions... You ask them their name, that's all. And if they don't want to tell you, never mind. Don't insist...

FLUGEL. Ya, ya!

CASIMIR. Now, in the morning, when the postman brings my letters and my papers, or maybe a package, you don't just bring them in and hand them to me like that... You put them on a little plate. And you say: "The mail, monsieur."

FLUGEL, *vigorously picking his nose as he listens.* A plate?

CASIMIR. I'll show you...

FLUGEL, *nodding.* Sehr gut...

CASIMIR, *trying not to lose his patience.* And for heaven's sake, Flugel! You don't stick your fingers in your nose when I'm talking to you! (FLUGEL *gives him a puzzled look.*) Or when anyone else is talking to you either!

FLUGEL. Hoo-hah!

CASIMIR. Or even when nobody is talking to you, understand?

FLUGEL. Ach, Gott! So many tings to remember!... So many!

CASIMIR. Yes, well... you try!

FLUGEL. Ya, ya! I do mein best...

CASIMIR. Good!... Now, about your wages... Fifty francs a month... (FLUGEL *nods.*) Plus your laundry...

FLUGEL, *with a wave and a shrug.* Pfff!

CASIMIR. And two meals a day...

FLUGEL, *with more enthusiasm.* So!

CASIMIR. With wine, of course...

FLUGEL. Nein!... Bock, bitte! Bock!

CASIMIR, *after a moment, understanding.* All right... Beer instead of wine...

FLUGEL. Und mein Milchkaffee in de morning?

CASIMIR, *quizzically.* Your...

FLUGEL. Milchkaffee!... Kaffee mit Milch!

CASIMIR. Aha! You mean café au lait...

FLUGEL. Dat's right... Café au lett...

CASIMIR, *correcting his pronunciation.* Au lait...

FLUGEL. Au lait, au lett... Vat difference?... I get?

CASIMIR. Yes, yes... I'm sure that can be arranged...

FLUGEL. Sehr gut! (*Going toward the door, up center.*) I go now for mein liver?

CASIMIR, *moving center stage, chuckling.* Your liver can wait! (*Pointing to the square table, up right.*) First bring that table and put it over here... with the chairs...

FLUGEL *complies.*

FLUGEL. Like so?

CASIMIR. Fine!

FLUGEL, *scratching his head, then pointing to the bowl of salad.* Und dat's all vat you eat?

CASIMIR. No, no! Don't be silly... The rest is on the way. They'll be sending it right up... We're going to have squab...

FLUGEL, *overjoyed.* Ve are? (*Knitting his brow.*) Vat's dat?

CASIMIR, *shaking his head, smiling.* Not "we," Flugel... A lady friend and myself...

FLUGEL. Ach, so... (*Pointing to the picture of* MIMI *on the mantle.*) Dat vun, maybe?

CASIMIR. Yes, as a matter of fact. If it's any of your business...

FLUGEL, *going over and picking up the picture, admiringly.* Ach du lieber! Sehr schön! Dat's vun fine hunk voman!

CASIMIR, *aside.* His eloquence overwhelms me!

FLUGEL, *with a broad wink.* You go to bett mit, ya?

CASIMIR, *abashed.* Flugel! Now really... Is that any way to—

FLUGEL. Never mind... I know vat kind tings goes on dese days... Und mit such a pretty, young vun yet... Believe me, I vouldn't blame you...

CASIMIR, *with a note of pride.* I daresay you'll find that all my lady friends are young and pretty, Flugel. But that doesn't give you the right to ask—

FLUGEL. Ya, ya! (*Holding up the picture.*) But dis vun... Hoo-hah! Dat's someting shpecial!... A shame de glass is so dirty only...

He spits on the picture several times, then goes to the table, center stage, picks up a napkin from one of the settings, and begins shining the glass.

CASIMIR, *unable to believe his eyes.* What do you think you're... Give me that!

He grabs the picture, puts it back on the mantle, then rips the napkin out of FLUGEL's *hands, goes over to the sideboard, angrily throws it down, and picks up a clean one, which he puts in its place on the table.*

FLUGEL, *puzzled.* Casimir?

CASIMIR, *struggling not to lose his aplomb.* For God's sake, don't you know the first thing about good manners?

FLUGEL. But I tought... So dirty it vas...

CASIMIR. Yes, yes, yes... (*The doorbell rings.*) There! That must be my lunch. Go let the boy in. I'll be in my study.

He goes toward the door, up right.

FLUGEL. Ya, ya! I go...

He moves to leave.

CASIMIR, *stopping him.* Oh, and... (*Pointing to his boots, next to the writing desk.*) Bring me my boots when you get a minute, Flugel.

He goes toward the door, up right.

FLUGEL. Sehr gut, sehr gut...

CASIMIR, *shaking his head, aside.* He's going to be harder to train than I thought!

He exits, up right. FLUGEL *goes and picks up the boots, then exits, up center. The stage is empty for a few moments.*

FLUGEL'S VOICE, *approaching.* So who you vant to see already?

MADAME PRÉVALLON'S VOICE, *stammering.* M-monsieur... M-monsieur...

FLUGEL'S VOICE. Ya, ya! Monsieur who?

MADAME PRÉVALLON *strides in, followed by* FLUGEL, *still carrying the boots.*

MADAME PRÉVALLON. M-monsieur Ca-ca... Ca-ca... Ca-ca...

FLUGEL, *gawking.* Vat? Vat kind talk...

MADAME PRÉVALLON. M-monsieur Ca-casimir Fe-ferret!

FLUGEL. Ach, so! Casimir!... So vy you don't tell me... (*Brusquely.*) Und vat's your name, voman?

MADAME PRÉVALLON, *shocked.* I b-beg y-your p-pardon!

FLUGEL. Bitte?

MADAME PRÉVALLON. Just who-who... who-who... who-who...

FLUGEL. Hoo-hah!

MADAME PRÉVALLON. Just who-who d-do you th-think y-you are?

FLUGEL. Nein! Dat's vat I ask you, remember?

MADAME PRÉVALLON. Y-young m-man! I am M-madame de Pré-pré-pré-va-vallon!

FLUGEL, *naïvely.* Matame Prépréprévavallon?

MADAME PRÉVALLON. N-n-n-n-n-no! (*Making a supreme effort, articulating slowly.* Pré-val-lon, ni-nin-com-poop!

FLUGEL. So, Matame Prévallon-Ninincompoop... A big difference dat makes!

MADAME PRÉVALLON, *fuming with frustration.* Oh!

FLUGEL. Und you come to see Casimir?... Casimir Ferret?

MADAME PRÉVALLON. Y-yes! N-n-now an-n-nou... an-n-nou... an-n-nounce me, y-you...

FLUGEL, *confidentially.* Listen, don't vaste your time. (*With a wave of the hand.*) Mit you he vouldn't go to bett, believe me—

MADAME PRÉVALLON, *nonplussed.* Wh-wh-what?

FLUGEL. Comes here for Casimir only young und pretty ladies!... Maybe try next door better...

MADAME PRÉVALLON, *livid with rage, stamping her foot.* Oh!... Ca-ca... Ca-ca... Ca-ca... Ca-ca...

FLUGEL. Vat, again?

MADAME PRÉVALLON. Ca-casimir has s-seen the l-last of m-me!

FLUGEL. Ya, ya!

MADAME PRÉVALLON. And m-m-my B-ba-bette t-too!

FLUGEL. Ya, ya, ya!

She storms out, up center, and slams the door.

FLUGEL, *calling after her through the closed door.* Your bett!... Ha ha!... In your bett he vouldn't be caught dead already! (*Shaking his head, laughing.*) Young und pretty!... Gott in Himmel! (*Realizing that he is still holding the boots, he moves toward the study door, up right, stops, reflects for a moment, goes to the table and takes a plate, and sets the boots on it with an air of evident satisfaction.*) So!

CASIMIR *opens the door, up right, and appears at the threshold.*

CASIMIR. Flugel! What about my boots?

FLUGEL, *presenting them.* Ya, ya, Casimir... Here! Just like you tell me...

CASIMIR, *with a start.* On a plate? You... Give me those!

He grabs the boots, disappears back into his study, and returns a few seconds later without them.

FLUGEL, *abashed, gazing at the plate in his hands.* But... You said—

CASIMIR, *pulling the plate away from him, going to the sideboard and exchanging it for a clean one.* Never mind what I said. Anyone with half a brain...

He puts the clean plate on the table.

FLUGEL. I tought...

CASIMIR, *looking around.* All right, where is it?... Where's my lunch?

FLUGEL. Your lunch?

CASIMIR. Yes... Wasn't that the boy with my lunch at the door?

FLUGEL. Nein, nein... Some crazy old lady it vas, vat talks funny... I kick her out good!

CASIMIR, *suspecting.* Oh no!... Not...

FLUGEL. Matame Préprépré... someting.

CASIMIR, *jumping.* Good God! (*Aside.*) Babette's mother!... My Babette!... (*To* FLUGEL.) You kicked her out?

FLUGEL. Ya, ya! She vouldn't bodder you no more, don't vorry!

CASIMIR, *in a rage.* You... you imbecile!... You idiot! You... (*Wringing his hands.*) Madame Prévallon!... Babette!...

FLUGEL, *taken aback, aside.* Vat's mit him all of a sudden?

CASIMIR. How... how could you?... Madame Prévallon!... She'll be fit to be tied!

FLUGEL. But you tell me, comes here only young und pretty ladies... Und dis vun... (*Grimacing.*) Yechhh!

CASIMIR, *pacing back and forth.* Oh, quiet, you... you... (*Aside.*) What on earth am I going to tell her? (*To* FLUGEL, *who has been looking on, uncomprehending.*) Do you realize what you've done?

FLUGEL, *with a glimmer of pride.* Ach, ya! You vouldn't see her no more. Dat's vat she said.

CASIMIR, *groaning.* Oh...

FLUGEL, *laughing.* Und her bett you vouldn't see no more neither! (*Waving his hand.*) Ha ha! You should care! Her bett!... I fix it good, ya?

CASIMIR. Oh yes! You fixed it fine! Just fine!... You're not even here half an hour, and already you've practically destroyed my love life!

The doorbell rings.

FLUGEL, *scratching his head.* I done vat, Casimir?

CASIMIR. Never mind, never mind!... Go see who's at the door!

FLUGEL. Ya, ya! (*Perplexed, aside.*) Vat he could vant mit an old goat like dat?

He shrugs his shoulders and hurries out, up center, leaving the door open.

CASIMIR, *pacing.* A nice mess he's gotten me into, that idiot!

He keeps pacing, obviously distraught.

FLUGEL'S VOICE, *offstage, shouting.* Vat? How much?... For dat?... Und dis piece shvill, how much yet?... Hoo-hah!... You tink here it grows maybe money on trees?...

The outside door is heard to slam shut.

CASIMIR, *stopping in his tracks, up center, listening.* God in heaven! What now? (*Calling out the open door.*) Flugel!... Flugel!...

FLUGEL, *entering, slapping his hands together, up and down, as if to say "That's that!"* I show him, dat bummer! Dat tief!

CASIMIR. Who?... What?...

FLUGEL. Six francs for a chicken... (*Holding out a fist.*) Big like mein fist, so... Und vat's dead from old age yet!

CASIMIR. You mean, the boy with my lunch?

FLUGEL. Ya, ya!... Und five francs for some brown shtuff vat shtinks, vat he calls "putty... putty mit troubles."

CASIMIR. Pâte... pâté...

FLUGEL. Ha! Mit troubles who needs?...

CASIMIR. Truffles, you idiot!

FLUGEL. ... und vat even to de pigs I vouldn't feed!

CASIMIR, *looking around.* So? Where is it? Where's my lunch?

FLUGEL. Vat you talking, Casimir?... You tell me vatch de money, de most important ting. So de money I vatch! Flugel vouldn't let nobody cheat you, don't worry! At home you get a chicken vat's a chicken, not a pigeon. Und it vouldn't cost an arm und a leg, Gott in Himmel!... I kick him out, de shvindler!

CASIMIR. You kicked him... (*Sarcastically.*) Is that all you can do? Kick people out?

FLUGEL, *taking him literally.* Nein, nein! I could clean, und cook, und do de dishes...

CASIMIR. Yes, well... Thanks to you there may not be any dishes...

FLUGEL. Never mind, Casimir. Better you go hungry dan you should pay for such shvill...

CASIMIR. Oh really? Well, if it's all the same with you... Now you get yourself downstairs this minute. There's a shop around the corner... You can buy a cold roast chicken or something.

FLUGEL. Ya, ya!

CASIMIR. And for heaven's sake, get dressed! Your supposed to be in livery! How many times do I have to tell you?

FLUGEL, *moving toward the door, up center, confused.* Ach! Put on mein chicken und buy a roast liver... Nein, put on mein liver und buy a roast chicken... Mein Gott! In dis house gives so much to remember!

The doorbell rings.

CASIMIR, *sharply*. And answer the door!

FLUGEL. Ya, ya! I go... I go...

He runs out, leaving the door open.

CASIMIR, *shaking his head*. Simply incredible!

He goes over and sits down at his writing desk, fanning himself with the letter. A moment later, FLUGEL comes bounding back in.

FLUGEL. It's de lover lady, Casimir. (CASIMIR *throws down the letter and jumps to his feet as* MIMI *enters, carrying a package.*) De vun vat you go to bett mit... on de mantle...

MIMI, *overhearing, aghast*. What?

CASIMIR. Flugel!

FLUGEL. From de picture I could tell...

CASIMIR, *flustered, to* FLUGEL. Is that any way to... (*To* MIMI.) Mimi... Please... You'll have to excuse him... He's—

MIMI, *eyeing* FLUGEL, *nodding*. Your diamond in the rough! I know...

FLUGEL, *to* CASIMIR. I go now, ya?

CASIMIR *nods*.

MIMI, *to* CASIMIR, *sarcastically*. Only not too many carats!

FLUGEL, *taking her remark to be directed at him*. Nein, nein! Chicken only... No carrots, no notting... (MIMI *casts a perplexed look at* CASIMIR *who shakes it off with a gesture.*) Und first mein liver, ya?

CASIMIR, *losing patience, motioning him off*. Ya, ya! Goddammit!... Ya!

FLUGEL *exits, up center.*

MIMI. What on earth...

CASIMIR. It's been like this since the minute he got here. He's simply beyond belief... You can't imagine...

MIMI, *laughing*. I must say, he's different!

CASIMIR. You can say that again!

MIMI *goes over to the sideboard, back to the audience, and begins unwrapping the package.* CASIMIR, *remembering the letter on the writing desk, rushes over to dispose of it while her back is turned, but in his haste juggles it clumsily between his hands during her ensuing remarks.*

MIMI. He's certainly no Etienne! I can tell that already... Of course, Etienne had his faults, but at least he was no fool... Not very discreet, but... (*She takes several pastries out of the package.*) There! (*She licks her fingers.*)

I think you're going to adore this dessert!... It's my absolute favorite... I just know you're going to love it!... (*Noticing that* CASIMIR *has remained strangely silent.*) Casimir?... (CASIMIR *finally stuffs the envelope into his inside pocket just before she turns around.*) I don't think you've heard a single word I've said!

CASIMIR. Who? Me?

MIMI, *going over to him.* What is it, love?... Is something wrong?

CASIMIR. Wrong? What do you mean?

MIMI. I don't know... You've been acting so... (*At a loss for words.*) You seem to be a million miles away these last few days.

CASIMIR. No, no... I was thinking... That's all, just thinking...

MIMI. About what, darling? (*Cajoling.*) Please, you can tell me...

CASIMIR. Oh... Things... Problems... You know...

MIMI, *pressing.* Problems? What kind of problems?

CASIMIR, *aside, to the audience.* Well, if she's going to insist! (*To* MIMI.) Look, Mimi... dearest... if you must know, I've reached a point in my life... (*Dramatically.*) There are times in a man's life when—

MIMI, *suddenly, sniffing.* What on earth is that smell?

CASIMIR. That what?

MIMI, *grimacing.* Something burning... Like a piece of rope... Don't you smell it?

CASIMIR, *aside.* Damn! I was off to such a good start too! (*To* MIMI.) It's that idiot Flugel and his blasted pipe!

MIMI. His pipe? You mean... you let him smoke his pipe? In here? In the... You must be joking!

CASIMIR, *shrugging, resigned.* I know...

MIMI, *fanning her face with her hand, looking around.* Don't you have an atomizer or something? Anything...

CASIMIR. An atomizer?... Yes, in the washroom... Just a second... (*He goes to the door, up center, and calls out.*) Flugel! Come in here this minute!

MIMI. Really! I never... You wouldn't catch Etienne smoking! Certainly not in the—

FLUGEL *appears suddenly in the doorway in his shirtsleeves. He is wearing no pants: only undershorts, long stockings, and garters.*

MIMI, *shocked.* Oh!

FLUGEL, *entering.* Ya? Vat gives?

MIMI *turns around and covers her eyes.*

CASIMIR. What the... You're practically naked, for God's sake! Is that any way to come into a room? Really!

FLUGEL. But Casimir… Just dressed I vas getting. You know, mit de liver… I don't vant you should vait, dat's all…

CASIMIR, *a little flustered.* Yes, well, next time… Look… (*Pointing to the door, down left.*) There's an atomizer in there on the table by the tub. Go get it…

FLUGEL. A vat?

CASIMIR. An atomizer! You know what that is?

FLUGEL. Adam who?

CASIMIR, *articulating, impatiently.* An a-to-mi-zer!… Like a bottle… a container… with a… a rubber thing at the end. You can't miss it.

FLUGEL. Ya, ya, Casimir. I find, don't vorry!

He runs off, down left.

MIMI, *turning back.* What did he call you?

CASIMIR. I know, I know… I've told him a dozen times. But he's new in Paris…

MIMI. Well, I must say… (*She notices the atomizer on the sideboard.*) Oh look, love! There it is… (*She goes over, picks it up, and begins spraying all around the room.*) Ah! Now I can breathe!

She takes a few deep breaths.

CASIMIR, *aside.* Back to the business at hand! Now or never!

MIMI. There! Isn't that better?

She puts the atomizer back on the sideboard.

CASIMIR, *very serious.* Come here, Mimi… (*He holds out his hands.*) Mimi, dearest… (*He takes her in his arms.*) There's something I've got to tell you… (*with exaggerated emotion.*) Oh Mimi, Mimi, Mimi!

MIMI. Casimir, love!

CASIMIR. You remember the letter… the letter I was writing… before, when you came in…

MIMI. The letter?… Yes…

He smothers her with kisses.

CASIMIR. Oh Mimi, Mimi, Mimi!

MIMI, *expectantly.* Yes, Casimir?… Yes…

CASIMIR. Well, dearest, that letter—

FLUGEL *bursts in from the washroom, leaving the door open. This time he has a bath towel wrapped around his waist, and is holding an object that neither the characters nor the audience can see clearly.*

MIMI, *startled by the interruption.* Oh!

She pushes herself free of CASIMIR's *embrace.*

FLUGEL. Nein, nein, you two! Don't shtop!

CASIMIR. Flugel! For heaven's—

FLUGEL. You couldn't do notting vat I never seen, believe me! Back home, on de farm, mit de cows und de pigs... Ach, ya! I see everyting und more, you bet!

MIMI. What?

FLUGEL. Listen, Casimir... All over de room I look... Dat's de ting vat you vant, ya?

He holds up an enema bag.

CASIMIR, *mortified, jumping.* Give me that!

He grabs the enema bag out of FLUGEL's *hands, throws it into the washroom, and slams the door.*

MIMI, *looking on, aghast.* I never...

FLUGEL, *shaking his head, quizzically.* Dat vasn't?

CASIMIR, *taking the atomizer from the sideboard, impatiently.* This, Flugel... This is an atomizer! See?

He squirts a few jets in FLUGEL's *face.*

FLUGEL. Pffffui! (*Sniffing.*) Vat makes it shmell like dat?

CASIMIR. How should I know?... Oil of peppermint or something...

He puts the atomizer back on the sideboard.

FLUGEL, *scratching his head.* Oil und pfeffer mit?... Ach, who vould tink?

CASIMIR. Now go on! Get out of here!

FLUGEL, *apologetically.* I do maybe someting wrong, Casimir?

CASIMIR. Never mind... Just get dressed and go downstairs, and do what I told you!

FLUGEL, *nodding.* Ya, ya! You bet... I go...

He exits, up center. There is a long moment of embarrassed silence.

CASIMIR, *with a nervous chuckle.* Well, I told you he was different!

MIMI, *shaking her head.* That's putting it mildly!... (*Another silence.*) You were saying, Casimir?

CASIMIR. Saying?... Saying what?

MIMI. About the letter...

CASIMIR. Oh! The letter...

MIMI. Yes... You were saying...

CASIMIR. I was saying... about the letter...

MIMI. Yes?

CASIMIR. The letter I was writing... before, when you came in... (*He pauses, summoning up his courage.*) Look, Mimi... I didn't want to write it, dearest... You've got to believe me... (MIMI's *expression gradually begins to betray her worst suspicions.*) Nothing in the world could make me write that letter... Wild horses, Mimi... But I had no choice... I... I'm... I've... I mean...

MIMI, *as the awful truth dawns.* Oh God! You're... you're telling me it's over!... That's it, isn't it?... You're telling me we're through!

CASIMIR, *trying to calm her.* Through? Who said we were through? We're just... just taking a break... A little break, that's all...

MIMI, *whimpering.* Don't bother, Casimir! You don't have to pretend!

CASIMIR. But...

MIMI. Come right out and say it! You don't love me, I can tell...

CASIMIR. But... but...

MIMI. I could feel it in my bones... I knew it all along...

CASIMIR. Please, Mimi! That's not true...

MIMI. I could see how you were acting...

CASIMIR, *holding out his arms.* Mimi, Mimi!

MIMI, *spurning him.* You can't fool a woman who's in love, Casimir... I know, I know...

CASIMIR, *aside.* Ay ay ay! Now the tears!

MIMI. And to think... (*She begins to sob.*) I... I was so sure it was something for my birthday... A surprise... (*Coyly, through her tears.*) After all, a girl doesn't turn twenty-two every day...

  She dries her eyes.

CASIMIR, *offhand.* Or twenty-three...

MIMI. Oh yes, a fine surprise! (*Sobbing again.*) But then, I should have known! You're all alike! You... (*Dramatically.*) you use a woman to your hearts' content... Any poor, simple fool... Then you throw her away and... and trample her love in the dust!

CASIMIR, *aside.* Ay ay ay!

MIMI, *waxing eloquent.* Oh! Why are we so blind? Why can't we see you for the beasts you are? (*Striding down right, the back of her hand poised dramatically against her forehead.*) Why, why? Oh, why?

  She lets herself collapse onto the love seat.

CASIMIR, *aside.* Really! Enough is enough! (*To* MIMI.) Look, Mimi... For heaven's sake... (*Going over to her.*) Please, love... Please! Listen to reason... (*Getting down on his knees, trying to take her hands in his.*) Let me explain...

MIMI, *drawing back sharply.* There's nothing to explain! Just leave me alone, you... you monster!

CASIMIR. Mimi! Love!

During the last exchange, the door up center flies open, and FLUGEL *appears at the threshold, unseen by* MIMI *and* CASIMIR. *He is wearing the latter's uniform—coat and trousers—and is holding the military cap in his hand.*

FLUGEL, *noticing the scene, aside.* Hoo-hah!

He closes the door quickly and quietly, and knocks a moment later.

CASIMIR, *standing up.* Yes?... What is it?

FLUGEL *opens the door discreetly and pokes his head through the opening, in such a way that* CASIMIR *doesn't notice what he is wearing.*

FLUGEL. Dat vas a cold chicken, Casimir, ya?

CASIMIR, *sharply.* Yes!

FLUGEL. Und vun ting else... I could take de umbrella? It's all of a sudden raining like you vouldn't believe...

CASIMIR, *waving him away.* Yes, yes, yes!

FLUGEL, *nodding.* Sehr gut! I go!

FLUGEL *pulls back his head and shuts the door.*

CASIMIR, *kneeling again, trying to recapture the mood.* Please, Mimi... Listen!... You're only a child... There are some things you don't understand... Please, believe me... It's... it's not that I don't still love you, dearest...

MIMI, *sarcastically.* Oh?

CASIMIR. It's just that... things have changed...

MIMI. Yes, I know! You've made that quite clear!

CASIMIR. No, no... Not us... Not you and me... Just me... My life... It's not the same... (*Pausing for a reaction from* MIMI, *but meeting with a stony silence.*) It's... it's... (*Dramatically.*) All right, if I have to tell you, I have to... I'm ruined, Mimi. Utterly ruined!... (*With mock pathos.*) There! Now you know!

MIMI, *surprised.* Ruined? You?

CASIMIR. Ruined! Not a centime to my name!... That's what I was trying to tell you in my letter.

MIMI. You mean, that's why... (*Throwing her arms around his neck.*) Oh, Casimir! Darling!... You're ruined... I'm so happy...

CASIMIR, *jumping to his feet.* I beg your pardon!

MIMI. No, no... I mean... if that's the reason... if you still really love me...

CASIMIR, *hypocritically.* Of course I do, silly! What ever made you think—

MIMI. Oh, you poor dear! How did it happen? (*Inviting him, with a gesture, to sit down beside her.*) Come... Tell your Mimi, darling!

CASIMIR, *sitting.* Well, what can I say? It was greed... pure greed... I thought I was going to make a killing in the market... A sure thing, someone told me... And instead... (*With a wave of the hand.*) Pfff! All gone...

MIMI. In the market?

CASIMIR. Yes, yes... Stocks, bonds... that kind of thing... You wouldn't understand...

MIMI. You mean, a bad investment?

CASIMIR. Exactly...

MIMI. Tsk tsk! In what?

CASIMIR, *eager to avoid an answer.* In... something... What's the difference? You never heard of it, I'm sure.

MIMI. Oh, I don't know. I've made my little investments now and then. (*Insisting.*) What was it, love?

CASIMIR, *with a sigh of resignation, blurting out the first name that comes to mind.* Caledonian Nickel!... See? I told you you never—

MIMI, *springing to her feet.* Caledonian... What are you talking about? I have thousands invested in Caledonian Nickel!

CASIMIR, *taken aback.* You do?

MIMI. Don't tell me it's gone down!... Good God! My whole life's savings...

CASIMIR. No... no... That is...

MIMI, *growing more and more excited.* It was going up, and up, and up... It can't have gone down!

CASIMIR. No, no... It's still up... Way up... Don't worry...

MIMI. But...

CASIMIR. It's just that I... I heard from my broker that it might go down. See?... And... and I sold it all and put everything I had into... into... (*At a loss.*) into something else...

MIMI. Oh?

CASIMIR. And that's what went down... All the way... Down, down, down!

MIMI, *embracing him, very much relieved.* Oh, thank you! Thank you, darling!

CASIMIR, *dryly.* Don't mention it.

MIMI, *sitting down, fanning herself with her hand.* I mean, it's bad enough that I'm losing you... But you and my savings... Both at the same time?

CASIMIR, *sitting down*. Perish the thought! I'm enough for one day...

MIMI. I should say! (*Sighing.*) What a fright! (*After a brief, embarrassed pause.*) But Casimir, darling... How ever will you manage? All alone, I mean... Because you're absolutely right... I couldn't possibly let myself be a burden to you now... Not now, poor love, when you don't have a centime to your name... (*Taking his hands in hers.*) Oh, I know how worried you are about me. But you needn't be, really. I'll muddle through somehow... And I'll always be just like a sister to you, dearest. You can always count on me...

CASIMIR, *kissing her hands, with mock gratitude and dejection*. Thank you, Mimi... Thank you! (*Aside.*) When there's nothing left to count!

MIMI. But you, poor dear... What on earth will you do?

CASIMIR. The only thing that's left, I'm afraid... I'm going to get married.

MIMI, *shocked*. You? Married?... Casimir!

CASIMIR. It's my only chance...

MIMI. But... but who?

CASIMIR, *with a casual shrug*. Oh...

MIMI, *not without a note of recrimination*. Some pretty young thing that you're madly in love with?

CASIMIR. Me? In love?... Mimi!... You know you're the only one... It's just that... (*Sighing.*) She's rich, and... and I'm... Well, you see what I mean...

MIMI, *coyly*. And she isn't pretty? Not even a little?

CASIMIR. Pretty? (*With a shudder and a grimace.*) Ugh! She's... she's ugly as sin!... She's a witch... an old hag... Why else would she make me marry her, for goodness' sake?

MIMI. Oh, thank you, Casimir! I knew I could trust you!

CASIMIR, *aside, with a sigh*. There! So far, so good!

A moment later the door, up center, opens, and FLUGEL, *bedraggled and dripping, appears at the threshold, still wearing* CASIMIR's *uniform, cap and all. In one hand he is carrying a wrapped package; in the other, a lady's dainty parasol, soaking wet*.

FLUGEL. Ach! Donner Wetter! Such a day!

CASIMIR *and* MIMI *jump up at the interruption*.

CASIMIR, *startled, to* FLUGEL. What... My uniform, you idiot?

MIMI. Good heavens! My parasol!...

CASIMIR. Just what do you think you're wearing? Who told you—

FLUGEL. Blue you said, Casimir. Mit gold buttons...

CASIMIR. But not my uniform! Not...

MIMI, *concerned for her parasol*. Look at it! It's ruined!

CASIMIR. Of all the stupid...

FLUGEL. Gott in Himmel! Vat a city! Vat kind crazy people dey let out in de shtreet! Back home it vouldn't happen, such a ting, believe me!... (CASIMIR *and* MIMI *exchange puzzled glances.*) Such a ting like dat? Never!... In a million years, never! In a tousand even!

CASIMIR, *to* FLUGEL. What on earth are you babbling about?

FLUGEL. Such a ting vat just happened... I do like you tell me... I go down und I buy... (*He holds up the package.*) Und de minute I come from de shtore out already, I bump into a man vat's dressed up just like me... Mit de same kind like mein liver... Und he shtops und yells: "Hey, sergeant! Vat you tink you doing, up und down de shtreet valking so, mit a uniform on, und no boots on de feet, und a crazy umbrella!"

CASIMIR. What?

FLUGEL. So I tell him his own business he should mind, danke schön!... Und vun two tree, all red in de face he gets... Red like mein pants even... Und he shtarts in mit de talk, like you vouldn't believe... All kinds crazy tings... Like I'm a drunken bummer, und a shame to mein country, und he's going to report me...

CASIMIR. Good God! The lieutenant!

During the ensuing dialogue, MIMI *goes up to* FLUGEL, *still in the doorway, and, taking her parasol, opens it and surveys the damage.*

FLUGEL. So I tell him: "Go, report!" Und he says: "Vat's your serial number?" Und I tell him: "Ha ha! You shtupid! Cereal I don't eat. Mit a number or mitout!" So he pulls from mein head yet mein hat off, und looks inside, und writes down someting...

CASIMIR, *furious*. You... Do you know what you've done?... Are you trying to make a... a shambles of my life, goddammit?

FLUGEL. Casimir?

CASIMIR. My serial number... A report... A court martial for all I know... I'll probably wind up behind bars thanks to you!

FLUGEL. I do someting wrong?

MIMI. A brand-new parasol... absolutely ruined!

FLUGEL, *perplexed, to* CASIMIR. I didn't ask you, Casimir, could I take de umbrella?

MIMI, shaking her head, goes over to the fireplace and lays the open parasol on the hearth to dry.

CASIMIR, *to* FLUGEL. Never mind, you... I've... (*Matching the gesture to the expression.*) I've had it up to here... You... you numbskull!

FLUGEL, *thoroughly confused, shrugging.* Mein Gott! Vat a city!

CASIMIR, *pointing to the uniform.* Now go take that off and put on what you're supposed to... In my closet, idiot!... And for heaven's sake, serve us our lunch! It's about time, don't you think?

FLUGEL. Ya, ya! Right avay!... Here! De chicken you got... (*He tosses the package to a startled* CASIMIR.) Vat a city!

He exits, up center, grumbling. CASIMIR, *with a look of disbelief at the package he has caught, watches him leave.*

MIMI. Chicken? But... I thought I ordered—

CASIMIR, *livid.* Do you believe... (*He slams the package angrily down on the sideboard.*) That... that... (*He starts pacing back and forth.*) A lovely mess he's gotten me into!... God knows if they'll believe me when I try to explain it!... Oh! That imbecile!... Me and my diamond in the rough! It serves me right!

MIMI, *joining him by the love seat.* Now, now, Casimir... Let's not get all upset. It's not his fault if he's not very bright. He's certainly no Etienne, but his heart's in the right place.

CASIMIR. I know. But his head...

MIMI. And he means well, I'm sure.

CASIMIR. Yes... So does a bear when he hugs you to death!

MIMI, *laughing.* Only he's not a bear! He's a boor, poor thing!

CASIMIR. Boor, bear... What's the difference? His hug is just as deadly!

MIMI, *wagging her finger.* Temper, temper, temper!

CASIMIR, *gradually calming down.* Bah!

MIMI. You'd better learn how to have patience, love... (*Teasing.*) Now that you're going to get married, I mean...

CASIMIR, *good-naturedly.* That's right, rub it in! Much obliged! That's all I need... (*Hypocritically.*) Look, I know her, you don't. I know what I'm in for... (*With a grimace, shuddering.*) The ugly old hag!

MIMI, *with a note of complicity.* I'd give anything to see what she looks like... Really... The way you describe her... How old did you say she was?

CASIMIR. Old?... She's fifty if she's a day... Maybe closer to sixty... I told you, she's a witch!

MIMI. And it's strictly... platonic?

CASIMIR. My God, I should hope so! You think I'd lay a hand on a sixty-year-old? What kind of cad do you take me for?... I'm not marrying a woman, I'm marrying a walking checkbook. I won't have to lift a finger for the rest of my life.

MIMI. Tsk tsk! You lazy thing, you!

She snickers.

CASIMIR, *forcing a laugh.* Well, after all...

They continue laughing, back and forth, in a gradual crescendo that reaches its peak in a series of good guffaws, eventually subsiding and petering out in a few final chuckles.

MIMI, *sighing.* My, my, my!... (*Looking at her watch.*) Aren't we ever going to eat, dearest? I'm absolutely famished!

CASIMIR. My sentiments exactly! (*Going to the door, up center, and calling, sternly.*) Flugel!... Get in here!...

FLUGEL'S VOICE. Ya, ya... You vant I should come in mitout mein pants?

CASIMIR, *calling.* Get dressed and get in here! And don't take all day!

He shrugs his shoulders and gives MIMI *a look of utter resignation. A few moments later,* FLUGEL *enters, buttoning the last few buttons of his livery.*

FLUGEL. Ya? So? Vat gives?

CASIMIR. What... (*Controlling his temper.*) We're ready for lunch, Flugel. That's "what gives"...

He and MIMI *stand by the table, waiting for* FLUGEL *to hold their chairs for them.*

FLUGEL. So vy you don't say? (*With a click of the heels and a grand gesture toward the table.*) Sit down, sit down... (CASIMIR *and* MIMI, *resigned, take their seats opposite one another, as* FLUGEL *goes to the sideboard and unwraps the chicken.*) Now dat's vat I call a chicken vat's a chicken!

He brandishes it in the air by one leg. MIMI, *still half-expecting squab, gives a puzzled look.*

CASIMIR, *still very subdued.* I'll thank you not to wave it around the room, Flugel... (FLUGEL *puts it on the serving platter on the sideboard.*) Just bring it over here and let me take care of it... (FLUGEL *complies.*) Here, you can fix the salad...

He puts down the platter and hands him the bowl of salad from the table.

FLUGEL. Ya, ya... Sehr gut... (*He returns to the sideboard and lays down the bowl, as* CASIMIR *begins carving the chicken, explaining sotto voce to*

MIMI *why there is chicken instead of squab.*) Sehr gut... (*Aside.*) Gives first mit de vinegar... (*He pours the contents of the vinegar cruet into the salad.*) Und den a shprinkle salt... (*He shakes out some salt.*) Und den... Und den... (*Spotting the atomizer.*) Ach, ya!... De oil und pfeffer mit... (*He takes it and sprays the salad generously with its contents.*) More maybe... (*He sprays a few more jets, puts back the atomizer, gives the salad a few good tosses, then stands back, satisfied.*) So! Fit for a king even!

CASIMIR, *putting down the carving knife and fork.* All right, Flugel. You may serve the chicken now.

FLUGEL, *nodding, lays the salad bowl down on the table, picks up the platter of chicken, and offers it to* CASIMIR.

CASIMIR, *pointing.* Madame first, Flugel.

FLUGEL, *offering the platter to* MIMI. Matame?

MIMI. Thank you.

She serves herself.

FLUGEL, *offering it to* CASIMIR. Und you, Casimir?

CASIMIR, *echoing him as he serves himself.* "Und you, Casimir?..." (*Shaking his head.*) He's incredible...

FLUGEL *puts the platter back on the sideboard and takes himself a drumstick, unseen by the others.*

MIMI, *laughing.* He's certainly—

CASIMIR, *interrupting, nodding.* No Etienne! I know!... (*He snaps his fingers.*) Flugel! The wine!

FLUGEL, *approaching.* Ya, ya!

He awkwardly fills both glasses, spilling as he pours.

CASIMIR, *to* MIMI. Salad, darling?

MIMI. Please.

CASIMIR *serves her, then himself, as* FLUGEL *withdraws to the sideboard, chomping on his drumstick, unnoticed.* CASIMIR *and* MIMI *begin to eat the salad.*

CASIMIR, *suddenly, with a grimace.* Pfffaw!... What on earth...

MIMI, *putting her napkin to her mouth, coughing.* Ugh!... That... It tastes like... like toilet water, or something...

FLUGEL, *obviously misunderstanding.* Toilet vater? (*He pulls an imaginary toilet-chain, with a quizzical look.*) In mein salad?... Vat kind a ting...

CASIMIR, *coughing.* What... what on earth did you put in this... It's... it's absolutely vile!

FLUGEL, *as* CASIMIR *and* MIMI *gradually regain their composure.* I put vinegar, und a shprinkle salt, und... (*Pointing to the atomizer.*) und plenty oil und pfeffer mit...

CASIMIR, *with a start.* Plenty of what?

MIMI. You didn't!

They both have another coughing and choking spasm at the thought.

FLUGEL. But I tought... (*Pointing again, this time with the drumstick.*) Vinegar, salt, oil, pfeffer...

CASIMIR. You mean...

FLUGEL *casually bites off a big piece of chicken.*

MIMI. Of all the...

CASIMIR, *having noticed* FLUGEL's *move, jumping to his feet shouting.* What are you eating?

FLUGEL, *startled, gags on his mouthful. After coughing and sputtering for a few moments, he runs over to the table and gulps down* MIMI's *wine.*

MIMI, *looking on in disbelief.* What...

FLUGEL, *with a deep breath.* Ach, dat's better... (*Holding out the drumstick and answering* CASIMIR's *question, naïvely.*) A piece chicken, Casimir... Only a piece chicken...

CASIMIR, *sitting down, slapping his hand on the table.* Now I've seen everything!

MIMI. Really!

CASIMIR. No... That's the last straw!... Simply the last straw!

MIMI. Never in my life...

FLUGEL, *innocently.* Casimir?... Mimi?... Vat I do now?

MIMI, *to* FLUGEL. I beg your pardon! Kindly don't you "Mimi" me!

FLUGEL. I shouldn't do vat?

MIMI. "Mimi" me, "Mimi" me...

FLUGEL. Vat vat vat?

MIMI. Oh...

She shakes her head, resigned.

CASIMIR, *drumming on the table, sarcastically, to* MIMI. Lovely lunch!... A perfectly lovely lunch!...

FLUGEL, *confused.* Danke schön, Casimir...

CASIMIR, *to* FLUGEL. Oh... Quiet!

FLUGEL *shrugs and moves back toward the sideboard, scratching his head.*

MIMI, *to* CASIMIR. Especially when it may be our last...

CASIMIR. Please, dearest...

MIMI. Our very, very last...

CASIMIR. Please... Don't say things like that... (*Hypocritically.*) I... I can't bear the thought... You can see what I'm going through... You know how I feel...

He wipes an imaginary tear from his cheek.

MIMI, *with a slightly skeptical drawl.* Well... that's what you say...

CASIMIR. And that's what I mean!

MIMI. And this... this walking checkbook of yours... You're sure she's not really some pretty young thing? You're sure you're not marrying some twenty-year-old...

CASIMIR. Mimi! I told you... Some pretty young thing? Some twenty-year-old? (*He puts his hand on his heart.*) I'd never marry a twenty-year-old! Even if I were offered one on a silver platter!

MIMI. Never?

CASIMIR, *raising his hand as if to swear.* Never!

FLUGEL, *who has been following the dialogue.* Never, Mimi! Never! If Casimir tells you never, dat means never, don't you vorry!

CASIMIR, *to* FLUGEL. You... Who's asking you?

MIMI, *to* CASIMIR. Because, if you ever did...

The doorbell rings. FLUGEL *remains at the sideboard, still munching on his drumstick.*

CASIMIR, *to* FLUGEL. Well? Are you just going to stand there? Go see who's at the door!

FLUGEL, *moving toward the door, up center, drumstick in hand.* Ya, ya! I go...

CASIMIR. And put down that chicken!

FLUGEL *returns, finally puts the drumstick down on the sideboard, and exits, leaving the door open.*

MIMI, *continuing.* Well, I simply couldn't find it in my heart to forgive you, Casimir.

CASIMIR, *taking her hands across the table.* Mimi, dearest... I'm telling you... She's old, and ugly, and rich... I mean, why would I marry some pretty young thing when I could have you?

MIMI *smiles briefly, then screws up her brow and looks askance, not quite certain how to take the last remark.*

FLUGEL'S VOICE. Ya! I tell him... I tell him...

He enters.

CASIMIR, *to* FLUGEL. Well?

FLUGEL. It's dat same old goat... De vun vat vas here bevore... Matame Préprépré... someting.

CASIMIR, *springing to his feet, aside.* Good God! Babette's mother! (*Seizing an inspiration of the moment, to* MIMI.) Speak of the devil!... You wanted to see that pretty young thing?... That twenty-year-old?... (*To* FLUGEL.) All right, show her in.

FLUGEL *exits, up center.*

MIMI. You mean...

CASIMIR. Quick... (*He pulls her up out of her chair.*) In here, so she can't see you. (*He pushes her toward the door, down left.*) You can peek through the keyhole and see for yourself...

MIMI *exits quickly into the washroom, and* CASIMIR *hurriedly removes her setting from the table to the sideboard, then frantically shuts the door behind her, as* FLUGEL *reappears, followed by* MADAME PRÉVALLON.

FLUGEL, *elbowing his way in front of her, motioning.* Come in... Come in...

He moves center stage.

MADAME PRÉVALLON, *to* CASIMIR. Ah! Th-th-there y-you are! Ca-ca... Ca-ca... Ca-ca...

FLUGEL, *aside.* More "caca" yet!

CASIMIR, *going quickly to meet her, leading her to the love seat, far right, to keep* MIMI *from overhearing, almost in a whisper.* Mother! What a pleasure!... Please... Come... Sit down...

FLUGEL, *surprised, aside.* Vat's dat he calls her?

MADAME PRÉVALLON, *resisting* CASIMIR's *invitation, standing in front of the love seat.* I'm f-f-fu... f-f-fu... f-f-furious with you, Ca-ca... Ca-ca... Ca-ca...

FLUGEL *makes a gesture, unseen by the others, as if to say "Enough is enough!"*

CASIMIR, *nodding, solicitously.* Yes, I know... I know you are... And I don't blame you one bit... (*Pointing to* FLUGEL.) We have him to thank!

MADAME PRÉVALLON, *looking* FLUGEL *up and down.* In-d-deed w-we d-do!

FLUGEL, *misunderstanding.* Don't mention!... Bitte schön!

CASIMIR. There's simply no excuse for his being so rude.

MADAME PRÉVALLON. S-so r-rude... And c-crude... And v-vulgar... And—

CASIMIR. No excuse, Mother! Simply no excuse!

MADAME PRÉVALLON. Why, he shat... he sh-shat... he sh-shat...

FLUGEL, *startled*. I vat?

MADAME PRÉVALLON. ... he sh-shattered e-every r-rule of g-good m-manners!

FLUGEL. Oh...

MADAME PRÉVALLON. He th-threw m-me out l-like s-some c-common t-t-tra... t-t-tra...

FLUGEL, *under his breath*. Tramp?

MADAME PRÉVALLON. ... t-t-traveling s-s-salesman...

FLUGEL, *aside*. Donner Wetter! She vould pray, und Gott could fall ashleep vaiting!

CASIMIR. I know, Mother... I know...

MADAME PRÉVALLON. I'm v-very s-se... s-se... s-se...

FLUGEL, *under his breath*. Sexy, maybe?

MADAME PRÉVALLON. ... s-sensi-t-t-tive, and I l-left.

CASIMIR. Yes, Mother... But you came back. That's the important thing. You're back... That's all that matters...

He invites her again, with a gesture, to sit down. This time she complies.

MADAME PRÉVALLON, *sitting*. W-well... I'm s-still a b-bit sh... I'm s-still a b-bit sh... a b-bit sh...

FLUGEL, *aside, nodding*. Dat she could say again!

MADAME PRÉVALLON. ... a b-bit sh-shaken b-by it all...

CASIMIR. Of course... Of course you are... (*He sits down beside her, facing the wall, down right, to be out of* MIMI'S *earshot.*) Please, try to relax... It was all just a terrible misunderstanding... Our dim-witted friend... (*He points to* FLUGEL, *who nods, smiling.*) You see, I gave him the strictest, strictest orders that if... Well, you know me. You know how I am... Serious, sensible, stable... (MADAME PRÉVALLON *nods.*) Just the right kind of man to make some lovely girl a perfect husband... And I told him: "Now look, whatever you do, don't open the door for any pretty young ladies..."

MADAME PRÉVALLON, *flattered*. O-o-oh?... W-well, h-how s-sweet!

CASIMIR. But he misunderstood. He thought I said: "... except for pretty young ladies..." And so he threw you out...

MADAME PRÉVALLON, *taken aback*. Wh-wh-what?

CASIMIR, *flustered, realizing his gaffe*. I mean... he thought... he thought I said: "... not even for pretty young ladies..." That's it... That's what he thought I said... "Not even," not "except"... And... and... (*Eager to change the subject, abruptly.*) Well now, Mother, how have you been? I'm so pleased you stopped by... Just what did you have in mind?

MADAME PRÉVALLON. I c-came a-ba-bout m-ma... a-ba-bout m-ma... m-ma... m-ma...

FLUGEL, *aside, as* MADAME PRÉVALLON *continues struggling.* She got a mamma shtill? Mein Gott! A hundred she must be, at least!

MADAME PRÉVALLON. ... a-ba-bout m-my d-daughter... T-to t-talk a-ba-bout y-your w-w-wedding, Ca-ca... Ca-ca...

CASIMIR, *finger to lips.* Shhh! Not so loud!

FLUGEL, *aside.* Hoo-hah!

MADAME PRÉVALLON, *to* CASIMIR. Wh-wh-why?

FLUGEL, *aside, nodding at the revelation.* Mit her daughter she vants he should marry! Ach, so!

CASIMIR, *to* MADAME PRÉVALLON, *glancing toward* FLUGEL. Not in front of the help... (*Standing up.*) Come, let's go into my study...

MADAME PRÉVALLON, *getting to her feet.* W-w-well...

She follows him to the door, up right. He opens it and steps aside to let her pass. MADAME PRÉVALLON *exits.*

CASIMIR, *quickly, to* FLUGEL. Now listen, for heaven's sake... (*Pointing to the washroom door, down left.*) Go tell madame I said she should make her escape... This is her perfect chance...

FLUGEL, *about to move down left.* Ya, ya...

CASIMIR, *holding him back.* And tell her I was all choked up... Tell her you even saw me crying...

FLUGEL. Crying?

MADAME PRÉVALLON'S VOICE, *calling.* Ca-ca... Ca-ca... Ca-ca...

FLUGEL shrugs his shoulders.

CASIMIR, *at the door, up right.* Coming, Mother...

He exits, humming the first few bars of the "Marseillaise," and shuts the door.

FLUGEL, *watching him leave.* Dat's vat he calls crying? (*He crosses over and opens the door, down left, calling softly.*) Mimi!... (MIMI *pokes her head out.*) You could come out now... Casimir says dat's de chance you should make your escape...

MIMI, *entering.* Aha! (*She tiptoes over to the fireplace, takes her parasol, closes it, and prepares to leave.*) Was that all he said?

FLUGEL. Nein, Mimi... He says: "Tell her I vas all choked up... Tell her even I vas crying..."

MIMI. Tsk tsk! Poor dear!

FLUGEL. Ya! Und den he goes out... Und he vas singing even...

MIMI. Singing?

FLUGEL. Ya, ya! Like so...

He hums the same bars of the "Marseillaise."

MIMI, *shaking her head.* Trying to fight back the tears, poor darling... Always trying to be brave...

FLUGEL. Ach! Poor Casimir!

He wipes away a tear.

MIMI. Poor, poor Casimir!

She heaves a sigh and moves to leave, up center.

FLUGEL, *holding her back.* But... but vat's de matter, Mimi? Vy you got to leave us already? You don't like it no more here, mit Casimir und me?

MIMI, *smiling wanly at his naïve presumptuousness.* I'm afraid I don't have much choice in the matter Flugel. Things have a way of changing, you know. And we have to accept them...

FLUGEL. Tings? Vat tings?

MIMI. Now that Casimir... (*Correcting herself.*) Now that Monsieur Ferret has lost his fortune, I mean...

FLUGEL. Lost his... (*Smiling.*) Ach, dat's a good vun! Lost his fortune? Casimir?... (MIMI *looks at him, quizzically.*) You hear vat he writes in dat letter bevore?... Dat's it, ya?... Und you tink... (*Laughing.*) Ach, ya! Dat's a good vun!...

MIMI. What?

FLUGEL, *laughing.* He didn't tell you maybe dat vas all a joke, dat letter?

MIMI. A... a joke?

FLUGEL. Ya, ya! You I could tell, Mimi... You're like family already... (*Confidentially.*) Dat's a "business" letter, vat he says... (*Winking.*) A "funny business" letter! He got plenty money shtill, Casimir! All de money vat he needs... Und you tink... Ach du lieber, dat's a good vun!

He bursts out laughing.

MIMI, *flustered.* But... but... what are you saying? (*Pointing up right.*) That woman... That old woman he has to marry?

FLUGEL. Dat old goat?... Nein, nein, nein! It's her daughter she vants he should marry mit. Her daughter...

MIMI. Her daughter?... (*In a sudden flash of insight.*) Oh!

FLUGEL. Ya, ya!... But gives notting to vorry your head, Mimi liebchen! Casimir vouldn't marry no tventy-year-old! Nein, nein! Like he said... In a silver bladder even!... He vouldn't do! Never!

MIMI, *to herself.* And here I was, pitying that... that cad... that swine... that...

FLUGEL, *chuckling.* Und you tink he really lose his money... Und you tink he marry dat Matame Préprépré... Und you tink you got to go und leave Casimir und me...

He bursts out again in a hearty, good-natured laugh.

MIMI, *seething.* Oh!

FLUGEL. A lucky ting Flugel vas here und could fix!... A lucky ting, you bet! (*He takes her by the hand and pulls her down left.*) Come... Ve make a surprise for Casimir... A good vun... (*Urging her into the washroom.*) In... in...

MIMI. Oh!

She exits and FLUGEL *shuts the door.*

FLUGEL, *rubbing his hands, proudly, crossing up right.* Ach, so! Dis time Flugel fix everyting just right! (*He opens the study door and calls.*) Casimir... Casimir...

CASIMIR *pokes his head out, gingerly.*

CASIMIR, *in a whisper.* Is she gone?

FLUGEL. Ya, ya! (*Aside.*) A surprise vat's a surprise, already!

CASIMIR. Fine... (*Entering, to* MADAME PRÉVALLON.) Come, Mother...

MADAME PRÉVALLON, *following him in.* I'm s-so g-glad we h-had our l-l-little ch-ch-chat. I al-w-ways th-thought you would m-make a s-sup... m-make a s-sup... m-make a s-sup...

FLUGEL, *aside.* Vat she tinks he is? A cook?

MADAME PRÉVALLON. ... a s-superb y-young m-man for m-my B-b-ba-b-b-bette...

CASIMIR, *standing by the fireplace.* Thank you... Thank you, Mother!

MADAME PRÉVALLON. N-n-now I'm s-s-sure!

CASIMIR, *falsely modest.* What can I say?... Except that... (*Dramatically.*) I'm touched... truly touched...

MADAME PRÉVALLON. I kn-know, s-son... I kn-know... (*She goes to embrace him, but her eye is caught by* MIMI's *picture on the mantle.*) Oh m-my! Wh-what a b-beautif-f-ful p-picture!

CASIMIR, *with a start.* Picture? What picture?

He tries to turn it toward the wall.

MADAME PRÉVALLON, *grasping it and looking at it admiringly.* Wh-what a s-simply l-lovely f-f-face!... W-was th-that y-your m-m-mother, Ca-ca... Ca-ca... Ca-ca...

FLUGEL, *laughing.* Nein, ach du lieber! Dat's Mimi... Dat's his lover lady, Mimi!

MADAME PRÉVALLON, *shocked, dropping the picture on the floor.* Wh-wh-what?

CASIMIR, *aside.* Good God! (*Aloud, flustered.*) Yes... yes... A very lovely lady... (*Emphasizing.*) A lovely, lovely, dear old friend...

FLUGEL. Vat you talking, "old friend," Casimir?... Mimi? Old?

CASIMIR, *aside to* FLUGEL. Will you shut up!

FLUGEL, *pointing to* MADAME PRÉVALLON. Dat vun is old, ya! Not your Mimi, Gott in Himmel!

MADAME PRÉVALLON, *to* CASIMIR. Wh-wh-what did he s-say?

CASIMIR, *as casually as possible.* Who knows? I never understand a word...

MADAME PRÉVALLON. And th-that l-lovely l-lady, Ca-ca... Ca-ca... Ca-ca...

CASIMIR, *innocently.* Who?... Who?...

MADAME PRÉVALLON. Th-that d-dear old f-friend... Wh-where is she n-now?

CASIMIR, *dramatically.* Ah, it's all very sad... She... she left this vale of tears, I'm afraid...

FLUGEL, *beaming.* Nein, nein, Casimir! Dat's vat you tink only! She don't leave notting.

CASIMIR. What?

FLUGEL. Ya, ya! She's here shtill... Flugel fix it all up! Vait, I get her... You see...

He moves down left, toward the washroom door. CASIMIR's *jaw drops in a look of panic and consternation..*

MADAME PRÉVALLON, *taken aback.* She... she... she...

CASIMIR. Flugel! What in the name...

MADAME PRÉVALLON. In th-this h-house? A-n-no-th-ther w-woman? With... with... with y-you... you... Ca-ca... Ca-ca... Ca-casan-n-nova!

CASIMIR. Mother?

MADAME PRÉVALLON. N-n-no! N-no! The w-wedding is off! M-my daughter is n-not for y-you, m-m-monsieur!

CASIMIR. But... but...

FLUGEL, *returning center stage, to* MADAME PRÉVALLON, *ignoring* CASIMIR's *frequent attempts to silence him.* Vat you tink he vants mit your daughter, Donner Wetter? Keep her! Who needs?... Like vat he tells Mimi ten minutes ago maybe... Right here, in front mein ears, so!... He vouldn't vant your daughter in a silver bladder even!

MADAME PRÉVALLON. Oh! I... I...

FLUGEL. Only too much a gentleman, dat's his trouble... Und he vouldn't got de heart to tell you... So I tell you!

MADAME PRÉVALLON. I... I... I...

CASIMIR, *desperately.* Flugel!... Flugel!...

FLUGEL. Nein, Casimir... Don't tank me... You do for me sometimes someting...

He goes to the washroom door and opens it.

MADAME PRÉVALLON. I... I... I...

FLUGEL. Peek-a-boo!

MIMI *enters.*

CASIMIR, *stupefied.* You!

MIMI, *ostentatiously flinging her arms around his neck.* Casimir... darling!

MADAME PRÉVALLON, *scandalized.* I... I... Oh! It's fi-fi... it's fi-fi... it's fi-fi...

FLUGEL. Nein! Not Fifi... Mimi!

MADAME PRÉVALLON. It's fi-finished!... Th-this is the end!... I've s-s-seen en-n-ough!

She turns and stalks toward the door, up center.

CASIMIR. Mother! Please!...

He breaks free of MIMI *and tries to hold* MADAME PRÉVALLON *back.*

MADAME PRÉVALLON. L-let m-me g-g-go!

She storms out and slams the door, as MIMI *ambles down left, musing.*

CASIMIR, *aside to* FLUGEL, *furious.* I hope you're pleased with your handi-work, you...

FLUGEL, *naïvely.* Ach, ya...

CASIMIR. Months and months and months, for nothing!

MIMI, *sarcastically.* Oh, Casimir, love! I knew it!... I knew you were only trying to test me... That story about your money, and that woman, and... Oh!

She strides up and smothers him with hypocritical kisses.

CASIMIR, *between clenched teeth.* Of course, Mimi... Of course...

He embraces her, obviously without much relish.

FLUGEL, *sighing.* Ach, dat's pretty, so! Two lovebirds! Sehr schön!

CASIMIR, *finally exploding.* Sehr schön? Sehr schön my foot, goddammit!

He gives FLUGEL *a swift kick, sending him flying.*

FLUGEL, *on the floor, astonished.* Ayyy! Gott!... Vat I do dis time?

CASIMIR, *apostrophizing.* Etienne!... Etienne!...

MIMI *takes his hand tightly in hers and, with a cynical little smile, leads him to the love seat, where they both sit down.*

MIMI. Ah, Casimir, dearest...

CASIMIR, *mechanically.* Ah, Mimi, darling...

FLUGEL, *getting up, rubbing his behind and shaking his head.* Ach du lieber, vat a city! Vat a city! Vat a city!...

The curtain falls on a bewildered FLUGEL, *as* CASIMIR, *taking the envelope from his pocket, slowly and dejectedly rips it up into confetti.*

CURTAIN

CAUGHT WITH HIS
TRANCE DOWN

·

Dormez, je le veux!

CHARACTERS

BORIQUET

JUSTIN

MAX

VALENCOURT

FRANCINE

ANTOINETTE

The drawing room in BORIQUET's *elegant bachelor apartment. Upstage center, a double door. Next to it, either standing or on the wall, a clock. Downstage right, a door. Upstage left, an open doorway. Downstage left, a fireplace with logs and the usual utensils, including a broom in the corner and a feather duster on the mantle. Between the doorway and the fireplace, a coatrack. In front of the fireplace, parallel to the wall, a large, solid desk, appropriately equipped with books, inkwell, papers, etc. Between the desk and the wall, a chair. On the other side of the desk, an armchair, facing the audience. Upstage right, a sideboard. On top of it, a basket of bread and a bottle of wine. In front of it, a small square table, with two chairs, facing each other, left and right. Downstage right, a canape, not quite parallel with the footlights. Other furniture—lamps, bric-a-brac, pictures, etc.*—ad lib.

At rise, JUSTIN *enters, up center, followed by* MAX, *who is carrying a big trunk on his back.*

JUSTIN. Here... This way, this way... (*Pointing center stage.*) Put it over here.

MAX, *with a heavy German accent.* Ya, ya... (*Panting.*) Ach! Dat's vun heavy sonofabitch!... (*Laying down the trunk, heaving a sigh.*) Whew! Dat feels good to get dat ting off mein back a little!

JUSTIN, *shaking his head, with something of a sneer.* Believe me, you'd never catch me lugging around a load like that. I've got better things to do with my time.

MAX. Ha! You tink I don't got better tings too? But mein boss says do, so I do. Vat else?

JUSTIN. Well, he could tell me to do it until he was blue in the face... Not a chance... (MAX *casts a doubtful look.*) First of all, it's doctor's orders... Nothing heavy... That's what he told me...

MAX. Ach, so?

JUSTIN. "If it's heavy, don't touch it." (MAX *nods*.) Like lobster, for instance...
I can't go near lobster...

MAX. Bitte?

JUSTIN. Lobster...

MAX, *uncomprehending*. Ya... Vat about?

JUSTIN. Doctor's orders... Too heavy, he told me... So if I can't eat lobster,
I'll be damned if I go around lugging heavy trunks...

MAX, *scratching his head*. Vat you talking... I don't eat lobster too, but
dat vouldn't keep me from lugging, lugging, lugging!

JUSTIN. Well then, you should do like me. (*He looks around to make sure
nobody is listening*.) I make my boss do it.

MAX, *incredulous*. You vat?

JUSTIN. So help me!

MAX. You make your boss he should carry his bags?

JUSTIN. His, and mine too if I want!

MAX. Mein Gott! Vat kind a boss is dat? (JUSTIN *gives a modest little shrug,
as if it were the most natural thing in the world*.) Vat kind a saint he
must be, such a boss!

JUSTIN. Boriquet?.., A saint?... Don't make me laugh! He's the world's
worst grouch...

MAX. But I tought you said—

JUSTIN. I did. (*Looking around again*.) I have a special system.

MAX. A zystem?

JUSTIN. That's right. I do it with hypnotism.

MAX. You do it mit...

JUSTIN. Hypnotism... The fluid...

MAX. De flu?... Dat vouldn't be catching maybe?

JUSTIN. No, no... Not the flu!... The fluid! The hypnotic fluid... You
know... Mesmerism, magnetism...

MAX. Maggot vat?

JUSTIN, *enunciating*. Magnetism... (MAX *shakes his head*.) I'm telling you,
it's fantastic! (*Glancing toward the doorway, up left*.) Listen, here he
comes... You want to see me make him carry your trunk? Just watch...

He moves behind the trunk. BORIQUET *enters, up left.*

BORIQUET, *brusquely*. Well? What's all this? What's going on here?

JUSTIN. This is Max, monsieur. Doctor Valencourt sent him ahead with the
baggage. He and mademoiselle have just arrived from Strasbourg.

BORIQUET. Aha!

MAX, *with a click of the heels, bowing from the waist*. Monsieur! A pleasure...

   He holds out his hand to BORIQUET.

BORIQUET, *ignoring his hand, nodding*. I see... (*Glancing around the room, then at his watch*.) But... You mean the doctor and his daughter aren't coming for lunch?

MAX. Nein, monsieur. For lunch dey say you shouldn't expect. Dey vas going to get someting at de station a little. Later dey come und move in.

BORIQUET. Well, they're welcome any time, I'm sure... (*To* JUSTIN, *pointing to the trunk*.) Give the young man a hand, Justin. We'll put the doctor in the bedroom off the hall, and Mademoiselle Valencourt can use the little room next to it.

JUSTIN, *with a wry smile*. Yes, monsieur.

   JUSTIN *and* MAX *move up behind the trunk, whispering to each other, as* BORIQUET *sits down in the armchair, facing the audience*.

BORIQUET, *aside, sighing*. No turning back now! Just make it official, set the date, and wait for the wedding.

MAX, *in a whisper, aside to* JUSTIN, *who is eyeing* BORIQUET. Vell? I don't see notting yet...

JUSTIN, *whispering*. Just watch... (*He sneaks up behind* BORIQUET *and makes several Svengali-like passes behind his back*.) You'll see!

   Little by little, as JUSTIN *continues,* BORIQUET *falls into a hypnotic trance*.

MAX, *still in a whisper, awkwardly duplicating* JUSTIN's *gestures*. But vat's mit so?

JUSTIN. Shhh! It's the fluid! (*To* BORIQUET, *still standing behind him*.) Can you hear me?

BORIQUET, *hypnotized*. Yes.

JUSTIN. "Yes" what?

BORIQUET. Yes, monsieur.

JUSTIN. Are you asleep?

BORIQUET. Yes, monsieur.

JUSTIN. Are you in my power?

BORIQUET. Yes, monsieur.

MAX. Mein Gott! He's sick!

JUSTIN, *turning to* MAX. Not at all. He's just under the influence...

MAX. Vat?... Vat you talking? Sober he vas, like a judge... Mit mein own eyes I see...

JUSTIN. No, no, no! I mean the influence of the fluid. It's hypnotism. I told you...

MAX, *still not comprehending.* Ach, so...

JUSTIN, *to* BORIQUET, *as* MAX *looks on in disbelief.* All right now, stupid! Up! On your feet! (BORIQUET *stands up, motionless.*) Now come with me. (*He motions with his forefinger and leads* BORIQUET *center stage, in front of the trunk.*) You're turning into a dog... a dog... You're turning into a dog... (*As he speaks,* BORIQUET *gradually gets down on all fours.*) There! Very good!... (*To* MAX.) See?

MAX. Mein Gott!

JUSTIN, *to* BORIQUET. You're a dog, understand?

BORIQUET, *barking.* Woof woof! Woof woof!

JUSTIN. Good! Give me your paw. (BORIQUET *complies.*) Fine! Nice dog!... Now sit up and beg. (*Again* BORIQUET *obeys.*) Very good! That's fine!

MAX. Gott in Himmel! In de circus you should be already! Draining de elephants... Und de lions, und de tigers...

JUSTIN, *still to* BORIQUET. All right... Now I'm going to turn you into a woman... a pretty, young woman... (BORIQUET *gets up and begins to assume a feminine stance.*) A pretty, young woman... Understand?

BORIQUET, *in a high-pitched voice.* Yes, monsieur.

JUSTIN. Very good! And we're going for a walk... (*He leads him downstage, far left.*) A nice little walk... (*They stop by the fireplace.*) There! (JUSTIN *picks up the feather duster from the mantle.*) Now turn around and let's walk back.

BORIQUET *obeys.*

MAX, *shaking his head, laughing.* Never in mein life...

JUSTIN, *as* BORIQUET *reaches the trunk.* Careful! Careful, mademoiselle! Don't step in that puddle!

BORIQUET *stops short, makes a gesture as if to lift up a long skirt, and steps daintily over the trunk.*

MAX. Never, such a ting...

JUSTIN. Oh! Look at the pretty flower! (*He hands* BORIQUET *the feather duster.*) What a beautiful flower! What kind is it, mademoiselle?

BORIQUET, *smelling the feather duster with evident satisfaction, still in the same high voice.* A chrysanthemum.

JUSTIN. That's right. A chrysanthemum. Very good!... All right, now give it back... (BORIQUET *hesitates, clutching the feather duster to his bosom.*) I said give it back!

He pulls it out of BORIQUET's *grasp, goes over to the fireplace and puts it back on the mantle.*

MAX. Never... Never in a million years...

JUSTIN, *returning to* BORIQUET. There! That's enough of that, stupid! No more tricks... (*Holding out his hand.*) Give me twenty francs!

BORIQUET *reaches into his vest pocket and automatically complies.*

MAX, *dropping his jaw.* Gott in Himmel!

JUSTIN. Fine! Now just because you've been so good, you can carry that trunk into the bedroom off the hall. And be sure to come back when you're finished. (BORIQUET *laboriously loads the trunk on his back, staggers under its weight, and exits, up left.*) And don't take all day!

He gives him a swift kick in the behind as he leaves.

MAX. Never in mein life...

JUSTIN, *brushing his hands together, up and down, as if to say "that's that!"* Well, are you convinced?

MAX. Ach, ya!... I could see vy dey call dat business kicknotism already!

JUSTIN, *with a condescending smile, sitting down behind the desk.* Hypnotism, my friend... Hypnotism... (*Emphasizing.*) Hyp... hyp...

MAX, *clapping.* Hoorah!

He sits down in the armchair.

JUSTIN, *making himself comfortable, musing smugly.* Yes... That's the kind of work for me! I could do it all day!

MAX. Dat you could say again, mein Gott! A boss vat does de vork, vat breaks his back... (JUSTIN *nods.*) But... but vat you...? How you...?

JUSTIN, *pointing to his eyes.* The eyes, Max... The fluid, and the eyes... (MAX *scratches his head, puzzled.*) I give him a look... a long, hard look... like this... (*He demonstrates.*) And the fluid goes "pshhhh"...

MAX, *nodding.* "Pshhhh"?

JUSTIN. And that's all there is to it.

MAX. Ach, so? (*Admiringly.*) Und dat's a hard ting, to make de vluid go "pshhhh"?

JUSTIN. Not really... as long as you've got a good strong will... It happened to me one day... out of a clear blue sky... I was looking at this girl... A real beauty...

MAX. Ach, so?

JUSTIN. And I said to myself: "Damn! Will you take a look at that! I wouldn't mind getting to know that better!..."

MAX, *waxing enthusiastic.* Ya, ya...

JUSTIN. So I give her the eye, if you know what I mean...

MAX. Ya, ya...

JUSTIN. Just so she gets the message...

MAX. Und so?

JUSTIN. Well, all of a sudden, she's staring right back. And next thing I know she's almost on top of me, looking me in the eye, practically sticking her nose in my face... No matter which way I turn, I can't shake her... Back, forth, left, right... still there! So I tell myself: "Look, you've got to do something! You can't let her spend the whole goddamn night!..."

He gets up.

MAX, *getting up too.* Vat you talking? Dat's not vat you vas after a little?

JUSTIN. Of course! But not like that!... Besides, I was beginning to get crosseyed... So anyway, I take a chance and snap my fingers. (*Demonstrating.*) Like that... Pffft! One, two, three! She wakes right up...

MAX. Nein! Such a ting...

JUSTIN. And that's how I found out I had the magnetic fluid!

MAX, *shaking his head.* Ach, Gott! You tink dat maggot shtuff, vat you call... You tink J could maggotize mein boss too, de same like you?

JUSTIN. Who knows? It's worth a try. Like I say, Max... As long as you've got a good strong will... You just stand behind him and give a long, hard look... (MAX *tries.*) Harder!... Harder!... That's it... Then you aim your fingers and let the fluid go "pshhhh"... (*He makes a few passes, which* MAX *imitates as best he can.*) And you keep saying over and over to yourself: "Sleep, sleep, sleep, sleep..." Then you wait and see. If he starts going to sleep, you know you've got him, and you tell him to do anything you please.

He moves toward the doorway, up left, and listens.

MAX, *shaking his head in admiration.* Ach du lieber! Such a ting dat science business! I'm telling you, fantastisch!... Vell, I give a try. Today even. Und ve see vat happens... Ach, I show dat sonofabitch! I show vat it feels to break your neck already!

BORIQUET *enters, up left, still hypnotized.*

JUSTIN. Well, well! Look what's back! (*Leading him by the nose, downstage.*) All right, you! This way...

MAX, *still agog.* Fantastisch!

JUSTIN, *to* BORIQUET. Did you put the trunk in the bedroom, like I told you?

BORIQUET. Yes.

JUSTIN. "Yes" what?

BORIQUET. Yes, monsieur.

JUSTIN, *leading him to the armchair*. Good!... Here, sit down... (*To* MAX, *as* BORIQUET *obeys*.) Now we wake him up.

He snaps his fingers in BORIQUET's *face*.

BORIQUET, *waking up*. As I was saying...

JUSTIN, *obsequiously*. Monsieur called?

BORIQUET, *a little disoriented*. No... I... (*Looking around*.) What about the trunk?

JUSTIN. The trunk, monsieur?

BORIQUET. Yes. I told you two to put it in the bedroom off the hall.

JUSTIN. We did, monsieur.

BORIQUET. Already?

JUSTIN. Yes, monsieur.

He pretends to huff and puff, winking at MAX, *who proceeds, exaggeratedly, to do likewise*.

BORIQUET. Damn!... It didn't take you long! I hardly turned around...

JUSTIN, *with an air of false modesty*. Well, when I put my mind to something, monsieur...

BORIQUET, *aside*. He's got his faults, but at least he works fast!

MAX, *to* BORIQUET. I go now, monsieur, maybe?

He moves toward the doorway, up left.

BORIQUET, *waving him off*. Yes... Go ahead... (*To* JUSTIN, *who is about to follow* MAX *off*.) No, no, Justin. Not you... You stay here...

MAX *exits*.

JUSTIN. Monsieur has something he wants me to do?

BORIQUET, *standing up*. Yes, Justin. Mademoiselle Francine will be joining me for lunch...

He goes to the desk, picks out a cigar, and puts it into a cigar holder.

JUSTIN, *aside, between his teeth*. Ugh! That dull old—

BORIQUET, *overhearing him*. I beg your pardon?

JUSTIN. Monsieur?

BORIQUET. Did I hear you refer to my sister as "that doll"?

JUSTIN, *feigning shock*. Oh, monsieur! Me? Take a liberty like that? Why, I'd never—

BORIQUET. Well, I certainly hope not! (JUSTIN *turns aside with a meaningful grimace, as* BORIQUET *lights his cigar and sits down in the armchair*.) Now then, you'll set the table for two... (JUSTIN *takes a few steps upstage*.) But first I want you to give this place a thorough sweeping...

JUSTIN. Yes, monsieur.

BORIQUET. Thorough, understand?

JUSTIN. Of course, monsieur.

BORIQUET. Because yesterday, frankly, it looked as if you hardly lifted the broom. I'm sure you can do better!

JUSTIN, *obsequiously*. Much obliged for calling it to my attention, monsieur. I won't let it happen again.

BORIQUET. Please see that it doesn't!

JUSTIN. Was that all monsieur had to tell me?

BORIQUET. Yes, that's all... No, wait!... At twelve noon you'll go downstairs and pick up my mail. And at twelve thirty you'll go down to the cellar and bring up the firewood.

JUSTIN. Very good, monsieur. Is that all?

BORIQUET, *waving him away*. Yes, that's all...

JUSTIN *moves upstage, as if about to leave, then tiptoes back and plants himself behind* BORIQUET, *sitting in the armchair, facing the audience*.

JUSTIN, *hands on hips, aside*. Here we go! (*He performs his hypnotic passes once again, and* BORIQUET *gradually falls into a trance*.) There! (*To* BORIQUET.) Can you hear me?

BORIQUET. Yes.

JUSTIN. "Yes" what, goddammit!

BORIQUET. Yes, monsieur.

JUSTIN. That's better! How many times... Are you asleep?

BORIQUET. Yes, monsieur.

JUSTIN. Are you in my power?

BORIQUET. Yes, monsieur.

JUSTIN, *making him stand up*. All right, on your feet! (BORIQUET *stands up and* JUSTIN *hands him the broom from the fireplace*.) Here! It's time to give this place a thorough sweeping. Thorough, understand?

BORIQUET. Yes, monsieur.

JUSTIN. Because it seems you didn't think too much of the job you did yesterday. And it better not happen again, my friend!... I'll be damned if I want you to jump down my throat for your own sloppy housework! A little muscle this time! You hear?

BORIQUET. Yes, monsieur.

JUSTIN. Good!... Now get started! (BORIQUET *takes the broom.*) And after that you'll set the table... For two, don't forget... (*Peevishly.*) Because you had to go and invite that dull old hag... Oh!... That damn... Couldn't land herself a man with a meathook, and now we've got her on our hands for good... And you go and invite her for lunch... instead of just the two of us... (*Impatiently.*) Come on, get to work!... (*Noticing that* BORIQUET *has put his cigar in his mouth.*) Wait a minute! Who said you could smoke?... What do you think... I'll take that! (*He pulls the cigar out of* BORIQUET's *mouth, leaving the empty holder between his teeth.*) The nerve!... (*He sits down in the armchair, relaxes, puffing with obvious relish as* BORIQUET *begins sweeping, none too energetically.*) Ah, yes... No two ways about it, this is my kind of work!... (*He puffs away for several moments, finally noticing* BORIQUET's *lethargic performance.*) Come on, you! What do you think you're... I said "muscle," remember?... What kind of a... You're sweeping a floor, you're not painting a picture!... Come on, get your back into it! (BORIQUET *sweeps a little faster.*) Harder!... Harder!... (BORIQUET *begins working at breakneck speed.*) That's better... (*To the audience.*) You know how they are! If you don't keep after them... (*He takes a few puffs.*) Ah! I could work like this all day! He gets my blisters... (*Puffing.*) And I smoke his cigars. That's what I call a real fair trade!... (*Coughing, as* BORIQUET *begins sweeping up a cloud of dust right under his nose.*) Hey, goddammit! Watch what you're... Give me that broom! (*He grabs the broom and puts it back in the corner.*) That's clean enough for you! If you don't like the way you did it, you can let me know next time!... Now listen! I'm going to wake you up... Just one thing. At exactly twelve noon... Pshhh! Back to sleep! Understand?

BORIQUET, *through his teeth, which are still clenching the empty cigar holder.* Yes, monsieur.

JUSTIN. Good!... And you'll go downstairs and bring up the mail... nice and polite... like this... (*He goes through the motions of approaching the desk and laying down a pile of letters.*) "The mail, monsieur." Then you'll sit down and wake up, as if nothing ever happened. And at twelve thirty, same thing... Back to sleep, down to the cellar, get a pile of firewood, bring it upstairs, put it in the bedrooms, come back here, wake up, and that's that!... Is all that clear?

BORIQUET. Yes, monsieur.

JUSTIN. Good! (*Leading him to the armchair.*) All right now, sit down... (BORIQUET *obeys, as* JUSTIN, *looking around to make sure that everything is in order, is struck by a sudden afterthought.*) Ah! (*He takes a few more puffs on the cigar, then puts it back in the holder, still between* BORIQUET's *teeth.)* There!

He snaps his fingers.

BORIQUET, *waking up, taking the cigar from his mouth.* As I was saying...

JUSTIN. Will there be anything else, monsieur?

BORIQUET. No, I told you. That's all. You'll give this place a thorough sweeping, then you'll—

JUSTIN. I have, monsieur.

BORIQUET. I beg your pardon?

JUSTIN. I've already swept, monsieur.

BORIQUET, *surprised, looking around.* You have?

JUSTIN. Yes, monsieur.

BORIQUET. So fast?

JUSTIN. Yes, monsieur.

BORIQUET. But I never even noticed...

JUSTIN. I hardly ever notice it myself, monsieur.

BORIQUET, *shaking his head.* Well, I must say... *(Feeling his forehead.)* Good heavens, Justin! Is it warm in here, or is it me?

JUSTIN. I couldn't say, monsieur.

BORIQUET, *wiping the perspiration from his face.* I haven't budged, and I'm wringing wet.

JUSTIN. It must be spring fever, monsieur.

BORIQUET. Spring... What are you talking about? It's the middle of winter!

JUSTIN. Yes, monsieur. But I'm sure spring is on the way.

The doorbell rings.

BORIQUET, *at a loss, shrugging his shoulders.* Go see who that is.

JUSTIN. Yes, monsieur.

He exits, up center.

BORIQUET, *shaking his head.* There's something... I can't put my finger on it, but...

He gives another puzzled shrug.

JUSTIN, *returning.* Monsieur's sister, monsieur.

He steps aside as FRANCINE *enters, close behind.*

FRANCINE, *to* BORIQUET. Marcel, precious! Let me look at you...

BORIQUET. Francine!

FRANCINE. Goodness me, dear boy! Aren't we a little pale this morning!

She takes off her hat and coat and hangs them up on the coatrack, up left.

BORIQUET. Pale? Me?... I was just telling Justin... If anything, I feel flushed.

FRANCINE. Oh?

BORIQUET. All I do is sit here, smoke my cigar... And all of a sudden I'm sweating like a... I mean, I feel as if I've been running a race, or something!

During the preceding, JUSTIN *has taken the table in front of the sideboard, up right, and moved it center stage, along with the two chairs. He begins to set the table for two, with tablecloth, silverware and glasses, from the sideboard.*

FRANCINE, *wagging her finger*. It's those cigars, Marcel! I keep telling you not to smoke...

BORIQUET, *shrugging*. I don't know... It's the same thing every day. Always just about this time, too. Right, Justin?

JUSTIN, *observing* BORIQUET *while setting the table*. If monsieur says so, monsieur.

BORIQUET, *to* FRANCINE. See? (*To* JUSTIN.) As soon as you start to clean up the apartment.

JUSTIN. Yes, monsieur. Now that monsieur mentions it.

FRANCINE. Hmm! It sounds like your liver to me...

BORIQUET, *to* FRANCINE. Well, liver or not... One of these days I'll have to look into it. It's really becoming... (*To* JUSTIN, *waving him off, impatiently*.) Well? What are you waiting for?

JUSTIN. Monsieur?

BORIQUET. Serve us!

JUSTIN. Of course, monsieur.

He exits, up left.

FRANCINE, *looking at the table set for two*. But I thought... You mean... Doctor Valencourt and his daughter won't be joining us for lunch?

BORIQUET, *sitting on the canape, down right*. I'm afraid not. All night in the train, after all... By the time they would freshen up and get settled, they thought it would be too late. Their young man said they're having a bite at the station, but they'll be along shortly... (FRANCINE *looks at him for a long moment, in silence, fighting back her tears*.) Rather soon, I imagine... (*Noticing her*.) Francine?

FRANCINE, *holding out her arms, in a burst of emotion.* Oh! Marcel... Precious!... (BORIQUET *gives her a quizzical look as she sits down in the armchair by the desk.*) When I think that... that soon you'll be a married man, with a home of your own, and... and a family of your own, and...

BORIQUET, *nodding.* Ah yes! That's the way of the world, my dear...

FRANCINE, *whimpering.* Of course... But... but...

BORIQUET. But what, for heaven's sake?

FRANCINE, *reluctantly.* Well... me, Marcel... What about me?... Once you have a wife, that is... What will that make me?

BORIQUET, *not quite comprehending.* What will... Why, her sister-in-law, I should think...

FRANCINE. No, no... I mean...

BORIQUET, *understanding.* Aha... You mean... (*Reassuringly.*) Why, you'll still be my sister! (*Affectionately.*) And you'll always be my sister!

FRANCINE. I know... But...

BORIQUET. Nothing is going to change...

FRANCINE. But...

BORIQUET. Now, now... You'll see, Francine! Everything is going to be just the same.

FRANCINE. It is?

BORIQUET. Everything... I promise...

FRANCINE. Thank you, Marcel... It's just that I... (*Gradually cheering up.*) Please don't misunderstand... I'm terribly happy for you. Really I am! It's a wonderful marriage... I'm perfectly delighted... You couldn't have chosen a lovelier young bride...

BORIQUET. I know!

FRANCINE. And such a famous father!

BORIQUET. Doctor Valencourt? I should say! "Famous" is hardly the word! He's one of the giants in his field, Francine. Why, he and that Doctor Freud... It's amazing what they do with this hypnosis of theirs.

FRANCINE. I know. It's all the rage.

BORIQUET. The people they actually cure, I mean...

He taps his temple with his forefinger.

FRANCINE. Yes, it seems it really works. Though frankly, Marcel, I'll never understand it. Putting people to sleep the way they do... It doesn't seem possible.

BORIQUET, *authoritatively.* Well, you have to realize... It only works with certain kinds. You know... high-strung, weak-willed... It would never work with me, for example.

FRANCINE. I should hope not!... Still, it must be quite a sight, don't you think? (BORIQUET *nods*.) I'll have to ask the doctor to let me watch some time.

BORIQUET. Please, after the wedding! First things first!

FRANCINE. Why, of course, Marcel! I didn't mean today! He's only here for one thing today, after all. To... to... (*She starts whimpering again.*) To give you his blessing, and... and...

BORIQUET, *smiling.* And not one day too soon, believe me! At my age, Francine, every day counts. I'm not getting any younger.

All at once the clock begins to strike twelve. At the first chime BORI-QUET'*s expression suddenly freezes in a glassy stare.*

FRANCINE, *wiping her eyes.* No, I don't suppose... (*Noticing* BORIQUET'*s expression.*) Good heavens, Marcel! What ever is the matter?... (BORI-QUET *remains silent.*) Marcel, precious! What is it?... What's wrong? (*At the last chime,* BORIQUET *springs up from the canape and dashes out, up center.*) My God!... Marcel!... (*Running to the door, calling after him.*) Marcel!...

JUSTIN *enters, up left, carrying a platter with a chicken, and a bowl brimming with salad.*

JUSTIN. Luncheon is... (*Looking around for* BORIQUET.) Monsieur?

He places the platter and bowl on the sideboard, up right, next to the basket of bread and the bottle of wine already there.

FRANCINE. Justin! My brother... He just... We were sitting here talking, and all of a sudden he jumped up like a madman and... and ran out the door!

JUSTIN, *suddenly understanding, aside.* Aha! Twelve o'clock!

FRANCINE. Where on earth did he go?

JUSTIN. I really don't think madame need concern herself. It's just one of monsieur's harmless little quirks... He likes to run downstairs now and then...

FRANCINE. He what?

JUSTIN. But he always comes back. No problem... Really...

FRANCINE. But...

JUSTIN. If madame would take my advice, she wouldn't even mention it. Monsieur gets rather annoyed...

FRANCINE. Well, I must say, I can't help worrying! If you saw the way... It's not like Marcel! It's not like him at all!... I mean, one minute we're talking, and the next minute I look at him and... (*Her gaze meets* JUSTIN'*s.*)

I look at him and... (*Beginning to feel the unintentional effects.*) I look at him... (*Shaking her head in an effort to resist.*) Please, don't stare at me that way... It makes me dizzy...

JUSTIN, *aside*. Well, what do you know!

FRANCINE. It makes me feel all...

She shudders.

JUSTIN, *aside*. It must run in the family...

FRANCINE. Really... I just don't understand...

JUSTIN, *aside*. Let's find out!

He moves behind her and performs his hypnotic passes as she speaks.

FRANCINE. One minute we're talking... (*Gradually succumbing.*) and the next minute I... the next minute I... the next minute... I... I... I...

She stands there, motionless, as the trance takes effect.

JUSTIN, *clenching his fist in triumph*. Perfect! Both of them!... Well, that's going to come in handy, damn it!

He snaps his fingers in front of her face, then goes over to the table, pretending to arrange the settings.

FRANCINE, *waking*. What... what happened?

JUSTIN, *playing dumb*. Madame was saying?

FRANCINE, *passing her hand in front of her eyes*. I... I was saying... (*Still confused.*) What was I saying?

JUSTIN. Madame was a little concerned about Monsieur Boriquet. And I was telling her not to worry... (*Looking toward the door, up center.*) See? Here he comes now.

BORIQUET enters, carrying a tray with several letters and newspapers, his face still frozen in the same blank stare.

FRANCINE. Marcel! For heaven's sake...

BORIQUET, *walking slowly to the desk and laying down the tray*. The mail, monsieur...

He goes back to the canape and sits down.

FRANCINE, *to* BORIQUET, *as he crosses in front of her*. What? What did you say?

BORIQUET, visibly released from the trance by carrying out the command, wakes up.

BORIQUET. I beg your pardon?

FRANCINE. I said: "What did you say?"

BORIQUET, *smiling*. I said: "I'm not getting any younger."

FRANCINE. No you didn't! You said: "The mail, monsieur..."

BORIQUET. I said what?

FRANCINE. You said... (*Emphasizing*.) "The mail, monsieur..."

BORIQUET. Don't be silly! Why should I say a thing like that?

FRANCINE. I'm sure I can't imagine!

JUSTIN, *still over by the table, catches* FRANCINE's *eye and motions to her, subtly, not to belabor the point.*

BORIQUET, *to* JUSTIN. You tell her, Justin. Did I say: "The mail, monsieur..."?

JUSTIN. I'm sorry, monsieur. I really wasn't listening.

BORIQUET,. Why the devil should I say... (*To* FRANCINE.) No, no. I said: "I'm not getting any younger..." But you thought I said: "The mail, monsieur..."

FRANCINE. Oh?

BORIQUET, *aside*. She must be getting deaf.

FRANCINE, *casting an anxious look at* BORIQUET *and shaking her head*. Really, Marcel...

BORIQUET, *abruptly*. And anyway, it's time to eat. (*To* JUSTIN.) What are you waiting for, Justin? Where on earth is our lunch?

JUSTIN. Lunch, monsieur? (*Pointing to the sideboard*.) I beg monsieur's pardon, but it's been ready for the last ten minutes, monsieur.

BORIQUET. It... Well why didn't you say so? (*Standing, to* FRANCINE.) Come, Francine... before it gets cold...

FRANCINE, *getting up, still obviously concerned, sighing*. I just don't understand...

They sit down at the table, facing each other. BORIQUET *tucks his napkin inside his collar, as* JUSTIN *brings over the chicken, the salad, and the basket of bread.*

BORIQUET, *holding up his glass*. Justin!

JUSTIN. Of course, monsieur.

He takes the bottle of wine and fills both glasses.

BORIQUET, *cutting several slices of chicken, passing the platter to* FRANCINE. Some for you, my dear... (FRANCINE *serves herself and hands back the platter*.) Some for me...

He serves himself and puts down the platter.

JUSTIN, *standing behind the table, facing the audience, aside.* And some for you-know-who!

He performs his hypnotic passes toward both BORIQUET *and* FRANCINE, *as inconspicuously as possible.*

BORIQUET, *quickly feeling the effects, lifting his glass as if to toast.* To... To...

FRANCINE, *doing likewise.* To... To...

BORIQUET. To...

He falls into a trance, still holding his glass in the air.

FRANCINE, *succumbing in the same position.* To...

JUSTIN, *mimicking.* To, to, to... (*Triumphant.*) "Two" is right! Two is better than one any day!

MAX *enters, up left, and stands for a moment, agape, transfixed at the sight.*

MAX. Gott in Himmel! Vat you do now dis time already?

JUSTIN. Just doubling my staff, Max! Doubling my staff! (*To* BORIQUET *and* FRANCINE, *in a commanding tone.*) All right, you two! Up! Up on your feet!

They spring to their feet.

MAX. Fantastisch!

JUSTIN *takes the glasses out of their hands and puts them on the table.*

JUSTIN, *to* MAX. I was just going to sit down to lunch. Care to join me?

MAX, *wide-eyed.* Lunch? Ach, you bet!

He sits down in FRANCINE's *chair, rubbing his hands, as* JUSTIN *removes* BORIQUET's *napkin and tucks it inside his own collar.*

JUSTIN, *sitting in the other chair, to* BORIQUET *and* FRANCINE. Come on, you two! Come on!... Let's get busy! We want our lunch!

BORIQUET *and* FRANCINE, *hurrying to comply, begin a virtual tug of war with the platter of chicken.*

MAX. Such good vorkers dey are yet!

JUSTIN. What do you expect? They're still new at the job! (*To* BORIQUET.) You... Boriquet... You serve the chicken and let her serve the salad. (*To* FRANCINE.) Understand, Francine? The salad...

The two of them are quick to obey, plying MAX *and* JUSTIN *with their respective dishes.*

MAX, *digging in*. Ach, so! A horse I could eat already!

JUSTIN, *laughing*. Sorry! All we have on the menu today is chicken!

MAX, *laughing*. Please! You shouldn't vorry! I'll eat, I'll eat...

The proceed to eat, smacking their lips, licking their fingers, and making appropriate exclamations, as BORIQUET *and* FRANCINE *outdo each other to serve them.*

MAX. Better I tink ve should eat fast maybe. De doctor comes in no time... Und de mamzelle mit.

JUSTIN. I know... (*To* BORIQUET, *in a commanding tone.*) Boriquet, more wine!... (BORIQUET *hurries to refill their glasses.*) That reminds me... I meant to ask you... What is he doing in Paris?

MAX. He?... Who?

JUSTIN. Your boss... And why here, of all places?

MAX, *chewing a mouthful*. Ach, him!... Ding dong! Dat's vy!

JUSTIN. Ding... What?

MAX. Ding dong! Ding dong!... Soon it gives mit de vedding bells maybe, I tink.

JUSTIN. Oh? You mean his daughter...

MAX. Ya, ya! Mit some friend vat de doctor got in Paris here.

JUSTIN. Some friend... (*Suddenly almost choking, pointing to* BORIQUET.) Not him, I hope!

MAX. Him?... Dat old goat?... How could dat be, such a ting?

JUSTIN. Well, I hope not, goddammit! That's all I need! Some woman to come in and... (*With a wave of the hand.*) and ruin all this! After all my work...

MAX, *to* FRANCINE, *who, like* BORIQUET, *has continued serving throughout the dialogue.* More salad, bitte!... (FRANCINE *fails to react.*) You! Mamzelle!... More salad!... (*Still no reaction.*) Mamzelle!... (*To* JUSTIN.) So? Vat's mit? All of a sudden she don't listen no more?

JUSTIN. No, only when I tell her. Nobody else... (*To* FRANCINE.) Francine, monsieur wants more salad!

She rushes to serve him.

MAX. Mein Gott!... Fantastisch!... I try it mit mein boss, you can bet your life already!

The doorbell rings.

JUSTIN. Good God! Who's that?

He rips off the napkin.

MAX. Ach du lieber!... De doctor und de mamzelle maybe.

JUSTIN, *jumping up*. Damn!... I'd better wake them up... (*To* MAX.) Look, you go downstairs and let them in...

MAX, *getting up*. Ya, ya! I go...

He dashes off, up center.

JUSTIN, *calling after him*. And take your time!... (*To* BORIQUET *and* FRAN-CINE.) Listen, you two!... Both of you, sit down!... (*He has them sit in their original chairs*.) That's right... Now... (*He tucks the napkin inside* BORIQUET's *collar*.) Take these glasses... (*He puts a glass in each one's hand, fills them with wine, and raises their arms as they were before*.) Good!... All right, now...

He moves behind the table and prepares to assume his subservient pose. When he is sure that everything is in order, he snaps his fingers, waking both BORIQUET *and* FRANCINE *simultaneously*.

BORIQUET, *toasting*. To... To the future!

FRANCINE. To the future!

They clink glasses and drink. A moment later MAX *comes running back in*.

MAX, *waving his hands in front of* BORIQUET's *face to see if he is back to normal*. Monsieur!... Monsieur!...

BORIQUET. What on earth...

MAX. De doctor!... De doctor, monsieur... He comes... Und de mamzelle likevise.

BORIQUET, *springing to his feet*. Already? (*To* FRANCINE.) Good heavens, Francine! My fiancée and her father...

JUSTIN flinches at the word "fiancée."

FRANCINE, *jumping up, flustered*. Your father and his fiancée... I mean... Oh, my goodness! So soon?

They put down their glasses and throw their napkins down on the table.

BORIQUET, *to* JUSTIN, *pointing to the table*. Quick, Justin! Take care of all this!

He and FRANCINE *rush off, up center*.

JUSTIN, *fuming, replacing the table and chairs in their original position, near the sideboard*. Did you hear what he said?

MAX. To me it sounds like: "Mein fiancée..." Dat's vat.

JUSTIN. Exactly, goddammit!

MAX. Ach du lieber! Who vould tink...

JUSTIN. "Fiancée," my foot! Oh no! Not on your life!

MAX. An old fart like dat, mit a young mamzelle...

JUSTIN, *angrily laying the plates, napkins, silverware, etc. back on the side-board.* Who does he think he is? His "fiancée"... Just like that? One, two, three!... And he never says a word? Never tells me a thing about it? (*Apostrophizing the absent* BORIQUET.) Well, we'll see! You just wait!... A wife? Here?... Oh no! Over my dead body! No wife is going to break up our happy little home! Who the devil would do the housework? Who the devil—

MAX, *putting his finger to his lips.* Schweig!... Shhh!... Dey come now, I tink...

BORIQUET *enters, up center, and shows in* VALENCOURT *and* ANTOI-NETTE, *followed by* FRANCINE. VALENCOURT *is holding his coat and hat,* ANTOINETTE *is still wearing hers.*

BORIQUET. This way, Doctor... this way... What a pleasure to see you! Please, come right in!

VALENCOURT. Thank you, monsieur. The pleasure is all mine. (*Looking around, noticing* JUSTIN, *up right, still puttering with the dishes, etc.*) I'm glad to see you didn't wait for us for lunch...

BORIQUET. No, no, Doctor. (*Pointing to* MAX.) Your young man explained...

FRANCINE, *to* ANTOINETTE. I hope the trip wasn't too tiring, my dear?

ANTOINETTE. Oh, not for me, madame. But I'm afraid poor papa didn't sleep a wink all night.

BORIQUET, *to* VALENCOURT. Really, Doctor?

VALENCOURT, *covering a yawn.* Not a wink is right! You know how trains can be...

BORIQUET, *very solicitous.* Well then, please... don't stand on ceremony! Your rooms are ready. Why not go lie down...

VALENCOURT. Oh no! No need... A nap would finish me for the rest of the day!

FRANCINE, *to* ANTOINETTE. And you, my dear?

ANTOINETTE. Oh, I'm fine, madame. But I would like to put away my things and freshen up a bit. (*Dusting off her coat.*) After a whole night in that train...

BORIQUET. Of course! (*To* JUSTIN.) Show mademoiselle to her room, Justin.

JUSTIN. Yes, monsieur.

VALENCOURT, *yawning, to* MAX. And why don't you go unpack our bags...

He hands him his coat and hat. MAX *clicks his heels and gives a quick little nod.*

Justin, *up left, to* Antoinette. If mademoiselle would come this way...

He steps aside to let her pass.

Antoinette. Thank you.

She exits, with Max *close behind.*

Justin, *aside, sneering, under his breath.* Madame Boriquet? Well, we'll see about that!

He follows them out.

Boriquet, *approaching* Valencourt, *who, eyes closed, is almost asleep on his feet.* Now then, Doctor, since the three of us—

Valencourt, *opening his eyes with a start.* Hmm? What?... Who...? Oh, yes...

Boriquet, *with a nervous little laugh.* Doctor?

Valencourt. Monsieur?

Boriquet. You weren't sleeping, I hope...

Valencourt. No, no! Just resting my eyes... (*He rubs his eyes, shakes his head, yawning.*) There!... You were saying?

Boriquet, *pointing to the canape.* Please! (Valencourt *takes a seat on the canape,* Boriquet *sits down in the armchair, and* Francine *behind the desk.*) I was saying, Doctor, that since the three of us are here, we might as well chat about the... how shall I put it?... the... the matter closest to my heart...

Valencourt, *smiling.* Ah yes! By all means!... I should say!... Besides, it shouldn't take too long. I'm sure I don't have to tell you... I've always felt you would be the perfect son-in-law...

Boriquet, *obsequiously.* Why, thank you...

Valencourt. I only wanted to be sure that Antoinette... Well, you know what I mean...

Boriquet. Of course...

Valencourt. And I'm delighted to tell you that she accepts your proposal and looks forward to becoming Madame Boriquet...

Boriquet. Fine! Fine!

Valencourt. In fact, she says the sooner the better...

Boriquet, *enthusiastically.* She does?

Francine. How sweet!

Valencourt. Yes... It seems she has a bet with her cousin Madeleine...

Boriquet, *puzzled.* A bet?

Valencourt. Yes... She bet her that she'll be married by Christmas, and she'd really hate to lose...

BORIQUET, *somewhat taken aback*. Oh!... I see... I... (*Echoing* FRANCINE.) How sweet!

VALENCOURT. Yes... Dear child... (*Rather abruptly*.) Now then, monsieur... what say we talk figures?... You're...

BORIQUET, *aside*. Figures? (*To* VALENCOURT.) Thirty-eight... Thirty—

VALENCOURT. No, no... I mean, you're... you're comfortable, I assume?

BORIQUET, *settling back in his chair, uncomprehending*. Quite, thank you... And you?

VALENCOURT, *shaking his head, smiling*. I mean... (*Emphasizing*.) Comfortable... Well fixed, financially...

BORIQUET, *suddenly understanding*. Oh, financially!... I thought... (*Clearing his throat*.) Well, I think it's safe to say... If you consider twelve thousand francs a year "well fixed"... And that's only from my investments, of course.

VALENCOURT, *impressed*. Aha! Twelve thousand?

BORIQUET. Yes... Government bonds, municipal bonds, railroad stocks... (VALENCOURT *nods approval throughout the enumeration*.) Place Pigalle Gold Mines...

VALENCOURT, *interrupting*. Place Pigalle... That swindle? You're not serious! You weren't taken in by Place Pigalle Gold Mines!

BORIQUET, *sheepishly*. Well, I... Not too many shares...

VALENCOURT. I certainly hope not!

BORIQUET. One or two... (*Eager to change the subject*.) And besides, there's what I earn each year... Capital, that is... Between fifteen and twenty-five thousand, usually.

VALENCOURT. And... prospects for the future, I assume?...

BORIQUET. Why, yes... yes... (*Turning toward* FRANCINE.) My sister has a rather considerable estate...

FRANCINE. Please, Marcel! I'm still very much alive!

BORIQUET. I know, Francine. But some day, after all...

VALENCOURT. Well, monsieur... I'm happy to tell you that I'm able to give my daughter a very substantial dowry... (BORIQUET *affects an unconcerned shrug*.) Very substantial... Three hundred thousand francs, monsieur... (*Despite himself,* BORIQUET *is obviously impressed*.) Most of it, like yourself, in government bonds and railroad stocks. And the rest in petroleum, South African diamonds, industrial development, my real estate holdings, my shares in the Eiffel Tower...

BORIQUET, *with a start*. Your shares in the... You can't buy shares in the Eiffel Tower!

VALENCOURT, *ingenuously*. I can't?

BORIQUET. Good heavens, no! That's the oldest trick... They're not worth the paper they're printed on!

VALENCOURT, *embarrassed*. My, my... (*Reflecting.*) The gentleman looked so honest. I was sure...

BORIQUET. I know, but...

VALENCOURT, *with a wave of the hand*. And anyway, all the rest is as good as gold, believe me!

BORIQUET, *quick to agree, standing up*. Oh, I do! I do!... Besides, Doctor, I assure you... money is no object!

VALENCOURT, *standing up*. My sentiments exactly!... What more can I say?... (*He holds out his open arms to* BORIQUET *in an invitation to embrace*.) Welcome to the family!

FRANCINE, *misunderstanding, fighting back the tears, getting up and flinging herself into* VALENCOURT'*s arms*. Oh, Doctor! You dear...

VALENCOURT, *momentarily flustered*. I... I beg your pardon! I was... (*Pointing to* BORIQUET.) I was talking to him!

FRANCINE, *trying to cover her gaffe*. Of course... Of course you were! (*Pulling back and motioning* BORIQUET *into* VALENCOURT'*s arms*.) Go on, precious...

The two men embrace for a moment, as FRANCINE *looks on emotionally.*

VALENCOURT, *moving back to the canape*. Now then... (*Emphasizing.*) son! I think it's time you were having a little chat with Antoinette. Just the two of you, I mean... heart to heart... with my blessings.

BORIQUET. Why, certainly, Doctor! Of course!

VALENCOURT, *wagging his finger*. Please, please! It's "father" now, not "doctor"!

BORIQUET, *emotionally*. You... you don't know how happy you've made me... Father! You don't know how grateful, how... You... How can I find the words? How can I tell you all the things in my heart... all the love, all the...

VALENCOURT, *nodding*. I know, son. I know... You don't have to tell me.

BORIQUET. No, please, let me try. Let me just say... Let me just say that... that... (*The clock begins striking twelve thirty, and suddenly* BORIQUET'*s expression freezes in a hypnotic stare*.) I'm going down to bring up the firewood.

VALENCOURT, *startled*. What?

BORIQUET *turns and, robotlike, hurries off, up center, leaving the door open*.

FRANCINE, *nonplussed*. Good God! Not again!

VALENCOURT, *to* FRANCINE. What in the name of...

FRANCINE, *running to the door, calling after him*. Marcel!... Marcel!... (*She steps outside for a moment, then returns*.) No use... He must be down in the cellar by now.

VALENCOURT. Does he always do that sort of thing?

FRANCINE, *distraught*. No... Yes... I mean... (*Calling offstage*.) Justin!... Justin, come in here!

JUSTIN *appears at the doorway, up left*.

JUSTIN, *entering*. Madame?

FRANCINE, *peremptorily*. What is the meaning of this, Justin?

JUSTIN. Please?

FRANCINE. He... he just... (*Pointing to the door, almost at a loss for words*.) My brother... He just went running off again!... I mean, really!

JUSTIN, *ingenuously*. Monsieur Boriquet, madame?

FRANCINE. Of course, Monsieur Boriquet!

JUSTIN. Just like that, madame?

VALENCOURT, *interrupting, quizzically*. Something about bringing up the firewood, wasn't it?

FRANCINE. Exactly!

JUSTIN, *aside*. Aha! (*To* FRANCINE.) That's because it's twelve thirty, madame.

FRANCINE. So?

JUSTIN, *very matter-of-fact*. Monsieur always goes to the cellar at twelve thirty to bring up the firewood.

FRANCINE, *unable to believe her ears*. He what?

JUSTIN. Yes... It's another one of his little... what should I say?... one of his little quirks, madame...

FRANCINE. Indeed!

JUSTIN. At twelve noon it's the mail. At twelve thirty, the firewood.

FRANCINE. But...

JUSTIN. Really, there's no need to be concerned. If madame would take my advice, she would just let it pass. Monsieur hates to discuss it.

FRANCINE. But... It's not like him at all! (*To* VALENCOURT.) It's not normal, for heaven's sake!

VALENCOURT. Oh, I don't know... Some people... It's a personality trait. They like to be well organized... Everything right on schedule...

FRANCINE. But...

JUSTIN. And besides, it's for his health. Monsieur is a little anemic, and his
doctor told him he should get more exercise.

FRANCINE. Exercise? (*Pointing to the door, up center.*) That?

VALENCOURT, *with a little laugh.* I hardly think so!

BORIQUET *can be heard climbing the last few stairs outside the open
door, up center. He appears at the threshold, still in a hypnotic sleep,
carrying a heavy pile of wood on his back.* FRANCINE, *agape in disbelief,
looks at* VALENCOURT, *who seems more amused than surprised.*

FRANCINE, *to* BORIQUET. Marcel!... (*She moves upstage, trying to stop
him.*) Precious!...

BORIQUET *pushes her aside and, robotlike, exits through the doorway
up left.*

VALENCOURT. Well now!

FRANCINE, *following* BORIQUET. My God! Marcel!... (*Stopping at the
threshold, to* JUSTIN.) Help me, Justin... We've got to do something...

JUSTIN. Of course, madame.

He follows her out.

VALENCOURT, *shaking his head, chuckling.* Amusing chap, I must say! Him
and his firewood! (*Yawning.*) At least he's got a sense of humor... (*He
stretches, still yawning.*) My, my, my! I'm asleep on my feet...

*He goes over to the canape, stands with his hands on the backrest, and
closes his eyes. After a moment* MAX *appears at the doorway, up left.*

MAX, *entering.* All unpacked already! Just like you... (*Noticing* VALEN-
COURT, *aside.*) Ach! Mein boss, und nobody mit! (*He rubs his hands.*)
Vat a time like so to give a try mit de kicknotism! Mit de eyes, und de
fingers, und de "pshhhh, pshhhh, pshhhh"... (*He tiptoes up behind*
VALENCOURT, *awkwardly duplicating* JUSTIN'S *maneuvers, just as* VALEN-
COURT, *dozing, lets his head drop to his chest.*) Mein Gott! I tink... I
tink I done it yet! (*He goes around to the front of the canape and looks
at* VALENCOURT.) Fantastisch!... So!... Maggotized already!... Ach! Now
ve see maybe... (*He moves back behind* VALENCOURT, *gives him a kick
in the behind, and holds out his hand.*) All right, shtupid! Twenty francs,
bitte!

VALENCOURT, *waking up abruptly.* What?... I beg your... (*Turning
around.*) Max! What in the name...

MAX, *terrified.* Ach du lieber! I tought... I tought...

VALENCOURT. You thought what, you... you idiot!

He slaps his face several times with both sides of his hand.

MAX, *trying to fend off the blows.* Monsieur... Monsieur...

VALENCOURT, *still slapping.* You numbskull! You thought what...

MAX. Monsieur... Monsieur, please...

He tries to escape by running around the canape.

VALENCOURT, *chasing him.* Of all the... (*After several turns, back and forth, he catches up with him and gives him a good swift kick.*) There! How does that feel?

MAX. Ayyyy! Gott in Himmel!

VALENCOURT. Now get out of here, you... before I really lose my temper!

MAX. But monsieur—

VALENCOURT. Out, I said! I've got half a mind to fire you on the spot!

MAX, *limping off, up center.* Donner Wetter! I tought... I tought...

He exits.

VALENCOURT, *following him to the door, calling after him, still fuming.* You thought, you thought! (*He slams the door.*) Heaven knows what he thought!... That... that... (*Rubbing his behind.*) Of all the... He hasn't heard the last... (*Glancing out the doorway, up left, and noticing BORIQUET outside.*) Oh my! Boriquet! (*He makes an obvious effort to control himself, taking a few deep breaths, quickly adjusting his clothing, etc.*) There you are, son...

BORIQUET *enters, still hypnotized, but this time without the firewood.* FRANCINE *is close on his heels, with* JUSTIN *several steps behind.*

FRANCINE, *whining.* Please, Marcel!... Precious!...

BORIQUET, VALENCOURT, *and* FRANCINE *have returned to the exact spots where they were standing when the clock struck twelve thirty. Once back,* BORIQUET *is visibly released from the hypnotic suggestion, and his expression suddenly returns to normal, as* FRANCINE *and* VALENCOURT *look on.*

BORIQUET, *to* VALENCOURT, *naturally, as if continuing their conversation.* As I was saying, Father... I... (*Scratching his head.*) Hmm, what was I saying?

VALENCOURT. When?

BORIQUET. Just now.

VALENCOURT. Just now? You weren't saying anything. You were hauling a pile of logs.

BORIQUET, *startled*. I was what?

VALENCOURT. You were bringing up your firewood, if you'd rather put it that way.

BORIQUET, *amused*. My firewood?

He turns toward the audience, out of VALENCOURT's *sight, and taps his temple with his finger, smiling.*

JUSTIN, *aside to* VALENCOURT, *behind the canape.* Please, monsieur! I told monsieur how much he hates to discuss it.

He goes over to the sideboard, and without taking his eyes off the action, busies himself folding the napkins, etc. FRANCINE, *meanwhile, stands wringing her hands, looking at* BORIQUET *with obvious concern.*

VALENCOURT, *to* BORIQUET. Frankly, I think lifting weights would be better. Dumbbells... that sort of thing...

BORIQUET. Dumbbells?

VALENCOURT. Yes... You know...

He moves his arms up and down a few times, as if exercising, to illustrate.

BORIQUET. What for? Why dumbbells, for goodness' sake?

VALENCOURT. Well it's certainly better exercise than carrying a pile of logs on your back!

BORIQUET, *nodding quizzically.* Aha! No doubt...

VALENCOURT. And an iron tonic perhaps... Something with a little quinine...

BORIQUET *keeps nodding for a moment, then turns toward the audience with a blank expression and a shrug of the shoulders.*

BORIQUET, *to* VALENCOURT. Excuse me, Doctor... (*Correcting himself.*) Father... But I thought we were here to make plans for a wedding, not to talk about dumbbells and... and iron tonics. I mean...

VALENCOURT. Of course we are! I only thought, with your medical problem...

BORIQUET. My medical problem? Me?... My medical... (*Thumping his chest.*) Ha ha! I'm solid as a rock!

VALENCOURT. Oh?

BORIQUET, *a little obsequiously.* But thank you for being concerned. I'm touched.

VALENCOURT, *aside, nodding.* Yes, I'm beginning to think so!

BORIQUET. Now then, Father... about that little chat with Antoinette... heart to heart...

VALENCOURT. Yes, yes... You wait here. I'll send her right in. (*Aside.*) I'd better keep an eye on this son-in-law of mine!

He exits, up left.

FRANCINE, *to* BORIQUET. Really, Marcel! Are you sure you're quite all right?

BORIQUET. Am I sure... What's the matter with you people? Of course I'm all right! (*To* JUSTIN.) You tell her, Justin. How do I look to you?

JUSTIN, *still at the sideboard*. Solid as a rock, monsieur.

BORIQUET, *to* FRANCINE. There! You see?... Now be a dear, Francine... I'd like to speak with my fiancée... (*Emphasizing.*) Alone!

FRANCINE, *sighing*. Well, precious, if you're sure...

She exits, down right, shaking her head. BORIQUET *watches her leave, smiling at her solicitousness.*

BORIQUET, *after a few moments*. You too, Justin. (*Motioning him off.*) You can go now. I won't be needing you.

He sits down in the armchair, facing the audience, to wait for ANTOI-NETTE.

JUSTIN. Very good, monsieur. (*He pretends to go off, up left, looks out the doorway to make sure that no one is coming, then tiptoes back behind the chair, makes his hypnotic passes, and gradually puts* BORIQUET *into a trance.*) There!... (*Moving around and waving his hands in front of* BORIQUET's *glassy stare to be sure that he is hypnotized.*) Now we'll see who's going to get married! (*Glancing anxiously toward the doorway, up left, several times throughout the following exchanges.*) Better work fast... (*To* BORIQUET.) All right, can you hear me?

BORIQUET, *nodding*. Yes.

JUSTIN. And you're in my power?

BORIQUET. Yes.

JUSTIN. Good! Now listen carefully... Your fiancée is ugly! Very, very ugly! Understand?

BORIQUET. Yes.

JUSTIN. And you're going to tell her so!... You're going to tell her, aren't you? Right to her face!

BORIQUET. Yes.

JUSTIN. And you're going to say that you don't want to marry her. (*Empha-

sizing.) You don't want to marry her... Not for anything in the world...
As nasty as you can be! Right?

BORIQUET. Yes.

JUSTIN. Good! Now don't forget! She's ugly!... (*With a start, as he sees*
ANTOINETTE *outside the doorway, up left, approaching.*) Oh oh! Time to
go!

    He exits, up center, as ANTOINETTE *enters, but peeks surreptitiously
through the double door at the ensuing action.*

ANTOINETTE, *to* BORIQUET. Ah! There you are, monsieur... Papa says you
wanted to talk to me... (*Coyly.*) Just the two of us... alone...

BORIQUET, *grimacing.* Me? Me? Talk to you? What on earth about?

ANTOINETTE, *taken aback.* What on... Monsieur! I thought... I mean—

BORIQUET. I can't even stand the sight of you! Why should I want to talk
to you, for heaven's sake!

ANTOINETTE, *scandalized.* What... what are you saying?

BORIQUET. I'm saying that you're ugly! Ugly, ugly, ugly! Understand?

    *He makes a repulsive face, and sticks out his tongue at her with an
appropriate exclamation of disgust.*

ANTOINETTE. Monsieur! I don't—

BORIQUET. Ugly, ugly, ugly!

ANTOINETTE. I... I thought you wanted to marry me. I thought—

BORIQUET. Marry you? Marry... (*Pointing to the doorway, up left, through
which* VALENCOURT *exited a few moments before.*) And have an idiot for
a father-in-law?

ANTOINETTE, *moving up left.* Oh!

BORIQUET, *pointing at her.* And a scarecrow for a wife?

    He chases her toward the doorway.

ANTOINETTE, *stopping for a moment at the threshold, looking at* BORIQUET,
speechless, then turning around in a state of near panic and confusion.
Papa!... Papa!...

    She runs off.

BORIQUET, *with a grimace and a shudder as she leaves.* Ugly, ugly, ugly!

    He moves downstage and stands by the desk. JUSTIN, *as soon as he is
sure that* ANTOINETTE *has left, opens the double door and comes out of
hiding.*

JUSTIN, *rubbing his hands together, with a wry smile.* Perfect! Just perfect! I couldn't have done better myself! (*Anxiously eyeing the doorway, up left.*) Now to take care of the old man... (*Striding confidently up to* BORIQUET.) All right, you! Can you hear me?

BORIQUET. Yes.

JUSTIN. And you're still in my power?

BORIQUET. Yes.

JUSTIN. Good! Now listen! I'm turning you into a monkey. Understand? (BORIQUET *nods.*) Yes, you're a nice little monkey... (BORIQUET *begins to make appropriate gestures, scratching under his armpits and the like.*) A chimpanzee...

BORIQUET, *squealing.* Chee chee! Chee chee chee!

JUSTIN. Good! That's just right!... A chimpanzee... Don't forget...

JUSTIN *looks up left, sees* VALENCOURT *and* ANTOINETTE *about to enter, and moves upstage.* VALENCOURT *storms in, with* ANTOINETTE *close on his heels.*

ANTOINETTE, *on the verge of tears.* But Papa! I'm telling you—

VALENCOURT. Please, Antoinette! Let me handle this! (*Confronting* BORIQUET.) Now then, monsieur! My daughter tells me—

BORIQUET, *squatting on his haunches, squealing.* Chee chee! Chee chee chee!

He scratches a few times, then begins leaping wildly around the room, finally jumping up on the desk, still squealing. VALENCOURT *and* ANTOINETTE *look at each other in horrified disbelief.*

VALENCOURT. What in the name... (*Turning to* JUSTIN.) What on earth...

JUSTIN, *throwing his arms in the air, feigning deep concern.* Don't ask me, monsieur... I just came in and... and... (*Pointing to* BORIQUET.) Monsieur can see for himself!

VALENCOURT. Quick! Run and get his sister! It's some kind of attack!

JUSTIN. Right away, monsieur. (*Aside.*) Wait until he sees what I turn her into!

He runs off, down right, leaving the door open. BORIQUET, *still squatting on his desk, is absorbed in picking imaginary fleas, examining them minutely, and trying to eat them.*

VALENCOURT. Boriquet! For heaven's sake! What's got into you? What's the trouble?

Suddenly BORIQUET *jumps down from the desk and leaps over to* VALENCOURT. *He flings one arm around his neck, hangs with his feet off the ground, and, with his free hand, continues to pluck imaginary fleas, this time from* VALENCOURT.

ANTOINETTE, *terrified, taking refuge behind her father.* Oh, Papa!

VALENCOURT, *to* BORIQUET, *defending himself as best he can.* Get away! Get... Let me go! Let me... What do you think you're... Will you please...

ANTOINETTE, *screaming.* Papa! Papa!

VALENCOURT, *managing to break loose, to* ANTOINETTE. Shhh! Not so loud! He may be dangerous! (*Seeing* JUSTIN *outside the door, down right.*) Well? Where is she?

JUSTIN *enters, standing aside to observe the action.*

JUSTIN. She's coming, monsieur. She'll be right in.

He gives the audience a broad wink, as VALENCOURT *runs to the door to see for himself. A moment later* FRANCINE *comes bursting in, almost knocking* VALENCOURT *over, doing a caricature of a Spanish dance to the tune of the "Habañera" from* Carmen.

VALENCOURT. What...

FRANCINE, *clicking her heels and snapping her fingers.* Tra la la la, Tra la la la...

VALENCOURT, *agape.* Good God!

FRANCINE. Tra la la la la la la, Tra la la la...

ANTOINETTE, *huddling in* VALENCOURT'*s arms.* Papa! Papa!

FRANCINE. Tra la la la, Tra la la la, Tra la la la la la la, Tra la la la!

VALENCOURT. She's crazier than he is!

FRANCINE. Olé! Olé! Olé! (*Beginning again.*) Tra la la la, Tra la la la...

FRANCINE *continues, more and more frenetically, as* BORIQUET—*who, in the meantime, has jumped up on the armchair—claps his hands in rhythm, with frequent squeals of delight.*

VALENCOURT. Come, Antoinette! I think we've seen quite enough of this display! The wedding is off!

ANTOINETTE. Oh, Papa! Papa!

They exit, up left. As soon as they are gone, JUSTIN, *jubilant, raises his joined hands in a gesture of triumph.*

JUSTIN, *to* BORIQUET *and* FRANCINE, *both of whom are still carrying on.* All right, you two... Boriquet... Francine... That's enough! Settle down... (*They comply, as* BORIQUET *jumps down.*) Now that that's taken care of... From now on you're on your own!

He snaps his fingers in their faces and beats a quick retreat, exiting, down right, as they both wake up.

BORIQUET, *looking around, surprised to see* FRANCINE. Francine?... I thought you left...

FRANCINE, *puzzled.* I... I thought so too!

She stands for a few moments, out of breath, fanning herself with her hand, exchanging quizzical glances with BORIQUET, *who sits mopping his brow. A moment later,* VALENCOURT *returns, wearing his hat and coat.*

VALENCOURT, *entering.* Max!... Max!... (*Aside.*) Where is that imbecile?

BORIQUET, *standing up.* Father!

VALENCOURT. Don't "father" me, you... you madman!

BORIQUET, *taken aback.* What?

VALENCOURT. You... Oh! To think... (*Shuddering.*) I almost let Antoinette actually marry this lunatic!

BORIQUET, *going up to him.* But... but, Father... Monsieur... I mean, please...

VALENCOURT. Out of my way, monsieur! My daughter and I have stayed in this madhouse long enough! (*Opening the double door, calling.*) Max!... Max!...

BORIQUET. This... Please! I don't understand. I—

FRANCINE, *to* BORIQUET. Whatever does he mean, precious?

BORIQUET, *not knowing which way to turn.* I have no idea! I'm... I'm fit to be tied!

VALENCOURT, *overhearing.* Exactly! In a straitjacket! And the sooner the better! Before your next attack!

BORIQUET. My what?

VALENCOURT, *pointing to* FRANCINE. And that goes for your lunatic sister too!

FRANCINE, *scandalized.* Monsieur! I beg your—

VALENCOURT, *mimicking* FRANCINE's *dance, clicking his heels and snapping his fingers in the air several times.* Olé! Olé! Olé!

BORIQUET *and* FRANCINE *look at each other, nonplussed.*

BORIQUET. Monsieur?

VALENCOURT. You heard me! You're mad! The two of you!... (*He jumps up and down a few times, like a monkey, scratching under his arm.*) Mad, mad, mad!

He turns his back on them and looks out the door.

FRANCINE, *aside to* BORIQUET. Do you think he's dangerous?

BORIQUET, *aside to* FRANCINE. I don't know. But let's not wait to find out! (*To* VALENCOURT, *curtly.*) Of course, monsieur. Whatever you say...

He takes FRANCINE's *hand and they exit quickly, down right.*

VALENCOURT, *calling.* Max!... Max!...

MAX'S VOICE. Monsieur?

VALENCOURT. Get up here! (*Turning around, seeing that* BORIQUET *and* FRANCINE *have left, shaking his head.*) Thank goodness I found out in time! That's all I can say... Another few weeks, and... (*Shuddering.*) Oh!... Heaven help us!

ANTOINETTE *enters, up left, wearing her hat and coat.*

ANTOINETTE. I'm ready, Papa.

MAX *enters, up center.*

MAX, *timidly.* Monsieur?

VALENCOURT, *to* MAX. Go get our bags. We're leaving.

MAX. Monsieur?

VALENCOURT. I said: "Go get our bags. We're leaving."

MAX, *throwing his arms around* VALENCOURT's *neck.* Oh! Danke schön, monsieur! Danke schön!

VALENCOURT, *struggling out of his embrace.* What—

MAX. So monsieur don't got half his mind no more maybe?

VALENCOURT. What?

MAX. To fire me already... On de shpot, like he tells me...

VALENCOURT. We'll talk about that later. Just go get our bags.

MAX. Ach, please monsieur! Bitte!... Bitte!...

VALENCOURT, *impatiently.* I'll think about it! Now go get the bags!

MAX, *on the verge of tears, falling to his knees.* De whole ting vas Justin's fault, monsieur. All his idea it vas... Justin... Not me...

ANTOINETTE. What does he mean, Papa?

VALENCOURT, *to* MAX. Please—

MAX. Mit his vluid, und his... (*Awkwardly duplicating* JUSTIN's *hypnotic passes.*) his "pshhhh! pshhhh! pshhhh!"... Und his kicknotism business!

VALENCOURT, *with a start.* His what?

MAX. Kicknotism, monsieur... Vat he uses to make Boriquet go to shleep und do him all his vork inshtead already...

VALENCOURT, *suddenly comprehending.* "Make Boriquet..." Good God! You mean...

ANTOINETTE. Papa?

MAX. Und so, I tink... I tink... maybe if I try too a little...

VALENCOURT, *gradually moving up center, ignoring* MAX, *reflecting.* Of course! He hypnotized them...

MAX, *scuffling after him on his knees.* Just a little, monsieur...

VALENCOURT. That explains everything...

MAX, *pleading.* Monsieur...

VALENCOURT. Those attacks, those fits... (*Calling out the double door, up center.*) Justin!

ANTOINETTE. Papa?

VALENCOURT, *to* ANTOINETTE. I'll handle this... (*Moving to the doorway, up left, calling.*) Justin!

MAX, *following him, still on his knees.* Monsieur...

JUSTIN *enters, down right.*

JUSTIN. Someone called?

VALENCOURT, *crossing over to him, angrily.* There you are, you... you...

He grabs JUSTIN *by the collar and pulls him center stage, as* MAX, *still kneeling, and* ANTOINETTE *look on.*

JUSTIN, *stunned.* Monsieur...

VALENCOURT. You swine!

ANTOINETTE. Papa?

MAX. Mein Gott!

JUSTIN. Me, monsieur?

VALENCOURT. Oh, don't play dumb! I know what you've been up to! (*With his free hand, making a few exaggerated hypnotic passes, by way of illustration.*) I know your little game... Very clever... Now admit it!

JUSTIN, *struggling to free himself.* Let me go! Let me—

VALENCOURT. Admit it, I said! Admit it, you—

JUSTIN. Let me go, or I'll... I'll...

VALENCOURT, *still holding fast.* You'll what?

JUSTIN. I'll... Don't say I didn't warn you!

ANTOINETTE. Papa! Papa!

JUSTIN, *still in* VALENCOURT's *grip, begins staring into his eyes, and manages several hypnotic passes in his direction.*

MAX. Gott in Himmel! He's going to kicknotize him yet!

VALENCOURT, *with a wry laugh.* So that's the way you want to play... All right, my friend...

He fixes his gaze on JUSTIN *in return, and the two men engage in a long, intense hypnotic duel, each summoning all his skill to subdue the other.*

ANTOINETTE. Papa! Papa!... (*To* MAX.) Please, stop them, Max! Stop them!

MAX, *gradually getting up off his knees to follow the contest.* Ach du lieber, mamzelle! I vouldn't go near such a business! Such giants like dat!

ANTOINETTE. Oh...

VALENCOURT, *to* JUSTIN, *in the thick of the struggle.* You've met your match this time, young man! I've studied with Freud...

JUSTIN. We'll see about that...

The combat continues in silence, more and more intense, under the anxious gaze of ANTOINETTE. MAX, *now on his feet, looks on with evident admiration. After a few moments* JUSTIN *begins to weaken. Little by little he crumbles under* VALENCOURT'S *superior ability. Before long it is clear that he is completely in the doctor's power.* VALENCOURT *releases his grip on* JUSTIN *and, placing one finger between his eyes, turns him to face the audience.*

VALENCOURT. Voilà!

MAX, *applauding.* Bravo! Bravo, monsieur! Bravo!

ANTOINETTE, *relieved.* Oh, Papa!

VALENCOURT, *to* JUSTIN. All right, you! Down on your knees! (JUSTIN *docilely obeys, as* VALENCOURT *goes to the door, down right, and calls.*) Boriquet!... Madame!...

BORIQUET *and* FRANCINE *enter, rather tentatively.*

BORIQUET, *stiffly, to* VALENCOURT. Are you still here, monsieur?

VALENCOURT. Yes... And you'll never believe what I have to tell you.

FRANCINE, *pointing to* JUSTIN. What on earth... (*To* JUSTIN.) Justin! What are you—

VALENCOURT. Don't bother, madame. He can't hear you.

FRANCINE. He can't?

VALENCOURT. No, he's hypnotized. He can't hear anyone's voice but mine.

BORIQUET. Hypnotized? What for, for heaven's sake?

VALENCOURT. That's what I have to tell you...

FRANCINE. Hypnotized?

VALENCOURT. Please, if you let me explain... A few moments ago, you remember... I called you both some rather nasty names...

BORIQUET, *snidely.* "Lunatics," to be exact!

FRANCINE. Yes, we remember!

VALENCOURT. Well, now I find out that it wasn't your fault at all!

BORIQUET, *after a puzzled glance at* FRANCINE, *to* VALENCOURT. What wasn't our fault?

VALENCOURT. All those idiotic things you were doing.

FRANCINE, }
BORIQUET, } *together*. {I beg your pardon!
{What?

VALENCOURT. But it wasn't your fault, don't you see? He made you do them. You were hypnotized.

FRANCINE *and* BORIQUET *stand aghast*.

FRANCINE, }
BORIQUET, } *together*. {What?
{We were hyp—

VALENCOURT. That's right...

BORIQUET. You mean... (*Pointing to* JUSTIN.) He... he...

VALENCOURT. Precisely! When I caught him at his little game he tried to hypnotize me too. Only this time he met his match. (*Pointing to* JUSTIN.) You can see for yourselves...

BORIQUET, *still incredulous*. Hypnotized? Me?

FRANCINE. But... but why? I don't understand...

VALENCOURT. Listen... We'll let him tell you himself... (*To* JUSTIN, *sternly*.) All right, Justin. Tell us what you've been doing to Monsieur Boriquet.

JUSTIN. I've been hypnotizing him.

BORIQUET *and* FRANCINE. Oh!

VALENCOURT. How often?

JUSTIN. Every day.

FRANCINE, *to* BORIQUET. Marcel!

VALENCOURT. That's right. Now tell us why.

JUSTIN. To make him do the housework, and get the mail, and bring up the firewood, and—

BORIQUET's *jaw drops with each progressive revelation*.

VALENCOURT. Yes... And what else did you make him do today?

JUSTIN. I made him insult Mademoiselle Valencourt.

VALENCOURT. Then what?

JUSTIN. Then I made him jump around the room and act like a monkey.

BORIQUET, *outraged, hands on hips*. Like a what?

VALENCOURT. Right... And what did you do to Monsieur Boriquet's sister?

JUSTIN. I hypnotized her too. I made her think she was a crazy Spanish dancer.

FRANCINE. Oh!

VALENCOURT. Yes... And why did you make them do all those things today?

JUSTIN. To break up monsieur's wedding and keep him in my power.

BORIQUET, *moving menacingly toward* JUSTIN, *fists clenched.* Oh! Let me get my hands on that...

FRANCINE. Hypnotized!... And by a... a domestic!

VALENCOURT, *to* BORIQUET, *restraining him.* Now do you believe me?

FRANCINE. Good God! Who knows what he did while he had me in his power?

BORIQUET, *to* FRANCINE, *not without a tinge of sarcasm.* Really, Francine! I don't think you have to worry!

VALENCOURT represses a knowing smile.

VALENCOURT, *to* BORIQUET. At any rate, now that we've cleared up our... (*Clearing his throat.*) our misunderstanding... I hope nothing has changed between us... (*Emphasizing.*) son!

He holds out his hand.

BORIQUET, *shaking it.* Why... Father! Nothing would please me more! That is, I mean... (*With a doubtful glance at* ANTOINETTE.) If mademoiselle...

ANTOINETTE, *feigning pique.* Well, I'm not sure, monsieur. After all those horrible things you said... (*Smiling demurely.*) But since you didn't really mean them...

She holds out her hand to BORIQUET *over* JUSTIN's *head.*

BORIQUET, *taking her hand.* Antoinette!

ANTOINETTE. Marcel!

VALENCOURT, beaming, opens his arms in a gesture of embrace. MAX, who has been observing all the action with rapt attention, breaks out in applause.

MAX, *clapping.* Bravo! Bravo!

VALENCOURT, *pointing to* JUSTIN. Now, about our friend here...

BORIQUET. Just leave him to me! You wake him up, and... (*Pointing to the door, up center.*) He'll be out on his ear!

FRANCINE. I should hope so, precious!

ANTOINETTE. And the sooner the better!

MAX, *nodding*. Dat vould teach him a lesson already!

VALENCOURT. No, wait... Wait... I have a better idea... (*The others look at him inquisitively.*) As long as we've got the scoundrel where we want him, why not let me turn him into an absolutely model servant?

BORIQUET. What do you mean?

VALENCOURT. Watch!... You'll see... (*To* JUSTIN.) All right, Justin, are you listening to me?

JUSTIN. Yes.

VALENCOURT. "Yes" what?

JUSTIN. Yes, monsieur.

VALENCOURT. That's better!... Now listen carefully... You're never going to hypnotize anyone again. Understand?

JUSTIN. Yes, monsieur.

VALENCOURT. Not Monsieur Boriquet, or his sister, or anyone. Is that clear?

JUSTIN. Yes, monsieur.

VALENCOURT. And you're going to do the housework, aren't you? All the things you're supposed to do. Right?

JUSTIN. Yes, monsieur.

VALENCOURT. And you'll always work hard, won't you? As hard as you can?

JUSTIN. Yes, monsieur.

VALENCOURT. And you promise you'll be good from now on?

JUSTIN. Yes, monsieur.

VALENCOURT. No more tricks?

JUSTIN. No, monsieur.

VALENCOURT, *with a wink toward the others, who have been looking on admiringly*. All right, then. Say so!... Say: "I promise I'll be good."

JUSTIN, *without much conviction*. I promise I'll be good.

VALENCOURT. Louder!

JUSTIN, *raising his voice a little*. I promise I'll be good.

VALENCOURT. Better... Again...

JUSTIN, *louder*. I promise I'll be good!

VALENCOURT. Again... And show me that you mean it!

JUSTIN, *still louder, beating his breast*. I promise I'll be good!

ANTOINETTE. Poor thing!

VALENCOURT, *to* ANTOINETTE. He's got it coming! (*To* JUSTIN.) Again...

JUSTIN, *shouting*. I promise I'll be good!

VALENCOURT. And again...

JUSTIN. I promise I'll be good!
VALENCOURT. And again...
JUSTIN. I promise I'll be good!
MAX, *shaking his head in admiration.* Such a ting dat science business!
VALENCOURT. And again...
JUSTIN. I promise...

JUSTIN's *shouts continue, as the curtain slowly falls.*

CURTAIN

TOOTH AND CONSEQUENCES

OR

HORTENSE SAID:
"NO SKIN OFF MY ASS!"

•

Hortense a dit: "Je m'en fous!"

CHARACTERS

FOLLBRAGUET

MONSIEUR JEAN

VILDAMOUR

LEBOUCQ

ALBERT

MARCELLE FOLLBRAGUET

HORTENSE

MADAME BIZARRE

YVETTE

FOLLBRAGUET's *office. Upstage, a wall with two doors; one far left, lead-ing to the waiting room, the other far right, leading to the hall. Between the two, a sink. In the wall midstage left, a drape-covered doorway. Next to it, downstage, a small table with an autoclave. In the wall midstage right, the door to* MARCELLE FOLLBRAGUET's *room. Next to it, downstage, a fire-place. Downstage left, a desk, perpendicular to the footlights, with an arm-chair between it and the wall. Upstage, a coatrack with* FOLLBRAGUET's *hat and coat. Center stage, facing the audience, the dentist's chair, drill, and appropriate apparatus: bowl, saliva pump, etc. Close by, stage right, a small instrument cabinet with a number of drawers. Other incidental furniture ad lib.*

At rise, VILDAMOUR *is sitting in the dentist's chair, a napkin around his neck. A rubber gag is strapped tightly over his mouth, leaving only the crucial tooth exposed. The saliva pump is hanging from one corner. He is obviously in agony.* FOLLBRAGUET, *in his long smock, is busily drilling.*

VILDAMOUR. Aaaay! Aaa-aaa-aaaay!

FOLLBRAGUET. It's all right. All right... Just a little more now. Open wide.

VILDAMOUR. Aaa-aaa-aaaay!

FOLLBRAGUET, *drilling away.* Don't even think about it. Try and think of something pleasant.

VILDAMOUR, *grunting through the gag, just barely comprehensible.* Gakf ee-vee fuh oo kuh fay! ("That's easy for you to say!")

FOLLBRAGUET. Keep your head still. Please... Now open wide... It doesn't hurt a bit. Believe me.

VILDAMOUR, *louder.* Aaaaaaaay!

FOLLBRAGUET. You'll see. When it's going to hurt, I'll tell you. Don't worry.

He stops and changes the burr on the drill.

VILDAMOUR, *as before*. Frankf uh waw! A kahnk waik! ("Thanks a lot! I can't wait!")

FOLLBRAGUET. All right now. Open wide... Good. Now just relax. This time it's going to hurt a little.

VILDAMOUR, *terrified*. Haaa?

FOLLBRAGUET. See? I'm not trying to fool you... (VILDAMOUR *desperately shakes his head from side to side.*) Please! Keep your head still! I told you...

VILDAMOUR, *worn out*. Ho gik... Ho gik uh ngi-ik! Fuh gaw fake, ho gik! ("Hold it... Hold it a minute! For God's sake, hold it!")

FOLLBRAGUET. Just a little more now. We're almost finished. It's nothing... nothing at all...

VILDAMOUR. Aw ngaw! Ngaw fuh oo! Oo kahnk fee ik, gang ik! ("Oh no! Not for you! You can't feel it, damn it!")

FOLLBRAGUET, *mechanically agreeing*. Yes, that's right... I know...

VILDAMOUR. Ik feev ngike oor gri-i froo ngy graign! Froo ngy haw gaw-gi! ("It feels like you're drilling through my brain! Through my whole body!")

FOLLBRAGUET. I know... I know...

VILDAMOUR. Gaw-ga koo-fake! A ngike kuh gek ngy hangv aw guh fung-uv-uh-gikf hoo ing-veng-kug ik! ("Goddamn toothache! I'd like to get my hands on the son-of-a-bitch who invented it!")

FOLLBRAGUET. I know...

VILDAMOUR. A hag wung uh kuh-koo uh eev uh-gaw, guh ik wuv nguh-fing ike gif! ("I had one a couple of years ago, but it was nothing like this!")

FOLLBRAGUET. Yes, I know... (*About to begin drilling again.*) All right now, open wide.

VILDAMOUR. Fuh gaw fake! Ngaw guh gri uh-geng! ("For God's sake! Not the drill again!")

FOLLBRAGUET. Just once more. A little touch for good measure. (*Drilling.*) See? You can hardly feel it, now can you?

VILDAMOUR. Aaaaaay!

FOLLBRAGUET, *still drilling over* VILDAMOUR's *groans*. It's got to be done if you want to save the tooth... Open... Open wide... There! That's not so terrible, is it? Every day like this for a week, and I bet you'd get to like it.

VILDAMOUR, *with a desperate look, even louder*. Aaaaay! Aaaaay! Aaaaay!

FOLLBRAGUET. Don't worry, I'm only joking!... All right, there we are. All finished... (*He keeps on drilling.*) All finished...

VILDAMOUR. Aaaaay!

FOLLBRAGUET. There!

He finally stops.

VILDAMOUR, *starting to get up, sighing.* Ah!

FOLLBRAGUET, *pushing him back down.* Not yet. I'm not through.

He lights a little alcohol burner.

VILDAMOUR, *aghast.* Oo keek fay-ing "Aw fi-if, aw fi-if," guh oo ngo fkok! ("You keep saying 'All finished, all finished,' but you don't stop!")

FOLLBRAGUET, *heating a rubber bulb over the flame.* This won't hurt. Just a little hot air... Now open up nice and wide. (VILDAMOUR *winces with each jet.*) See?

VILDAMOUR. Ugh! Af aw-fl! ("That's awful!")

He begins to close his mouth.

FOLLBRAGUET, *quickly.* No, no! Open! Open! Don't close until I tell you! (*He prepares a cotton swab, dips it into a vial of liquid, and plugs it up into the tooth.*) Fine! That wasn't so bad, now was it? (*He undoes the rubber gag, removes the saliva-pump, and hands* VILDAMOUR *a small glass of mouthwash.*) Spit out!

VILDAMOUR, *rinsing his mouth a few times.* Whew! I wouldn't want to go through that again!

FOLLBRAGUET, *moving to his desk.* Don't be silly. It's all in the mind. It only hurts if you let yourself think so... Well now, we'll leave the medication in for a day or two. Then you'll come back and we'll put in the filling. (*Flipping through his appointment book.*) Let's see what my appointments look like... Hmmm... How about the day after tomorrow? Say five o'clock? Are you free?

VILDAMOUR. Day after tomorrow? Five o'clock?... No... no, there's this man I have to see...

FOLLBRAGUET. Well then... (*About to look for another time.*) How about...

VILDAMOUR. Never mind. That's all right... He's coming to collect a bill. He can go whistle for it!

FOLLBRAGUET. Oh? If you're sure... (*Jotting down the appointment.*) February the eleventh, five o'clock, Monsieur Vildamour. There! You won't forget...

VILDAMOUR. Me? Forget an appointment? Never!... Look, if I remember when somebody's coming to collect a bill... (*He pauses.*) Five o'clock, the eleventh... (*He pauses again, putting his hand to his cheek.*) You know, Doctor, this tooth is still killing me.

FOLLBRAGUET, *waiting for him to leave, indifferently.* Right, right...

VILDAMOUR. I mean, it hurts like the devil.

FOLLBRAGUET, *nodding.* Right...

VILDAMOUR. It really does.

FOLLBRAGUET. Right, right...

VILDAMOUR, *a little piqued at* FOLLBRAGUET'*s apparent lack of concern.* But it's killing me, Doctor. Is that all you can say?

FOLLBRAGUET. That's all I can say because it's perfectly normal. After all that drilling... It takes time to settle. Give it about fifteen minutes. It should start to let up.

VILDAMOUR. Aha?

FOLLBRAGUET, *ringing for the butler as he speaks.* Of course, if you keep having trouble, don't hesitate to come back. I'll manage to fit you in.

VILDAMOUR. Thank you, Doctor. I appreciate that. There aren't many like you, believe me. It's like I always tell my friends: "My dentist is a prince! He's one of a kind!... And painless? Absolutely painless!"

FOLLBRAGUET, *flattered.* And what do your friends say to that?

VILDAMOUR. They usually say: "So is mine."

FOLLBRAGUET, *taken aback.* Oh? Well...

ALBERT *enters from the hall, up right.*

ALBERT. Monsieur rang?

FOLLBRAGUET. Yes, Albert. Show Monsieur Vildamour out, will you please? (ALBERT *and* VILDAMOUR *move to leave.*) And while you're at it... (*Pointing off, left.*) step around and send in Monsieur Jean. (*Calling after* VILDAMOUR.) Day after tomorrow, then?

VILDAMOUR, *nodding.* Five o'clock...

FOLLBRAGUET. And be sure to keep your mouth covered. We don't want you catching a cold in that tooth. (*Suddenly noticing that* VILDAMOUR *still has the napkin around his neck.*) Just a minute! My napkin!

VILDAMOUR. Oh, sorry!

He takes it off and drapes it over the back of the dentist's chair. ALBERT *has already opened the door, up right.* MARCELLE *can be seen in the hall arguing with* HORTENSE, *who keeps trying to get a word in edgewise.*

MARCELLE. No, no, no! I've had all I'm going to take! When I tell you something, young lady, you can keep your mouth shut!

FOLLBRAGUET. What in the name... What's the matter?

VILDAMOUR *goes out the door with* ALBERT *close behind.*

VILDAMOUR, *squeezing by* MARCELLE. Madame!

MARCELLE, *curtly.* Monsieur!

FOLLBRAGUET. For heaven's sake, Marcelle! The hall is no place to be arguing with the help. Especially during office hours!

MARCELLE *stamps into the office, brandishing a fur muff. She heads straight for* FOLLBRAGUET *and holds it out to him.*

MARCELLE. Here! Feel this!

FOLLBRAGUET. I'm telling you, the hall is no place—

MARCELLE. Well, I'm not in the hall! I'm in your office! Now just feel this!

FOLLBRAGUET, *mechanically complying.* Why on earth... What is it? It's all wet.

MARCELLE, *triumphant.* Aha! (*Toward* HORTENSE, *still in the hall.*) See? (*To* FOLLBRAGUET.) You can feel how wet it is, can't you?

HORTENSE, *at the threshold.* So? I never said it wasn't.

FOLLBRAGUET, *instinctively sniffing his fingers.* A little water or something...

MARCELLE. Water? You really think it's water?

FOLLBRAGUET. Well? It's wet, isn't it?

HORTENSE, *to* MARCELLE. See!

MARCELLE. It's cat pee, that's what it is!

FOLLBRAGUET, *furious, holding up his hand.* It's what?

MARCELLE. That shows how much you know!

FOLLBRAGUET, *going to the sink and washing.* Then why in hell did you make me stick my fingers in it? What kind of a disgusting—

HORTENSE. Don't blame me, monsieur. It's madame... She's got this idea that my cat went and did a job on her muff. But it couldn't be my cat, monsieur. Everybody knows she never does it in the apartment. It just couldn't be...

MARCELLE. Good God, all you've got to do is smell it! (*Thrusting the muff under* FOLLBRAGUET's *nose.*) Here!

FOLLBRAGUET, *recoiling.* No, damn it!

MONSIEUR JEAN *enters through the draped doorway, stage left, in a long smock.*

MONSIEUR JEAN. You wanted to see me, Monsieur Follbraguet?

FOLLBRAGUET, *wiping his hands.* Yes... yes, I did.

MARCELLE, *holding out the muff.* Here, Monsieur Jean. Please smell this and tell me what you think it is.

FOLLBRAGUET. Oh no, for heaven's sake! You're not going to—

MARCELLE, *to* FOLLBRAGUET. Please! Don't say a word. Let him make up his own mind.

MONSIEUR JEAN, *taking a few polite whiffs.* Hmm! I can't say I care much for it...

MARCELLE. That's not what I asked you. What do you think it is?

FOLLBRAGUET *grits his teeth.*

MONSIEUR JEAN, *inhaling deeply, scratching his head.* Eucalyptus oil?

MARCELLE, *brandishing the muff in his face, categorically.* No, monsieur! It's cat pee!

MONSIEUR JEAN, *wiping his nose.* Hmm! I can't say I care much for it at all...

MARCELLE, *to* HORTENSE. You see? Everyone says so. Now that ought to shut you up!

FOLLBRAGUET, *trying to push them into the hall.* Look, I don't care what it is. Cat pee or not. Go argue somewhere else. I'll be damned if I want my patients to have to listen to your nonsense!

MARCELLE, *as* FOLLBRAGUET *pushes her out, to* HORTENSE. Now maybe you'll admit that that cat of yours—

HORTENSE, *still at the threshold.* What? Admit what? Why should I go and admit some stupid lie?

MARCELLE. Oh! Don't you dare... Don't you dare speak to me that way! When I tell you something—

FOLLBRAGUET, *finally pushing them out.* Damn it, you two! Get out and let me work in peace! (*He slams the door on them and grumbles to himself, as the argument, muffled, can be heard trailing off.*) Incredible! Always something... Not a day goes by... (*To* MONSIEUR JEAN.) Now then, what did I want to ask you?... Oh yes... (*Pointing to the draped doorway.*) Are you working on anyone in there?

MONSIEUR JEAN. Not anymore, monsieur. Madame Pavlova was here a few minutes ago...

FOLLBRAGUET. Madame Pavlova?

MONSIEUR JEAN. Yes, monsieur.

FOLLBRAGUET. *The* Madame Pavlova?

MONSIEUR JEAN. Yes, monsieur. A little trouble with a wisdom tooth...

FOLLBRAGUET. Oh?

MONSIEUR JEAN. I incised the gum for her. No problem...

FOLLBRAGUET. Aha! (*Muttering under his breath, impressed.*) Madame Pavlova! (*To* MONSIEUR JEAN.) What does she look like? Is she as pretty as her pictures?

MONSIEUR JEAN. Is she? I'll say!

FOLLBRAGUET. Then why on earth didn't you call me in? I'd give anything to see her.

MONSIEUR JEAN. Well, you were busy with a patient... And I knew I could handle her myself...

FOLLBRAGUET, *with a knowing wink.* I'll bet!

MONSIEUR JEAN. So...

FOLLBRAGUET, *facetiously.* Never miss a chance, do you, Monsieur Jean! Especially when they're pretty!

MONSIEUR JEAN, *suddenly understanding his veiled allusions, naïvely.* Oh, Monsieur Follbraguet! Really! Me? With Madame Pavlova?... I wouldn't dream... She wouldn't... We never even gave it a thought!

FOLLBRAGUET, *slyly.* Oh?

MONSIEUR JEAN, *solemnly.* Never! I swear!

FOLLBRAGUET. Well, if you say so... (*Getting back to business, after a few chuckles at* MONSIEUR JEAN's *expense.*) Look, I'd like you to run over to what's-his-name... The supplier...

MONSIEUR JEAN. Bringuet.

FOLLBRAGUET. Right, Bringuet... And tell him that last batch of amalgam he sent us wasn't worth a damn. Every filling I use it for breaks up and falls out. I'm not complaining, tell him. I just want him to exchange it.

MONSIEUR JEAN. Yes, monsieur. Anything else?

FOLLBRAGUET. No, that's all.

MONSIEUR JEAN *nods and is about to leave. Before he has a chance,* MARCELLE *bursts in, up right.*

MARCELLE. Look, will you please—

FOLLBRAGUET. Oh no! Not again!

MARCELLE, *looking around, pointing to the empty dentist's chair.* What's the matter? You're not busy...

FOLLBRAGUET. I beg your pardon! (*Gesturing up left.*) There are people out there waiting.

MARCELLE. Well, let them wait! When you've got a toothache, you expect to have to wait. This is more important. I want you to tell that girl she's fired. And I mean this very minute!

FOLLBRAGUET. What? What now?

MARCELLE. What now? I'll tell you "what now"! I was standing there giving her a piece of my mind, and you know what she comes out with? "No skin off my ass!" (*Hands on hips.*) Now how do you like that?

FOLLBRAGUET. Well... tell her it's no skin off yours either, damn it!

MARCELLE, *furious*. Tell her... You mean you're going to let her talk to your wife—

FOLLBRAGUET, *sarcastically*. She's lucky! She lets things roll off her back!

MONSIEUR JEAN *tries to stifle a little laugh*.

MARCELLE, *to* MONSIEUR JEAN. I suppose you think that's funny!

MONSIEUR JEAN. Me, madame?

MARCELLE, *to* FOLLBRAGUET. Oh yes, very clever! Of course, I'm not surprised. A lot you care how people insult me! You let them walk all over me... say anything they please... Everybody knows. That's why nobody thinks twice...

FOLLBRAGUET. What are you talking about? Walk all over you... If you'd just leave that poor child alone... Stop picking on her all the time...

MARCELLE. Oh, of course! Now it's my fault! Now I'm picking on her! Really!

MONSIEUR JEAN, *to* FOLLBRAGUET. Should I go now, monsieur?

FOLLBRAGUET. Yes, please, Monsieur Jean. I'm sure you don't want to have to listen to this.

MONSIEUR JEAN. Oh no, it's not that... I just thought...

FOLLBRAGUET. I know, I know... I understand...

He motions him off with several waves of the hand. MONSIEUR JEAN *exits through the draped doorway*.

MARCELLE. There! That's typical! Even someone like him can insult me! Just typical!

FOLLBRAGUET. What?

MARCELLE. And why not, when he sees the way you make fun of me yourself...

FOLLBRAGUET. What are you talking about? In the first place, he didn't insult you...

MARCELLE. No, but give him time. You'll see... The idea! Standing up for that... that tramp! Taking her side...

FOLLBRAGUET. Whose side? I'm not taking her side...

MARCELLE. Oh, forget it! I've learned my lesson. (*Sarcastically.*) From now on I'll remember that a fur muff is something for my maid's cat to pee on!

FOLLBRAGUET, *moving upstage*. Now look, I've had it up to here with that cat! You can grind her up into mincemeat for all I care, only let me have some peace!

MARCELLE, *after a brief pause*. Well?

FOLLBRAGUET. Well what?

MARCELLE. Are you going to fire her or aren't you?

FOLLBRAGUET. Marcelle, you're... you're impossible!

MARCELLE, *going to the door, up right, calling*. Hortense!... Hortense!

FOLLBRAGUET. Listen, that's enough!

MARCELLE. Hortense! Come here this minute!

HORTENSE'S VOICE. I'm coming!

FOLLBRAGUET *throws up his hands. The door, up right, opens and* HORTENSE *appears at the threshold*.

MARCELLE, *pointing*. Inside! Monsieur has something to tell you.

HORTENSE *enters*.

FOLLBRAGUET, *babbling*. What?... No... I mean...

MARCELLE. He wants to tell you that you're fired. (*Glowering at* FOLL-BRAGUET.) Doesn't he?

FOLLBRAGUET. I mean...

MARCELLE. I just told him the lovely way you answered me back, and he's perfectly furious.

FOLLBRAGUET, *losing patience*. Damn it! It's incredible!

MARCELLE, *to* HORTENSE. There! You see? He thinks it's incredible.

HORTENSE, *to* FOLLBRAGUET. Did monsieur mean me when he said that, monsieur?

MARCELLE, *to* HORTENSE. I suppose you have the nerve to suggest he meant me?

HORTENSE. Who can tell?

MARCELLE, *to* FOLLBRAGUET. There! You hear that? You hear the way she answers me back?

FOLLBRAGUET. Well...

MARCELLE. Go on. Tell her. Be man enough to say what you think for once.

FOLLBRAGUET. Like what, for instance?

MARCELLE. Like what? Like... She tells your wife "No skin off my ass!" and you think that's right? You're just going to stand there and let her get away with it?

FOLLBRAGUET, *without much conviction*. No...

MARCELLE. Well, prove it then. Tell her she's fired. (*Long pause*.) Well?

From the production of *Tooth and Consequences* at Los Angeles City College, February 19 directed by Dudley Knight (photographs by James Mathews).

FOLLBRAGUET. What's the hurry?

HORTENSE, *to* FOLLBRAGUET. I'm sure monsieur knows how much I'd hate to leave. He's always been so nice to me, I mean. But if monsieur says I have to...

FOLLBRAGUET. Look, Hortense... Why don't you show me exactly how you said it...

MARCELLE, *angrily*. Show you how... "No skin off my ass!" That's how! How many ways can you say a thing like that?

FOLLBRAGUET. Well...

MARCELLE. Well nothing! No maid is going to swear like a trooper at me! Not at me, understand?

FOLLBRAGUET. But—

MARCELLE. Shoot off her filthy mouth in my face, will she?

FOLLBRAGUET. But—

MARCELLE, *losing control*. Now kick her out, damn it! Kick her out on her ass! Once and for all!

FOLLBRAGUET, *to* HORTENSE, *resigned*. I'm afraid madame has her mind made up, Hortense. You heard what she said.

HORTENSE, *to* FOLLBRAGUET. Yes, monsieur. I understand. (*Long, uneasy pause.*) You know, I'm really going to miss monsieur. He's always been so good to the help, I mean, and—

MARCELLE, *sharply*. That's enough! Go on! Go get your account book, and monsieur will figure up what he still owes you. Go on!

    HORTENSE *exits, up right*.

FOLLBRAGUET, *standing by his desk*. Did you have to bite the poor child's head off just because she was trying to say something nice to me?

MARCELLE. Nice, my foot! How can you be so blind? That was just another one of her nasty pokes at me.

FOLLBRAGUET. Oh yes! That's you! That's you all over! Always looking for those deep, dark motives...

MARCELLE. Well, that's better than being a... a jellyfish, for heaven's sake!

FOLLBRAGUET. Of course! Dare disagree, and you're a jellyfish! What else! (*There is a knock at the door, up left.*) Come in!

    ALBERT *enters*.

ALBERT. Monsieur won't forget. He has a lady in the waiting room.

FOLLBRAGUET. I know. If madame here would get off my neck for one minute...

MARCELLE. Now that's really what I call tact!

FOLLBRAGUET. Well, it's true. (*To* ALBERT.) Show her in.

MARCELLE, *exiting to her room, stage right.* Jellyfish!

FOLLBRAGUET, *calling after her as she leaves.* Of course! You're right!

ALBERT, *opening the door, up left.* This way, madame...

MADAME BIZARRE *enters, carrying a handbag and a muff.*

FOLLBRAGUET. Please, madame. Come right in.

MADAME BIZARRE, *to* ALBERT, *as he steps aside.* Excuse me...

ALBERT *exits by the same door.*

FOLLBRAGUET, *consulting his appointment book.* Did you have an appointment, madame?

MADAME BIZARRE, *leaving her muff on the desk.* No, Doctor. This is my first visit. I hope you don't mind. You see, my regular dentist passed away...

FOLLBRAGUET. Oh, I'm sorry...

MADAME BIZARRE. Yes, I really have terrible luck when it comes to dentists. He's the third one I've lost already.

FOLLBRAGUET. The third... (*Half-seriously.*) Thanks for telling me!

MADAME BIZARRE, *realizing her gaffe.* Oh no, Doctor. That doesn't mean that... Well, besides, only time will tell.

FOLLBRAGUET. Much obliged!

MADAME BIZARRE. Anyway, Doctor, one of your patients is a very dear friend of mine, and I thought it would be all right. Monsieur Grosbourgeois...

FOLLBRAGUET, *nodding.* Aha...

MADAME BIZARRE. You do know the one I mean?

FOLLBRAGUET. Monsieur Grosbourgeois? Of course I know him. I've got a lawsuit going with Monsieur Grosbourgeois...

MADAME BIZARRE, *taken aback.* Oh! He didn't tell me...

FOLLBRAGUET. Yes. Nonpayment of bills...

MADAME BIZARRE, *relieved.* Oh, nothing serious then. Only money...

FOLLBRAGUET, *echoing.* Only money...

MADAME BIZARRE. Money isn't everything, after all.

FOLLBRAGUET. No...

MADAME BIZARRE. Like I always say, it can't buy happiness!

FOLLBRAGUET. It's a wonder the rich are so damned attached to theirs!

MADAME BIZARRE. Isn't it the truth!... (FOLLBRAGUET *nods.*) But I really shouldn't take your time chatting this way, Doctor. Let me tell you my problem. My little accident...

FOLLBRAGUET. Yes... please...

MADAME BIZARRE. It happened while I was eating some lentils, and...
Well, you know how careless the help can be these days... Anyway,
Doctor, to make a long story short, I bit into a little stone and broke a
tooth.

FOLLBRAGUET. My, my! That's a shame! Let's have a look. (*Pointing to the
dentist's chair.*) Here, make yourself comfortable.

MADAME BIZARRE. With pleasure...

She sits down.

FOLLBRAGUET, *ready to examine her mouth.* Now then, which tooth is it?

He raises the chair with several pumps of the pedal.

MADAME BIZARRE. Just a second, I'll show you. (*Taking a denture out of
her handbag.*) See?

FOLLBRAGUET, *surprised.* Oh, you mean... I thought...

MADAME BIZARRE, *a little embarrassed.* It goes without saying, I'd rather
no one knew.

FOLLBRAGUET. Of course, my dear lady. Medical ethics... I wouldn't
dream...

MADAME BIZARRE, *handing him the denture, admiringly.* Really a lovely
job, don't you think?

FOLLBRAGUET, *nodding approval.* Hmmm... Very nice...

MADAME BIZARRE. They were the last ones he ever made. Just before he
died.

FOLLBRAGUET. Your last dentist, you mean? Before me, that is...

MADAME BIZARRE. Yes, poor thing. I asked him to make me something
really special. Something... Well, I don't know if you feel the way I do,
Doctor, but I've always thought the first thing a woman should have is
beautiful teeth.

FOLLBRAGUET, *nodding.* As long as she can afford them.

MADAME BIZARRE. Exactly.

FOLLBRAGUET. You won't find a dentist in the world who'll disagree.

He lets the chair down.

MADAME BIZARRE, *amused.* Wheeee!

FOLLBRAGUET, *laughing.* Last stop. Everybody out!

MADAME BIZARRE. Oh, that was fun!

She stands up.

FOLLBRAGUET, *gradually getting back to business, examining the denture.*
Well now, this doesn't look so bad. We'll have to replace one tooth,

that's all. The only thing is, it's going to take a few days. I hope you don't need them right away.

MADAME BIZARRE. Oh no! Take your time. I'll just use my everyday set...

FOLLBRAGUET. Oh, you mean these are your Sunday best?

MADAME BIZARRE. Heavens no, Doctor! Nothing that pretentious! It's just that, when I go to a party, or a dinner... You know... But I have no parties or dinners in the offing.

FOLLBRAGUET. Fine! No problem then. (*Going to the draped doorway, calling.*) Monsieur Jean! Could you come in here, please?

He absentmindedly puts the denture in his pocket.

MONSIEUR JEAN'S VOICE. One moment, monsieur.

FOLLBRAGUET, *behind his desk, opening his appointment book, about to write.* Now then, if you'll just give me your name and address...

MADAME BIZARRE. Madame Bizarre, 8 rue Bugeaud.

FOLLBRAGUET. Bizarre? B-I-Z...

He pauses, uncertain.

MADAME BIZARRE, *continuing.* A-R-R-E. Madame Zsa-Zsa Bizarre.

FOLLBRAGUET, *shrugging his shoulders.* Bizarre! (*Speaking as he writes.*) "Madame Zsa-Zsa Bizarre, 8 rue Bugeaud, repair upper munch-munch..."

MADAME BIZARRE. What? "Repair upper munch-munch"?

FOLLBRAGUET. Yes. That's my code. After all, you wouldn't want someone to open my book, by mistake, and read: "Madame Zsa-Zsa Bizarre, repair upper denture..."

MADAME BIZARRE. Certainly not!

FOLLBRAGUET. That's why I write "munch-munch." I know what it means. But anyone who isn't in on the secret...

MADAME BIZARRE. I see! Very clever!

FOLLBRAGUET. I always do it in cases like this. You know... where it could be embarrassing.

MADAME BIZARRE. Of course.

FOLLBRAGUET. The same with all my patients. You're not the only one... (*Leafing through his book.*) See? Here's one. "Madame Rethel-Pajon: munch-munch..." (*Musing.*) Lower left incisor, if I remember...

MADAME BIZARRE. Madame Armand Rethel-Pajon?

FOLLBRAGUET. That's right.

MADAME BIZARRE. Why, she's one of my dearest friends. Don't tell me *she* has false teeth, doctor!

FOLLBRAGUET, *trying to cover his blunder.* Who? Madame Rethel... Why no! No! Not Madame Rethel-Pajon...

MADAME BIZARRE. But what about her "munch-munch"? You said—

FOLLBRAGUET. It was a mistake! I meant someone else!

MADAME BIZARRE, *unconvinced*. Come now, Doctor. You can trust me. I won't breathe a word...

FOLLBRAGUET, *resigned to his gaffe, sighing*. Please, Madame Bizarre... I... Really, I hope you'll be discreet.

MADAME BIZARRE. My lips are sealed.

FOLLBRAGUET. Besides, you're in no position... if you see what I mean...

MADAME BIZARRE, *reflecting*. Madame Rethel-Pajon! I never would have dreamt... I always thought she had such beautiful teeth. (FOLLBRAGUET *nods, smiling*.) Simply exquisite!

FOLLBRAGUET, *bowing slightly*. Thank you. You're much too kind.

MADAME BIZARRE. You mean they're yours?

FOLLBRAGUET. Yes, they're mine.

MADAME BIZARRE, *admiringly*. Oh, Doctor! You're an artist! An absolute artist!

> MONSIEUR JEAN *enters through the draped doorway*.

MONSIEUR JEAN. You wanted to see me, monsieur?

FOLLBRAGUET, *ringing for* ALBERT *the butler*. Yes, Monsieur Jean. Madame Bizarre is going to leave us her... (*Looking around for the denture*.) Where on earth are they?

MADAME BIZARRE. What?

FOLLBRAGUET. Your teeth... Where did I put them? (*Looking all over, and finally feeling in his pocket*.) Ah! Here they are. (*Handing the denture to* MONSIEUR JEAN.) Single replacement, second molar, upper left.

MONSIEUR JEAN. Very good, monsieur.

FOLLBRAGUET. And let's make it really extra fine. These are her special occasion teeth.

MONSIEUR JEAN. Of course, monsieur. (*To* MADAME BIZARRE.) Was madame thinking of a particular day for her bridge?

MADAME BIZARRE. For my...? Heavens, I don't even know how to play the game...

MONSIEUR JEAN. No, I mean madame's... (*Holding up the denture*.) madame's...

FOLLBRAGUET, *to* MADAME BIZARRE. Yes, we call that type a "bridge."

MADAME BIZARRE. Oh, I didn't know...

FOLLBRAGUET, *to* MONSIEUR JEAN. That's fine, Monsieur Jean. You can go. I'll arrange a time...

Monsieur Jean *exits through the draped doorway, just as* Albert *enters, up right.*

Albert. Monsieur rang?

Follbraguet. Yes. Show madame out, will you please?

Albert. Certainly, monsieur.

Madame Bizarre. Thank you so much, Doctor. You've been very kind.

She goes to the desk and picks up her muff.

Follbraguet, *to* Albert. Do I have anybody waiting, Albert?

Albert. No, monsieur. Only Hortense. She'd like a word with monsieur as soon as he has a minute.

Follbraguet, *grimacing.* Oh? (*Controlling his obvious impatience in front of* Madame Bizarre.) Fine. First show madame out, then I'll see what she wants.

Albert *moves to comply.* Madame Bizarre *hesitates, reluctant to leave.*

Madame Bizarre. Well, Doctor?

Follbraguet, *preoccupied.* Madame?

Madame Bizarre. When will it be ready?

Follbraguet. When will what be ready?

Madame Bizarre. My... (*Inhibited by* Albert's *presence, giving* Follbraguet *a knowing glance.*) My "munch-munch"...

Albert *stifles a little guffaw.*

Follbraguet. Oh yes... Your... Well, I'd say about a week... But that's all right. I'll send it. I have your address.

Madame Bizarre. Oh? Why, thank you!

Follbraguet, *eager to be rid of her.* Not at all! My pleasure!

Madame Bizarre, *exiting, up right, with* Albert *at her heels.* Bye-bye, Doctor. And thank you again...

Follbraguet, *at the door, nodding.* Madame... (*To* Hortense, *as soon as* Madame Bizarre *is out of earshot.*) All right, come in!

Hortense, *entering.* I'm bringing monsieur my book, like madame told me.

Follbraguet. Good. Let's have it.

He takes the account book to his desk and sits down.

Hortense. Monsieur can see for himself. It only goes to the end of January. And today's the ninth of February, so that means expenses for... (*Counting on her fingers.*) for nine more days.

FOLLBRAGUET, *scanning the pages*. Right... Right...

HORTENSE. Plus my wages... Monsieur knows they go from the fifteenth of the month. So if this is the ninth, that adds up to a month, minus... (*Laboring*.) minus six days. But monsieur has to give me a whole week's notice. So that makes... That makes a month and one day altogether. And its sixty francs for a month, and... (*More complicated calculations*.) and two francs for the extra day... So that makes sixty-two francs...

FOLLBRAGUET, *hardly listening, more absorbed in his wife's expenses*. Look at this! Day after day, all this useless junk! Ribbons, lace, ribbons, lace, ribbons, ribbons, ribbons...

HORTENSE, *quick to defend herself*. Oh, monsieur! Madame insisted...

FOLLBRAGUET. Yes, I'm sure she did! I know only too well...

HORTENSE. Thank you, monsieur. I knew monsieur knew.

FOLLBRAGUET. But why so much, for goodness' sake?

HORTENSE, *sarcastically*. Madame loves pretty things, monsieur!

FOLLBRAGUET *shakes his head in resignation, still scanning the book*.

FOLLBRAGUET, *stopping at another item*. What on earth is this?

HORTENSE, *looking over his shoulder*. I'm sorry I write so bad, monsieur. I never had a chance—

FOLLBRAGUET. That's not the problem. I can read it all right. I just don't know what it means: "Ingredients for poultry, 80 centimes."

HORTENSE. Oh, that was one night when monsieur was away, and madame had the grippe. She sent me to the druggist's so she could make a poultry to put on her chest.

FOLLBRAGUET. A what?

HORTENSE. A poultry, monsieur. Like a... a kind of plaster.

FOLLBRAGUET, *smiling in spite of himself*. Aha!

HORTENSE. The druggist had everything except for the mouse turd...

FOLLBRAGUET. Except for the what?

HORTENSE. The mouse turd. Madame said it had to be a mouse turd plaster... I don't know how she managed...

FOLLBRAGUET, *trying to keep a straight face, figuring*. Well now, that gives us eighty-six francs, twenty centimes in expenses. Plus your sixty-two francs. Or a total of one hundred forty-eight francs and twenty centimes. (*Putting the book on the desk and handing her a piece of paper*.) Here... just write what I tell you: "Received in full payment of all indebtedness heretofore incurred, the sum of one hundred forty-eight francs, twenty centimes." Then date it and sign your name.

HORTENSE. Oh... If it's all the same, I wish monsieur would write it himself. With all those foreign words, I mean...

FOLLBRAGUET, *indulgent*. If you'd rather...

He begins writing.

HORTENSE. And monsieur won't forget my reference, I hope!

FOLLBRAGUET, *writing*. Not today. You can send for it tomorrow. (*Finishing the receipt.*) "...the sum of one hundred forty-eight francs, twenty centimes. February 9, 1915." There! Now you sign it.

HORTENSE, *taking the pen*. Thank you, monsieur. I was never too good at spelling.

FOLLBRAGUET. That's all right...

HORTENSE. Or puncturating either.

FOLLBRAGUET. I know... Just sign the receipt.

HORTENSE. I never knew where the commas and semaphores went, and all those things...

FOLLBRAGUET. Please, Hortense. Just sign it.

HORTENSE, *finally complying, laboriously*. There you are, monsieur.

FOLLBRAGUET, *standing up*. Good! Now I'll go get your money.

HORTENSE, *sheepishly*. I hope monsieur isn't angry with me.

FOLLBRAGUET. Angry? Why should I be angry? (*Sarcastically*.) I'm having a fine time, thanks to you!

HORTENSE. But it's not my fault, monsieur. If only...

FOLLBRAGUET. If only what?

HORTENSE. Well, if only madame didn't say what she did. About my cat, I mean... going on her muff...

FOLLBRAGUET. So what? Who cares? Why get so insulted? It's only your cat, after all. You'd think it was your sister, or your mother, the way you're carrying on! You're blowing the whole thing up into a national crisis, for heaven's sake!

HORTENSE. I'm sorry, monsieur. But just because a girl is somebody's maid, that doesn't mean she should let somebody talk to her any way they please!

FOLLBRAGUET. What's the difference? Let her rave all she wants!... (HORTENSE *bows her head*.) No! Instead, you've always got to answer her back!

HORTENSE. I know, monsieur. I try, but I just can't help it. Monsieur knows how madame can be... how she talks to people, I mean...

FOLLBRAGUET. All right, but still...

HORTENSE. You'd think monsieur never noticed it himself. And after the awful way she treats him, too!

FOLLBRAGUET. Oh? Well, I... Really, I don't think—

HORTENSE. And in front of the help! It's so embarrassing, monsieur!

FOLLBRAGUET, *beginning to squirm*. Yes, I'm sure... I... Really...

HORTENSE. We were talking about it in the pantry, just the other day. Albert was simply furious...

FOLLBRAGUET. He was?

HORTENSE. And he said... Well, monsieur knows it takes a lot to get Albert to talk, but he's nobody's fool. And he said: "You know, I really admire monsieur. I wouldn't put up with a woman like that for even one day."

FOLLBRAGUET. Well, I do my best...

HORTENSE. Take yesterday, for instance... while we were serving dinner... All the nasty things she screamed at monsieur... Like his "belly's full of jelly!", and he's "nothing but a unit..."

FOLLBRAGUET, *correcting*. K... k...

HORTENSE. Monsieur?

FOLLBRAGUET. "Eunuch"... The word was "eunuch"...

HORTENSE. Well, I knew what she meant.

FOLLBRAGUET. And besides, it's not true!

HORTENSE. True or not, monsieur. I don't care. That's none of my business.

FOLLBRAGUET. No, but I don't want you to think—

HORTENSE, *incensed at the thought*. Really! Is that any way to talk in front of the help?

FOLLBRAGUET. I know...

HORTENSE. I mean, how are we supposed to respect monsieur when she says such things?

FOLLBRAGUET. You're right...

HORTENSE. Your kind don't realize how something like that can hurt them. I mean, would the help ever talk that way in front of them? We wouldn't be caught dead...

FOLLBRAGUET. You're right. I only wish you could tell that to her!

HORTENSE. Oh, that'll be the day!

FOLLBRAGUET, *waxing confidential*. I don't know how many times I've tried to stop her. But you know, she just can't help it. The minute she's got an audience... Heaven help me if I say something that rubs her the wrong way... If I find fault with her dress, or her hair, or whatever... That's enough to get her started. Me... My family... (*Imitating.*) "Oh, of course! You'd rather see me dress up like some slut, I suppose! Like that sister of yours!"

HORTENSE, *feigning outrage*. Oh! Not monsieur's sister!

FOLLBRAGUET. You were here the other day, when she made that scene... (*Very matter-of-fact.*) Please, sit down... Sit down... (HORTENSE *takes the seat behind the desk.*) You remember... about her clothes... how I never give her enough money, and she doesn't have a thing to wear... You remember...

HORTENSE, *shaking her head, as if to say "Incredible!"* Tsk, tsk, tsk!

FOLLBRAGUET. And if anyone knows it's not true, I'm sure you do. You know how much I pay, day in day out. (*Picking up the account book from the desk, and brandishing it.*) Bills, bills, bills! And what for? For foolishness!

HORTENSE, *nodding*. Ribbons, lace, ribbons, lace...

FOLLBRAGUET. Exactly! Ribbons, ribbons, ribbons!

HORTENSE. But... Then why doesn't monsieur put his foot down for a change?

FOLLBRAGUET. How? I've tried everything.

HORTENSE. Monsieur should just tell madame, once and for all: "That's it! That's enough! So much for clothes, and not one centime more!"

FOLLBRAGUET. That's easy to say. But when the bills come in, the clothes are all bought!

HORTENSE. Then monsieur should say: "Too bad! I'm sorry, I just won't pay it!" The next time madame will know better!

FOLLBRAGUET, *pondering*. I suppose so...

HORTENSE. Monsieur is too good. He lets people walk all over him. That's his trouble.

FOLLBRAGUET. Well, what can I do? It's better to give in sometimes for a little peace and quiet.

HORTENSE. Maybe monsieur thinks so...

FOLLBRAGUET. And it wouldn't have done you any harm either, frankly. Instead of talking back like that, and picking a fight.

HORTENSE. Well, I guess I've just got a worse temper than monsieur.

FOLLBRAGUET. Besides, you know madame... You know how she blows up at the least little thing. But it's over in no time, if you just let it pass. Why, tomorrow... I'll bet when she sees you here, same as always, she won't even remember that she wanted to fire you.

HORTENSE. Well, I don't know... I hope monsieur sees my point... But I just don't see how I can stay. Not the way things are...

FOLLBRAGUET. Oh, come now, Hortense! Now who's being stubborn?

HORTENSE. It's not that, monsieur. It's just that... well, when you know that somebody doesn't appreciate your work... For example, monsieur, when I first took this job, I asked madame for seventy francs. And she told me: "No, sixty. And after six months, if I'm pleased with your work, I'll give you ten more." Well, I didn't want to argue, so I said all right.

FOLLBRAGUET, *waiting for her to make her point*. So?

HORTENSE. So? It's been eight months already, and I still haven't had my raise.

FOLLBRAGUET. Oh? Madame must have forgotten...

HORTENSE. No, monsieur. She couldn't have. I reminded her about it. All she said was: "Not now. We can talk about it later!"

FOLLBRAGUET. Just for ten measly francs?

HORTENSE, *wheedling*. I'm sure monsieur wouldn't tell me no. I'm sure...

FOLLBRAGUET. Of course not! What's ten francs?

HORTENSE. Oh, thank you, monsieur! Thank you! Thank you!

FOLLBRAGUET. For what?

HORTENSE. For my raise!

FOLLBRAGUET. For your... (*Clearing his throat.*) Don't mention it!... Just be sure you behave from now on. I don't want any more scenes, you understand? They get on my nerves, and that's one thing I don't need!

HORTENSE. Oh yes, monsieur!

FOLLBRAGUET, *noticing the account book, still in his hand*. Now I'll get you your money, as long as your book is up to date...

HORTENSE. If monsieur thinks he should...

FOLLBRAGUET *moves toward the draped doorway. A knock is heard*.

FOLLBRAGUET, *stopping in his tracks*. Come in!

YVETTE *the cook enters, up right, appropriately dressed*.

YVETTE. It's me, monsieur.

FOLLBRAGUET, *looking at her in surprise*. What are you doing here? Why aren't you in the kitchen, where you belong?

YVETTE. Because I just got through helping madame get dressed, monsieur, since she doesn't have anyone else to do it now, and she told me to come in...

FOLLBRAGUET, *with several impatient gestures*. Fine! That's fine!

He exits.

YVETTE, *as soon as he has left, to* HORTENSE. Well?

HORTENSE. Well what?

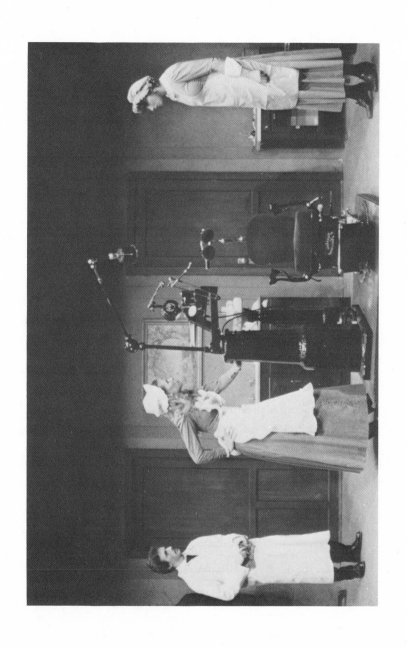

YVETTE. How come you're still here?

HORTENSE. Why not?

YVETTE. I thought you got fired.

HORTENSE. I did.

YVETTE. For talking dirty to madame.

HORTENSE. That's right.

YVETTE. So?

HORTENSE. So monsieur just gave me a raise. Ten francs!

YVETTE, *astonished*. He didn't!

FOLLBRAGUET *returns with the money*.

FOLLBRAGUET, *to* YVETTE. Are you still here?

YVETTE. Like I was telling monsieur... madame told me to come in...

FOLLBRAGUET, *shrugging*. What now?

YVETTE. ...and ask monsieur if... (*Trying to remember verbatim*.) if "it's all taken care of."

FOLLBRAGUET *gives* HORTENSE *a knowing glance*.

FOLLBRAGUET, *to* YVETTE. Thank you! That's fine! Go tell madame I'll speak to her myself.

YVETTE. Yes, monsieur.

She exits, up right.

FOLLBRAGUET, *gritting his teeth*. She just can't leave me alone!

HORTENSE, *with a gesture as if to say "What did you expect?"* No, monsieur.

FOLLBRAGUET, *sighing*. Anyway... here you are, Hortense. We said one hundred forty-eight francs, twenty centimes.

HORTENSE. Yes, monsieur.

FOLLBRAGUET, *paying her piecemeal*. First the twenty centimes... Then the one hundred francs... and... three twenties make sixty. Do you have change from sixty?

HORTENSE. Yes, monsieur. (*Taking some coins from her purse*.) There! Two francs.

FOLLBRAGUET. Two? No, no. Twelve... Forty-eight from sixty leaves twelve. Twelve francs.

HORTENSE. But monsieur... My raise... Ten francs, remember?

FOLLBRAGUET. Your... Oh yes... yes, of course...

HORTENSE. Thank you, monsieur.

Suddenly MARCELLE *bursts onstage from her room, midstage right. She is obviously shocked to see* HORTENSE *sitting at* FOLLBRAGUET's *desk.*

MARCELLE, *to* HORTENSE, *sarcastically.* Well, well! Aren't we making ourselves right at home! (HORTENSE *jumps up.*) No, please! Don't mind me! (*Glowering at* FOLLBRAGUET.) I didn't know you had a guest!

FOLLBRAGUET. Please, Marcelle! I was talking to the child...

MARCELLE. And we let the help sit down now, do we? Just so we can talk?

FOLLBRAGUET. Well for goodness' sake, I couldn't keep her standing. It was going to take time.

MARCELLE. Yes, I'm sure.

FOLLBRAGUET. Besides, Marcelle, I wish you wouldn't be so hard on her. Down deep, she's got a heart of gold... Believe me, she... Really, she...

He pauses, groping for more convincing arguments.

MARCELLE, *archly.* Are you through? (FOLLBRAGUET *sighs and throws up his hands.*) Now then, did you give her her money?

FOLLBRAGUET, *hesitant.* Yes... yes, I did... I gave her her money. (*To* HORTENSE.) Didn't I, Hortense?

HORTENSE. Yes, monsieur.

MARCELLE. Then what is she waiting for? Why doesn't she get out?

FOLLBRAGUET. Why doesn't she... Well, as a matter of fact... the two of us were talking just now, and... Actually, you know, she thinks the world of you, Marcelle... A real lady, I mean... That's what she thinks...

MARCELLE, *coldly.* Very touching, I'm sure. Who asked for her opinion?

FOLLBRAGUET. That's not the point. What she meant was... Well, sometimes... Even you'll admit, sometimes you can blow up at people...

MARCELLE. What?

FOLLBRAGUET. Even at me, sometimes. I know you don't mean it... but it's like Hortense was saying. There are some things you just shouldn't say in front of the help.

MARCELLE, *scandalized.* Oh? And since when do you ask the help to pass judgment on your wife?

FOLLBRAGUET. No, no. It's not that. We were talking, that's all. Just one of those things. Like... like the raise you promised her when she first came to work... The ten-franc raise...

MARCELLE. What about it?

FOLLBRAGUET. Well, I mean... you did promise, after all. So I thought it was only right, and...

MARCELLE. And?

FOLLBRAGUET. And I told her she could have it.

MARCELLE, *with a start*. You what?

FOLLBRAGUET. I'm sure you see my point...

MARCELLE, *furious*. Now isn't that lovely! I tell you to fire her, and you give her a raise!

FOLLBRAGUET. But—

MARCELLE. No! That's the last straw! That's just the last straw!

FOLLBRAGUET. But Marcelle—

MARCELLE. Don't "but Marcelle" me! I know what I've got to do!

FOLLBRAGUET. But—

MARCELLE. Never mind! I see how much I count in this house! (*Pointing to* HORTENSE.) I see whose word you take instead of mine!

FOLLBRAGUET. Marcelle—

MARCELLE. I see who's running things around here now!

FOLLBRAGUET. For heaven's sake, calm down! Don't go flying off the handle!

MARCELLE. Oh, I'm calm! I'm calm! I just know what I've got to do, that's all... The same as any self-respecting woman in my place... I'm leaving! Understand?

FOLLBRAGUET. Marcelle! For heaven's sake—

MARCELLE. No! My mind is made up!

FOLLBRAGUET. But—

MARCELLE. I'm leaving! That's final!

FOLLBRAGUET, *fed up*. All right, damn it! Leave! Go ahead! I'm not holding you back!

MARCELLE, *going toward her room*. Don't worry, you won't have to tell me twice!

FOLLBRAGUET, *to* HORTENSE. What a temper! My goodness!

HORTENSE *looks up at the ceiling and raises her eyebrows, as if to say "You're telling me!"*

HORTENSE. I always said monsieur has the patience of a saint.

MARCELLE, *returning, looking* FOLLBRAGUET *straight in the eye*. And you can have my room too... For your precious Hortense! That way you won't have so far to go when you take your maid to bed!

FOLLBRAGUET, *scandalized*. What?

HORTENSE, *unable to believe her ears*. What did she say?

MARCELLE *stalks off into her room and slams the door*.

FOLLBRAGUET. She's out of her mind! That's all there is to it!

HORTENSE, *incensed*. Well, I never, monsieur!... Never in all my born days!...

FOLLBRAGUET. Please, Hortense...

HORTENSE. I don't have to let anyone talk to me that way!

FOLLBRAGUET. Please... Don't listen to her...

HORTENSE, *on the verge of tears*. I mean, just because someone's a maid, monsieur, that doesn't mean people can say anything they like!

FOLLBRAGUET. Of course not... But you know madame. You know what I've had to put up with all these years.

HORTENSE. Well, maybe monsieur has to put up with it, but I don't! Not me, monsieur! I'm sorry, but I'm leaving! I won't stay in this house another minute!

FOLLBRAGUET. Hortense, please...

HORTENSE, *sobbing*. No, monsieur! I'm leaving!

FOLLBRAGUET, *distraught*. Good God, what a mess! (*A knock is heard at the door, up left.*) Come in!

ALBERT *enters, leaving the door open.*

ALBERT. Monsieur Leboucq would like to see monsieur. He thinks he has an abscess.

FOLLBRAGUET. Damn him and his abscess!

HORTENSE *moves to leave, up right.*

ALBERT, *to* HORTENSE, *seeing her whimpering*. What's the matter with you?

HORTENSE, *petulantly brushing him aside as she exits*. Nothing! Leave me alone!

ALBERT, *following her out*. What is it? What's the matter?

HORTENSE'S VOICE. Nothing, I told you...

FOLLBRAGUET, *pacing*. Goddamn!... Oh!... Goddamn!... (*Brusquely, to* LEBOUCQ, *appearing at the open door, up left, a bandage around his swollen jaw.*) What do you want?

LEBOUCQ. My jaw, Doctor... It's killing me! It's swollen up twice the size! I must have an abscess.

FOLLBRAGUET, *still fuming*. You don't have to tell me! I can see for myself! (*Pointing to the dentist's chair.*) Here, sit down! Take off the bandage!

LEBOUCQ *complies*. FOLLBRAGUET *goes to the sink and fills a little glass with mouthwash.*

LEBOUCQ. I think I must have caught it last night, at the theater. I was sitting in a terrible draft, and—

FOLLBRAGUET. That has nothing to do with it! Absolutely nothing!

LEBOUCQ, *sheepishly, taken aback*. Oh?... I thought...

FOLLBRAGUET, *placing the glass on his instrument cabinet*. Open your mouth! (*Grumbling, as* LEBOUCQ *obeys*.) Enough is enough, damn it! I've had it up to here!

He joins the gesture to the expression.

LEBOUCQ, *quizzically*. Doctor?

FOLLBRAGUET. Nothing, nothing!... Open your mouth!

LEBOUCQ, *pointing to the offending tooth*. It's this one...

FOLLBRAGUET. I can see! (*After a cursory glance at the tooth, very matter-of-fact*.) It'll have to come out.

LEBOUCQ. What?

FOLLBRAGUET. It's too far gone...

LEBOUCQ. But...

FOLLBRAGUET. It'll have to come out!

LEBOUCQ. But Doctor, can't you save it?

FOLLBRAGUET. Save it? Why in hell should I save it? You think I collect them?

LEBOUCQ. No, I mean... (*Emphasizing*.) save it... For me...

FOLLBRAGUET. Look, if you want the damn thing that much, you can keep it!

LEBOUCQ, *timidly*. Really, Doctor... You don't have to growl...

FOLLBRAGUET, *taking the forceps from his instrument cabinet*. Oh? If you'd been through what I've been through... Open your mouth!

He plunges the forceps into LEBOUCQ'*s mouth and begins to pull the tooth.*

LEBOUCQ, *caught unawares, screaming*. Ayyyyyy!

FOLLBRAGUET, *tugging*. Not so loud, damn it! I've had all I can take for one day, thank you!

The tooth finally gives.

LEBOUCQ. Ohhhhh!

FOLLBRAGUET, *over* LEBOUCQ'*s protracted moans and groans*. There! Very pretty!... (*Sarcastically*.) I think you ought to keep it!

He puts the tooth into a little pillbox, then takes the glass of mouthwash and hands it to LEBOUCQ.

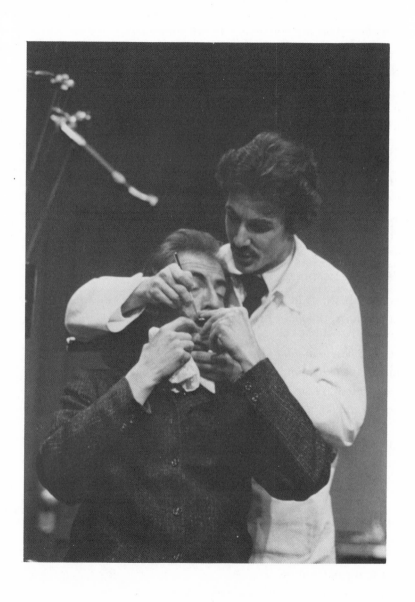

LEBOUCQ, *panting*. Good God in heaven!

FOLLBRAGUET. Here, rinse your mouth. (LEBOUCQ, *ready to faint, takes the glass and gulps down the contents, as* FOLLBRAGUET *tries in vain to stop him*.) What are you doing? You're not supposed to drink it!

LEBOUCQ, *feebly*. No... Leave me alone...

He gets up from the chair, totters, almost collapses.

FOLLBRAGUET. Hold on! You're not going to get sick on me, I hope! That's all I need!

LEBOUCQ. I... I think I'm going to faint...

FOLLBRAGUET. No, no!... Hold on! Don't faint!... Not in here... (*Running to the draped doorway and calling*.) Monsieur Jean!... Monsieur Jean!

He runs back to LEBOUCQ, *trying to hold him up*. MONSIEUR JEAN *appears at the door*.

MONSIEUR JEAN. Monsieur?

FOLLBRAGUET, *pointing off, left*. Here, take monsieur out and have him lie down.

He passes LEBOUCQ, *reeling, over to* MONSIEUR JEAN.

MONSIEUR JEAN, *nodding*. Of course... (*To* LEBOUCQ.) Please... This way...

FOLLBRAGUET, *stopping* LEBOUCQ *as they reach the doorway*. Oh, just a minute...

LEBOUCQ, *barely audible*. Doctor?

FOLLBRAGUET, *handing him the little pillbox*. You're forgetting your tooth! You wanted to save it, remember?

LEBOUCQ, *taking it half-heartedly*. Who needs it now? (*Putting the box in his pocket*.) I... I think I'm going to faint...

FOLLBRAGUET. Yes... Well, just don't faint in here.

MONSIEUR JEAN, *leading* LEBOUCQ *off*. This way, monsieur...

They exit.

FOLLBRAGUET, *sitting down at his desk, sighing*. Good God, what a day! (*There is a knock at the door, up right*.) Come in!

ALBERT *opens the door and appears at the threshold*.

ALBERT. It's me, monsieur.

FOLLBRAGUET, *after a quizzical pause*. So?

ALBERT, *very stiff and proper*. There's a matter I'd like to discuss with monsieur.

FOLLBRAGUET. What? What now?

ALBERT. I waited for monsieur to finish with his patient. When I heard him call for Monsieur Jean to take him out, I knocked at the door.

FOLLBRAGUET. All right, go ahead. I'm listening.

ALBERT. Very good, monsieur... (*Stepping into the office, moving downstage.*) Certainly monsieur is aware that madame has insulted Mademoiselle Hortense... Cut her to the quick, I might add...

FOLLBRAGUET. Oh no! Please! Not you too! Not another earful!

ALBERT, *still very correct.* I'm sorry to be giving monsieur another earful. It's not something I enjoy. But monsieur must know that Mademoiselle Hortense and I have been seeing one another...

FOLLBRAGUET. Oh?

ALBERT. I can go so far as to say that we haven't seen fit to resist temptation.

FOLLBRAGUET. I see...

ALBERT. Even so, monsieur can rest assured that I still have every intention of making her my wife.

FOLLBRAGUET. Of course! Of course!... (*Waiting for* ALBERT's *conclusion.*) So what?

ALBERT. Well, as mademoiselle's husband, so to speak, I can't stand by and let madame say that my wife, as it were, goes to bed with monsieur! It's outrageous!

FOLLBRAGUET. Damn right it's outrageous! I hope you don't believe it!

ALBERT. Of course not, monsieur. I know Mademoiselle Hortense too well.

FOLLBRAGUET, *wryly.* Much obliged, I'm sure!

ALBERT. Besides, wasn't it just yesterday that madame informed monsieur that he was nothing but a eunuch?

FOLLBRAGUET, *with a start.* Now just you wait one minute!...

ALBERT. Nothing personal, monsieur. I only bring the matter up to point out how illogical women can be.

FOLLBRAGUET. Maybe so, but—

ALBERT. At any rate, monsieur, given the present state of affairs, I'm afraid I have to tell monsieur that I have no choice but to leave his employ.

FOLLBRAGUET. Well, leave it then! What do you expect me to say?

ALBERT. Very good, monsieur. (*Drawing himself up to his full height.*) And now, since I'm no longer monsieur's social unequal, we can speak man to man.

FOLLBRAGUET, *cocking his head, incredulously.* I beg your pardon!

ALBERT. I'm just another husband, monsieur, defending his wife's honor.

FOLLBRAGUET. Of course!

ALBERT. Now, either madame takes back what she said and apologizes to Mademoiselle Hortense...

FOLLBRAGUET, *with a nervous little laugh.* Ha! That I'd like to see!

ALBERT. ... or else... Well, monsieur, I haven't forgotten my regimental days... (*Another quizzical cock of the head from* FOLLBRAGUET.) As assistant fencing master...

FOLLBRAGUET. Oh?

ALBERT. And I beg to inform monsieur that my seconds will be paying him a visit in the morning.

FOLLBRAGUET. Your seconds? Your... (*Standing up.*) What kind of a joke... You really expect me to fight a duel with my butler?

ALBERT. Excuse me, monsieur. I've stopped being monsieur's butler.

FOLLBRAGUET, *striding up to him.* Too bad! I'll toss your seconds right out on their ears!

ALBERT. In that case monsieur will be publicly disgraced. It will have to be reported—officially, of course—that monsieur provokes people, then refuses to duel. He'll lose by default.

FOLLBRAGUET, *convulsed.* Default? Default, my... Fine! Let it be reported! You think I give a damn?

ALBERT, *very calmly.* That's up to monsieur, I'm sure.

FOLLBRAGUET, *ready to tear his hair.* Good God! Why me? What on earth have I done? Why is everyone on my neck?

ALBERT. Oh, it's not monsieur's fault. I know he's not to blame. It's just that a husband has to answer for his wife, and, that being the case... Well, I'll wait until tonight for monsieur to decide. Either madame takes back what she said...

FOLLBRAGUET. You can't really believe—

ALBERT. ... or two of my friends will come by in the morning.

FOLLBRAGUET. Look, if you imagine for one moment that she would even dream—

ALBERT. Well, it's not for me to say, but perhaps if monsieur started putting his foot down... Perhaps if he stopped giving in to her, I mean... After all, the law says a wife is supposed to obey her husband. Perhaps if he told madame, once and for all: "That's enough! I'm the boss, and what I say goes!"...

FOLLBRAGUET. Ha! That's easier said than done.

ALBERT. Well anyway, monsieur, as I was saying... Monsieur has until this evening. After that, I send my seconds.

HORTENSE *has appeared at the door, up right, still ajar since* ALBERT'S *entrance, and has apparently overheard the last exchange.*

HORTENSE, *running in, flinging her arms around* ALBERT'S *neck.* Seconds? What seconds? Don't tell me you've got a duel?

ALBERT, *breaking away, sharply.* Who asked you, woman? This is man to man. Now quiet!

HORTENSE. But Albert... Not a duel... Not with the likes of them!

ALBERT. That's enough! I'm the boss, and what I say goes!

HORTENSE, *meekly.* Yes, Albert...

The doorbell rings offstage.

ALBERT, *changing his tone, to* FOLLBRAGUET. I'll remain in monsieur's employ until this evening. If monsieur will excuse me, I'll go see who's at the door.

He moves off, up right, taking HORTENSE *with him. Before they reach the door,* MARCELLE *comes bursting out of her room.*

MARCELLE. Here's the key...

FOLLBRAGUET, *startled.* Marcelle!

At the sight of HORTENSE, MARCELLE *stops in her tracks. She looks her up and down with obvious contempt, until the pair, never losing their aplomb, are out the door.*

MARCELLE, *throwing the key onto* FOLLBRAGUET'S *desk.* Here's the key to my room. Now you two can use my bed to your heart's content!

FOLLBRAGUET. Your key? Your... (*Picking it up.*) Here's what I'll do with your goddamn key!

He hurls it across the room, into the fireplace.

MARCELLE, *utterly indifferent.* You can do what you please...

FOLLBRAGUET, *fuming.* Do you know what your foolishness has gotten me into?

MARCELLE. I don't know, and I don't care.

FOLLBRAGUET. Oh no? Well I'll tell you! I've got myself a duel, that's what! And with my butler, no less!

MARCELLE, *sarcastically.* My, my! Fancy that!

FOLLBRAGUET, *mimicking.* "Fancy that! Fancy that!..." What do you expect? Hortense is practically married to Albert. You insult Hortense. So he challenges me to a duel. What else?

MARCELLE. Of course! Some men stand up for their women when someone insults them. At least Albert has blood in his veins! Good for him!

FOLLBRAGUET. Yes, well in the meantime I'll thank you to tell Hortense you're sorry, and you take back what you said...

MARCELLE, *incredulous*. Tell her what?

FOLLBRAGUET. And right this minute!

MARCELLE, *needling him*. Well, well! Don't tell me we're afraid of our butler!

FOLLBRAGUET. What kind of talk... (*Summoning up all his authority*.) Besides, that's enough! I'm the boss, and what I say goes!

ALBERT *appears at the door, up left. He stops short at the threshold*.

MARCELLE, *to* FOLLBRAGUET. Oh, really? You don't say! (*She gives him a resounding slap across the face*.) I'll try to remember!

She strides off, up right.

FOLLBRAGUET, *agape, rubbing his cheek, to* ALBERT. There! You see what happens when I put my foot down!

ALBERT. Monsieur has an uphill struggle, if I may say so.

FOLLBRAGUET. Goddamn!

ALBERT. But he does have the rest of the day... until tonight... After that...

FOLLBRAGUET, *exasperated*. I know! I know!... Now what did you want to tell me?

ALBERT. That gentleman is back, monsieur.

FOLLBRAGUET. Who? What gentleman?

ALBERT. The one who was here just before the lady, monsieur... The lady with the "munch-munch"...

FOLLBRAGUET. Oh?

ALBERT. He says his tooth still hurts, monsieur.

FOLLBRAGUET. So? It hurts! Too bad!

MARCELLE *enters, up right.* YVETTE *is close behind, stopping at the threshold*.

MARCELLE, *to* FOLLBRAGUET. Here, I brought you the cook. She's all yours too!

FOLLBRAGUET. What? What now?

MARCELLE, *to* YVETTE. Don't just stand there, Yvette. Come in, come in! (*To* FOLLBRAGUET, *as* YVETTE *enters*.) Since I don't seem to count in this house anymore...

FOLLBRAGUET, *gnashing his teeth*. Marcelle!

MARCELLE. Since you seem to think more of the help than your wife...

FOLLBRAGUET. Marcelle!

MARCELLE. Oh no, don't try to deny it!

FOLLBRAGUET. Marcelle!

MARCELLE. Well, they're all yours. I'm through! Here, you can run the house, buy the food, plan the meals... (*To* YVETTE.) From now on monsieur will be giving you your orders. (*To* FOLLBRAGUET.) I quit!

FOLLBRAGUET. But, for heaven's sake—

MARCELLE. Q-U-I-T, quit! Understand?

She storms out the open door, up right.

FOLLBRAGUET, *running to the door*. Marcelle!

MARCELLE'S VOICE. And that's that!

YVETTE, *after a brief, embarrassed pause*. Monsieur?

FOLLBRAGUET. What is it?

YVETTE. I have no idea what to make monsieur for dinner.

FOLLBRAGUET, *beside himself*. Well, that's no skin off my ass, damn it!

YVETTE, *snippily, giving him tit for tat*. Well, it's certainly no skin off mine, monsieur!

FOLLBRAGUET, *exploding*. What? What did you say?

YVETTE. I said—

FOLLBRAGUET. You dare talk to me like that? You dare...

YVETTE, *suddenly losing her composure*. But monsieur—

FOLLBRAGUET. Never mind! Go pack your bags and get out of here! You're fired!

YVETTE. But I didn't mean any offense, monsieur. I just thought—

FOLLBRAGUET. Too bad! You're still fired! (*Pointing to the open door, up right.*) You heard me! Get out!

YVETTE, *beginning to whimper*. But I thought monsieur would give me a raise. Like Hortense, I mean—

FOLLBRAGUET. Out, I said! Out! Out! (*Pushing her bodily out the door and slamming it behind her.*) What in hell do they take me for? What kind of an idiot...

ALBERT, *still standing discreetly in the corner, up left*. Shall I show the gentleman in, monsieur?

FOLLBRAGUET. Yes!... No!... Yes, yes, goddammit!

ALBERT, *opening the door, up left, calling out*. Monsieur, the doctor can see you now.

VILDAMOUR *enters, obviously in pain*.

VILDAMOUR. Oh, thank heaven! (*To* FOLLBRAGUET, *as* ALBERT *exits, up right*.) Doctor, I'm sorry to bother you like this, but I just can't stand it. It's worse than before.

FOLLBRAGUET, *pointing to the dentist's chair.* Fine!... Sit down!

VILDAMOUR, *sitting.* Thank you...

FOLLBRAGUET, *visibly distraught, shaking his clenched fists in an uncontrollable outburst, under his breath.* Damn! Damn! Damn! Damn!

VILDAMOUR. Please?

FOLLBRAGUET. Nothing! I wasn't talking to you!... Sit still!

He attaches the napkin around VILDAMOUR's *neck, catching his chin.*

VILDAMOUR, *pointing to his chin.* Doctor...

FOLLBRAGUET, *brusquely pulling the napkin into the proper position.* Watch what you're doing!

He picks up the rubber gag.

VILDAMOUR. Do you have to put all that stuff back in my mouth?

FOLLBRAGUET. If I have to, I have to!

VILDAMOUR. Good God, what a pain! It's killing me, Doctor!

FOLLBRAGUET, *thinking of his own situation.* Some people have worse, believe me!

VILDAMOUR. Well, mine's bad enough! I can't worry about theirs!

FOLLBRAGUET. Of course not! Why should you give a damn?... Open your mouth!

VILDAMOUR. It's not going to hurt, is it?

FOLLBRAGUET, *impatient.* No, no, no! Come on, open up!

He arranges the rubber gag and the saliva pump. Then he goes to the sink and fills a glass with mouthwash.

VILDAMOUR, *grunting, as before.* A foo uhv ag gif koof fikfk wong uh-gaw, guh a faw a koo waik, av wong av ik wawv-nk gaw-vuh-ing ngee. ("I should have had this tooth fixed long ago, but I thought I could wait, as long as it wasn't bothering me.")

FOLLBRAGUET, *coming back with the glass, placing it on the instrument cabinet.* Fine! Fine!

VILDAMOUR. Guh wak ngyk ik wuv faw gag, a faw a wuv gaw-nguh ngy! ("But last night it was so bad, I thought I was going to die!")

FOLLBRAGUET. Fine! Open your mouth!

VILDAMOUR complies. FOLLBRAGUET *pulls out the cotton swab left in the tooth and throws it aside.*

VILDAMOUR. A gi-gnk fweek uh wink. A faw ngy heg wuv gaw-nguh gurfk! ("I didn't sleep a wink. I thought my head was going to burst!")

FOLLBRAGUET, *on edge*. Please! Shut up! I can't do anything if you keep on blabbing!

VILDAMOUR, *cowed*. Aaaah...

FOLLBRAGUET, *musing aloud as he works on the tooth*. Go get married and see what it gets you, goddammit! (VILDAMOUR *stares at him quizzically*.) Open your mouth!

He takes the drill and sets it in motion.

VILDAMOUR, *grimacing, trying in vain to close his mouth*. Ngaw! Ngaw! ("No! No!")

FOLLBRAGUET. I said open your mouth!

He begins drilling the tooth, over VILDAMOUR's *groans. After a moment,* MARCELLE *bursts in, up right.*

MARCELLE. Now what's this all about? Yvette says you fired her...

FOLLBRAGUET, *jumping at the sudden intrusion*. Marcelle!... Please!

He inadvertently lets the drill slip.

VILDAMOUR, *in agony*. Ayyyyy!

FOLLBRAGUET, *to* VILDAMOUR, *realizing that he is drilling his cheek*. Sorry! (*To* MARCELLE.) Leave me alone. Can't you see I'm busy?

MARCELLE. That's too bad! You're not firing Yvette, understand? I've never had even the slightest bit of trouble—

FOLLBRAGUET. Listen, when a cook talks dirty to me, I throw her out! That's that! Now I'm busy! This is no time—

MARCELLE. I see! (*To* VILDAMOUR, *still groaning*.) I'm sure monsieur will excuse me... (*To* FOLLBRAGUET.) You haven't heard the end of this! Not by a long shot!

She exits, up right, leaving the door open.

FOLLBRAGUET. Incredible! Just incredible! The whole damn day... (*To* VILDAMOUR.) Open your mouth!

He hangs up the drill and begins poking away at the tooth with another instrument.

MARCELLE'S VOICE, *just outside the door*. Don't you worry, Yvette. Monsieur Follbraguet just isn't himself. You mustn't listen to a thing he says. (FOLLBRAGUET *bites his lip and struggles to hold back his rage*.) It's all right when somebody insults his wife, but say one word to him... (*Appearing at the threshold*.) Besides, I don't care what he told you. I give the orders here, and I say you're staying! (*Obviously aiming the remark at* FOLLBRAGUET.) I hope that's clear!

FOLLBRAGUET *flings down the instrument and dashes out into the hall, closing the door behind him.*

FOLLBRAGUET'S VOICE. Over my dead body!

MARCELLE'S VOICE, *snickering.* Don't make me laugh!

FOLLBRAGUET'S VOICE. You can laugh your damn head off! You give the orders when I let you give the orders! That's when you give the orders! And don't you forget it! And in case you don't believe me, I just fired your cook, and I'll thank her to get the hell out of my house!

YVETTE'S VOICE. But monsieur, it's not my fault...

FOLLBRAGUET'S VOICE. Too bad! Out of my house!

MARCELLE'S VOICE. I told you, Yvette. Don't listen. He's out of his mind.

FOLLBRAGUET'S VOICE. Maybe so. But she'll do what I tell her, understand? (*He returns, grumbling, and slams the door.*) Of all the goddamn... Who does she think she is? (*To* VILDAMOUR.) Open your mouth! (*Handing him the glass of mouthwash.*) Here!

YVETTE'S VOICE, *whimpering.* But madame...

MARCELLE'S VOICE. Now, now... Don't you worry... Don't pay any attention. Just leave everything to me.

FOLLBRAGUET *makes another dash for the door, opens it, and sticks his head out.*

FOLLBRAGUET, *at the top of his voice.* I said leave me alone! I'm sick of the two of you standing out here yapping! Enough is enough!

MARCELLE'S VOICE. I beg your pardon!

FOLLBRAGUET. You heard me, woman! Go do as you're told! (*He returns again, slamming the door behind him.*) Why me, for God's sake? Why in hell... (*To* VILDAMOUR.) Spit out!

VILDAMOUR *obeys.*

MARCELLE'S VOICE, *furious.* Now that's the last straw! I won't stay in this house! I won't stay here another minute!...

FOLLBRAGUET, *opening the door.* Fine! Get out! Who's stopping you? (*Mimicking.*) "I won't stay in this house! I won't stay in this house!" That's all you ever say! But you're still here, goddammit!

MARCELLE'S VOICE. Oh? Well, this time I mean it!

FOLLBRAGUET. That suits me just fine! (*Slamming the door.*) Nagging bitch!

MARCELLE, *flinging the door open.* What was that?

FOLLBRAGUET, *turning her around bodily and giving her a push.* Out! Out! Out!

He closes the door and this time bolts it shut. MARCELLE, *outside, pounds in vain to get it open.*

MARCELLE'S VOICE. Let me in! Let me in!

FOLLBRAGUET *heaves a disgusted sigh.*

FOLLBRAGUET, *to* VILDAMOUR. I hope you'll excuse this ludicrous display...

VILDAMOUR *replies with an indulgent wave of the hand. Just at that moment,* MARCELLE *bursts in through the other door, up left, and heads straight for* VILDAMOUR.

MARCELLE, *to* VILDAMOUR. You heard him, monsieur! You heard what he called me! (VILDAMOUR *tries to give a noncommittal shrug.*) You heard him order me out of this house. You heard... You heard...

FOLLBRAGUET. Yes! He heard, he heard, he heard!

MARCELLE, *arms akimbo.* Well, that's just too bad! I'm not budging one inch! This is *my* house, remember? It's in *my* name, not yours!... You and your fancy little legal tricks!... So if anyone gets out, it's going to be you!

FOLLBRAGUET. Then it's going to be me! Damn right I'll get out! If you think I'm working my fingers to the bone... For what? For you?... You want to run the show? Well, that's fine with me! It's yours! Lock, stock, and barrel! Patients and all! I'm through, damn it! Here!

He scoops up a bunch of instruments and plants them squarely in MAR-CELLE'S *hands.*

MARCELLE. Me? (VILDAMOUR *grimaces in horror at the prospect.*) Me? Stick my fingers in all those filthy, repulsive mouths? (*Wincing.*) That's all right for you, but—

FOLLBRAGUET, *ripping off his smock and going to the coatrack to put on his hat and coat.* Yes, well just don't forget... You can thank those filthy, repulsive mouths that I stick my fingers in, day in day out... (*Pointing unthinkingly to* VILDAMOUR.) You can thank them for all your fancy clothes... And your goddamn lace! And your ribbons, ribbons, ribbons! From now on, you can earn them yourself! I quit!

MARCELLE. Go ahead! Only don't be surprised when you come home tonight and I'm gone!

FOLLBRAGUET. Same here! Good-bye!

He storms out, up right.

MARCELLE. Good-bye!

The outside door is heard to slam. MARCELLE *throws the instruments down on the cabinet and exits to her room.* VILDAMOUR, *having followed the last few exchanges with mounting concern, sits up straight, appalled at being left all alone with a mouthful of apparatus.*

VILDAMOUR, *not knowing which way to turn.* Wuh a-gou ngee?... Wuh a-gou ngee?... ("What about me?... What about me?...")

CURTAIN

Library of Congress Cataloging in Publication Data

FEYDEAU, GEORGES, 1862–1921.
  Feydeau, first to last.

  Contents: Ladies' man—Wooed and viewed—
Romance in a flat—[etc.]
  I. Shapiro, Norman R.   II. Title.
PQ2611.E86F44   1982   842'.8   81-15182
ISBN 0-08014-1295-1   AACR2